Greek
PHRASEBOOK & DICTIONARY

D0830289

Acknowledgments

Product Editors Kate Mathews, Amanda Williamson
Production Support Chris Love
Cover Researcher Naomi Parker
Language Writer Thanasis Spilias

Thanks

James Hardy, Valentina Kremenchutskaya, Angela Tinson, Tony Wheeler

Published by Lonely Planet Publications Pty Ltd
ABN 36 005 607 983

6th Edition – March 2016
ISBN 978 1 74321 729 0
Text © Lonely Planet 2016

Cover Image Restaurant and bars along the waterfront, Mykonos, Greece. Maurizio Rellini / 4Corners ©

Printed in China 10 9 8 7 6 5 4

Contact lonelyplanet.com/contact

acknowledgments

This 6th edition of Lonely Planet's *Greek phrasebook* is based on the previous edition by the Lonely Planet Language Products team and translator Dr Thanasis Spilias.

Thanasis studied in Greece (University of Thessaloniki) and Australia (University of Melbourne, La Trobe University and University of New England). He has taught Greek language and culture at Deakin and La Trobe Universities and worked as the State Consultant for Greek Language (Victoria, Australia). Thanasis' main research interests are in Greek language and literature, Greek–Australian literature and literary translation. He has published articles in both Greece and Australia, and has co-edited *Reflections: Selected Works from Greek Australian Literature*. With G Betts and S Gauntlett, he has translated Vitsentzos Kornaros' *Erotokritos* into English.

Thanks also to the Lonely Planet Language Products team who produced previous editions of the *Greek phrasebook* on which this one is based: Vanessa Battersby, Francesca Coles, Margie Jung, Yukiyoshi Kamimura, David Kemp, Jodie Martire and Meladel Mistica.

make the most of this phrasebook ...

Anyone can speak another language! It's all about confidence. Don't worry if you can't remember your school language lessons or if you've never learnt a language before. Even if you learn the very basics (on the inside covers of this book), your travel experience will be the better for it. You have nothing to lose and everything to gain when the locals hear you making an effort.

finding things in this book

For easy navigation, this book is in sections. The Basics chapters are the ones you'll thumb through time and again. The Practical section covers basic travel situations like catching transport and finding a bed. The Social section gives you conversational phrases, pick-up lines, the ability to express opinions – so you can get to know people. Food has a section all of its own: gourmets and vegetarians are covered and local dishes feature. Safe Travel equips you with health and police phrases, just in case. Remember the colours of each section and you'll find everything easily; or use the comprehensive Index. Otherwise, check the two-way traveller's Dictionary for the word you need.

being understood

Throughout this book you'll see coloured phrases on each page. They're phonetic guides to help you pronounce the language. You don't even need to look at the language itself, but you'll get used to the way we've represented particular sounds. The pronunciation chapter in Basics will explain more, but you can feel confident that if you read the coloured phrase slowly, you'll be understood.

communication tips

Body language, ways of doing things, sense of humour – all have a role to play in every culture. 'Local talk' boxes show you common ways of saying things, or everyday language to drop into conversation. 'Listen for ...' boxes supply the phrases you may hear. They start with the Greek translation (so a Greek speaker can look up the phrase they want to say to you) and then lead in to the pronunciation guide and the English translation.

CONTENTS

5

social 107

greek

official language

For more details, see the **introduction**.

ristotle, Homer, Plato, Sappho, Herodotus and Alexander the
reat can't all be wrong in their choice of language – if you've
ver come across arcane concepts such as 'democracy', exotic
sciplines like 'trigonometry' or a little-known neurosis termed
he Oedipus complex', then you'll have some inkling of the wide-
pread influence of Greek language and culture. With just a little
odern Greek under your belt, you'll have a richer understanding
f this language's impact on contemporary Western culture.

Greek is the official language of Greece and a co-official lan-
uage of Cyprus, in addition to being spoken by emigrant commu-
ties in Turkey, Australia, Canada, Germany and the United States.
In total, there are over 13 million Greek speakers worldwide.

at a glance ...

language name: Greek

name in language:
Ελληνικά e·li·ni·ka,
Νέα Ελληνικά ne·a e·li·ni·ka
(Greek, Modern Greek)

language family:
Indo-European
(Hellenic branch)

key countries:
Greece, Cyprus

approximate number of speakers:
13 million worldwide

close relatives:
Ancient Greek

donations to English:
anarchy, astronomy,
cosmos, democracy,
drama, logic, politics ...

Modern Greek constitutes a
separate branch of the Indo-
European language family, with
Ancient Greek its only (extinct)
relative. The first records of written Ancient Greek were found in
the fragmentary Linear B tablets,
dating from the 14th to the 12th
centuries BC. By the 9th century
BC, the Greeks had adapted the
Phoenician alphabet to include
vowels – the first alphabet to do
so – and the script in use today
came to its final form some time
in the 5th century BC. The Greek
script was the foundation for
the Cyrillic script (used in Slavic
languages) and the Latin alphabet (used in English and other
European languages).

Although written Greek may
have been remarkably stable

introduction

9

over the millennia, the spoken language has evolved considerab
In the 5th century, the dialect spoken around Athens (known
'Attic') became the dominant speech as a result of the city-state
cultural and political prestige. Attic gained even greater influen
as the medium of administration for the vast empire of Alexa
der the Great, and remained the official language of the Easte
Roman Empire and the Orthodox Church after the demise of th
Hellenistic world. Once the Ottoman Turks took Constantinop
in 1453, the Attic dialect lost its official function. In the meantim
the common language – known as *Koine* (Κοινή ki·ni) – continue
to evolve. It developed a rich history of popular songs (δημοτι
τραγούδια ţhi·mo·ti·ka tra·ghu·ţhia) and absorbed vocabula
from Turkish, Italian, Albanian and other Balkan languages.

When an independent Greece returned to the world stage
1832, it needed to choose a national language. Purists advocate
a slightly modernised version of Attic known as *Καθαρεύου*
ka·tha·re·vu·sa (from the Greek word for 'clean'), which no long
resembled the spoken language. *Koine*, or *laiki* as it was also know
(λαϊκή la·i·ki means 'popular'), had strong support as it was spoke
and understood by the majority of Greeks – in the end, this was th
language which gained official recognition. By the mid-20th ce
tury, *Koine/laiki* was known as 'demotic' and continued in daily us
It was banned during Greece's military dictatorship (1967-74) b
then reinstated as the official language of the Hellenic Republic.

This book gives you the practical phrases you need to get by
Greek, as well as all the fun, spontaneous phrases that can lead
a better understanding of Greeks and their culture. Once you'v
got the hang of how to pronounce Greek words, the rest is ju
a matter of confidence. Local knowledge, new relationships ar
a sense of satisfaction are on the tip of your tongue. So don't ju
stand there, say something!

abbreviations used in this book

a	adjective	n	neuter (after Greek)
acc	accusative	n	noun (after English)
f	feminine	nom	nominative
gen	genitive	pl	plural
inf	informal	pol	polite
lit	literal	sg	singular
m	masculine	v	verb

The pronunciation of Greek is easy to master, as most of the sounds correspond to those found in English. Use the coloured pronunciation guides to become familiar with them, and then read directly from the Greek when you feel more confident.

vowel sounds

Greek vowels are pronounced separately even when they're written in sequence, eg ζώο *zo·o* (animal). You'll see though in the table below that some letter combinations correspond to a single sound – ουρά (queue) is pronounced u·*ra*.

When a word ending in a vowel is followed by another word that starts with the same or a similar vowel sound, one vowel is usually omitted and the two words are pronounced as if they were one – Σε ευχαριστώ se ef·kha·ris·*to* becomes Σ' ευχαριστώ sef·kha·ris·*to* (Thank you). Note that the apostrophe (') is used to show that two words have been joined together.

symbol	english equivalent	greek example	transliteration
a	car	αλλά	a·*la*
e	bet	πλένομαι	ple·no·me
i	lid	πίσω, πόλη, υποφέρω, είδος, οικογένεια, υιός	pi·so, po·li, i·po·fe·ro, i·thos, i·ko·ye·ni·a, i·os
o	lot	πόνος, πίσω	po·nos, pi·so
u	put	ουρά	u·*ra*
ia	nostalgia	ζητιάνος	zi·*tia*·nos
io	ratio	πιο	pio

consonant sounds

Most Greek consonant sounds are also found in English – only the guttural gh and kh might need a bit of practice. Double consonants are only pronounced once – άλλος *a*·los (other).

symbol	english equivalent	greek example	trans-literation
b	bed	μπαρ	bar
d	dog	ντομάτα	do·*ma*·ta
dz	adds	τζαμί	dza·*mi*
f	fit	φως, αυτή	fos, af·*ti*
g	gap	γκαρσόν	gar·*son*
gh	guttural sound, between goat and loch	γάτα	*gha*·ta
h	heat	χέρι	*he*·ri
k	kit	καλά	ka·*la*
kh	loch (guttural sound)	χαλί	kha·*li*
l	let	λάδι	*la*·thi
m	mat	μαζί	ma·*zi*
n	not	ναός	na·os
ng	singer	ελέγχω	e·*leng*·kho
p	pin	πάνω	*pa*·no
ps	lapse	ψάρι	*psa*·ri
r	red (trilled)	ράβω	*ra*·vo
s	sad	στυλό	sti·*lo*
t	top	τι	ti
th	theatre	θέα	*the*·a
ṭh	the	δεν	ṭhen
ts	hats	τσέπη	*tse*·pi
v	vase	βίζα, αύριο	*vi*·za, *av*·ri·o
y	yes	γέρος	*ye*·ros
z	zoo	ζέστη	*ze*·sti

BASICS

word stress

Most Greek words have only one stressed syllable, but some have two. Stress can fall on any of the last three syllables. In our pronunciation guides, the stressed syllable is always in italics, but in written Greek, the stressed syllable is always indicated by an accent over the vowel, eg καλά ka·*la*.

If a vowel is represented by two letters, it's written on the second letter, eg ζητιάνος zi·*tia*·nos (beggar). If the accent is marked on the first of these two letters, they should be read separately, like in Μάιος *ma*·i·os (May). Where two vowels occur together but are not stressed, a diaeresis (¨) is used to indicate that they should be pronounced separately, eg λαϊκός la·i·*kos* (popular). When stress falls on a capitalised vowel (like in Έχασα *e*·ha·sa (I lost)), the accent is written to the left of the letter.

intonation

Intonation in mainland Greece is rather flat, except in questions, when the voice is raised at the end of the sentence. Many island dialects have a more 'singing' intonation.

spellbound

You may have noticed that sometimes two Greek letters in combination form one single consonant sound – the combination of the letters μ and π makes the sound b, and the combination of the letters ν and τ makes the sound d. This is particularly the case when each combination appears at the start of a word – in the middle of a word they sound more like the 'mb' in 'amber' and the 'nd' in 'indigo' respectively. In this book, we've used the same symbols regardless of the position of these letters within a word – you'll be understood just fine if you follow our pronunciation guides.

reading & writing

The Greek writing system was simplified in 1982, when the old stress symbols and aspiration marks (ie an accent indicating that a sound is pronounced with a puff of air before it) were abolished, although they may still be found in old books.

The modern Greek alphabet consists of 24 letters. Their pronunciation is shown in the box below for spelling purposes, eg when you need to spell your name to book into a hotel. Many of the letters of the Greek alphabet are also used in the Roman alphabet. Some letters, however, are a little misleading – they look like English letters but are pronounced very differently. For more information, see the consonant table on page 12 and the box on page 34.

Greek punctuation uses the same symbols as in English, except for the question mark – this is written as a semicolon (;).

greek alphabet			
A α *al*·pha	B β *vi*·ta	Γ γ *gha*·ma	Δ δ *thel*·ta
E ε *ep*·si·lon	Z ζ *zi*·ta	H η *i*·ta	Θ θ *thi*·ta
I ι *yio*·ta	K κ *ka*·pa	Λ λ *lam*·tha	M μ mi
N ν ni	Ξ ξ ksi	O o *o*·mi·kron	Π π pi
P ρ ro	Σ σ/ς* *sigh*·ma	T τ taf	Υ υ *ip*·si·lon
Φ φ fi	X χ hi	Ψ ψ psi	Ω ω *o·me·gha*

* The letter Σ has two forms for the lower case – σ and ς. The second one is used at the end of words.

contents

The index below shows the grammatical structures you can use to say what you want. Look under each function – in alphabetical order – for information on how to build your own phrases. For example, to tell the taxi driver where your hotel is, look for **giving instructions** and you'll be directed to information on **negatives**, **prepositions** and **requests**. A glossary of grammatical terms is included at the end of this chapter to help you.

Abbreviations like **nom** and **acc** in the literal translations for each example refer the case of the noun or pronoun – this is explained in the glossary and in **case**.

making statements

naming people/things

negating

pointing things out

possessing

adjectives & adverbs

Adjectives in Greek normally come before the noun, just like in English. They take different endings to agree with the noun they qualify (see **case**, **gender** and **plurals**) – we've given their standard forms below. Adjectives are shown in the nominative form in lists throughout this book and in the **dictionary** – these forms won't always be strictly correct within a sentence, but you'll still be understood. To find out more, see **case**.

	masculine	feminine	neuter
singular	καλός δρόμος ka·*los* thro·mos good road	καλή τύχη ka·*li* ti·hi good fortune	καλό ποτό ka·*lo* po·to good drink
plural	καλοί δρόμοι ka·*li* thro·mi good roads	καλές τύχες ka·*les* ti·hes good fortunes	καλά ποτά ka·*la* po·ta good drinks

Adverbs normally end with the sound a (eg καλά ka·*la* 'well').

He filled in the form quickly.

Συμπλήρωσε το έντυπο   si·*bli*·ro·se to e·di·po
γρήγορα.   ghri·gho·ra
(lit: filled-in the-acc form-acc quickly)

articles

The Greek words for 'a' and 'an' change form to agree in gender and case with the noun they refer to.

		masculine	feminine	neuter
indefinite article (a/an)	nom	ένας e·*nas*	μια mia	ένα e·na
	acc	ένα(ν) e·*na(n)*	μια mia	ένα e·na
	gen	ενός e·*nos*	μιας *mi*·as	ενός e·nos

a–z phrasebuilder

17

The Greek equivalents of 'the' also change form according to the noun – see also **case**, **gender** and **plurals**.

			masculine		feminine		neuter	
definite article (the)	nom	sg	ο	o	η	i	το	to
		pl	οι	i	οι	i	τα	ta
	acc	sg	το(ν)	to(n)	τη(ν)	ti(n)	το	to
		pl	τους	tus	τις	tis	τα	ta
	gen	sg	του	tu	της	tis	του	tu
		pl	των	ton	των	ton	των	ton

Articles alway come before the noun:

a road	**ένας** δρόμος	*e·nas thro·mos*
the road	**ο** δρόμος	*o thro·mos*

be

The verb είμαι *i·me* (be) changes depending on who or what is the subject (doer) of the sentence. These are the forms for the present and past tenses.

present			past		
I am	είμαι	*i·me*	**I was**	ήμουν	*i·mun*
you are sg inf	είσαι	*i·se*	**you were** sg inf	ήσουν	*i·sun*
you are sg pol	είστε	*i·ste*	**you were** sg pol	ήσαστε	*i·sa·ste*
he/she/it is	είναι	*i·ne*	**he/she/it was**	ήταν	*i·tan*
we are	είμαστε	*i·ma·ste*	**we were**	ήμαστε	*i·ma·ste*
you are pl	είστε	*i·ste*	**you were** pl	ήσαστε	*i·sa·ste*
they are	είναι	*i·ne*	**they were**	ήταν	*i·tan*

The future tense is formed by placing the word θα tha (will) in front of the present tense forms.

I'll be there tomorrow.

    Θα είμαι εκεί αύριο.   tha *i*·me e·*ki* av·ri·o
    (lit: will be there tomorrow)

case

**doing things · indicating location ·
naming people/things · possessing**

Greek uses four different cases, usually shown by word endings, to indicate a noun's role and its relationship to other words in the sentence. Adjectives, articles, demonstratives and pronouns also change their form to agree with the noun they go with.

---

nominative **nom** – shows the subject of a sentence

The car won't start.

    Το αυτοκίνητο δεν αρχίζει.   to af·to·*ki*·ni·to then ar·*hi*·zi
    (lit: the-**nom** car-**nom** not starts)

accusative **acc** – shows the direct object of a sentence

Please bring the menu.

    Παρακαλώ φέρε το μενού.   pa·ra·ka·*lo* fe·re to me·*nu*
    (lit: please bring the-**acc** menu-**acc**)

genitive **gen** – shows possession or the indirect object of a sentence

What's the address of the hotel?

    Ποια είναι η διεύθυνση του   pia *i*·ne i *thi*·ef·thin·si tu
    ξενοδοχείου;   kse·no·tho·*hi*·u
    (lit: which is the-**nom** address-**nom** the-**gen** hotel-**gen**)

vocative **voc** – to address someone directly

Officer, I think there's been a mistake.

    Κύριε, νομίζω ότι έχει γίνει   *ki*·ri·e no·*mi*·zo o·ti e·xi yi·ni
    κάποιο λάθος   *ka*·pio *la*·thos
    (lit: sir-**voc** I-think that has been some-**nom** mistake-**nom**)

Greek nouns in the **dictionaries**, the **menu decoder** and word lists in this book are given in the nominative case. You can use this form as a default and, although this won't always be grammatically correct within sentences, you'll still be understood.

demonstratives

indicating location • naming people/things • pointing things out

The words for 'this' and 'that' in Greek change their endings depending on the form of the noun they determine (see **case**, **gender** and **plurals**). We've only given the nominative forms here – in most cases you'll be understood just fine.

		masculine		feminine		neuter	
this	sg	αυτός	af·tos	αυτή	af·ti	αυτό	af·to
	pl	αυτοί	af·ti	αυτές	af·tes	αυτά	af·ta
that	sg	εκείνος	e·ki·nos	εκείνη	e·ki·ni	εκείνο	e·ki·no
	pl	εκείνοι	e·ki·ni	εκείνες	e·ki·nes	εκείνα	e·ki·na

Does this train go to Lamia?

Πηγαίνει αυτό το τρένο   pi·ye·ni af·to to tre·no
στη Λαμία;   sti la·mi·a
(lit: goes this-nom the-nom train-nom to Lamia-acc)

That bag is mine.

Εκείνη η τσάντα είναι   e·ki·ni i tsa·da i·ne
δική μου.   thi·ki mu
(lit: that-nom the-nom bag-nom is mine)

This is my bag.

Αυτή η σάκα είναι δική μου.   af·ti i sa·ka i·ne thi·ki mu
(lit: this-nom the-nom bag-nom is mine)

gender

Greek nouns have gender – masculine **m**, feminine **f** or neuter **n**. You need to learn the grammatical gender for each noun as you go, but you can often identify it by the noun's ending as shown in the table below. Adjectives, articles and pronouns take the same gender to agree with the noun they qualify.

common noun endings				
masculine	sg	**-ας** πατέρας pa·*te*·ras father	**-ης** ναύτης *naf*·tis sailor	**-ος** δρόμος *thro*·mos road
	pl	**-ες** πατέρες pa·*te*·res fathers	**-ες** ναύτες *naf*·tes sailors	**-οι** δρόμοι *thro*·mi roads
feminine	sg	**-α** πόρτα *por*·ta door	**-η** τύχη *ti*·hi fortune	
	pl	**-ες** πόρτες *por*·tes doors	**-ες** τύχες *ti*·hes fortunes	
neuter	sg	**-μα** όνομα o·*no*·ma name	**-ι** αγόρι a·*gho*·ri boy	**-ο** ποτό po·*to* drink
	pl	**-τα** ονόματα o·*no*·ma·ta names	**-α** αγόρια a·*gho*·ria boys	**-α** ποτά po·*ta* drinks

have

The verb έχω *e*·kho (have) only changes form according to who or what is the subject (doer) of the sentence. To form the future tense (as in the example on page 22), just place the word θα tha (will) in front of the present tense forms.

present			past		
I have	έχω	e·kho	**I had**	είχα	i·kha
you have sg inf	έχεις	e·his	**you had** sg inf	είχες	i·hes
you have sg pol	έχετε	e·he·te	**you had** sg pol	είχατε	i·kha·te
he/she/it has	έχει	e·hi	**he/she/it had**	είχε	i·he
we have	έχουμε	e·khu·me	**we had**	είχαμε	i·kha·me
you have pl	έχετε	e·he·te	**you had** pl	είχατε	i·kha·te
they have	έχουν	e·khun	**they had**	είχαν	i·khan

I'll have no money by the end of my trip!

Δεν θα έχω χρήματα με   ᵵhen tha e·kho khri·ma·ta me
το τέλος του ταξιδιού!   to te·los tu tak·si·ᵵhiu
(lit: not will I-have money-acc with
the-acc end-acc the-gen trip-gen)

negatives

To make a statement negative, add the word δεν ᵵhen (not)
before the verb:

I speak Greek.

Μιλώ Ελληνικά.   mi·lo e·li·ni·ka
(lit: speak Greek)

I don't speak Greek.

Δεν μιλώ Ελληνικά.   ᵵhen mi·lo e·li·ni·ka
(lit: not speak Greek)

In commands, use the word μην min (not) instead:

Don't swim here.

Μην κολυμπάς εδώ.   min ko·li·bas e·ᵵho
(lit: not swim here)

Note that, unlike English, Greek has double negatives:

I don't want anything.
Δεν θέλω τίποτε.   then *the*·lo *ti*·po·te
(lit: not want nothing)

personal pronouns

doing things · making statements

In Greek, there are two words for 'you' – an informal one, εσύ e·*si* (used with friends, younger people or family members), and a formal one, εσείς e·*sis* (used when addressing strangers, authority figures or older people). In this phrasebook we've used the form of 'you' (and the verb form) appropriate for each situation.

	subject nom	
I	εγώ	e·*gho*
you sg inf	εσύ	e·*si*
you sg pol	εσείς	e·*sis*
he/she/it	αυτός/αυτή/αυτό	af·*tos*/af·*ti*/af·*to*
we	εμείς	e·*mis*
you pl	εσείς	e·*sis*
they m/f/n	αυτοί/αυτές/αυτά	af·*ti*/af·*tes*/af·*ta*

	direct object acc		**indirect object** gen	
me	με	me	μου	mu
you sg inf	σε	se	σου	su
you sg pol	σας	sas	σας	sas
him/her/it	τον/την/το	ton/tin/to	του/της/του	tu/tis/tu
us	μας	mas	μας	mas
you pl	σας	sas	σας	sas
them m/f/n	τους/τις/τα	tus/tis/ta	τους	tus

Greek pronouns vary according to case – the subject or doer of an action is in the nominative case while the object is in the accusative or genitive case.

Both direct and indirect object pronouns are placed before the verb. If you have both in a sentence, the indirect pronoun comes first. In commands, they come after the verb.

I gave my passport to him.
Του έδωσα το
διαβατήριό μου.
tu e·țho·sa to
țhia·va·*ti*·ri·o mu
(lit: him-**gen** I-gave the-**acc** passport-**acc** my)

I gave it to him.
Του το έδωσα.
tu to e·țho·sa
(lit: him-**gen** it-**acc** I-gave)

It's not necessary to use a subject pronoun in Greek, as verb endings show who the subject is. A subject pronoun can be used for emphasis or when there's no verb in the sentence.

I go to school everyday.
Πηγαίνω στο σχολείο
κάθε μέρα.
pi·*ye*·no sto skho·*li*·o
ka·the *me*·ra
(lit: go-I to school-**acc** every day)

I **did it.**
Εγώ το έκανα.
e·*gho* to e·ka·na
(lit: I-**nom** it-**acc** did)

plurals

naming people/things

Plural nouns take different endings depending on gender – see the table under **gender** for the most common ones. Adjectives, articles, demonstratives and pronouns also have plural forms to agree with the plural noun.

possessives

Possession can be expressed not only with the verb 'have' but with possessive pronouns and adjectives as well.

The possessive adjectives (my, your, his etc) are placed after the noun, with the definite article before the noun (also see **articles**). They don't change for case, gender or number.

possessive adjectives		
my	μου	mu
your sg inf	σου	su
your sg pol	σας	sas
his/her/its	του/της/του	tu/tis/tu
our	μας	mas
your pl	σας	sas
their	τους	tus

I've lost my car keys.

Έχασα τα κλειδιά *e·kha·sa ta kli·thia*
του αυτοκινήτου μου. *tu af·to·ki·ni·tu mu*
(lit: lost the-acc keys-acc the-gen car-gen my)

Possessive pronouns (mine, yours etc) are formed by adding the word δικός/δική/δικό thi·*kos*/thi·*ki*/thi·*ko* m/f/n in front of the possessive adjective. This word agrees in gender and case with the noun it refers to – endings are the same as those the adjectives take (see **adjectives & adverbs**). To keep things simple we've only given the nominative case in the next table.

possessive pronouns			
	masculine	**feminine**	**neuter**
mine	δικός μου thi·*kos* mu	δική μου thi·*ki* mu	δικό μου thi·*ko* mu
yours sg inf	δικός σου thi·*kos* su	δική σου thi·*ki* su	δικό σου thi·*ko* su
yours sg pol	δικός σας thi·*kos* sas	δική σας thi·*ki* sas	δικό σας thi·*ko* sas
his/hers/its	δικός του/της/του thi·*kos* tu/tis/tu	δική του/της/του thi·*ki* tu/tis/tu	δικό του/της/του thi·*ko* tu/tis/tu
ours	δικός μας thi·*kos* mas	δική μας thi·*ki* mas	δικό μας thi·*ko* mas
yours pl	δικός σας thi·*kos* sas	δική σας thi·*ki* sas	δικό σας thi·*ko* sas
theirs	δικός τους thi·*kos* tus	δική τους thi·*ki* tus	δικό τους thi·*ko* tus

Those bags are ours.

Εκείνες οι τσάντες είναι   e·*ki*·nes i *tsa*·des *i*·ne
δικές μας.   thi·*kes* mas
(lit: those-nom the-nom bags-nom are ours)

prepositions

giving instructions • indicating location •
pointing things out

Many prepositions require the noun used after them to be in
a particular case (see **case**) – σε se (to/at/in), από a·*po* (from),
με me (with), για yia (for), προς pros (towards), κάτω από ka·to
a·*po* (under), πάνω σε *pa*·no se (on) are all followed by the accusative. The genitive is used after μεταξύ me·tak·*si* (between).

I'd like to book a seat to Athens.

Θα ήθελα να κρατήσω   tha *i*·the·la na kra·*ti*·so
μια θέση για την Αθήνα.   mia *the*·si yia tin a·*thi*·na
(lit: I-would like to book
a seat-acc for the-acc Athens-acc)

What's the difference between 1st and 2nd class?

Ποια είναι η διαφορά μεταξύ   pia *i*·ne i thia·fo·*ra* me·tak·*si*
πρώτης και δεύτερης θέσης;   *pro*·tis ke *thef*·te·ris *the*·sis
(lit: which is the-nom difference-nom between
first-gen and second-gen class-gen)

questions

asking questions

To ask a yes/no question, just raise the intonation at the end of a sentence. Note that Greek uses a semicolon (;) instead of a question mark.

The bus stop is over there.

Η στάση του λεωφορείου   i *sta*·si tu le·o·fo·*ri*·u
είναι εκεί πέρα.   *i*·ne e·*ki* pe·ra
(lit: the-nom stop-nom the-gen bus-gen is there over)

Is the bus stop over there?

Η στάση του λεωφορείου   i *sta*·si tu le·o·fo·*ri*·u
είναι εκεί πέρα;   *i*·ne e·*ki* pe·ra
(lit: the-nom stop-nom the-gen bus-gen is there over)

The subject and the verb are often reversed in questions (see **word order**). You can also start a question with a question word – the verb comes in the second place, just like in English. The table on the next page lists the main question words.

question words		
How?	Πώς;	pos
How many?	Πόσοι/Πόσες/Πόσα; m/f/n pl	po·si/po·ses/po·sa
How much?	Πόσος/Πόση/Πόσο; m/f/n	po·sos/po·si/po·so
What?	Τι;	ti
When?	Πότε;	po·te
Where?	Πού;	pu
Who?	Ποιος/Ποια/Ποιο; m/f/n sg Ποιοι/Ποιες/Ποια; m/f/n pl	pios/pia/pio pii/pies/pia
Which?	Ποιος/Ποια/Ποιο; m/f/n sg Ποιοι/Ποιες/Ποια; m/f/n pl	pios/pia/pio pii/pies/pia
Why?	Γιατί;	yi·a·ti

How do you pronounce this?

Πώς προφέρεις αυτό;   pos pro·fe·ris af·to
(lit: how you-pronounce this-acc)

How much is it?

Πόσο κάνει;   po·so ka·ni
(lit: how-much makes)

When's the first bus?

Πότε είναι το πρώτο   po·te i·ne to pro·to
λεωφορείο;   le·o·fo·ri·o
(lit: when is the-nom first-nom bus-nom)

Who is that?

Ποιος είναι εκείνος;   pios i·ne e·ki·nos
(lit: who-nom is that-nom)

Why can't I board this train?

Γιατί δεν μπορώ να ανεβώ   yia·ti then bo·ro na a·ne·vo
σ'αυτό το τρένο;   saf·to to tre·no
(lit: why not can to board to-this-acc the-acc train-acc)

requests

giving instructions

A simple and polite way to make a request is to use the verb
as found in the table on page 30, in its second-person present
form, followed by παρακαλώ pa·ra·ka·*lo* ('please'). Use the
informal (singular) form with people you know well, and the
polite (plural) form with others.

Would you please open the window?

ανοίγεις το παράθυρο,	a·*ni*·yis to pa·*ra*·thi·ro
παρακαλώ; sg inf	pa·ra·ka·*lo*

(lit: open the window please)

Would you please open the window?

ανοίγετε το παράθυρο,	a·*ni*·ye·te to pa·*ra*·thi·ro
παρακαλώ; pl pol	pa·ra·ka·*lo*

(lit: open the window please)

For the negative form, see **negatives**.

verbs

doing things

The dictionary form of all Greek verbs ends in -ω ·o or -ομαι
o·me, which is the present tense form of the first person singular (like in 'I eat'). The ending -ω represents 'active' verbs (which
show someone actively doing something – πηγαίνω pi·*ye*·no
'go'), while -ομαι is for 'stative' verbs (which show a state or
condition, and don't require movement – κάθομαι *ka*·tho·me
'sit'). These endings change according to the subject of the
sentence. Sometimes changes in the verb stem (the form of
the verb before the ending) occur, but if you use the endings
shown on the next page, you'll be understood just fine.

present

Active and stative verbs have different sets of endings.

	active verb eg 'write'		**stative verb** eg 'think'	
dictionary form	γράφω	*ghra·fo*	σκέφτομαι	*skef·to·me*
I	γράφ**ω**	*ghra·fo*	σκέφτομαι	*skef·to·me*
you sg inf	γράφ**εις**	*ghra·fis*	σκέφτ**εσαι**	*skef·te·se*
you sg pol	γράφ**ετε**	*ghra·fe·te*	σκέφτ**εστε**	*skef·tes·te*
he/she/it	γράφ**ει**	*ghra·fi*	σκέφτ**εται**	*skef·te·te*
we	γράφ**ουμε**	*ghra·fu·me*	σκεφτ**όμαστε**	*skef·to·ma·ste*
you pl	γράφ**ετε**	*ghra·fe·te*	σκέφτ**εστε**	*skef·tes·te*
they	γράφ**ουν**	*ghra·fun*	σκέφτ**ονται**	*skef·ton·de*

past

The past tense endings for all verbs are provided below. There are some irregularities, however – as the stress in the verb moves back to the third syllable from the end, the prefix ε e· (augment) is added to the verb when there are less than three syllables. Also, the final letter before the ending sometimes changes.

	all verbs eg 'write'	
I	έγραψα	*e·ghra·psa*
you sg inf	έγραψες	*e·ghra·pses*
you sg pol	γράψατε	*ghra·psa·te*
he/she/it	έγραψε	*e·ghra·pse*
we	γράψαμε	*ghra·psa·me*
you pl	γράψατε	*ghra·psa·te*
they	έγραψαν	*e·ghra·psan*

future

The easiest way to express an action in the future is by using the present tense forms and adding the word θα tha (will) in front of them.

I'll send you a postcard everyday.

Θα σου στέλνω μία κάρτα κάθε μέρα.

tha su *stel*·no mia *kar*·ta *ka*·the *me*·ra

(lit: will you-gen send a-acc postcard-acc every day)

word order

asking questions • making statements • negating

While the sentence order of subject–verb–object is most common in Greek, all other combinations are correct too – the word order is relatively free as Greek uses case (meaning that different word endings express the role of a word in the sentence). You might notice, however, that emphasised words are usually at the beginning of the sentence (see also **negatives** and **questions**).

The cashier didn't give me the correct change.

Ο ταμίας δεν μου έδωσε τα σωστά ρέστα.

o ta·*mi*·as then mu *e*·tho·se ta so·*sta re*·sta

(lit: the-nom cashier-nom not me-gen gave the-acc correct-acc change-acc)

The cashier didn't give me the correct change.

Δεν μου έδωσε τα σωστά ρέστα ο ταμίας.

then mu *e*·tho·se ta so·*sta re*·sta o ta·*mi*·as

(lit: not me-gen gave the-acc correct-acc change-acc the-nom cashier-nom)

Note that the indirect object comes before the direct object.

glossary

active verb	a verb that involves someone actively doing something – 'he **travelled** for many moons'
adjective	a word that describes something – '**ancient** hero'
adverb	a word that explains how an action was done – 'he **heroically** set out to find his father'
article	the words 'a', 'an' and 'the'
case (marking)	word ending that shows the role of the thing or person in the sentence
demonstrative	a word that means 'this' or 'that'
gender	Greek nouns can be masculine, feminine or neuter
imperative	a command – '**prove** to me that you are Odysseus'
noun	a thing, person or idea – 'an **odyssey**'
number	whether a word is singular or plural – 'journey' or 'journeys'
object (direct)	the thing or person that's directly affected by the action – 'Penelope offered **dinner** to her suitors'
object (indirect)	the person in the sentence that benefits from an action – 'Penelope offered **them** dinner'
personal pronoun	a word that means 'I', 'you', etc
possessive pronoun	a word that means 'mine', 'yours', etc
preposition	a word like 'for' or 'before' in English
stative verb	a verb that doesn't require movement – 'Penelope **missed** her husband very much'
subject	the thing or person that does the action – '**the suitors** took advantage of her hospitality'
tense	marking on the verb that tells you whether the action is in the present, past or future – 'travel**led**'
verb	the word that tells you what action happened – 'Odysseus **disguises** himself as a beggar'
verb stem	the part of a verb which does not change – like 'charm' in 'charmed' and 'charming'

Do you speak (English)?
Μιλάς (Αγγλικά);   mi·*las* (ang·gli·*ka*)

Does anyone speak (English)?
Μιλάει κανείς (Αγγλικά);   mi·*la*·i ka·*nis* (ang·gli·*ka*)

Do you understand?
Καταλαβαίνεις;   ka·ta·la·*ve*·nis

Yes, I understand.
Ναι, καταλαβαίνω.   ne ka·ta·la·*ve*·no

No, I don't understand.
Όχι, δεν καταλαβαίνω.   *o*·hi ʒen ka·ta·la·*ve*·no

I (don't) understand.
(Δεν) καταλαβαίνω.   (ʒen) ka·ta·la·*ve*·no

Pardon?
Συγνώμη;   sigh·*no*·mi

I speak (English).
Μιλώ (Αγγλικά).   mi·*lo* (ang·gli·*ka*)

I don't speak Greek.
Δεν μιλώ Ελληνικά.   ʒen mi·*lo* e·li·ni·*ka*

I speak a little.
Μιλώ λίγο.   mi·*lo li*·gho

Let's speak Greek.
Ας μιλήσουμε Ελληνικά.   as mi·*li*·su·me e·li·ni·*ka*

---

tongue-tied

If you're after a challenge, try this tongue twister for size.

Ο παπάς ο παχύς έφαγε παχιά φακή.
Γιατί, παπά παχύ, έφαγες παχιά φακή;
o pa·*pas* o pa·*his* e·fa·ye pa·*hia* fa·*ki*
yia·*ti* pa·*pa* pa·*hi* e·fa·yes pa·*hia* fa·*ki*
(The fat priest ate thick lentil soup.
Why, fat priest, did you eat thick lentil soup?)

I would like to practise Greek.

Θα ήθελα να εξασκήσω   tha *i*·the·la na ek·sa·*ski*·so
τα Ελληνικά μου.   ta e·li·ni·*ka* mu

What does (μώλος) mean?

Τι σημαίνει (μώλος);   ti si·*me*·ni (*mo*·los)

How do you …?   Πώς …;   pos …
  pronounce this   προφέρεις αυτό   pro·*fe*·ris af·*to*
  write 'Madhuri'   γράφεις   *ghrap*·sis
                         'Μαδουρή'   ma·thu·*ri*

Could you   Θα μπορούσες   tha bo·*ru*·ses
please …?   παρακαλώ να …;   pa·ra·ka·*lo* na …
  repeat that   το επαναλάβεις   to e·pa·na·*la*·vis
  speak more   μιλάς πιο αργά   mi·*las* pio ar·*gha*
  slowly
  write it down   το γράψεις   to *ghrap*·sis

---

alphabet soup

Some Greek letters might look like English ones, but they're pronounced quite differently.

upper case	lower case	pronunciation
Β	β	v
Η	η	i
Ρ	ρ	r
Υ	υ	i
Χ	χ	h
Ν	ν	n
Ξ	ξ	ks
Σ	σ/ς	s
Ω	ω	o

See the box on page 14 for the full Greek alphabet.

numbers & amounts

cardinal numbers

απόλυτοι αριθμοί

In Greek, some numbers (one, three, four, and numbers linked to them like 21 and 13) change according to gender – that is, they have different forms when the noun they're associated with is masculine m, feminine f or neuter n. When simply counting, you use the neuter form.

1	ένας/μία/ένα m/f/n	e·nas/mi·a/e·na
2	δύο	thi·o
3	τρεις/τρία m&f/n	tris/tri·a
4	τέσσερις m&f	te·se·ris
	τέσσερα n	te·se·ra
5	πέντε	pe·de
6	έξι	ek·si
7	εφτά	ef·ta
8	οχτώ	okh·to
9	εννέα	e·ne·a
10	δέκα	the·ka
11	έντεκα	e·de·ka
12	δώδεκα	tho·the·ka
13	δεκατρείς m&f	the·ka·tris
	δεκατρία n	the·ka·tri·a
14	δεκατέσσερις m&f	the·ka·te·se·ris
	δεκατέσσερα n	the·ka·te·se·ra
15	δεκαπέντε	the·ka·pe·de
16	δεκαέξι	the·ka·ek·si
17	δεκαεφτά	the·ka·ef·ta
18	δεκαοχτώ	the·ka·okh·to
19	δεκαεννέα	the·ka·e·ne·a
20	είκοσι	i·ko·si
21	είκοσι ένας/μία m/f	i·ko·si e·nas/mi·a
	είκοσι ένα n	i·ko·si e·na

22	είκοσι δύο	i·ko·si thi·o
30	τριάντα	tri·a·da
40	σαράντα	sa·ra·da
50	πενήντα	pe·ni·da
60	εξήντα	ek·si·da
70	εβδομήντα	ev·tho·mi·da
80	ογδόντα	ogh·tho·da
90	ενενήντα	e·ne·ni·da
100	εκατό	e·ka·to
200	διακόσια	thia·ko·sia
1000	χίλια	hi·lia
1,000,000	ένα εκατομμύριο	e·na e·ka·to·mi·rio

ordinal numbers

Ordinals agree in gender with the noun they're associated with.

1st	πρώτος/πρώτη m/f	pro·tos/pro·ti
	πρώτο n	pro·to
2nd	δεύτερος/δεύτερη m/f	thef·te·ros/thef·te·ri
	δεύτερο n	thef·te·ro
3rd	τρίτος/τρίτη/τρίτο m/f/n	tri·tos/tri·ti/tri·to
4th	τέταρτος/τέταρτη m/f	te·tar·tos/te·tar·ti
	τέταρτο n	te·tar·to
5th	πέμπτος/πέμπτη m/f	pem·tos/pem·ti
	πέμπτο n	pem·to
6th	έκτος/έκτη/έκτο m/f/n	ek·tos/ek·ti/ek·to
7th	έβδομος/έβδομη m/f	ev·tho·mos/ev·tho·mi
	έβδομο n	ev·tho·mo
8th	όγδοος/όγδοη m/f	ogh·tho·os/ogh·tho·i
	όγδοο n	ogh·tho·o
9th	ένατος/ένατη/ένατο m/f/n	e·na·tos/e·na·ti/e·na·to
10th	δέκατος/δέκατη m/f	the·ka·tos/the·ka·ti
	δέκατο n	the·ka·to

fractions

κλάσματα

a quarter	ένα τέταρτο n	e·na te·tar·to
a third	ένα τρίτο n	e·na tri·to
a half	μισό n	mi·so
three-quarters	τρία τέταρτα n pl	tri·a te·tar·ta
all	όλα n pl	o·la
none	τίποτε	ti·po·te

useful amounts

χρήσιμα ποσά

The words for 'How much?' and 'How many?' take different forms for the gender of the noun they refer to, as shown below.

How much?	Πόσος/Πόση m/f	po·sos/po·si
	Πόσο; n	po·so
How many?	Πόσοι/Πόσες m/f	po·si/po·ses
	Πόσα; n	po·sa
How much water?	Πόσο νερό; n	po·so ne·ro
How much sugar?	Πόση ζάχαρη; f	po·si za·kha·ri
How many men?	Πόσοι άντρες; m	po·si a·dres
How many women?	Πόσες γυναίκες; f	po·ses yi·ne·kes

numbers & amounts

37

I'd like (a) ...	Θα ήθελα ...	tha *i*·the·la ...
Please give	Παρακαλώ	pa·ra·ka·*lo*
me (a) ...	δώσε μου ...	*tho*·se mu ...
(100) grams	(εκατό)	(e·ka·*to*)
	γραμμάρια	ghra·*ma*·ria
half a dozen	μισή ντουζίνα	mi·*si* du·*zi*·na
dozen	μια ντουζίνα	mia du·*zi*·na
half a kilo	μισό κιλό	mi·*so* ki·*lo*
kilo	ένα κιλό	*e*·na ki·*lo*
bottle	ένα μπουκάλι	*e*·na bu·*ka*·li
jar	ένα βάζο	*e*·na *va*·zo
tin	ένα κουτί	*e*·na ku·*ti*
packet	ένα πακέτο	*e*·na pa·*ke*·to
slice	μια φέτα	mia *fe*·ta
few	λίγα	*li*·gha
less	λιγότερο	li·*gho*·te·ro
(just) a little	(μόνο) λιγάκι	(*mo*·no) li·*gha*·ki
lot	πολύ	po·*li*
many	πολλά	po·*la*
more	πιο πολύ	pio po·*li*
some ...	μερικά ...	me·ri·*ka* ...

To find out how to put these amounts to use, see **self-catering**, page 171.

---

what's in a name?

Although Greeks have moved around their own country and emigrated worldwide, you can sometimes tell from their surnames where they originally come from. People whose name ends in -ακης -a·kis are from Crete, -ατος -a·tos from Cephallonia, -ιδης -i·this from Macedonia, and -πουλος -pu·los from the Peloponnese.

time & dates
ώρα και ημερομηνίες

telling the time

Telling the time in Greek is straightforward. For 'It's … o'clock' simply say είναι *i*·ne (lit: it-is) followed by the number, then η ώρα i *o*·ra (lit: the-hour). Note that η ώρα is optional. To give times after the hour say the number of hours, then και ke (lit: and) and the number of minutes. For times before the hour say the number of hours, then παρά pa·*ra* (lit: minus) and the minutes. Instead of 30 or 15 minutes, say μισή mi·*si* (half) for the half hour and τέταρτο te·tar·to (quarter).

What time is it?
Τι ώρα είναι; ti *o*·ra *i*·ne

It's (ten) o'clock.
Είναι (δέκα) η ώρα. *i*·ne (*the*·ka) i *o*·ra

Five past (ten).
(Δέκα) και πέντε. (*the*·ka) ke *pe*·de

Quarter past (ten).
(Δέκα) και τέταρτο. (*the*·ka) ke te·tar·to

Half past (ten).
(Δέκα) και μισή. (*the*·ka) ke mi·*si*

Quarter to (ten).
(Δέκα) παρά τέταρτο. (*the*·ka) pa·*ra* te·tar·to

Twenty to (ten).
(Δέκα) παρά είκοσι. (*the*·ka) pa·*ra* i·ko·si

At what time …?
Τι ώρα …; ti *o*·ra …

At (ten).
Στις (δέκα). stis (*the*·ka)

At (7.57pm).
Στις (7.57μ.μ.). stis (ef·*ta* ke pe·*ni*·da ef·*ta* me·*ta* to me·si·*me*·ri)

The times 'am' and 'pm' are written 'π.μ.' and 'μ.μ.', but you always say the full name – πριν το μεσημέρι prin to me·si·me·ri (am) and μετά το μεσημέρι me·ta to me·si·me·ri (pm).

the calendar

το ημερολόγιο

days

Monday	Δευτέρα	thef·te·ra
Tuesday	Τρίτη	tri·ti
Wednesday	Τετάρτη	te·tar·ti
Thursday	Πέμπτη	pem·ti
Friday	Παρασκευή	pa·ra·ske·vi
Saturday	Σάββατο	sa·va·to
Sunday	Κυριακή	ki·ria·ki

months

January	Ιανουάριος	i·a·nu·a·ri·os
February	Φεβρουάριος	fev·ru·a·ri·os
March	Μάρτιος	mar·ti·os
April	Απρίλιος	a·pri·li·os
May	Μάιος	ma·i·os
June	Ιούνιος	i·u·ni·os
July	Ιούλιος	i·u·li·os
August	Αύγουστος	av·ghu·stos
September	Σεπτέμβριος	sep·tem·vri·os
October	Οκτώβριος	ok·tov·ri·os
November	Νοέμβριος	no·em·vri·os
December	Δεκέμβριος	the·kem·vri·os

dates

What date is it today?

Τι ημερομηνία είναι σήμερα; ti i·me·ro·mi·ni·a i·ne si·me·ra

It's (18 October).

Είναι (18 Οκτωβρίου). i·ne (the·ka·okh·to ok·tov·ri·u)

seasons

spring	άνοιξη f	*a*·nik·si
summer	καλοκαίρι n	ka·lo·*ke*·ri
autumn	φθινόπωρο n	fthi·*no*·po·ro
winter	χειμώνας m	hi·*mo*·nas

present

παρόν

now	τώρα	*to*·ra
today	σήμερα	*si*·me·ra
tonight	το βράδι	to *vra*·thi
this week	αυτή την εβδομάδα	af·*ti* tin ev·tho·*ma*·tha
this ...	αυτό το ...	af·*to* to ...
morning	πρωί	pro·*i*
afternoon	απόγευμα	a·*po*·yev·ma
month	μήνα	*mi*·na
year	χρόνο	*khro*·no

past

παρελθόν

(three days) ago	(τρεις μέρες) πριν	(tris *me*·res) prin
day before yesterday	προχτές	prokh·*tes*
since (May)	από (το Μάιο)	a·*po* (to *ma*·i·o)
yesterday ...	χτες το ...	khtes to ...
morning	πρωί	pro·*i*
afternoon	απόγευμα	a·*po*·yev·ma
evening	βράδι	*vra*·thi

last night/week
την περασμένη
νύχτα/εβδομάδα

tin pe·raz·*me*·ni
nikh·ta/ev·tho·*ma*·tha

last month/year
τον περασμένο μήνα/χρόνο

ton pe·raz·*me*·no *mi*·na/*khro*·no

future

tomorrow ...	αύριο το ...	*av*·ri·o to ...
morning	πρωί	pro·*i*
afternoon	απόγευμα	a·*po*·yev·ma
evening	βράδι	*vra*·ṭhi
tomorrow	αύριο	*av*·ri·o
day after tomorrow	μεθαύριο	me·*thav*·ri·o
next week	την επόμενη εβδομάδα	tin e·*po*·me·ni ev·ṭho·*ma*·ṭha
next month	τον επόμενο μήνα	ton e·*po*·me·no *mi*·na
next year	τον επόμενο χρόνο	ton e·*po*·me·no *khro*·no
in (six days)	σε (έξι μέρες)	se (*ek*·si *me*·res)
until (June)	μέχρι (τον Ιούνιο)	*meh*·ri (ton i·*u*·ni·o)

during the day

afternoon	απόγευμα n	a·*po*·yev·ma
dawn	αυγή f	av·*yi*
day	ημέρα f	i·*me*·ra
evening	βράδι n	*vra*·ṭhi
midday	μεσημέρι n	me·si·*me*·ri
midnight	μεσάνυχτα n pl	me·*sa*·nikh·ta
morning	πρωί n	pro·*i*
night	νύχτα f	*nikh*·ta
sunrise	ανατολή του ήλιου f	a·na·to·*li* tu *i*·liu
sunset	δύση του ήλιου f	*ṭhi*·si tu *i*·liu

but the most important time of day ...

... is probably the μεσημεριανή ανάπαυση me·si·*me*·ria·*ni* a·*na*·paf·si (siesta). Don't miss out!

How much is it?
Πόσο κάνει; *po*·so *ka*·ni

It's (12) euros.
Κάνει (δώδεκα) ευρώ. *ka*·ni (*tho·*the·ka) ev·*ro*

It's free.
Είναι δωρεάν. *i*·ne tho·re·*an*

Can you write down the price?
Μπορείς να γράψεις την τιμή; bo·*ris* na *ghrap*·sis tin ti·*mi*

Do you accept ...?	Δέχεσαι ...;	*the*·he·se ...
credit cards	πιστωτικές	pi·sto·ti·*kes*
	κάρτες	*kar*·tes
debit cards	χρεωτικές	khre·o·ti·*kes*
	κάρτες	*kar*·tes
travellers	ταξιδιωτικές	tak·si·thio·ti·*kes*
cheques	επιταγές	e·pi·ta·*yes*
Where's a/an ...?	Πού είναι ...;	pu *i*·ne ...
automated	μια αυτόματη	mia af·*to*·ma·ti
teller machine	μηχανή	mi·kha·*ni*
	ανάληψης	a·*na*·lip·sis
	χρημάτων	khri·*ma*·ton
foreign exchange	ένα γραφείο	*e*·na ghra·*fi*·o
office	αλλαγής	a·la·*yis*
	χρημάτων	khri·*ma*·ton

The official currency in Greece is the ευρώ ev·ro (euro),
which is made up of 100 λεπτά lep·ta (euro cents). Some
vendors are also happy to take foreign currencies.

What's the …?	Πόσο είναι …;	po·so i·ne …
charge	το κόστος	to kos·tos
exchange rate	η τιμή	i ti·mi
	συναλλάγματος	si·na·lagh·ma·tos

I'd like to …	Θα ήθελα να …	tha i·the·la na …
cash a cheque	εξαργυρώσω	ek·sar·yi·ro·so
	μια επιταγή	mia e·pi·ta·yi
change money	αλλάξω χρήματα	a·lak·so khri·ma·ta
change a	αλλάξω μια	a·lak·so mia
travellers	ταξιδιωτική	tak·si·thio·ti·ki
cheque	επιταγή	e·pi·ta·yi
get a cash	κάμω μια	ka·mo mia
advance	ανάληψη	a·na·lip·si
	σε μετρητά	se me·tri·ta
withdraw	αποσύρω	a·po·si·ro
money	χρήματα	khri·ma·ta

I'd like …,	Θα ήθελα …,	tha i·the·la …
please.	παρακαλώ.	pa·ra·ka·lo
my change	τα ρέστα μου	ta re·sta mu
a refund	μια επιστροφή	mia e·pi·stro·fi
	χρημάτων	khri·ma·ton
to return this	να επιστρέψω αυτό	na e·pi·strep·so af·to

There's a mistake in the bill.
Υπάρχει κάποιο λάθος   i·par·hi ka·pio la·thos
στο λογαριασμό.   sto lo·gha·riaz·mo

Do I need to pay upfront?
Χρειάζεται να πληρώσω   khri·a·ze·te na pli·ro·so
από πριν;   a·po prin

I don't have that much money.
Δεν έχω τόσα πολλά   then e·kho to·sa po·la
χρήματα.   khri·ma·ta

getting around

κυκλοφορώντας

Which ... goes to (Athens)?	Ποιο ... πηγαίνει στην (Αθήνα)	pio ... pi·ye·ni stin (a·thi·na)
Is this the ... to (Athens)?	Είναι αυτό το ... για την (Αθήνα);	i·ne af·to to ... yia tin (a·thi·na)
boat	πλοίο	pli·o
bus	λεωφορείο	le·o·fo·ri·o
ferry	φέρυ	fe·ri
plane	αεροπλάνο	a·e·ro·pla·no
train	τρένο	tre·no
When's the ... (bus)?	Πότε είναι το ... (λεωφορείο);	po·te i·ne to ... (le·o·fo·ri·o)
first	πρώτο	pro·to
last	τελευταίο	te·lef·te·o
next	επόμενο	e·po·me·no

What time does it leave?
Τι ώρα φεύγει;   ti o·ra fev·yi

What time does it get to (Thessaloniki)?
Τι ώρα φτάνει στη   ti o·ra fta·ni sti
(Θεσσαλονίκη);   (the·sa·lo·ni·ki)

How long will it be delayed?
Πόση ώρα θα καθυστερήσει;   po·si o·ra tha ka·thi·ste·ri·si

Is this seat free?
Είναι αυτή η θέση ελεύθερη;   i·ne af·ti i the·si e·lef·the·ri

That's my seat.
Αυτή η θέση είναι δική μου.   af·ti i the·si i·ne thi·ki mu

transport

45

Please tell me when we get to (Thessaloniki).

Παρακαλώ πέστε μου
όταν φτάσουμε στη
(Θεσσαλονίκη).

pa·ra·ka·lo pe·ste mu
o·tan fta·su·me sti
(the·sa·lo·ni·ki)

How long do we stop here?

Πόση ώρα θα
σταματήσουμε εδώ;

po·si o·ra tha
sta·ma·ti·su·me e·tho

Are you waiting for more people?

Περιμένεις για
περισσότερο κόσμο;

pe·ri·me·nis yia
pe·ri·so·te·ro koz·mo

Can you take us around the city, please?

Μπορείς να μας πάρεις
γύρω στην πόλη,
παρακαλώ;

bo·ris na mas pa·ris
yi·ro stin po·li
pa·ra·ka·lo

How many people can ride on this?

Πόσοι άνθρωποι μπορούν
να ανεβούν σ'αυτό;

po·si an·thro·pi bo·run
na a·ne·vun saf·to

Can you take me as well?

Μπορείς να πάρεις
και εμένα;

bo·ris na pa·ris
ke e·me·na

tickets

Where do I buy a ticket?

Πού αγοράζω εισιτήριο;

pu a·gho·ra·zo i·si·ti·ri·o

Do I need to book?

Χρειάζεται να κλείσω θέση;

khri·a·ze·te na kli·so the·si

A bunch of (10) tickets, please.

Μια δέσμη από (δέκα)
εισιτήρια, παρακαλώ.

mia thez·mi a·po (the·ka)
i·si·ti·ri·a pa·ra·ka·lo

Do you have a timetable (in English)?

Έχεις ένα πρόγραμμα
(στα αγγλικά);

e·his e·na pro·ghra·ma
(sta ang·gli·ka)

Can I get a tourist rail pass?

Μπορώ να έχω ένα		bo·ro na e·kho e·na
τουριστικό πάσο		tu·ri·sti·ko pa·so
για το τρένο;		yia to tre·no

A ... ticket	Ένα εισιτήριο ...	e·na i·si·ti·ri·o ...
to (Patras).	για την (Πάτρα).	yia tin (pa·tra)
1st-class	πρώτη θέση	pro·ti the·si
2nd-class	δεύτερη θέση	thef·te·ri the·si
child's	παιδικό	pe·thi·ko
deck class (boat)	κατάστρωμα	ka·ta·stro·ma
one-way	απλό	a·plo
return	με επιστροφή	me e·pi·stro·fi
student's	μαθητικό	ma·thi·ti·ko
tourist class	τουριστική θέση	tu·ri·sti·ki the·si

I'd like a/an ...	Θα ήθελα μια	tha i·the·la mia
seat.	θέση ...	the·si ...
aisle	στο διάδρομο	sto thia·thro·mo
(non)smoking	στους (μη)	stus (mi)
	καπνίζοντες	kap·ni·zo·des
window	στο παράθυρο	sto pa·ra·thi·ro

transport

47

Is there (a) …?	Υπάρχει …;	i·*par*·hi …
air conditioning	έρκοντίσιον	e·kon·*di*·si·on
blanket	κουβέρτα	ku·*ver*·ta
sick bag	σακούλα εμετού	sa·*ku*·la e·me·*tu*
toilet	τουαλέτα	tu·a·*le*·ta

Can I get a sleeping berth?

Μορώ να έχω μια θέση	bo·*ro* na *e*·kho mia *the*·si
με κρεβάτι	me kre·*va*·ti

How much is it?

Πόσο κάνει;	*po*·so *ka*·ni

How long does the trip take?

Πόσο διαρκεί το ταξίδι;	*po*·so thi·ar·*ki* to tak·*si*·thi

Is it a direct route?

Πηγαίνει κατ'ευθείαν;	pi·*ye*·ni ka·tef·*thi*·an

Can I get a stand-by ticket?

Μπορώ να μπω στον	bo·*ro* na bo ston
κατάλογο αναμονής	ka·*ta*·lo·gho a·na·mo·*nis*
για εισιτήριο;	yia i·si·*ti*·ri·o

What time should I check in?

Τι ώρα να έρθω στον	ti *o*·ra na *er*·tho ston
έλεγχο;	*e*·leng·kho

I'd like to … my ticket, please.	Θα ήθελα να … το εισιτήριό μου παρακαλώ.	tha *i*·the·la na … to i·si·*ti*·ri·o mu pa·ra·ka·*lo*
cancel	ακυρώσω	a·ki·*ro*·so
change	αλλάξω	a·*lak*·so
confirm	επικυρώσω	e·pi·ki·*ro*·so

---

it's not roulette

If Athenian locals talk about μονά-ζυγά mo·*na*·zi·*gha* (odds-evens) and δακτύλιος thak·*ti*·lios (rings), they refer to traffic restrictions put in place in Athens to help minimise the notorious νέφος *ne*·fos (smog). The system is called 'odd-evens' because certain cars can enter the 'ring' (a restricted zone) on even or odd days of the month. The boundaries of the thak·*ti*·lios are marked with yellow hexagonal signs.

luggage

Where can I find a/the …?	Πού μπορώ να βρω …;	pu bo·ro na vro …
baggage claim	το χώρο αποσκευών	to kho·ro a·pos·ke·von
left-luggage office	φύλαξη αποσκευών	fi·lak·si a·pos·ke·von
luggage locker	τη φύλαξη αντικειμένων	ti fi·lak·si a·di·ki·me·non
trolley	ένα καροτσάκι	e·na ka·rot·sa·ki

My luggage has been …	Οι αποσκευές μου έχουν …	i a·pos·ke·ves mu e·khun …
damaged	πάθει ζημιά	pa·thi zi·mia
lost	χαθεί	kha·thi
stolen	κλαπεί	kla·pi

That's (not) mine.
Αυτό (δεν) είναι δικό μου.   af·to (then) i·ne thi·ko mu

Can I have some coins/tokens?
Μπορώ να έχω μερικά   bo·ro na e·kho me·ri·ka
κέρματα/κουπόνια;   ker·ma·ta/ku·po·nia

listen for ...

αποσκευές χειρός f pl	a·pos·ke·ves hi·ros	carry-on baggage
διαβατήριο n	thia·va·ti·ri·o	passport
κάρτα επιβίβασης f	kar·ta e·pi·vi·va·sis	boarding pass
κουπόνι n	ku·po·ni	token
μεταβίβαση f	me·ta·vi·va·si	transfer
πτήση τσάρτερ f	pti·si tsar·ter	charter flight
τράνζιτ n	tran·zit	transit
υπέρβαρο n	i·per·va·ro	excess baggage

plane

Where does flight (10) arrive/depart?
Πού προσγειώνεται/   pu pros·yi·o·ne·te/
απογειώνεται η πτήση (δέκα);   a·po·yi·o·ne·te i pti·si (the·ka)

Where's (the) …?   Πού είναι …;   pu i·ne …
   airport shuttle   το λεωφορείο   to le·o·fo·ri·o
        του αεροδρομίου   tu a·e·ro·thro·mi·u
   arrivals hall   η αίθουσα των   i e·thu·sa ton
        αφίξεων   a·fik·se·on
   departures hall   η αίθουσα των   i e·thu·sa ton
        ανα χωρήσεων   a·na kho·ri·se·on
   duty-free shops   τα αφορολόγητα   ta a·fo·ro·lo·yi·ta
   gate (9)   η θύρα (εννέα)   i thi·ra (e·ne·a)

bus, trolley bus & coach

How often do buses come?
Κάθε πότε έρχονται τα   ka·the po·te er·kho·de ta
λεωφορεία;   le·o·fo·ri·a

Does it stop at (Iraklio)?
Σταματάει στο (Ηράκλειο);   sta·ma·ta·i sto (i·ra·kli·o)

What's the next stop?
Ποια είναι η επόμενη στάση;   pia i·ne i e·po·me·ni sta·si

I'd like to get off (at Iraklio).
Θα ήθελα να κατεβώ   tha i·the·la na ka·te·vo
(στο Ηράκλειο).   (sto i·ra·kli·o)

Where's the trolley bus stop?
Πού είναι η στάση του τρόλεϋ;   pu i·ne i sta·si tu tro·le·i

city a   αστικό   a·sti·ko
intercity a   υπεραστικό   i·pe·ra·sti·ko
local a   τοπικό   to·pi·ko

train & metro

Where's the nearest metro station?
Πού είναι ο πιο κοντινός   pu *i*·ne o pio ko·di·*nos*
σταθμός του μετρό;   stath·*mos* tu me·*tro*

Which line goes to (the port)?
Ποια γραμμή πηγαίνει   pia ghra·*mi* pi·ye·ni
(στο λιμάνι);   (sto li·*ma*·ni)

What station is this?
Ποιος σταθμός είναι αυτός;   pios stath·*mos* i·ne af·tos

What's the next station?
Ποιος είναι ο επόμενος   pios i·ne o e·*po*·me·nos
σταθμός;   stath·*mos*

Does it stop at (Kalamata)?
Σταματάει στην (Καλαμάτα);   sta·ma·*ta*·i stin (ka·la·*ma*·ta)

Do I need to change?
Χρειάζεται να αλλάξω;   khri·*a*·ze·te na a·*lak*·so

Is it direct/express?
Είναι κατ'ευθείαν/εξπρές;   i·ne ka·tef·*thi*·an/eks·*pres*

Which carriage is ...?	Ποια άμαξα είναι (για) ...;	pia *a*·mak·sa i·ne (yia) ...
1st class	πρώτη θέση	*pro*·ti *the*·si
for dining	φαγητό	fa·yi·*to*
for (Kalamata)	την (Καλαμάτα)	tin (ka·la·*ma*·ta)

north & south

On Greek maps and road signs, 'N' stands for Νότια *no*·ti·a
(south) and 'B' stands for Βόρια *vo*·ri·a (north).

boat

βάρκα

Where's the port/port police?
Πού είναι το λιμάνι/
λιμεναρχείο;
pu *i*·ne to li·*ma*·ni/
li·me·nar·*hi*·o

Can I have the ferry timetable?
Μπορώ να έχω το
πρόγραμμα του φέρι;
bo·*ro* na *e*·kho to
pro·ghra·ma tu *fe*·ri

Where does the boat to (Chios) leave from?
Από πού φεύγει το πλοίο
για τη (Χίο);
a·*po* pu *fev*·yi to *pli*·o
yia ti (*hi*·o)

When is the next boat for (Naxos)?
Πότε είναι το επόμενο
πλοίο για τη (Νάξο);
po·te *i*·ne to e·*po*·me·no
pli·o yia ti (*nak*·so)

Does this ferry go to (Rhodos)?
Πηγαίνει αυτό το φέρι
στη (Ρόδο);
pi·*ye*·ni af·*to* to *fe*·ri
sti (*ro*·ţho)

How many hours is it to (Milos)?

Πόσες ώρες είναι για
τη (Μήλο);

po·ses o·res i·ne yia ti (mi·lo)

How many stops does the boat make?

Πόσες στάσεις κάνει
το πλοίο;

po·ses sta·sis ka·ni to pli·o

Where can I get a taxi boat?

Πού μπορώ να νοικιάσω
μια βάρκα με βαρκάρη;

pu bo·ro na ni·kia·so mia var·ka me var·ka·ri

Where can we hire an uncrewed boat?

Πού μπορώ να νοικιάσω
μόνο μια βάρκα;

pu bo·ro na ni·kia·so mo·no mia var·ka

I'd like a/an ...	Θα ήθελα ...	*tha i·the·la ...*
cabin for	μια καμπίνα για	*mia ka·bi·na yia*
one/two	ένα/δύο	*e·na/thi·o*
inside/outside	μια εσωτερική/	*mia e·so·te·ri·ki/*
cabin	εξωτερική καμπίνα	*ek·so·te·ri·ki ka·bi·na*

What's the sea like today?

Πώς είναι η θάλασσα
σήμερα;

pos i·ne i tha·la·sa si·me·ra

Are there life jackets?

Υπάρχουν σωσίβια;

i·par·khun so·si·vi·a

What island is this?

Ποιο νησί είναι αυτό;

pio ni·si i·ne af·to

What beach is this?

Ποια παραλία είναι αυτή;

pia pa·ra·li·a i·ne af·ti

I feel seasick.

Αισθάνομαι ναυτία.

es·tha·no·me naf·ti·a

cabin	καμπίνα f	ka·bi·na
caïque (large fishing boat)	καΐκι n	ka·i·ki
captain	καπετάνιος m	ka·pe·ta·nios
car deck	χώρος για αυτοκίνητο στο κατάστρωμα m	kho·ros yia af·to·ki·ni·to sto ka·ta·stro·ma
catamaran	σχεδία καταμαράν f	she·thi·a ka·ta·ma·ran
cruise	κρουαζέρα f	kru·a·ze·ra
deck	κατάστρωμα n	ka·ta·stro·ma
excursion boat	εκδρομική βάρκα f	ek·thro·mi·ki var·ka
ferry	φέρι n	fe·ri
hammock	αιώρα f	e·o·ra
hydrofoil	ιπτάμενο δελφίνι n	ip·ta·me·no thel·fi·ni
inter-island boat	πλοίο συγκοινωνίας μεταξύ νησιών n	pli·o si·gi·no·ni·as me·tak·si ni·sion
jolly roger	βάρκα πλοίου f	var·ka pli·u
lifeboat	ναυαγοσωστική λέμβος f	na·va·gho·so·sti·ki lem·vos
life jacket	σωσίβιο n	so·si·vi·o
muster station	χώρος συγκέντρωσης m	kho·ros si·ge·dro·sis
purser's office	γραφείο λογιστή n	ghra·fi·o lo·yi·sti
sailing boat	ιστιοφόρο n	i·sti·o·fo·ro
small fishing boat	μικρή βάρκα για ψάρεμα f	mi·kri var·ka yia psa·re·ma
yacht	γιωτ n	yiot

taxi

ταξί

I'd like a taxi …	Θα ήθελα ένα ταξί …	tha i·the·la e·na tak·si …
at (9am)	στις (εννέα π.μ.)	stis (e·ne·a prin to me·si·me·ri)
now	τώρα	to·ra
tomorrow	αύριο	av·ri·o

Where's the taxi rank?
Πού είναι η στάση για ταξί;   pu *i*·ne i *sta*·si yia tak·*si*

Is this taxi available?
Είναι αυτό το ταξί ελεύθερο;   *i*·ne af·*to* to tak·*si* e·*lef*·the·ro

Please put the meter on.
Παρακαλώ βάλε το   pa·ra·ka·*lo va*·le to
ταξίμετρο.   tak·*si*·me·tro

How much is it (to Petroupoli)?
Πόσο κάνει (για Πετρούπολη);   *po*·so *ka*·ni (yia pe·*tru*·po·li)

Please take me to (this address).
Παρακαλώ πάρε με σε   pa·ra·ka·*lo pa*·re me se
(αυτή τη διεύθυνση).   (af·*ti* ti thi·*ef*·thin·si)

How much do you charge for the luggage?
Πόσο χρεώνεις για   *po*·so khre·*o*·nis yia
τις αποσκευές;   tis a·pos·ke·*ves*

Please …	Παρακλώ …	pa·ra·ka·*lo* …
slow down	πήγαινε πιο σιγά	*pi*·ye·ne pio si·*gha*
stop here	σταμάτα εδώ	sta·*ma*·ta e·*tho*
wait here	περίμενε εδώ	pe·*ri*·me·ne e·*tho*

car & motorbike

car & motorbike hire

I'd like to hire a/an …	Θα ήθελα να ενοικιάσω ένα …	tha *i*·the·la na e·ni·ki·*a*·so *e*·na …
4WD	4W ντράιβ	for·ghu·*il dra*·iv
automatic	αυτόματο	af·*to*·ma·to
car	αυτοκίνητο	af·to·*ki*·ni·to
manual	με ταχύτητες	me ta·*hi*·ti·tes
motorbike	μοτοσακό	mo·to·sa·*ko*
with …	με …	me …
air conditioning	έρκοντίσιον	e·kon·*di*·si·on
a driver	οδηγό	o·thi·*gho*

How much for daily/weekly hire?

Πόσο νοικάζεται την
ημέρα/εβδομάδα;

*po·so ni·kia·ze·te tin
i·me·ra/ev·tho·ma·tha*

Does that include insurance/mileage?

Αυτό συμπεριλαμβάνει
ασφάλεια/χιλιόμετρα;

*af·to si·be·ri·lam·va·ni
as·fa·li·a/hi·lio·me·tra*

Can I take the car on a ferry?

Μπορώ να πάρω το
αυτοκίνητο στο φέρι;

*bo·ro na pa·ro to
af·to·ki·ni·to sto fe·ri*

Do you have a guide to the road rules in English?

Έχετε οδικό κώδικα
κυκλοφορίας στα Αγγλικά;

*e·he·te o·thi·ko ko·thi·ka
ki·klo·fo·ri·as sta ang·gli·ka*

Do you have a road map?

Έχετε οδικό χάρτη;

e·he·te o·thi·ko khar·ti

on the road

What's the speed limit?

Ποιο είναι το όριο ταχύτητας; *pio i·ne to o·ri·o ta·hi·ti·tas*

Is this the road to (Lamia)?

Είναι αυτός ο δρόμος για
(τη Λαμία);

*i·ne af·tos o thro·mos yia
(ti la·mi·a)*

Where's a petrol station?

Πού είναι ένα πρατήριο
βενζίνας;

*pu i·ne e·na pra·ti·ri·o
ven·zi·nas*

Fill it up, please.

Γεμίστε το, παρακαλώ. *ye·mis·te to pa·ra·ka·lo*

signs		
Απαγορεύεται η είσοδος	a·pa·gho·re·ve·te i i·so·thos	**No Entry**
Διόδια	thi·o·thi·a	**Toll**
Είσοδος	i·so·thos	**Entrance (Freeway)**
Έξοδος Εθνικής Οδού	ek·so·thos e·th·ni·kis o·thu	**Exit Freeway**
Προσοχή	pro·so·hi	**Drive With Care**
Μονόδρομος	mo·no·thro·mos	**One-Way**

άδεια οδήγησης f	a·thi·a o·thi·yi·sis	drivers licence
βενζίνα f	ven·zi·na	petrol (gas)
δωρεάν	tho·re·an	free a
επί τόπου	e·pi to·pu	on-the-spot
ασφάλεια f	as·fa·li·a	insurance
παρκόμετρο n	par·ko·me·tro	parking meter
Πράσινη κάρτα f	pra·si·ni kar·ta	Green Card (international third-party insurance)
χιλιόμετρα n pl	hi·lio·me·tra	kilometres

diesel	ντίζελ n	di·zel
leaded	μολυβδούχος f	mo·liv·thu·khos
LPG	υγραέριο n	igh·ra·e·ri·o
premium	σούπερ	su·per
unleaded	αμόλυβδος f	a·mo·liv·thos
regular	απλή f	ap·li
unleaded	αμόλυβδος f	a·mo·liv·thos

Can you check the ...?	Μπορείς να κοιτάξεις ...;	bo·ris na ki·tak·sis ...
oil	το λάδι	to la·thi
tyre pressure	την πίεση των τροχών	tin pi·e·si ton tro·khon
water	το νερό	to ne·ro

(How long) Can I park here?

(Πόση ώρα) Μπορώ να
παρκάρω εδώ;

(po·si o·ra) bo·ro na
par·ka·ro e·tho

Do I have to pay?

Πρέπει να πληρώσω;

pre·pi na pli·ro·so

problems

I need a mechanic.
Χρειάζομαι μηχανικό.
khri·*a*·zo·me mi·kha·ni·*ko*

I've had an accident.
Είχα ένα ατύχημα.
i·kha *e*·na a·*ti*·hi·ma

The car/motorbike has broken down (at Corinth).
Το αυτοκίνητο/μοτοσακό
χάλασε (στην Κόρινθο).
to af·to·*ki*·ni·to/mo·to·sa·*ko*
ha·la·se (stin *ko*·rin·tho)

The car/motorbike won't start.
Το αυτοκίνητο/μοτοσακό
δεν αρχίζει.
to af·to·*ki*·ni·to/mo·to·sa·*ko*
then ar·*hi*·zi

I have a flat tyre.
Μ'έπιασε λάστιχο.
me·pia·se *la*·sti·kho

I've lost my car keys.
Έχασα τα κλειδιά του
αυτοκινήτου μου.
e·ha·sa ta kli·*thia* tu
af·to·ki·*ni*·tu mu

petrol
βενζίνα f
ven·*zi*·na

windscreen
παμπρίζ n
pab·*riz*

battery
μπαταρία f
ba·ta·*ri*·a

engine
μηχανή f
mi·kha·*ni*

tyre
λάστιχο n
las·ti·kho

headlight
φως n
fos

I've locked the keys inside.
Κλείδωσα τα κλειδιά μου   *kli·ṭho·sa ta kli·ṭhia mu*
στο αυτοκίνητου.   *sto af·to·ki·ni·to*

I've run out of petrol.
Μου τελείωσε η βενζίνα.   *mu te·li·o·se i ven·zi·na*

Can you fix it (today)?
Μπορείς να το   *bo·ris na to*
επισκευάσεις (σήμερα);   *e·pis·ke·va·sis (si·me·ra)*

How long will it take?
Πόση ώρα θα κάμει;   *po·si o·ra tha ka·mi*

bicycle

ποδήλατο

I'd like ...	Θα ήθελα ...	tha *i·*the·la ...
my bicycle	να επισκευάσω	na e·pis·ke·*va·*so
repaired	το ποδήλατό μου	to po·*ṭhi·*la·to mu
to buy a bicycle	να αγοράσω ένα	na a·gho·*ra·*so e·na
	ποδήλατο	po·*ṭhi·*la·to
to hire a bicycle	να νοικιάσω ένα	na ni·*kia·*so e·na
	ποδήλατο	po·*ṭhi·*la·to

I'd like a ... bike.	Θα ήθελα ένα ...	tha *i·*the·la e·na ...
mountain	ποδήλατο για	po·*ṭhi·*la·to yia
	βουνό	vu·*no*
racing	ποδήλατο	po·*ṭhi·*la·to
	κούρσας	*kur·*sas
second-hand	μεταχειρισμένο	me·ta·hi·riz·*me·*no
	ποδήλατο	po·*ṭhi·*la·to

How much is it per day?
Πόσο κοστίζει την ημέρα;   *po·so ko·sti·zi tin i·me·ra*

How much is it per hour?
Πόσο κοστίζει την ώρα;   *po·so ko·sti·zi tin o·ra*

Do I need a helmet?
Χρειάζομαι κράνος;　　　　khri·a·zo·me kra·nos

Is there a bicycle-path map?
Υπάρχει χάρτης για δρόμο　　i·par·hi khar·tis yia thro·mo
ποδηλάτου;　　　　　　　　po·thi·la·tu

Is this road OK for bicycles?
Είναι αυτός ο δρόμος　　　　i·ne af·tos o thro·mos
κατάλληλος για ποδήλατα;　　ka·ta·li·los yia po·thi·la·ta

I have a puncture.
Τρύπησε η ρόδα μου.　　　　tri·pi·se i ro·tha mu

Greeks tend to get pretty physical when they talk about their emotions:

I'm not impressed.
Δεν μου γεμίζει το μάτι.　　　then mu ye·mi·zi to ma·ti
(lit: It doesn't fill my eye.)

I can't stand him/her.
Δεν τον/την χωνεύω.　　　　then ton/tin tso·ne·vo
(lit: I can't digest him/her.)

I've had enough of you.
Μ'έπρηξες.　　　　　　　　me·prik·ses
(lit: You've made me swollen.)

I regretted it.
Μου βγήκε από τη μύτη.　　　mu vyi·ke a·po ti mi·ti
(lit: It came out of my nose.)

He/She put me under pressure.
Μου βαλε τα δυο πόδια　　　mu va·le ta thio po·thia
σ' ένα παπούτσι.　　　　　　se·na pa·put·si
(lit: He/She put both my feet in one shoe.)

border crossing

περνώντας τα σύνορα

I'm ...	Είμαι ...	*i*-me ...
in transit	τράνζιτ	*tran*-zit
on business	για δουλειά	yia thu-*lia*
on holiday	σε διακοπές	se thia-ko-*pes*

I'm here for	Είμαι εδώ για	*i*-me e-*tho* yia
(three) ...	(τρεις) ...	(tris) ...
days	μέρες	*me*-res
weeks	εβδομάδες	ev-tho-*ma*-thes
months	μήνες	*mi*-nes

I'm going to (Limassol).
Πηγαίνω στη (Λεμεσό).   pi-*ye*-no sti (le-me-*so*)

I'm staying at (the Xenia).
Μένω στο (Ξενία).   *me*-no sto (kse-*ni*-a)

The children are on this passport.
Τα παιδιά είναι σ'αυτό   ta pe-*thia i*-ne saf-*to*
το βιαβατήριο.   to thia-va-*ti*-ri-o

listen for ...

άδεια **f**	*a*-thi-a	export permit
εξαγωγής	ek-sa-gho-*yis*	
βίζα **f**	*vi*-za	visa
διαβατήριο **n**	thia-va-*ti*-ri-o	passport
μόνος **m**	*mo*-nos	alone
οικογένεια **f**	i-ko-*ye*-ni-a	family
ομάδα **f**	o-*ma*-tha	group
ταυτότητα **f**	taf-*to*-ti-ta	ID card

Can you stamp a separate paper instead of the passport?

Μπορείτε να σφραγίσετε
ένα χωριστό χαρτί αντί
για το διαβατήριο;

bo·*ri*·te na sfra·*yi*·se·te
e·na kho·ri·*sto* khar·*ti* a·*di*
yia to thia·va·*ti*·ri·o

Where can I get a travel permit for (Mt Athos)?

Πού μπορώ να πάρω μια
άδεια ταξιδιού για (το
Άγιο Όρος);

pu bo·*ro* na *pa*·ro mia
a·thi·a tak·si·*thiu* yia (to
a·yi·o *o*·ros)

at customs

I have nothing to declare.

Δεν έχω τίποτε να δηλώσω. then e·kho *ti*·po·te na thi·*lo*·so

I have something to declare.

Έχω κάτι να δηλώσω. e·kho *ka*·ti na thi·*lo*·so

Do I have to declare this?

Πρέπει να το δηλώσω αυτό; *pre*·pi na to thi·*lo*·so af·*to*

That's (not) mine.

Αυτό (δεν) είναι δικό μου. af·*to* (then) *i*·ne thi·*ko* mu

I didn't know I had to declare it.

Δεν ήξερα πως έπρεπε να
το δηλώσω.

then *ik*·se·ra pos e·*pre*·pe na
to thi·*lo*·so

I have a doctor's certificate for this medication.

Έχω πιστοποιητικό γιατρού
για αυτό το φάρμακο.

e·kho pis·to·pi·i·ti·*ko* yia·*tru*
yia af·*to* to *far*·ma·ko

signs

Αφορολόγητα	a·fo·ro·*lo*·yi·ta	**Duty-Free**
Έλεγχος	e·len·ghos	**Passport Control**
Διαβατηρίων	thia·va·ti·*ri*·on	
Καραντίνα	ka·ran·*di*·na	**Quarantine**
Τελωνείο	te·lo·*ni*·o	**Customs**
Μετανάστευση	me·ta·*na*·stef·si	**Immigration**

PRACTICAL

Where's (the tourist office)?
Πού είναι (το τουριστικό γραφείο);
pu *i*·ne (to tu·ri·sti·*ko* ghra·*fi*·o)

What's the address?
Ποια είναι η διεύθυνση;
pia *i*·ne i thi·*ef*·thin·si

How far is it?
Πόσο μακριά είναι;
po·so ma·kri·*a i*·ne

How do I get there?
Πώς πηγαίνω εκεί;
pos pi·*ye*·no e·*ki*

What street is this?
Ποιος δρόμος είναι αυτός;
pios *thro*·mos *i*·ne af·*tos*

What village is this?
Ποιο χωριό είναι αυτό;
pio kho·*rio i*·ne af·*to*

Can you show me (on the map)?
Μπορείς να μου δείξεις (στο χάρτη);
bo·*ris* na mu *thik*·sis (sto *khar*·ti)

It's …	Είναι …	*i*·ne …
close	κοντά	ko·*da*
behind …	πίσω …	*pi*·so …
here	εδώ	e·*tho*
in front of …	μπροστά από …	bros·*ta* a·*po* …
near …	κοντά	ko·*da* …
next to …	δίπλα από …	*thip*·la a·*po* …
on the corner	στη γωνία	sti gho·*ni*·a
opposite …	απέναντι …	a·*pe*·na·di …
straight ahead	κατ'ευθείαν	ka·tef·*thi*·an
there	εκεί	e·*ki*

north	βόρια	*vo*·ri·a
south	νότια	*no*·ti·a
east	ανατολικά	a·na·to·li·*ka*
west	δυτικά	thi·ti·*ka*

χιλιόμετρα	hi·*lio*·me·tra	**kilometres**
λεπτά	lep·*ta*	**minutes**
μέτρα	*me*·tra	**metres**

avenue	λεωφόρος f	le·o·*fo*·ros
lane	πάροδος f	*pa*·ro·thos
street	οδός f	o·*thos*

| **by bus/taxi** | με λεωφορείο/ταξί | me le·o·fo·*ri*·o/tak·*si* |
| **on foot** | με πόδια | me *po*·thia |

Turn ...	Στρίψε ...	*strip*·se ...
at the corner	στη γωνία	sti gho·*ni*·a
at the traffic lights	στα φανάρια	sta fa·*na*·ria
left	αριστερά	a·ris·te·*ra*
right	δεξιά	thek·si·*a*

traffic lights
φανάρια n pl
fa·*na*·ria

shop
κατάστημα n
ka·*tas*·ti·ma

pedestrian crossing
διάβαση πεζών f
thi·*a*·va·si pe·*zon*

bus
λεωφορείο n
le·o·fo·*ri*·o

intersection
διασταύρωση f
thi·a·*stav*·ro·si

corner
γωνία f
gho·*ni*·a

taxi
ταξί n
tak·*si*

PRACTICAL

64

finding accommodation

βρίσκοντας κατάλυμα

Where's (a) ...?	Πού είναι ...;	pu *i*·ne ...
bed and	κατάλυμα με	ka·*ta*·li·ma me
breakfast	πρόγευμα	*pro*·ghev·ma
camping	χώρος για	*kho*·ros yia
ground	κάμπινγκ	*kam*·ping
guesthouse	ξενώνας	kse·*no*·nas
(3-star) hotel	ξενοδοχείο	kse·no·*tho*·*hi*·o
	(τριών αστέρων)	(tri·*on* a·*ste*·ron)
mountain	ορεινό	o·ri·*no*
refuge	καταφύγιο	ka·ta·*fi*·yi·o
pension	πανσιόν	pan·*sion*
room for	δωμάτιο για	tho·*ma*·ti·o yia
rent	νοίκιασμα	*ni*·kiaz·ma
self-contained	ξεχωριστό	kse·kho·ri·*sto*
apartment	διαμέρισμα	thi·a·*me*·riz·ma
some traditional	παραδοσιακό	pa·ra·tho·si·a·*ko*
accommodation	κατάλυμα	ka·*ta*·li·ma
youth hostel	γιουθ χόστελ	yiuth *kho*·stel

dive	βουτιά f	vu·*tia*
rat-infested	γεμάτο ποντίκια	ye·*ma*·to po·*di*·kia
top spot	ωραιότατο σημείο n	o·re·o·ta·to si·*mi*·o

Can you	Μπορείτε να	bo·*ri*·te na
recommend	συστήσετε	si·*sti*·se·te
somewhere ...?	κάπου ...;	*ka*·pu ...
cheap	φτηνό	fti·*no*
good	καλό	ka·*lo*
nearby	κοντινό	ko·di·*no*
romantic	ρομαντικό	ro·ma·di·*ko*

What's the address?

Ποια είναι η διεύθυνση;   pia *i*·ne i thi·*ef*·thin·si

For responses, see **directions**, page 63.

booking ahead & checking in

I'd like to book a room, please.

Θα ήθελα να κλείσω ένα   tha *i*·the·la na *kli*·so *e*·na
δωμάτιο, παρακαλώ.   tho·*ma*·ti·o pa·ra·ka·*lo*

I have a reservation.

Έχω κάμει κάποια κράτηση.   *e*·kho *ka*·mi *ka*·pia *kra*·ti·si

My name's ...

Με λένε ...   me *le*·ne ...

For (three) nights/weeks.

Για (τρεις) νύχτες/   yia (tris) *nikh*·tes/
εβδομάδες.   ev·tho·*ma*·thes

From (2 July) to (6 July).

Από (τις δύο Ιουλίου)   a·*po* (tis *thi*·o i·u·*li*·u)
μέχρι (τις έξι Ιουλίου).   *me*·khri (tis *ek*·si i·u·*li*·u)

listen for ...

Πόσες νύχτες;	*po*·ses *nikh*·tes	**How many nights?**
διαβατήριο n	thia·va·*ti*·ri·o	**passport**
γεμάτο	ye·*ma*·to	**full** a
κλειδί n	kli·*thi*	**key**
ρεσεψιόν f	re·sep·*sion*	**reception**

PRACTICAL

66

Ελεύθερα δωμάτια	e-lef-the-ra tho-ma-ti-a	**Vacancy**
Μπάνιο	ba-nio	**Bathroom**
Πλήρες	pli-res	**No Vacancy**

Do you have	Έχετε ένα ...	e-he-te e-na ...
a ... room?	δωμάτιο	tho-ma-ti-o
single	μονό	mo-no
double	διπλό	thi-plo
twin	δίκλινο	thi-kli-no

How much is it	Πόσο είναι για	po-so i-ne yia
per ...?	κάθε ...;	ka-the ...
night	νύχτα	nikh-ta
person	άτομο	a-to-mo
week	εβδομάδα	ev-tho-ma-tha

Can I see it?
Μπορώ να το δω;   bo-ro na to tho

I'll take it.
Θα το πάρω.   tha to pa-ro

Do I need to pay upfront?
Χρειάζεται να πληρώσω   khri-a-ze-te na pli-ro-so
από πριν;   a-po prin

Can I pay by ...?	Μπορώ να	bo-ro na
	πληρώσω με ...;	pli-ro-so me ...
credit card	πιστωτική κάρτα	pi-sto-ti-ki kar-ta
travellers	ταξιδιωτική	tak-si-thio-ti-ki
cheque	επιταγή	e-pi-ta-yi

For other methods of payment, see **shopping**, page 77.

accommodation

requests & queries

When/Where is breakfast served?

Πότε/Πού σερβίρεται το πρόγευμα;	po·te/pu ser·vi·re·te to pro·yev·ma

Please wake me at (seven).

Παρακαλώ ξύπνησέ με στις (εφτά).	pa·ra·ka·lo ksip·ni·se me stis (ef·ta)

Do you ... here? ... εδώ; ... e·*tho*

arrange tours	Κανονίζετε ξεναγήσεις	ka·no·*ni*·ze·te kse·na·*yi*·sis
change money	Αλλάζετε χρήματα	a·*la*·ze·te *khri*·ma·ta

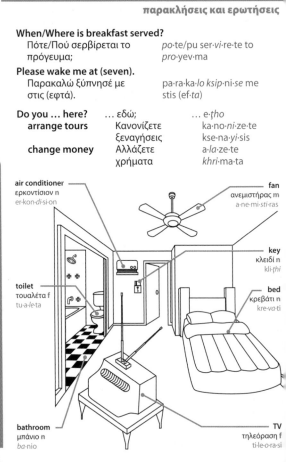

air conditioner
ερκοντίσιον n
er·kon·*di*·si·on

fan
ανεμιστήρας m
a·ne·mi·*sti*·ras

key
κλειδί n
kli·*thi*

toilet
τουαλέτα f
tu·a·*le*·ta

bed
κρεβάτι n
kre·*va*·ti

bathroom
μπάνιο n
ba·nio

TV
τηλεόραση f
ti·le·*o*·ra·si

Can I use the ...?	Μπορώ να χρησιμοποιήσω ...;	bo·ro na khri·si·mo·pi·i·so ...
kitchen	την κουζίνα	tin ku·zi·na
laundry	το πλυντήριο	to pli·di·ri·o
telephone	το τηλέφωνο	to ti·le·fo·no

Do you have a/an ...?	Έχετε ...;	e·he·te ...
elevator	ασανσέρ	a·san·ser
laundry service	υπηρεσία πλυντηρίου	i·pi·re·si·a pli·di·ri·u
message board	πίνακα μηνυμάτων	pi·na·ka mi·ni·ma·ton
safe	χρηματοκιβώτιο	khri·ma·to·ki·vo·ti·o
swimming pool	πισίνα	pi·si·na

Could I have (a/an) ..., please?	Μπορώ να έχω ... παρακαλώ;	bo·ro na e·kho ... pa·ra·ka·lo
extra blanket	μια κουβέρτα ακόμη	mia ku·ver·ta a·ko·mi
my key	το κλειδί μου	to kli·thi mu
mosquito net	μια κουνουπιέρα	mia ku·nu·pie·ra
receipt	μια απόδειξη	mia a·po·thik·si

Is there hot water all day?
Υπάρχει ζεστό νερό όλη την ημέρα;
i·par·hi ze·sto ne·ro o·li tin i·me·ra

Is there a message for me?
Υπάρχει μήνυμα για μένα;
i·par·hi mi·ni·ma yia me·na

Can I leave a message for someone?
Μπορώ να αφήσω ένα μήνυμα για κάποιον;
bo·ro na a·fi·so e·na mi·ni·ma yia ka·pion

I'm locked out of my room.
Κλειδώθηκα έξω από το δωμάτιό μου.
kli·tho·thi·ka ek·so a·po to tho·ma·ti·o mu

69

complaints

It's too ...	Είναι πάρα πολύ ...	i·ne pa·ra po·li ...
bright	φωτεινό	fo·ti·no
cold	κρύο	kri·o
dark	σκοτεινό	sko·ti·no
expensive	ακριβό	a·kri·vo
noisy	θορυβώδες	tho·ri·vo·thes
small	μικρό	mi·kro

The ... doesn't work.	... δεν δουλεύει.	... then thu·le·vi
air conditioner	Το ερκοντίσιον	to er·kon·di·si·on
fan	Ο ανεμιστήρας	o a·ne·mi·sti·ras
toilet	Η τουαλέτα	i tu·a·le·ta

Can I get another (blanket)?
Μπορώ να πάρω μια άλλη (κουβέρτα);
bo·ro na pa·ro mia a·li (ku·ver·ta)

This (pillow) isn't clean.
Αυτό (το μαξιλάρι) δεν είναι καθαρό.
af·to (to mak·si·la·ri) then i·ne ka·tha·ro

---

a knock at the door ...

Who is it?
Ποιος είναι;
pios i·ne

Just a moment.
Μια στιγμή.
mia stigh·mi

Come in.
Περάστε.
pe·ra·ste

Come back later, please.
Έλα αργότερα, παρακαλώ.
e·la ar·gho·te·ra pa·ra·ka·lo

checking out

What time is checkout?
Τι ώρα είναι η αναχώρηση; ti *o*·ra *i*·ne i a·na·*kho*·ri·si

Can I have a late checkout?
Μπορώ να φύγω αργά; bo·*ro* na *fi*·gho ar·*gha*

Can you call a taxi for me (for 11 o'clock)?
Μπορείτε να καλέσετε ένα bo·*ri*·te na ka·*le*·se·te *e*·na
ταξί (για τις έντεκα); tak·*si* (yia tis *e*·de·ka)

I'm leaving now.
Φεύγω τώρα. *fev*·gho *to*·ra

Can I leave my bags here?
Μπορώ να αφήσω τις bo·*ro* na a·*fi*·so tis
βαλίτσες μου εδώ; va·*lit*·ses mu e·*tho*

There's a mistake in the bill.
Υπάρχει κάποιο λάθος i·*par*·hi *ka*·pio *la*·thos
στο λογαριασμό. sto lo·gha·riaz·*mo*

Could I have	Μπορώ να έχω ...	bo·*ro* na *e*·kho ...
my ..., please?	παρακλώ;	pa·ra·ka·*lo*
deposit	την προκατα-	tin pro·ka·ta·
	βολή μου	vo·*li* mu
passport	το διαβατήριο	to thia·va·*ti*·rio
	μου	mu
valuables	τα κοσμήματά	ta koz·*mi*·ma·*ta*
	μου	mu

I'll be back ...	Θα επιστρέψω ...	tha e·pi·*strep*·so ...
in (three) days	σε (τρεις) μέρες	se (tris) *me*·res
on (Tuesday)	την (Τρίτη)	tin *tri*·ti

I had a great stay, thank you.
Είχα υπέροχη διαμονή, *i*·kha i·*pe*·ro·hi thi·a·mo·*ni*
ευχαριστώ. ef·kha·ri·*sto*

I'll recommend it to my friends.
Θα το συστήσω στους tha si·*sti*·so stus
φίλους μου. *fi*·lus mu

camping

Do you have (a) …?	Έχετε …	e·he·te …
electricity	ηλεκτρισμό	i·lek·triz·mo
laundry	πλυντήριο	pli·di·ri·o
site	χώρο	kho·ro
shower	εγκαταστάσεις	e·ga·ta·sta·sis
facilities	για ντουζ	yia duz
tents for hire	τέντες για	te·des yia
	νοίκιασμα	ni·kiaz·ma

How much is it per …?	Πόσο κοστίζει για κάθε …;	po·so ko·sti·zi yia ka·the …
caravan	τροχόσπιτο	tro·kho·spi·to
person	άτομο	a·to·mo
tent	τέντα	te·da
vehicle	αυτοκίνητο	af·to·ki·ni·to

Can I camp here?
Μπορώ να
κατασκηνώσω εδώ;
bo·ro na
ka·ta·ski·no·so e·tho

Can I park next to my tent?
Μπορώ να παρκάρω
δίπλα στην τέντα μου;
bo·ro na par·ka·ro
thi·pla stin te·da mu

Who do I ask to stay here?
Ποιον ρωτάω για να
μείνω εδώ;
pion ro·ta·o yia na
mi·no e·tho

Could I borrow …?
Μπορώ να δανειστώ …;
bo·ro na tha·ni·sto …

Is it coin-operated?
Λειτουργεί με κέρματα;
li·tur·yi me ker·ma·ta

Is the water drinkable?
Είναι το νερό πόσιμο;
i·ne to ne·ro po·si·mo

When you're making a request, make it sound more polite by starting your question with μήπως *mi*·pos, the equivalent of the English 'Do you, by any chance, …?'.

Do you, by any chance, have a room with a view?
Μήπως έχετε ένα
δωμάτιο με θέα;
mi·pos *e*·hete *e*·na
tho·*ma*·tio me *the*·a

See the **phrasebuilder** for more on requests.

renting

νοικιάζοντας

I'm here about the … for rent.	Είμαι εδώ για το … που νοικιάζεται.	*i*·me e·*tho* yia to … pu ni·*kia*·ze·te
Do you have a/an … for rent?	Έχεις ένα … για νοίκιασμα;	*e*·his *e*·na … yia ni·*kiaz*·ma
apartment	διαμέρισμα	thi·a·*me*·riz·ma
house	σπίτι	*spi*·ti
room	δωμάτιο	tho·*ma*·ti·o
I'm here about the … for rent.	Είμαι εδώ για την … που νοικιάζεται.	*i*·me e·*tho* yia tin … pu ni·*kia*·ze·te
Do you have a … for rent?	Έχεις μια … για νοίκιασμα;	*e*·his mia … yia ni·*kiaz*·ma
cabin	καμπίνα	ka·*bi*·na
villa	έπαυλη	*e*·pav·li
furnished	με έπιπλα	me *e*·pi·pla
partly furnished	με λίγα έπιπλα	me *li*·gha *e*·pi·pla
unfurnished	χωρίς έπιπλα	kho·*ris* *e*·pi·pla

accommodation

73

staying with locals

Can I stay at your place?
Μπορώ να μείνω στο
σπίτι σου;

bo·ro na mi·no sto
spi·ti su

Is there anything I can do to help?
Μπορώ να κάνω κάτι για
να βοηθήσω;

bo·ro na ka·no ka·ti yia
na vo·i·thi·so

I have my own ...	Έχω το δικό μου ...	e·kho to thi·ko mu ...
mattress	στρώμα	stro·ma
sleeping bag	σλίπινγκ μπαγκ	sli·ping bag

Can I ...?	Μπορώ να ...;	bo·ro na ...
bring anything for the meal	φέρω κάτι για το φαγητό	fe·ro ka·ti yia to fa·yi·to
do the dishes	πλύνω τα πιάτα	pli·no ta pia·ta
set/clear the table	στρώσω/μαζέψω το τραπέζι	stro·so/ma·zep·so to tra·pe·zi
take out the rubbish	βγάλω έξω τα σκουπίδια	vgha·lo ek·so ta sku·pi·thia

Thanks for your hospitality.
Ευχαριστώ για τη
φιλοξενία σας.

ef·kha·ri·sto yia ti
fi·lok·se·ni·a sas

If you're dining with your hosts, see **eating out**, page 157, for additional phrases.

see **eating out**, page 157

---

foreign visitors

Punctuality for social engagements is not taken as seriously as you might be used to. An invitation for 9pm means that most people won't show up before 9.30pm. An evening coffee can sometimes extend to dinner, and not end until after midnight. Such a long visit is known in Greek as an αρμένικη βίζιτα ar·me·ni·ki vi·si·ta (Armenian visit).

looking for ...

ψάχνοντας για ...

Where's ...?	Πού είναι ...;	pu *i*·ne ...
a department store	ένα κατάστημα	*e*·na ka·*ta*·sti·ma
the flea market	το παζάρι	to pa·*za*·ri
the food market	η αγορά τροφίμων	i a·gho·*ra* tro·*fi*·mon
a kiosk	ένα περίπτερο	*e*·na pe·*rip*·te·ro
the street market	η λαϊκή αγορά	i la·i·*ki* a·gho·ra
a supermarket	ένα σούπερ-μάρκετ	*e*·na *su*·per *mar*·ket
a souvenir shop	ένα κατάστημα με σουβενίρ	*e*·na ka·*ta*·sti·ma me su·ve·*nir*

On which day is the street market held?
Ποια μέρα έχει λαϊκή;   pia *me*·ra e·hi la·i·*ki*

Where can I buy (a padlock)?
Πού μπορώ να αγοράσω   pu bo·*ro* na a·gho·*ra*·so
(μια κλειδαριά);   (mia kli·tha·*ria*)

For phrases on directions, see **directions**, page 63.

listen for ...

Μπορώ να σας βοηθήσω; bo·*ro* na sas vo·i·*thi*·so	**Can I help you?**
Τίποτε άλλο; *ti*·po·te *a*·lo	**Anything else?**
Όχι, δεν έχουμε. *o*·hi then *e*·khu·me	**No, we don't have any.**
Να το τυλίξω; na to ti·*lik*·so	**Shall I wrap it?**

making a purchase

I'm just looking.
Απλά κοιτάζω.
a·*pla* ki·*ta*·zo

I'd like to buy (an adaptor plug).
Θα ήθελα να αγοράσω
(ένα μετασχηματιστή).
tha i·*the*·la na a·gho·*ra*·so
(*e*·na me·ta·shi·ma·ti·*sti*)

Can I look at it?
Μπορώ να το κοιτάξω;
bo·*ro* na to ki·*tak*·so

Do you have any others?
Έχετε άλλα;
e·he·te *a*·la

How much is it?
Πόσο κάνει;
po·so *ka*·ni

Can you write down the price?
Μπορείς να γράψεις την τιμή;
bo·*ris* na *ghrap*·sis tin ti·*mi*

Does it have a guarantee?
Έχει εγγύηση;
e·hi e·*gi*·i·si

Could I have it wrapped?
Μπορείς να μου το τυλίξεις;
bo·*ris* na mu to ti·*lik*·sis

Could I have a bag/receipt, please?
Μπορώ να έχω μια τσάντα/
απόδειξη, παρακαλώ;
bo·*ro* na *e*·kho mia *tsa*·da/
a·*po*·thik·si pa·ra·ka·*lo*

Can I have it sent overseas?
Μπορείς να το στείλεις
στο εξωτερικό;
bo·*ris* na to *sti*·lis
sto ek·so·te·ri·*ko*

Can you order it for me?
Μπορείς να το παραγγείλεις
για μένα;
bo·*ris* na to pa·ra·*gi*·lis
yia *me*·na

Can I pick it up later?
Μπορώ να το πραλάβω
αργότερα;
bo·*ro* na to pa·ra·*la*·vo
ar·*gho*·te·ra

It's faulty.
Είναι ελαττωματικό.
i·ne e·la·to·ma·ti·*ko*

Do you accept ...?	Δέχεστε ...;	*the*·he·ste ...
credit cards	πιστωτικές κάρτες	pi·sto·ti·*kes kar*·tes
debit cards	χρεωτικές κάρτες	khre·o·ti·*kes kar*·tes
travellers cheques	ταξιδιωτικές επιταγές	tak·si·*thio*·ti·*kes* e·pi·ta·*yes*
I'd like ..., please.	Θα ήθελα ..., παρακαλώ.	tha *i*·the·la ... pa·ra·ka·*lo*
a refund	επιστροφή χρημάτων	e·pi·stro·*fi* khri·*ma*·ton
my change	τα ρέστα μου	ta *re*·sta mu
to return this	να επιστρέψω αυτό	na e·pi·*strep*·so af·*to*

bargaining

παζάρεμα

That's too expensive.
Είναι πάρα πολύ ακριβό.   *i*·ne *pa*·ra po·*li* a·kri·*vo*

I don't have that much money.
Δεν έχω τόσα πολλά   *then* e·kho *to*·sa po·*la*
χρήματα.   khri·*ma*·ta

Do you have something cheaper?
Έχεις κάτι πιο φτηνό;   e·his *ka*·ti pio fti·*no*

Can you lower the price?
Μπορείς να κατεβάσεις
την τιμή;

bo·*ris* na ka·te·*va*·sis
tin ti·*mi*

How much for (two)?
Πόσο κάνει για (δύο);

po·so *ka*·ni yia (*thi*·o)

I'll give you (five euros).
Θα σου δώσω (πέντε ευρώ).

tha su *tho*·so (*pe*·de ev·*ro*)

books & reading

βιβλία και διάβασμα

Is there an English-language bookshop/section?
Υπάρχει ένα βιβλιοπωλείο/
τμήμα Αγγλικής γλώσσας;

i·*par*·hi e·na viv·li·o·po·*li*·o/
tmi·ma ang·gli·*kis* ghlo·sas

Can you recommend a book for me?
Μπορείς να μου συστήσεις
ένα βιβλίο;

bo·*ris* na mu si·*sti*·sis
e·na viv·*li*·o

Do you have Lonely Planet guidebooks?
Έχετε βιβλία-οδηγούς του
Λόνλι Πλάνετ;

e·he·te viv·*li*·a·o·*thi*·*ghus* tu
lon·li *pla*·net

Do you have ...?	Έχεις ένα ...;	e·his e·na ...
a book by (Nikos Kazantzakis)	βιβλίο (του Νίκου Καζαντζάκη)	viv·*li*·o (tu *ni*·ku ka·za·*dza*·ki)
an entertainment guide	οδηγό διασκεδάσεων	o·*thi*·*gho* thias·ke·*tha*·se·on

I'd like a ...	Θα ήθελα ...	tha *i*·the·la ...
dictionary	ένα λεξικό	e·na lek·si·*ko*
newspaper (in English)	μια εφημερίδα (στα Αγγλικά)	mia e·fi·me·*ri*·tha (sta ang·gli·*ka*)
notepad	ένα μπλοκ για σημειώσεις	e·na blok yia si·mi·o·sis

clothes

ρούχα

My size is …	Το νούμερό μου είναι …	to *nu·me·ro* mu *i·*ne …
(40)	(σαράντα)	(sa·*ra·*da)
small	μικρό	mi·*kro*
medium	μεσαίο	me·*se·*o
large	μεγάλο	me·*gha·*lo

Can I try it on?
Μπορώ να το προβάρω;   bo·*ro* na to pro·*va·*ro

It doesn't fit.
Δε μου κάνει.   ţhe mu *ka·*ni

electronic goods

ηλεκτρονικά είδη

Where can I buy duty-free electronic goods?
Πού μπορώ να αγοράσω   pu bo·*ro* na a·gho·*ra·*so
αφορολόγητα ηλεκτρονικά   a·fo·ro·*lo·*yi·ta i·lek·tro·ni·*ka*
είδη;   *i·*ţhi

Is this the latest model?
Είναι αυτό το τελευταίο   *i·*ne af·*to* to te·lef·*te·*o
μοντέλο;   mo·*de·*lo

Is this (240) volts?
Είναι αυτό   *i·*ne af·*to*
(240) βολτ;   (ţhia·*ko·*sia sa·*ra·*da) volt

I need an adaptor plug.
Χρειάζομαι ένα   khri·*a·*zo·me *e·*na
μετασχηματιστή.   me·ta·shi·ma·ti·*sti*

shopping

79

hairdressing

I'd like (a) ...	Θα ήθελα ένα ...	tha *i*·the·la *e*·na ...
blow wave	στέγνωμα	*stegh*·no·ma
	με πιστολάκι	me pis·to·*la*·ki
colour	βάψιμο	*vap*·si·mo
haircut	κούρεμα	*ku*·re·ma
my beard	ψαλίδισμα	psa·*li*·thiz·ma
trimmed	στο μούσι μου	sto *mu*·si mu
shave	ξύρισμα	*ksi*·riz·ma

Don't cut it too short.
Μην τα κόψεις πολύ κοντά.   min ta *kop*·sis po·*li* ko·*da*

Please use a new blade.
Παρακαλώ χρησιμοποίησε   pa·ra·ka·*lo* khri·si·mo·*pi*·i·se
καινούργιο ξυράφι.   ke·*nur*·yio ksi·*ra*·fi

Shave it all off!
Ξύρισέ τα όλα.   *ksi*·ri·se ta *o*·la

I should never have let you near me!
Δεν θα έπρεπε ποτέ να σε   ţhen tha *e*·pre·pe po·*te* na se
αφήσω κοντά μου!   a·*fi*·so ko·*da* mu

barber	κουρέας m	ku·*re*·as
beauty salon	ινστιτούτο	in·sti·*tu*·to
	αισθητικής n	es·thi·ti·*kis*
for both sexes	και για τα δύο φύλα	ke yia ta *ţhi*·o *fi*·la
men's	κομμωτής	ko·mo·*tis*
hairdresser	για άντρες m	yia *a*·dres
women's	κομμωτής	ko·mo·*tis*
hairdresser	για γυναίκες m	yia yi·*ne*·kes

music & DVD

I'd like a CD/DVD.
Θα ήθελα ένα CD/DVD.   tha *i*·the·la *e*·na si·*di*/di·vi·*di*

I'm looking for something by (Anna Vissi).
Ψάχνω για κάτι   *psakh*·no yia *ka*·ti
(της Άννας Βίσση).   (tis *a*·na *vi*·si)

What's his/her best recording?
Ποια είναι η καλύτερη   pia *i*·ne i ka·*li*·te·ri
ηχογράφησή του/της;   i·kho·*ghra*·fi·si tu/tis

Does this work on all DVD players?
Παίζει σε όλα τα DVD;   *pe*·zi se *o*·la ta di·vi·*di*

Is this for a (PAL/NTSC) system?
Είναι κατάλληλο για   *i*·ne ka·*ta*·li·lo yia
σύστημα (PAL/NTSC);   *si*·sti·ma (pal/en·ti·es·*si*)

video & photography

Can you ...?	Μπορείς να ...;	bo·*ris* na ...
develop	εμφανίσεις	em·fa·*ni*·sis
digital	ψηφιακές	psi·fi·a·*kes*
photos	φωτογραφίες	fo·to·ghra·*fi*·es
develop this	εμφανίσεις	em·fa·*ni*·sis
film	αυτό το φιλμ	af·*to* to film
load my film	βάλεις το φιλμ	*va*·lis to film
	στη μηχανή μου	sti mi·kha·*ni* mu
recharge the	φορτίσεις την	for·*ti*·sis tin
battery for	μπαταρία για την	ba·ta·*ri*·a yia tin
my digital	ψηφιακή μου	psi·fi·a·*ki* mu
camera	μηχανή	mi·kha·*ni*
transfer	μεταφέρεις	me·ta·*fe*·ris
photos from	φωτογραφίες από	fo·to·ghra·*fi*·es a·*po*
my camera	την φωτογραφική	ti fo·to·ghra·fi·*ki*
to CD	μου μηχανή στο CD	mu mi·kha·*ni* sto si·*di*

I need ... film for this camera.	Χρειάζομαι φιλμ ... για αυτή τη μηχανή.	khri·a·zo·me film ... yia af·ti ti mi·kha·ni
APS	APS	e·i·pi·es
B&W	μαυρόασπρο	mav·ro·a·spro
colour	έγχρωμο	eng·khro·mo
slide	σλάιντ	sla·id
(200) speed	ταχύτητα (200)	ta·hi·ti·ta (thia·ko·si·on)

Do you have ... for this camera?	Έχεις ... για αυτή τη φωτογραφική μηχανή;	e·his ... yia af·ti ti fo·to·ghra·fi·ki mi·kha·ni
batteries	μπαταρίες	ba·ta·ri·es
memory cards	κάρτες μνήμης	kar·tes mni·mis

I need a cable to connect my camera to a computer.

Χρειάζομαι ένα καλώδιο για να συνδέσω τη μηχανή μου στο κομπιούτερ.

khri·a·zo·me e·na ka·lo·thi·o yia na sin·the·so ti mi·kha·ni mu sto kom·piu·ter

I need a cable to recharge this battery.

Χρειάζομαι ένα καλώδιο για να φορτίσω αυτή τη μπαταρία.

khri·a·zo·me e·na ka·lo·thi·o yia na for·ti·so af·ti ti ba·ta·ri·a

I need a video cassette for this camera.

Χρειάζομαι μια βιντεοκασέτα για αυτή τη μηχανή.

khri·a·zo·me mia vi·de·o·ka·se·ta yia af·ti ti mi·kha·ni

Do you have disposable (underwater) cameras?

Έχεις (υποβρύχιες) φωτογραφικές μηχανές μιας χρήσης;

e·his (i·pov·ri·hi·es) fo·to·ghra·fi·kes mi·kha·nes mias khri·sis

When will it be ready?

Πότε θα είναι έτοιμο; po·te tha i·ne e·ti·mo

How much is it?

Πόσο κάνει; po·so ka·ni

I need a passport photo taken.

Θέλω να βγάλω φωτογραφία για διαβατήριο.

the·lo na vga·lo fo·to·ghra·fi·a yia thia·va·ti·ri·o

I'm not happy with these photos.

Δεν είμαι ικανοποιημένος/
ικανοποιημένη με αυτές
τις φωτογραφίες. **m/f**

then i·me i·ka·no·pi·i·*me*·nos/
i·ka·no·pi·i·*me*·ni me af·*tes*
tis fo·to·ghra·*fi*·es

I don't want to pay the full price.

Δεν θέλω να πληρώσω
ολόκληρη την τιμή.

then *the*·lo na pli·*ro*·so
o·*lo*·kli·ri tin ti·*mi*

repairs

Can I have my …	Μπορώ να	bo·*ro* na
repaired here?	επισκευάσω εδώ …;	e·pi·ske·*va*·so e·*tho* …
backpack	το σάκο μου	to *sa*·ko mu
camera	τη φωτογραφική	ti fo·to·ghra·fi·*ki*
	μηχανή μου	mi·kha·*ni* mu
shoes	τα παπούτσια μου	ta pa·*pu*·tsia mu
sunglasses	τα γιαλιά μου	ta yia·*lia* mu
	του ήλιου	tu *i*·liu
When will my …	Πότε θα είναι	*po*·te tha *i*·ne
be ready?	έτοιμα τα …;	e·*ti*·ma ta …
glasses	γιαλιά μου	yia·*lia* mu
shoes	παπούτσια μου	pa·*put*·sia mu
sunglasses	γιαλιά μου	yia·*lia* mu
	του ήλιου	tu *i*·liu

When will my camera be ready?

Πότε θα είναι έτοιμη η
φωτογραφική μηχανή μου;

po·te tha *i*·ne e·*ti*·mi i
fo·to·ghra·fi·*ki* mi·kha·*ni* mu

When will my backpack be ready?

Πότε θα είναι έτοιμος
ο σάκος μου;

po·te tha *i*·ne e·*ti*·mos
o *sa*·kos mu

backgammon board	τάβλι n	*tav·li*
baskets	καλάθια n pl	ka·*la*·thia
bouzouki	μπουζούκι n	bu·*zu*·ki
bronzeware	μπρούτζινα n pl	*bru*·dzi·na
carpets	χαλιά n pl	kha·*lia*
ceramics	κεραμικά n pl	ke·ra·mi·*ka*
copperware	χάλκινα n pl	*khal*·ki·na
cushion covers	μαξιλαροθήκες f pl	mak·si·la·ro·*thi*·kes
evil eye (blue eye warding off evil spirits)	φυλαχτό n	fi·lakh·*to*
icons	εικόνες f pl	i·*ko*·nes
lace	δαντέλλα f	than·*te*·la
leather work	δερμάτινα n pl	ther·*ma*·ti·na
pottery	είδη	*i*·thi
	αγγειοπλαστικής n pl	a·gi·o·pla·sti·*kis*
rugs	τάπητες m pl	*ta*·pi·tes
sculptures	γλυπτά n pl	ghlip·*ta*
worry beads	κομπολόγια n pl	ko·bo·*lo*·yia
woven shoulder bag	υφαντή τσάντα ώμου f	i·fa·*di* tsa·da *o*·mu
… jewellery	… κοσμήματα n pl	… koz·*mi*·ma·ta
filigree	φιλιγκράν	fi·li·*gran*
gold	χρυσά	khri·*sa*
silver	ασημένια	a·si·*me*·nia

post office

I want to send a ...	Θέλω να στείλω ...	*the*·lo na *sti*·lo ...
fax	ένα φαξ	*e*·na faks
letter	ένα γράμμα	*e*·na *ghra*·ma
parcel	ένα δέμα	*e*·na *the*·ma
postcard	μια κάρτα	mia *kar*·ta
telegram	ένα τηλεγράφημα	*e*·na ti·le·*ghra*·fi·ma
I want to buy a/an ...	Θέλω να αγοράσω ένα ...	*the*·lo na a·gho·*ra*·so *e*·na ...
aerogram	αερόγραμμα	a·e·*ro*·ghra·ma
envelope	φάκελο	*fa*·ke·lo
stamp	γραμματόσημο	ghra·ma·*to*·si·mo
customs declaration	δήλωση τελωνείου f	*thi*·lo·si te·lo·*ni*·u
domestic a	εσωτερικό	e·so·te·ri·*ko*
fragile a	εύθραυστο	*ef*·thraf·sto
international a	διεθνές	thi·eth·*nes*
mail	αλληλογραφία f	a·li·lo·ghra·*fi*·a
mailbox	ταχυδρομικό κουτί n	ta·hi·thro·mi·*ko* ku·*ti*
postcode	ταχυδρομικός τομέας m	ta·hi·thro·mi·*kos* to·*me*·as

snail mail

airmail	αεροπορικώς	a·e·ro·po·ri·*kos*
express mail	εξπρές	eks·*pres*
registered mail	συστημένο	si·sti·*me*·no
sea mail	ατμοπλοϊκώς	at·mo·plo·i·*kos*
surface mail	δια ξηράς	thi·*a* ksi·*ras*

Please send it by airmail to (Australia).

Παρακαλώ στείλτε το
αεροπορικώς στην
(Αυστραλία).

pa·ra·ka·*lo stil*·te to
a·e·ro·po·ri·*kos* stin
(af·stra·*li*·a)

Please send it by surface mail to (New Zealand).

Παρακαλώ στείλτε το δια
ξηράς στην (Νέα Ζηλανδία).

pa·ra·ka·*lo stil*·te to ţhi·*a*
ksi·*ras* stin (*ne*·a zi·nan·*thi*·a)

It contains (souvenirs).

Περιέχει (σουβενίρ).

pe·ri·e·hi (su·ve·*nir*)

Where's the poste restante section?

Πού είναι το ποστ ρεστάντ;

pu *i*·ne to post re·*stant*

Is there any mail for me?

Υπάρχουν γράμματα
για μένα;

i·*par*·khun ghra·ma·ta
yia *me*·na

I'd like to collect a parcel.

Θα ήθελα να παραλάβω
ένα δέμα.

tha *i*·the·la na pa·ra·*la*·vo
e·na *the*·ma

Where can I find a fax and telegram service?

Πού μπορώ να βρω
υπηρεσία για φαξ και
για τηλεγράφημα;

pu bo·*ro* na vro
i·pi·re·*si*·a yia faks ke
yia ti·le·*ghra*·fi·ma

How much is a fax per page?

Πόσο κοστίζει το φαξ
η σελίδα;

po·so ko·*sti*·zi to faks
i se·*li*·ţha

Do you have Internet services?

Έχετε υπηρεσία
Διαδικτύου;

e·he·te i·pi·re·*si*·a
ţhi·a·ţhik·*ti*·u

---

medusa

Medusa, famous for turning mortals to stone, had hair much like the tentacles of a jellyfish. In fact the jellyfish is named after her in Greek (μέδουσα me·ţhu·sa), French (*méduse* me·*dooz*) and Spanish (*medusa* me·*doo*·sa), to name just a few languages.

phone

τηλέφωνο

What's your phone number?
Τι αριθμό τηλεφώνου έχεις;   ti a·rith·*mo* ti·le·*fo*·nu *e*·his

Where's the nearest public phone?
Πού είναι το πιο κοντινό   pu *i*·ne to pio ko·di·*no*
δημόσιο τηλέφωνο;   thi·*mo*·si·o ti·*le*·fo·no

Where's the nearest telephone office?
Πού είναι το πιο κοντινό   pu *i*·ne to pio ko·di·*no*
τηλεφωνικό κέντρο;   ti·le·fo·ni·*ko* *ke*·dro

Do you have a metered phone?
Έχεις τηλέφωνο με μετρητή;   *e*·his ti·*le*·fo·no me me·tri·*ti*

Can I look at a phone book?
Μπορώ να κοιτάξω τον   bo·*ro* na ki·*tak*·so ton
τηλεφωνικό κατάλογο;   ti·le·fo·ni·*ko* ka·*ta*·lo·gho

I want to ...	Θέλω να ...	*the*·lo na ...
buy a (2000 unit) phonecard	αγοράσω μια τηλεφωνική κάρτα (2000 μονάδων)	a·gho·*ra*·so mia ti·le·fo·ni·*ki* *kar*·ta (thi·o hi·*lia*·thon mo·*na*·thon)
buy a discount card	αγοράσω μια κάρτα με έκπτωση	a·gho·*ra*·so mia *kar*·ta me *ek*·pto·si
call (Singapore)	τηλεφωνήσω (στη Σιγγαπούρη)	ti·le·fo·*ni*·so (sti sing·ga·*pu*·ri)
make a (local) call	κάμω ένα (τοπικό) τηλέφωνο	*ka*·mo *e*·na (to·pi·*ko*) ti·*le*·fo·no
reverse the charges	αντιστρέψω τα έξοδα	a·di·*strep*·so ta *ek*·so·tha
speak for (three) minutes	μιλήσω για (τρία) λεπτά	mi·*li*·so yia (*tri*·a) lep·*ta*

Ποιος μιλάει; pios mi·*la*·i	**Who's calling?**
Σε ποιον θέλετε να μιλήσετε; se pion *the*·le·te na mi·*li*·se·te	**Who do you want to** **speak to?**
Μια στιγμή. mia stigh·*mi*	**One moment.**
Δεν είναι εδώ. then *i*·ne e·*tho*	**He's/She's not here.**
Λάθος αριθμός. *la*·thos a·rith·*mos*	**Wrong number.**

How much	Πόσο κοστίζει ...;	*po*·so ko·*sti*·zi ...
does ... cost?		
a (three)-	ένα τηλεφώνημα	*e*·na ti·le·*fo*·ni·ma
minute call	(τριών) λεπτών	(tri·*on*) lep·*ton*
each extra	κάθε έξτρα λεπτό	*ka*·the *eks*·tra lep·*to*
minute		

The number is ...
Ο αριθμός είναι ...   o a·rith·*mos i*·ne ...

What's the code for (New Zealand)?
Ποιος είναι ο κωδικός   pios *i*·ne o ko·thi·*kos*
αριθμός για   a·rith·*mos* yia
(τη Νέα Ζηλανδία);   (ti *ne*·a zi·lan·*thi*·a)

It's engaged.
Είναι κατειλημμένη.   *i*·ne ka·ti·li·*me*·ni

I've been cut off.
Με διέκοψαν.   me thi·e·*kop*·san

The connection's bad.
Η σύνδεση είναι κακή.   i *sin*·the·si *i*·ne ka·*ki*

Hello.
Εμπρός.   e·*bros*

It's ...
Είμαι ...   *i*·me ...

Is … there?
Είναι … εκεί;   *i*·ne … e·*ki*

Can I speak to …?
Μπορώ να μιλήσω με …;   bo·*ro* na mi·*li*·so me …

Can I leave a message?
Μπορώ να αφήσω ένα μήνυμα;   bo·*ro* na a·*fi*·so e·na *mi*·ni·ma

Please tell him/her I called.
Παρακαλώ πες του/της   pa·ra·ka·*lo* pes tu/tis
ότι τηλεφώνησα.   *o*·ti ti·le·*fo*·ni·sa

My number is …
Ο αριθμός μου είναι …   o a·rith·*mos* mu *i*·ne …

I don't have a contact number.
Δεν έχω αριθμό για   then *e*·kho a·rith·*mo* yia
επικοινωνία.   e·pi·ki·no·*ni*·a

I'll call back later.
Θα τηλεφωνήσω αργότερα.   tha ti·le·fo·*ni*·so ar·*gho*·te·ra

mobile/cell phone

κινητό τηλέφωνο

I'd like a …	Θα ήθελα …	tha *i*·the·la …
charger for	ένα φορτιστή για	e·na for·ti·*sti* yia
my phone	το τηλέφωνό μου	to ti·*le*·fo·no mu
mobile/cell	να νοικιάσω ένα	na ni·*kia*·so e·na
phone for hire	κινητό τηλέφωνο	ki·ni·*to* ti·*le*·fo·no
prepaid mobile/	ένα	e·na
cell phone	προπληρωμένο	pro·pli·ro·*me*·no
	κινητό τηλέφωνο	ki·ni·*to* ti·*le*·fo·no
SIM card for	μια κάρτα SIM	mia *kar*·ta sim
your network	για το δίκτυό σας	yia to *thik*·tio sas

What are the rates?
Ποιες είναι οι τιμές;   pies *i*·ne i ti·*mes*

(40c) per (30) seconds.
(40λ) για (30)   (sa·*ra*·da lep·*ta*) yia (tri·*a*·da)
δευτερόλεπτα.   *thef*·te·ro·lep·ta

the internet

Where's the local Internet cafe?

Πού είναι το τοπικό	pu *i*·ne to to·pi·*ko*
καφενείο με διαδίκτυο;	ka·fe·*ni*·o me thi·a·*thik*·ti·o

I'd like to …	Θα ήθελα να …	tha *i*·the·la na …
check my	ελέγξω την	e·*leng*·so tin
email	ηλεκτρονική	i·lek·tro·ni·*ki*
	αλληλογραφία μου	a·li·lo·ghra·*fi*·a mu
get Internet	έχω πρόσβαση	e·kho *pros*·va·si
access	στο Διαδίκτυο	sto thi·a·*thik*·ti·o
use a printer	χρησιμοποιήσω	khri·si·mo·pi·*i*·so
	έναν εκτυπωτή	e·nan ek·ti·po·*ti*
use a scanner	χρησιμοποιήσω	khri·si·mo·pi·*i*·so
	ένα σκάνερ	e·na *ska*·ner

Do you have …?	Έχετε …;	e·he·te …
Macs	Κομπιούτερ Mac	kom·*piu*·ter mak
PCs	Κομπιούτερ PC	kom·*piu*·ter pi si
a Zip drive	Zip drive	zip *dra*·iv

How much	Πόσο κοστίζει	*po*·so ko·*sti*·zi
per …?	κάθε …;	*ka*·the …
hour	ώρα	*o*·ra
page	σελίδα	se·*li*·tha

How do I log on?

Πώς μπαίνω μέσα;	pos *be*·no *me*·sa

Please change it to the (English)-language setting.

Παρακαλώ άλλαξέ το στην	pa·ra·ka·*lo* a·lak·*se* to stin
(αγγλική) γλώσσα.	(ang·gli·*ki*) *glo*·sa

Do you have (English) keyboards?

έχεις (Αγγλικό) πληκτρολόγιο;	e·his (ang·gli·*ko*) plik·tro·*lo*·yi·o

It's crashed.

κατέρρευσε.	ka·*te*·ref·se

I've finished.

Τελείωσα.	te·*li*·o·sa

What time does the bank open?

Τι ώρα ανοίγει η τράπεζα; ti *o*·ra a·*ni*·yi i *tra*·pe·za

Where's a/an ...?	Πού είναι ...;	pu *i*·ne ...
automated teller machine	μια αυτόματη μηχανή χρημάτων	mia af·*to*·ma·ti mi·kha·*ni* khri·*ma*·ton
foreign exchange office	ένα γραφείο αλλαγής χρημάτων	*e*·na ghra·*fi*·o a·la·*yis* khri·*ma*·ton

Where can I ...?	Πού μπορώ να ...;	pu bo·*ro* na ...
I'd like to ...	Θα ήθελα να ...	tha *i*·the·la na ...
cash a cheque	εξαργυρώσω μια επιταγή	ek·sar·yi·*ro*·so mia e·pi·ta·*yi*
change money	αλλάξω χρήματα	a·*lak*·so khri·ma·ta
change a travellers cheque	αλλάξω μια ταξιδιωτική επιταγή	a·*lak*·so mia tak·si·*thio*·ti·*ki* e·pi·ta·*yi*
get a cash advance	κάμω μια ανάληψη σε μετρητά	*ka*·mo mia a·*na*·lip·si se me·tri·*ta*
withdraw money	αποσύρω χρήματα	a·po·*si*·ro *khri*·ma·ta

What's the ...?	Ποια είναι ... ;	pia *i*·ne ...
exchange rate	η τιμή συναλλάγματος	i ti·*mi* si·na·*lagh*·ma·tos
charge for that	η χρέωση για αυτό	i *khre*·o·si yia af·*to*

Has my money arrived yet?

| Έχουν φτάσει τα | e·khun fta·si ta |
| χρήματά μου; | khri·ma·ta mu |

How long will it take to arrive?

| Σε πόσο καιρό θα φτάσουν; | se po·so ke·ro tha fta·sun |

The automated teller machine took my card.

Η αυτόματη μηχανή	i af·to·ma·ti mi·kha·ni
χρημάτων κράτησε	khri·ma·ton kra·ti·se
την κάρτα μου.	tin kar·ta mu

I've forgotten my PIN.

| Ξέχασα τον κωδικό | kse·ha·sa ton ko·thi·ko |
| αριθμό μου. | a·rith·mo mu |

Can I use my credit card to withdraw money?

Μπορώ να χρησιμοποιήσω	bo·ro na khri·si·mo·pi·i·so
την πιστωτική μου κάρτα	tin pi·sto·ti·ki mu kar·ta
για να αποσύρω χρήματα;	yia na a·po·si·ro khri·ma·ta

I'd like a/an …	Θα ήθελα …	tha i·the·la …
audio set	ακουστικά	a·ku·sti·ka
catalogue	ένα κατάλογο	e·na ka·ta·lo·gho
guide	έναν οδηγό	e·nan o·thi·gho
guidebook in (English)	έναν οδηγό στα (Αγγλικά)	e·nan o·thi·gho sta (ang·gli·ka)
(local) map	ένα (τοπικό) χάρτη	e·na (to·pi·ko) khar·ti

Do you have information on … sights?	Έχετε πληροφορίες για … χώρους;	e·he·te pli·ro·fo·ri·es yia … kho·rus
ancient	αρχαίους	ar·he·us
archaic	αρχαϊκούς	ar·kha·i·kus
archeological	αρχαιολογικούς	ar·he·o·lo·yi·kus
architectural	αρχιτεκτονικούς	ar·hi·tek·to·ni·kus
Byzantine	Βυζαντινούς	vi·za·di·nus
classical	κλασσικούς	kla·si·kus
cultural	πολιτιστικούς	po·li·ti·sti·kus
Hellenistic	Ελληνιστικούς	e·li·ni·sti·kus
historical	ιστορικούς	i·sto·ri·kus
neoclassical	νεοκλασσικούς	ne·o·kla·si·kus
Orthodox	Ορθόδοξους	or·tho·dok·sus
Ottoman	Οθωμανικούς	o·tho·ma·ni·kus
religious	θρησκευτικούς	thris·kef·ti·kus
Roman	Ρωμαϊκούς	ro·ma·i·kus

signs

Ανδρών	an·thron	Men
Είσοδος	i·so·thos	Entrance
Έξοδος	ek·so·thos	Exit
Τουαλέτες	tu·a·le·tes	Toilets
Γυναικών	yi·ne·kon	Women

I'd like to see (the) …	Θα ήθελα να δω …	tha *i*·the·la na tho …
Acropolis	την Ακτόπολη	tin ak·*ro*·po·li
amphitheatre	το αμφιθέατρο	to am·fi·*the·a*·tro
Archeological Museum	το Αρχαιολογικό Μουσείο	to ar·he·o·lo·yi·*ko* mu·*si*·o
Byzantine frescoes	Βυζαντινά φρέσκο	vi·za·di·*na* *fres*·ko
labyrinth	τον λαβύρινθο	ton la·*vi*·rin·tho
mosaics	τα μωσαϊκά	ta mo·sa·i·*ka*
Mt Athos monasteries	τα μοναστήρια του Αγίου Όρους	ta mo·na·*sti*·ria tu a·*yi*·u *o*·rus
Mycaenian tombs	Μυκηναϊκούς τάφους	mi·ki·na·i·*kus* *ta*·fus
oracle of Delphi	το μαντείο των Δελφών	to ma·*di*·o ton thel·*fon*
palace	το παλάτι	to pa·*la*·ti
ruins	τα ερείπια	ta e·*ri*·pi·a
sculptures	τα γλυπτά	ta ghlip·*ta*
statues	τα αγάλματα	ta a·*ghal*·ma·ta
temple	το ναό	to na·*o*

What's that?
Τι είναι εκείνο;   ti *i*·ne e·*ki*·no

Who made it?
Ποιος το έκαμε;   pios to *e*·ka·me

How old is it?
Πόσο χρονώ είναι;   *po*·so khro·*no i*·ne

When was this discovered?
Πότε ανακαλύφτηκε αυτό;   *po*·te a·na·ka·*lif*·ti·ke af·*to*

When were the excavations done?
Πότε έγιναν οι ανασκαφές;   *po*·te *e*·yi·nan i a·nas·ka·*fes*

Could you take a photograph of me?
Μπορείς να μου πάρεις   bo·*ris* na mu *pa*·ris
μια φωτογραφία;   mia fo·to·ghra·*fi*·a

Can I take a photo (of you)?
Μπορώ να (σου) πάρω   bo·*ro* na (su) *pa*·ro
μια φωτογραφία;   mia fo·to·ghra·*fi*·a

getting in

What time does it open?
Τι ώρα ανοίγει;   ti *o*·ra a·*ni*·yi

What time does it close?
Τι ώρα κλείνει;   ti *o*·ra *kli*·ni

Is it open every day?
Είναι ανοιχτό κάθε μέρα;   *i*·ne a·nikh·*to ka*·the *me*·ra

What's the admission charge?
Πόσο κοστίζει η είσοδος;   *po*·so ko·*sti*·zi i *i*·so·ṭhos

Can I go in wearing these clothes?
Μπορώ να μπω με αυτά   bo·*ro* na bo me af·*ta*
τα ρούχα;   ta *ru*·kha

Is there a discount for …?	Υπάρχει έκπτωση για …;	i·*par*·hi ek·pto·si yia …
children	παιδιά	pe·*thia*
families	οικογένειες	i·ko·ye·ni·es
groups	γκρουπ	grup
older people	υπερήλικους	i·pe·*ri*·li·kus
pensioners	συνταξιούχους	si·dak·si·*u*·khus
students	σπουδαστές	spu·tha·*stes*

tours

Can you recommend a tour?
Μπορείς να συστήσεις κάποια περιήγηση;
bo·*ris* na si·*sti*·sis *ka*·pia pe·ri·*i*·yi·si

When's the next tour?
Πότε είναι η επόμενη περιήγηση;
po·te *i*·ne i e·*po*·me·ni pe·ri·*i*·yi·si

How long is the tour?
Πόσην ώρα διαρκεί η περιήγηση;
po·sin o·ra thi·ar·*ki* i pe·ri·*i*·yi·si

The guide will pay.
Ο/Η οδηγός θα πληρώσει. m/f
o/i o·thi·*ghos* tha pli·*ro*·si

The guide has paid.
Ο/Η οδηγός έχει πληρώσει. m/f
o/i o·thi·*ghos* e·hi pli·*ro*·si

What time should we be back?
Τι ώρα πρέπει να επιστρέψουμε;
ti o·ra *pre*·pi na e·pi·*strep*·su·me

I'm with them.
Είμαι με αυτούς.
i·me me af·*tus*

I've lost my group.
Έχασα την ομάδα μου.
e·*kha*·sa tin o·*ma*·tha mu

doing business

επιχειρησήσεις

I'm attending a ...	Παρακολουθώ ...	pa·ra·ko·lu·*tho* ...
conference	ένα συνέδριο	*e*·na sin·*e*·thri·o
course	μια σειρά μαθημάτων	mia si·*ra* ma·thi·*ma*·ton
meeting	μια συνεδρίαση	mia sin·e·*thri*·a·si
trade fair	μια εμπορική έκθεση	mia e·bo·ri·*ki* ek·the·si

I'm with ...	Είμαι με ...	*i*·me me ...
(Olympiaki)	(την Ολυμπιακή)	(tin o·li·bi·a·*ki*)
my colleague	τον συνάδελφό μου m	ton sin·*a*·thel·*fo* mu
	την συναδέλφισσά μου f	tin sin·a·*thel*·fi·sa mu
my colleagues	τους συναδέλφους μου	tus sin·a·*thel*·fus mu

I'm alone.
Είμαι μόνος/μόνη. m/f   *i*·me *mo*·nos/*mo*·ni

I have an appointment with ...
Έχω ένα ραντεβού με ...   *e*·kho *e*·na ra·de·*vu* me ...

I'm staying at (the Xenia), room (10).
Μένω στο (Ξενία), δωμάτιο (10).   *me*·no sto (kse·*ni*·a) tho·*ma*·ti·o (*the*·ka)

I'm here for (two) days/weeks.
Είμαι εδώ για (δύο) μέρες/εβδομάδες.   *i*·me e·*tho* yia (*thi*·o) *me*·res/ev·tho·*ma*·thes

Here's my business card.
Ορίστε η κάρτα μου.   o·*ri*·ste i *kar*·ta mu

Can I have your business card?
Μπορώ να έχω την κάρτα σου;   bo·*ro* na *e*·kho tin *kar*·ta su

Here's my ...	Ορίστε ... μου.	o·ri·ste ... mu
What's your ...?	Ποια είναι η δική σου η ...;	pia i·ne i thi·ki su i ...
address	διεύθυνση	thi·ef·thin·si
email address	ηλεκτρονική διεύθυνση	i·lek·tro·ni·ki thi·ef·thin·si

Here's my ... number.	Εδώ είναι ο αριθμός ... μου.	e·tho i·ne o a·rith·mos ... mu
What's your ... number?	Ποιος είναι ο δικός σου ο αριθμός ...;	pios i·ne o thi·kos su o a·rith·mos ...
fax	του φαξ	tu faks
mobile	του κινητού	tu ki·ni·tu
pager	του τηλεειδοποιητή	tu ti·le·i·tho·pi·i·ti
work	της δουλειάς	tis thu·lias

Where's the ...?	Πού είναι ...;	pu i·ne ...
business centre	ο χώρος εργασίας	o kho·ros er·gha·si·as
conference	το συνέδριο	to sin·e·thri·o
meeting	η συνεδρίαση	i sin·e·thri·a·si

I need (a/an) ...	Χρειάζομαι ...	khri·a·zo·me ...
computer	ένα κομπιούτερ	e·na kom·piu·ter
Internet connection	σύνδεση στο διαδίκτιο	sin·the·si sto thi·a·thik·ti·o
interpreter	διερμηνέα	thi·er·mi·ne·a
more business cards	περισσότερες κάρτες	pe·ri·so·te·res kar·tes
some space to set up	χώρο να τοποθε- τήσω τα πράγματα	kho·ro na to·po·the- ti·so ta ragh·ma·ta
to send a fax	να στείλω ένα φαξ	na sti·lo e·na faks

Thank you for your time.
Ευχαριστώ για το χρόνο σου. ef·kha·ri·sto yia to khro·no su

That went very well.
Πήγε πολύ καλά. pi·ye po·li ka·la

Shall we go for a drink/meal?
Πάμε για ποτό/φαγητό; pa·me yia po·to/fa·yi·to

looking for a job

Where are jobs advertised?
Πού διαφημίζονται   pu thi·a·fi·*mi*·zo·de
οι δουλειές;   i thu·*lies*

I'm enquiring about the position advertised.
ζητώ πληροφορίες για τη   zi·*to* pli·ro·fo·*ri*·es yia ti
θέση που διαφημίστηκε.   the·si pu thi·a·fi·*mi*·sti·ke

I've had experience.
Έχω πείρα.   e·kho *pi*·ra

What's the wage?
Τι μισθό έχει;   ti mi·*stho* e·hi

I'm looking for ... work.	Ψάχνω για δουλειά ...	*psakh*·no yia thu·*lia* ...
bar	σε μπαρ	se bar
casual	προσωρινή	pro·so·ri·*ni*
English-teaching	να διδάσκω αγγλικά	na thi·*tha*·sko ang·gli·*ka*
fruit-picking	να μαζεύω φρούτα	na ma·*ze*·vo *fru*·ta
full-time	με πλήρη απασχόληση	me *pli*·ri a·pa·*skho*·li·si
labouring	χειρωνακτική	hi·ro·nak·ti·*ki*
office	γραφείου	ghra·*fi*·u
part-time	μερικής απασχόλησης	me·ri·*kis* a·pa·*skho*·li·sis
waitering	γκαρσόν	gar·*son*

Do I need (a/an)...?	Χειάζομαι ...;	khri·*a*·zo·me ...
contract	συμβόλαιο	sim·*vo*·le·o
experience	πείρα	*pi*·ra
insurance	ασφάλεια	as·*fa*·li·a
my own transport	δικό μου μεταφορικό μέσο	thi·*ko* mu me·ta·fo·ri·*ko* me·so
paperwork	ντοκουμέντα	do·ku·*men*·ta
uniform	στολή	sto·*li*
work permit	άδεια εργασίας	a·thi·a er·gha·*si*·as

Here is/are my ...	Ορίστε ...	o·ri·ste ...
bank account	ο τραπεζικός μου	o tra·pi·zi·kos mu
details	λογαριασμός	lo·gha·riaz·mos
CV/résumé	το βιογραφικό	to vi·o·ghra·fi·ko
	μου σημείωμα	mu si·mi·o·ma
residency	η άδεια	i a·thi·a
permit	παραμονής μου	pa·ra·mo·nis mu
visa	η βίζα μου	i vi·za mu
work permit	η άδεια	i a·thi·a
	εργασίας μου	er·gha·si·as mu

What time do I ...?	Τι ώρα ...;	ti o·ra ...
finish	τελειώνω	te·li·o·no
have a break	έχω διάλειμμα	e·kho thia·li·ma
start	αρχίζω	ar·hi·zo

I can start ...	Μπορώ να	bo·ro na
	αρχίσω ...	ar·hi·so ...
Can you start ...?	Μπορείς να	bo·ris na
	αρχίσεις ...;	ar·hi·sis ...
at (eight) o'clock	στις (οχτώ)	stis (okh·to)
next week	την επόμενη	tin e·po·me·ni
	εβδομάδα	ev·tho·ma·tha
today	σήμερα	si·me·ra
tomorrow	αύριο	av·ri·o
advertisement	διαφήμιση f	thi·a·fi·mi·si
contract	συμβόλαιο n	sim·vo·le·o
employee	υπάλληλος m&f	i·pa·li·los
employer	εργοδότης m	er·gho·tho·tis
	εργοδότρια f	er·gho·tho·tri·a
job	δουλειά f	thu·lia
work experience	πείρα στη δουλειά f	pi·ra sti thu·lia

I have a disability.
Έχω μια αναπηρία.   *e*·kho mia a·na·pi·*ri*·a

I need assistance.
Χρειάζομαι βοήθεια.   khri·*a*·zo·me vo·*i*·thi·a

What services do you have for people with a disability?
Τι υπηρεσίες έχετε για   ti i·pi·re·*si*·es *e*·he·te yia
άτομα με ειδικές ανάγκες;   *a*·to·ma me i·thi·*kes* a·*na*·ges

Are there disabled toilets?
Υπάρχουν τουαλέτες για   i·*par*·khun tu·a·*le*·tes yia
άτομα με ειδικές ανάγκες;   *a*·to·ma me i·thi·*kes* a·*na*·ges

Are there disabled parking spaces?
Υπάρχει πάρκνιγκ για   i·*par*·hi *par*·king yia
άτομα με ειδικές ανάγκες;   *a*·to·ma me i·thi·*kes* a·*na*·ges

Is there wheelchair access?
Υπάρχει δρόμος για   i·*par*·hi *thro*·mos yia
αναπηρικές καρέκλες;   a·na·pi·ri·*kes* ka·*re*·kles

How wide is the entrance?
Πόσο πλατιά είναι η είσοδος;   *po*·so pla·*tia i*·ne i *i*·so·thos

Is there somewhere I can sit down?
Υπάρχει κάπου να καθίσω;   i·*par*·hi *ka*·pu na ka·*thi*·so

I'm deaf.
Είμαι κουφός.   *i*·me ku·*fos*

I have a hearing aid.
Έχω ακουστικά.   *e*·kho a·ku·sti·*ka*

Are guide dogs permitted?
Επιτρέπεται στα σκυλιά   e·pi·*tre*·pe·te sta ski·*lia*
για τυφλούς;   yia ti·*flus*

How many steps are there?
Πόσα σκαλοπάτια υπάρχουν;   *po*·sa ska·lo·*pa*·tia i·*par*·khun

Is there a lift?
Υπάρχει ασανσέρ;   i·*par*·khi a·san·*ser*

Are there rails in the bathroom?

Υπάρχουν στηρίγματα i·*par*·khun sti·*righ*·ma·ta
στο μπάνιο; sto *ba*·nio

Could you call me a disabled taxi?

Μπορείς να καλέσεις bo·*ris* na ka·*le*·sis
ένα ταξί για άτομα με *e*·na tak·*si* yia *a*·to·ma me
ειδικές ανάγκες; i·thi·*kes a*·na·ges

Could you help me cross the street safely?

Μπορείς να με βοηθήσεις bo·*ris* na me vo·i·*thi*·sis
να περάσω το δρόμο na pe·*ra*·so to *thro*·mo
με ασφάλεια; me as·*fa*·li·a

guide dog	σκυλί για τυφλούς n	ski·*li* yia ti·*flus*
older person	υπερήλικος m	i·pe·*ri*·li·kos
	υπερήλικη f	i·pe·*ri*·li·ki
person with a disability	άτομο με ειδικές ανάγκες n	*a*·to·mo me i·thi·*kes a*·na·ges
ramp	ράμπα f	*ram*·pa
walking frame	περπατούσα f	per·pa·*tu*·sa
walking stick	μπαστούνι n	ba·*stu*·ni
wheelchair	αναπηρική καρέκλα f	a·na·pi·ri·*ki* ka·*re*·kla

gobbledy gook

So you're having one of those days when you can't make heads or tails of the Greek signs around you, and you're dying to say 'It's all Greek to me!'. In your shoes, a Greek speaker would say:

This is Chinese to me.

Αυτά για μένα είναι Κινέζικα. af·*ta* yia *me*·na *i*·ne ki·*ne*·zi·ka

travelling with children

ταξιδεύοντας με παιδιά

Is there a ...?	Υπάρχει ...;	i·*par*·hi ...
baby change room	δωμάτιο για άλλαγμα μωρών	tho·*ma*·ti·o yia *a*·lagh·ma mo·*ron*
child-minding service	υπηρεσία διαφύλαξης παιδιών	i·pi·re·*si*·a thi·a·*fi*·lak·sis pe·*thion*
children's menu	παιδικό μενού	pe·thi·*ko* me·*nu*
child's portion	παιδική μερίδα	pe·thi·*ki* me·*ri*·tha
crèche	βρεφοκομείο	vre·fo·ko·*mi*·o
discount for children	έκπτωση για παιδιά	*ek*·pto·si yia pe·*thia*
family ticket	οικογενειακό εισιτήριο	i·ko·ye·ni·a·*ko* i·si·*ti*·ri·o

I need a/an ...	Χρειάζομαι ...	khri·*a*·zo·me ...
baby seat	κάθισμα μωρού	*ka*·thiz·ma mo·*ru*
(English-speaking) babysitter	(αγγλομαθή) μπέημπι σίτερ	(ang·glo·ma·*thi*) be·i·bi *si*·ter
booster seat	ανυψωμένο κάθισμα	a·nip·so·*me*·no *ka*·thiz·ma
cot	παιδικό κρεβάτι	pe·thi·*ko* kre·*va*·ti
highchair	παιδική καρέκλα	pe·thi·*ki* ka·*re*·kla
plastic sheet	πλαστικό σεντόνι	pla·sti·*ko* se·*do*·ni
plastic bag	πλαστική σακούλα	pla·sti·*ki* sa·*ku*·la
potty	γιογιό	yio·*yio*
pram	παιδικό καροτσάκι	pe·thi·*ko* ka·rot·*sa*·ki
sick bag	σακούλα εμετού	sa·*ku*·la e·me·*tu*
stroller	καροτσάκι	ka·rot·*sa*·ki

Where's the nearest …?	Πού είναι το πιο κοντινό …;	pu *i*·ne to pio ko·di·*no* …
park	πάρκο	*par*·ko
playground	γήπεδο	*yi*·pe·do
toy shop	κατάστημα παιγνιδιών	ka·*ta*·sti·ma pegh·ni·*thion*

Where's the nearest …?	Πού είναι η πιο κοντινή …;	pu *i*·ne i pio ko·di·*ni* …
drinking fountain	βρύση με πόσιμο νερό	*vri*·si me *po*·si·mo ne·*ro*
swimming pool	πισίνα	pi·*si*·na
tap	βρύση	*vri*·si
theme park	παιδική χαρά	pe·thi·*ki* kha·*ra*

Do you sell …?	Πουλάτε …;	pu·*la*·te …
baby wipes	πετσέτες για σκούπισμα μωρών	pet·*se*·tes yia *sku*·piz·ma mo·*ron*
painkillers for infants	παυσίπονα για μωρά	paf·*si*·po·na yia mo·*ra*
disposable nappies/diapers	πάνες μιας χρήσης	*pa*·nes mias *khri*·sis
tissues	χαρτομάντηλα	khar·to·*ma*·di·la

Do you hire out …?	Νοικιάζετε …;	ni·*kia*·ze·te …
prams	παιδικά καροτσάκια	pe·thi·*ka* ka·rot·*sa*·kia
strollers	καροτσάκια	ka·rot·*sa*·kia

Are there any good places to take children around here?

Υπάρχουν καλά μέρη εδώ κοντά για τα παιδιά;

i·*par*·khun ka·*la* me·ri e·*tho* ko·*da* yia ta pe·*thia*

Is there space for a pram?

Υπάρχει χώρος για το παιδικό καροτσάκι;

i·*par*·hi *kho*·ros yia to pe·thi·*ko* ka·rot·*sa*·ki

Are children allowed?

Επιτρέπεται στα παιδιά;

e·pi·*tre*·pe·te sta pe·*thia*

Where can I change a nappy?

Πού μπορώ να αλλάξω την πάνα;

pu bo·*ro* na a·*lak*·so tin *pa*·na

Do you mind if I breast-feed here?

Σε πειράζει αν θηλάσω	se pi·*ra*·zi an thi·*la*·so
εδώ το μωρό;	e·*tho* to mo·*ro*

Could I have some paper and pencils, please?

Μπορώ να έχω λίγο χαρτί	bo·*ro* na *e*·kho *li*·gho khar·*ti*
και μολύβια, παρακαλώ;	ke mo·*li*·via pa·ra·ka·*lo*

Is this suitable for (five)-year-old children?

Είναι αυτό κατάλληλο για	*i*·ne af·*to* ka·ta·li·lo yia
παιδιά (πέντε) χρονών;	pe·*thia* (*pe*·de) khro·*no*

Do you know a dentist/doctor who is good with children?

Ξέρεις ένα οδοντίατρο/	*kse*·ris *e*·na o·*tho*·*di*·a·tro/
γιατρό που είναι καλός	yia·*tro* pu *i*·ne ka·*los*
με τα παιδιά;	me ta pe·*thia*

If your child is sick, see **health**, page 195.

talking with children

μιλώντας με τα παιδιά

What's your name?

Πώς σε λένε;	pos se *le*·ne

How old are you?

Πόσο χρονώ είσαι;	*po*·so khro·*no i*·se

When's your birthday?

Πότε είναι τα	*po*·te *i*·ne ta
γενέθλιά σου;	ye·*neth*·li·*a* su

Do you go to school/kindergarten?

Πηγαίνεις στο σχολείο/	pi·*ye*·nis sto skho·*li*·o/
νηπιαγωγείο;	ni·pi·a·gho·*yi*·o

What grade are you in?

Σε ποια τάξη είσαι;	se pia *tak*·si *i*·se

Do you like ...?

	Σου αρέσει ...;	su a·*re*·si ...
music	η μουσική	i mu·si·*ki*
school	το σχολείο	to skho·*li*·o
your teacher	ο δάσκαλός σου m	o *tha*·ska·los su
	η δασκάλα σου f	i *tha*·*ska*·la su

Do you like sport?
Σου αρέσουν τα σπορ; su a·*re*·sun ta spor

What do you do after school?
Τι κάνεις μετά το σχολείο; ti *ka*·nis me·*ta* to skho·*li*·o

Do you learn English?
Μαθαίνεις αγγλικά; ma·*the*·nis ang·gli·*ka*

talking about children

μιλώντας για παιδιά

When's the baby due?
Πότε είναι να γεννηθεί *po*·te *i*·ne na ye·ni·*thi*
το μωρό; to mo·*ro*

What are you going to call the baby?
Πώς θα το ονομάσεις pos tha to·o·no·*ma*·sis
το μωρό; to mo·*ro*

Is this your first child?
Είναι το πρώτο σου παιδί; *i*·ne to *pro*·to su pe·*thi*

How many children do you have?
Πόσα παιδιά έχεις; *po*·sa pe·*thia* e·his

What a beautiful child!
Τι όμορφο παιδί! ti o·*mor*·fo pe·*thi*

Is it a boy or a girl?
Είναι αγόρι ή κορίτσι; *i*·ne a·*gho*·ri i ko·*rit*·si

How old is he/she?
Πόσο χρονώ είναι; *po*·so khro·*no* *i*·ne

Does he/she go to school?
Πηγαίνει στο σχολείο; pi·*ye*·ni sto skho·*li*·o

What's his/her name?
Πώς τον/την λένε; pos ton/tin *le*·ne

Is he/she well-behaved?
Είναι καλό παιδί; *i*·ne ka·*lo* pe·*thi*

He/She has your eyes.
Έχει τα μάτια σου. e·hi ta *ma*·tia su

He/She looks like you.
Σου μοιάζει. su *mia*·zi

basics

βασικά

Yes.	Ναι.	ne
No.	Όχι.	o·hi
Please.	Παρακαλώ.	pa·ra·ka·lo
Thank you (very much).	Ευχαριστώ (πολύ).	ef·kha·ri·sto (po·li)
You're welcome.	Παρακαλώ.	pa·ra·ka·lo
Sorry.	Συγνώμη.	si·ghno·mi
Excuse me.	Με συγχωρείτε.	me sing·kho·ri·te
I beg your pardon?	Ορίστε;/Συγνώμη;	o·ri·ste/si·ghno·mi
Here you are.	Ορίστε.	o·ri·ste

greetings & goodbyes

χαιρετισμοί και αποχαιρετισμοί

Greeks shakes hands when greeting each other and saying goodbye. When greeting friends, male or female, they kiss each other on both cheeks.

Hello/Hi.	Γεια σου.	yia su
Good afternoon.	Χαίρετε.	he·re·te
Good morning.	Καλή μέρα.	ka·li me·ra
Good evening.	Καλή σπέρα.	ka·li spe·ra

when in greece ...

Be sure not to turn up empty-handed when you visit a Greek friend's house. It's customary to bring ένα κουτί γλυκά e·na ku·ti ghli·ka (a box of sweets) or μια ανθοδέσμη mia an·tho·thes·mi (a bunch of flowers).

meeting people

How are you?
Τι κάνεις; · ti *ka*·nis

So-so.
Έτσι και έτσι. · *et*·si ke *et*·si

Fine. And you?
Καλά. Εσύ; · ka·*la* e·*si*

What's your name?
Πώς σε λένε; · pos se *le*·ne

My name is …
Με λένε … · me *le*·ne …

I'm pleased to meet you.
Χαίρω πολύ. · *he*·ro po·*li*

I'd like to introduce you to … (a man).
Θα ήθελα να σε · tha *i*·the·la na se
συστήσω στο … · si·*sti*·so sto …

I'd like to introduce you to … (a woman).
Θα ήθελα να σε · tha *i*·the·la na se
συστήσω στη … · si·*sti*·so sti …

This is my …	Από εδώ …	a·*po* e·*tho* …
child	το παιδί μου	to pe·*thi* mu
colleague	ο συνάδελφός μου m	o sin·*a*·thel·*fos* mu
	η συναδέλφισσά μου f	i sin·a·*thel*·fi·*sa* mu
friend	ο φίλος μου m	o *fi*·los mu
	η φίλη μου f	i *fi*·li mu
husband	ο σύζυγός μου	o *si*·zi·ghos mu
partner	ο σύντροφός μου m	o *si*·dro·fos mu
(intimate)	η σύντροφός μου f	i *si*·dro·fos mu
wife	η σύζυγός μου	i *si*·zi·ghos mu

For other family members, see **family**, page 114.

See you later/Goodbye/Bye.
Αντίο. · a·*di*·o

Good night.
Καλή νύχτα. · ka·*li nikh*·ta

Bon voyage!
Καλό ταξίδι! · ka·*lo* tak·*si*·thi

addressing people

The Greek language has two forms of the word 'you'. Use the polite form εσείς *e·sis* with adult strangers, elders, or those in a position of authority. In all other cases, you can use the informal form εσύ *e·si*. The polite form is simply the plural form of 'you', and you use it even when addressing one person. In this book we've chosen the appropriate form for the situation that the phrase is used in – it's normally the polite form unless we've marked it otherwise. For phrases where either form might be suitable, we've given both.

Also note that when speaking to older people you know well, their first name comes after Κύριε *ki·ri·e* (Sir), or Κυρία *ki·ri·a* (Madam).

Mr/Sir	Κύριε	*ki·ri·e*
Ms/Mrs	Κα	*ki·ri·a*
Miss	Δις	*thes·pi·nis*
Madam	Κυρία	*ki·ri·a*

on friendly terms

People will indicate when you can use the informal form of the word 'you' (εσύ *e·si*). If you want to initiate a more informal conversation with a Greek acquaintance, say:

Please speak to me in the singular.
Μίλα μου στον ενικό.　　*mi·*la mu ston e·ni·*ko*

And here are a few casual terms to address your Greek pals:

friend	φίλε/φίλη **m/f**	*fi·*le/*fi·*li
dude	ρε μάγκα	re *ma·*ga
mate (Cyprus only)	κουμπάρε	ku·*ba·*re

making conversation

How are you going?
Πώς πάμε;   pos *pa*·me

What's happening?
Τι γίνεται;   ti *yi*·ne·te

What's new?
Τι νέα;   ti *ne*·a

What a beautiful day!
Τι όμορφη μέρα!   ti o·mor·fi *me*·ra

Nice/Awful weather, isn't it?
Καλός/απαίσιος καιρός,   ka·*los*/a·*pe*·si·os ke·*ros*
έτσι δεν είναι;   *et*·si then *i*·ne

Where are you going?
Πού πηγαίνεις;   pu pi·*ye*·nis

What are you doing?
Τι κάνεις;   ti *ka*·nis

What's this called?
Πώς το λένε αυτό;   pos to *le*·ne af·*to*

That's (beautiful), isn't it!
Είναι (όμορφο),   *i*·ne (o·*mor*·fo)
έτσι δεν είναι!   *et*·si then *i*·ne

---

don't mention the war

Sometimes, discretion is the better part of conversation – these topics are best avoided:

• anything linked to Το Μακεδονικό to ma·ke·tho·ni·*ko* (the Macedonian issue). A northern region of Greece is called Macedonia, and many Greek patriots object to the Former Yugoslav Republic of Macedonia usurping 'their' name.

• any mention of Το Κυπριακό to kip·ri·a·*ko* (the Cyprus problem). Displaced Greek Cypriots object to the Turkish occupation of Northern Cyprus.

Can I take a photo (of you)?
Μπορώ να (σου) πάρω
μια φωτογραφία;
bo·*ro* na (su) *pa*·ro
mia fo·to·ghra·*fi*·a

Do you live here?
Μένεις εδώ;
me·nis e·*tho*

Are you here on holiday?
Είσαι εδώ για διακοπές;
i·se e·*tho* yia thia·ko·*pes*

I'm here …	Είμαι εδώ για …	*i*·me e·*tho* yia …
for a holiday	διακοπές	thia·ko·*pes*
on business	δουλειά	thu·*lia*
to study	σπουδές	spu·*thes*

How long are you here for?
Πόσον καιρό θα είσαι εδώ;
po·son ke·*ro* tha *i*·se e·*tho*

I'm here for (four) weeks/days.
Θα είμαι εδώ για (τέσσερις)
εβδομάδες/μέρες.
tha *i*·me e·*tho* yia (*te*·se·ris)
ev·tho·*ma*·thes/*me*·res

Do you like it here?
Σου αρέσει εδώ;
su a·*re*·si e·*tho*

I love it here.
Μου αρέσει εδώ.
mu a·*re*·si e·*tho*

nationalities

Where are you from?
Από πού είσαι;
a·*po* pu *i*·se

I'm from …	Είμαι από …	*i*·me a·*po* …
Australia	την Αυστραλία	tin af·stra·*li*·a
Canada	τον Καναδά	ton ka·na·*tha*
Singapore	τη Σιγγαπούρη	ti si·ga·*pu*·ri

age

How old ...?	Πόσο χρονώ ...;	*po·so* khro·*no* ...
are you	είσαι	*i·se*
is your son	είναι ο γιος σου	*i·*ne o yios su
is your daughter	είναι η κόρη σου	*i·*ne i *ko·*ri su

I'm ... years old.
Είμαι ... χρονώ. — *i·*me ... khro·*no*

He/She is ... years old.
Αυτός/αυτή είναι ... χρονών. — af·*tos*/af·*ti i·*ne ... khro·*no*

I'm younger than I look.
Είμαι νεώτερος/νεώτερη — *i·*me ne·*o·*te·ros/ne·*o·*te·ri
από ό,τι φαίνομαι. **m/f** — a·*po* o·ti *fe·*no·me

For your age, see **numbers & amounts**, page 35.

local talk

Absolutely!	Απολύτως!	a·po·*li·*tos
Don't stress!	Μην κάνεις έτσι!	min *ka·*nis et·si
Enough!	Αρκετά!	ar·ke·*ta*
Exactly!	Ακριβώς!	a·kri·*vos*
Great!	Απίθανο!	a·*pi·*tha·no
Hey!	Εε!	e·e
I don't care.	Δεν με νιάζει.	then me *nia·*zi
I don't give a stuff.	Δεν δίνω δεκάρα.	then *thi·*no the·*ka·*ra
It's OK.	Είναι εντάξει.	*i·*ne e·*dak·*si
Just a minute.	Μισό λεπτό.	mi·*so* lep·*to*
Just joking.	Αστειεύομαι.	a·sti·e·vo·me
Maybe.	Ίσως.	*i·*sos
No problem.	Δεν υπάρχει	then i·*par·*hi
	πρόβλημα.	*prov·*li·ma
No way!	Αποκλείεται!	a·po·*kli·*e·te
Rubbish!	Σαχλαμάρες!	sakh·la·*ma·*res
Sure.	Σίγουρα.	*si·*ghu·ra
Well now ...	Λοιπόν ...	li·*pon* ...
You're wrong.	Κάνεις λάθος.	*ka·*nis *la·*thos

the call of the wild ... and the domesticated

Dogs in Greece don't 'woof' – instead, they say ghav. Greek cows, on the other hand, seem to speak English. Here are some animal noises as they sound to Greek ears:

bird	τσίου-τσίου	*tsi*·u *tsi*·u
cat	νιάου	*nia*·ou
chick	κο-κο-κο	ko·ko·*ko*
cow	μου	mu
crow	κρα	kra
dog	γαβ	ghav
hen	κα-κα-κα	ka·ka·*ka*
rooster	κι-κιρίκου	ki·ki·*ri*·ku

occupations & studies

επαγγέλματα και σπουδές

What's your occupation?
Τι δουλειά κάνεις;   ti thu·*lia* ka·nis

I'm a ...	Είμαι ...	*i*·me ...
businessperson	επιχειρηματίας m&f	e·pi·hi·ri·ma·*ti*·as
journalist	δημοσιογράφος m&f	thi·mo·si·o·*ghra*·fos
salesperson	πωλητής m	po·li·*tis*
	πωλήτρια f	po·*li*·tri·a
student	σπουδαστής m	spu·tha·*stis*
	σπουδάστρια f	spu·*tha*·stri·a
teacher	δάσκαλος m	*tha*·ska·los
	δασκάλα f	*tha*·ska·la
waiter	γκαρσόν	gar·*son*
waitress	γκαρσόνα	gar·*so*·na

I work in ...	Δουλεύω ...	thu·*le*·vo ...
administration	στη διοίκηση	sti thi·*i*·ki·si
health	στην υγεία	stin i·*yi*·a
sales &	στις πωλήσεις	stis po·*li*·sis
marketing	και μάρκετινγκ	ke *mar*·ke·ting

meeting people

I'm ...	Είμαι ...	*i*-me ...
retired	συνταξιούχος m/f	si-dak-si-*u*-khos
self-employed	ιδιωτικός/ιδιωτική	i-thi-o-ti-*kos*/i-thi-o-ti-*ki*
	υπάλληλος m/f	i-*pa*-li-los
unemployed	άνεργος/άνεργη m/f	*an*-er-ghos/*an*-er-yi

What are you studying?	Τι σπουδάζεις;	ti spu-*tha*-zis

I'm studying ...	Σπουδάζω ...	spu-*tha*-zo ...
Greek	Ελληνικά	e-li-ni-*ka*
languages	γλώσσες	*ghlo*-ses
science	θετικές επιστήμες	the-ti-*kes* e-pi-*sti*-mes

family

οικογένεια

Are you married? (to a man)
Είσαι παντρεμένος;   *i*-se pa-dre-*me*-nos

Are you married? (to a woman)
Είσαι παντρεμένη;   *i*-se pa-dre-*me*-ni

I live with someone. (with a woman)
Ζω με κάποια.   zo me *ka*-pia

I live with someone. (with a man)
Ζω με κάποιον.   zo me *ka*-pion

I'm ...	Είμαι ...	*i*-me ...
married	παντρεμένος m	pa-dre-*me*-nos
	παντρεμένη f	pa-dre-*me*-ni
separated	χωρισμένος m	kho-riz-*me*-nos
	χωρισμένη f	kho-riz-*me*-ni
single	ανύπαντρος m	a-*ni*-pa-dros
	ανύπαντρη f	a-*ni*-pa-dri

Do you have a/an ...?
Έχεις ...;   *e*-his ...

I (don't) have a/an ...
(Δεν) έχω ...   (then) *e*-kho ...

aunt	θεία f	*thi*·a
brother	αδερφό m	a·*ther*·fo
brother-in-law	γαμπρό m	gha·*bro*
cousin	ξάδερφο m	ksa·*ther*·fo
	ξαδέρφη f	ksa·*ther*·fi
daughter	κόρη f	*ko*·ri
daughter-in-law	νύφη f	*ni*·fi
family	οικογένεια f	i·ko·*ye*·ni·a
father	πατέρα m	pa·*te*·ra
father-in-law	πεθερό m	pe·the·*ro*
granddaughter	εγγονή f	e·go·*ni*
grandfather	παπού m	pa·*pu*
grandmother	γιαγιά f	yia·*yia*
grandson	εγγονό m	e·go·*no*
husband	σύζυγο m	*si*·zi·gho
mother	μητέρα f	mi·*te*·ra
mother-in-law	πεθερά f	pe·the·*ra*
nephew	ανιψιό m	a·nip·*sio*
niece	ανιψιά f	a·nip·*sia*
partner (intimate)	σύντροφο m&f	*si*·dro·fo
sister	αδερφή f	a·*ther*·fi
sister-in-law	νύφη f	*ni*·fi
son	γιο m	yio
son-in-law	γαμπρό m	gha·*bro*
uncle	θείο m	*thi*·o
wife	σύζυγο f	*si*·zi·gho

farewells

Tomorrow is my last day here.
Αύριο είναι η τελευταία
μέρα μου εδώ.

av·ri·o *i*·ne i te·lef·*te*·a
me·ra mu e·*tho*

It's been great meeting you.
Είναι υπέροχο που σε
συνάντησα.

i·ne i·*pe*·ro·kho pu se
si·*na*·di·sa

If you come to (Scotland) you can stay with me.

Αν έρθεις (στη Σκωτία)   an er·this (sti sko·ti·a)
μπορείς να μείνεις μαζί μου.   bo·ris na mi·nis ma·zi mu

Here's my address.

Εδώ είναι η διεύθυνσή μου.   e·tho i·ne i thi·ef·thin·si mu

What's your address?

Ποια είναι η δική σου   pia i·ne i thi·ki su
διεύθυνση;   thi·ef·thin·si

What's your ...?	Ποιο είναι το ... σου;	pio i·ne to ... su
Here's my ...	Εδώ είναι το ... μου.	e·tho i·ne to ... mu
phone number	τηλέφωνό	ti·le·fo·no
email address	ημέιλ	i·me·il

Keep in touch!

Μη χαθούμε!   mi kha·thu·me

We'll talk again soon.

Θα τα πούμε.   tha ta pu·me

Farewell.

Γεια χαρά.   yia ha·ra

Adieu.

Αντίο.   a·di·o

---

well-wishing

Bless you!	Ο Θεός να σε	o the·os na se
	φυλάει!	fi·la·i
Bon voyage!	Καλό ταξίδι!	ka·lo tak·si·thi
Congratulations!	Συγχαρητήρια!	sing·kha·ri·ti·ri·a
Good luck!	Καλή τύχη!	ka·li ti·hi
Happy Birthday!	Χαρούμενα	kha·ru·me·na
	γενέθλια!	ye·ne·thli·a
Have a nice/	Καλά/Ωραία να	ka·la/or·e·a na
good time!	περάσεις!	pe·ra·sis
Merry Christmas!	Καλά Χριστούγεννα!	ka·la khri·stu·ye·na

If you're lost for words on a special occasion, just wish people Χρόνια πολλά! *khro*·nia po·*la* (Many years!) – this works for just about any festive occasion.

common interests

κοινά ενδιαφέροντα

What do you do in your spare time?

Τι κάνεις τον ελεύθερο χρόνο σου;		ti *ka*·nis ton e·*lef*·the·ro *khro*·no su

Do you like ...?	Σου αρέσει ...;	su a·*re*·si ...
I (don't) like ...	(Δεν) μου αρέσει ...	(ṭhen) mu a·*re*·si ...
billiards	το μπιλιάρδο	to bi·*liar*·ṭho
chess	το σκάκι	to *ska*·ki
cooking	η μαγειρική	i ma·yi·ri·*ki*
dancing	ο χορός	o kho·*ros*
dominoes	το ντόμινο	to *do*·mi·no
drawing	το σχέδιο	to *she*·ṭhi·o
gardening	η κηπουρική	i ki·pu·ri·*ki*
music	η μουσική	i mu·si·*ki*
painting	η ζωγραφική	i zo·ghra·fi·*ki*
reading	το διάβασμα	to *ṭhia*·vaz·ma

Do you like ...?	Σου αρέσουν ...;	su a·*re*·sun ...
I (don't) like ...	(Δεν) μου αρέσουν τα ...	(ṭhen) mu a·*re*·sun ta ...
films	φιλμ	film
sport	σπορ	spor

Do you like ...?	Σου αρέσει να ...;	su a·*re*·si na ...
shopping	ψωνίζεις	pso·*ni*·zis
travelling	ταξιδεύεις	tak·si·*the*·vis

I (don't) like ...	(Δεν) μου αρέσει να ...	(ṭhen) mu a·*re*·si na ...
shopping	ψωνίζω	pso·*ni*·zo
travelling	ταξιδεύω	tak·si·*the*·vo

For sporting activities, see **sport**, page 141.

astrology	αστρολογία f	a·stro·lo·*yi*·a
backgammon	τάβλι n	*tav*·li
bouzouki (instrument)	μπουζούκι n	bu·*zu*·ki
current affairs	επίκαιρα θέματα n pl	e·*pi*·ke·ra *the*·ma·ta
playing cards	χαρτιά n pl	khar·*tia*
politics	πολιτική f	po·li·ti·*ki*
sirtaki (Greek dancing)	συρτάκι n	sir·*ta*·ki

music

What music do you like?

Τι μουσική σου αρέσει;   ti mu·si·*ki* su a·*re*·si

Which bands/singers do you like?

Τι μπάντες/τραγουδιστές   ti *ba*·des/tra·ghu·thi·*stes*
σου αρέσουν;   su a·*re*·sun

traditional greek dances

Many traditional dances are specific to certain regions of Greece, while others are popular throughout the country. The most common ones are the Ζεμπέκικο ze·*be*·ki·ko (Zembekiko), the Τσάμικο *tsa*·mi·ko (Tsamiko), Καλαματιανό ka·la·ma·tia·*no* (Kalamatiano) – also called the Συρτό sir·*to* (Sirto) – and the Χασαποσέρβικο ha·sa·po·*ser*·vi·ko (Zorba Dance).

In most of these dances, the participants hold hands to form a semicircle and, moving in repetitive steps, they follow the lead dancer in an anticlockwise direction. The one exception is the Zembekiko, which is danced by individuals – although sometimes called the 'drunken sailor's dance' for its seeming clumsiness, it actually takes great skill to perform.

Other popular dances are the Κότσαρι *kot*·sa·ri (Kotsari), the Κρητικός kri·ti·*kos* (Kritikos) and the Ποντιακός po·di·a·*kos* (Pontiakos).

Do you ...?		
dance	Χορεύεις;	kho·*re*·vis
go to concerts	Πηγαίνεις σε κονσέρτα;	pi·*ye*·nis se kon·*ser*·ta
listen to music	Ακούς μουσική;	a·*kus* mu·si·*ki*
play an instrument	Παίζεις κανένα όργανο;	*pe*·zis ka·*ne*·na *or*·gha·no
sing	Τραγουδάς;	tra·ghu·*thas*

blues	μπλουζ n	bluz
classical music	κλασσική μουσική f	kla·si·*ki* mu·si·*ki*
electronic music	ηλεκτρονική μουσική f	i·lek·tro·ni·*ki* mu·si·*ki*
Greek folk music	Ελληνική παραδοσιακή μουσική f	e·li·ni·*ki* pa·ra·tho·si·a·*ki* mu·si·*ki*
jazz	τζαζ f	tzaz
pop music	ποπ f	pop
rembetika	ρεμπέτικα n pl	re·*be*·ti·ka
rock music	μουσική ροκ f	mu·si·*ki* rok
traditional music	παραδοσιακή μουσική f	pa·ra·tho·si·a·*ki* mu·si·*ki*

Planning to go to a concert? See **tickets**, page 46, and **going out**, page 127.

cinema & theatre

I feel like going to a ...	Θέλω να πάω σε ...	*the*·lo na *pa*·o se ...
ballet	μπαλέτο	ba·*le*·to
film	φιλμ	film
play	έργο	*er*·gho

What's showing at the cinema/theatre tonight?

| Τι παίζει στο σινεμά/ | ti *pe*·zi sto si·ne·*ma*/ |
| θέατρο απόψε; | *the*·a·tro a·*pop*·se |

Is it in English/Greek?

| Είναι στα Αγγλικά/Ελληνικά; | *i*·ne sta ang·gli·*ka*/e·li·ni·*ka* |

Does it have (English) subtitles?

| Έχει (Αγγλικούς) υπότιτλους; | *e*·hi (ang·gli·*kus*) i·*po*·tit·lus |

Is this seat taken?

| Είναι αυτή η θέση πιασμένη; | *i*·ne af·*ti* i *the*·si piaz·*me*·ni |

Have you seen …?

| Έχεις δει …; | *e*·his thi … |

Who's in it?

| Ποιος παίζει σ' αυτό; | pios *pe*·zi saf·*to* |

Did you like the (film)?

| Σου άρεσε το (φιλμ); | su *a*·re·se to (film) |

I thought it was …	Νομίζω πως ήταν …	no·*ni*·zo pos *i*·tan …
excellent	εξαιρετικό	ek·se·re·ti·*ko*
long	μεγάλο	me·*gha*·lo
OK	εντάξει	e·*dak*·si

I (don't) like …	(Δεν) μου αρέσουν …	(then) mu a·*re*·sun …
action movies	οι ταινίες δράσης	i te·*ni*·es *thra*·sis
animated films	τα φιλμ κινουμένων σχεδίων	ta film ki·nu·*me*·non she·*thi*·on
comedies	οι κωμωδίες	i ko·mo·*thi*·es
documentaries	τα ντοκυμαντέρ	ta do·ki·man·*ter*
drama	τα δραματικά έργα	ta thra·ma·ti·*ka* *er*·gha
Greek cinema	τα ελληνικά έργα	ta e·li·ni·*ka* *er*·gha
horror movies	τα έργα τρόμου	ta *er*·gha *tro*·mu
sci-fi	τα έργα επιστημονικής φαντασίας	ta *er*·gha e·pi·sti·mo·ni·*kis* fa·da·*si*·as
short films	τα φιλμ μικρής διάρκειας	ta film mi·*kris* thi·*ar*·ki·as
thrillers	τα θρίλερ	ta *thri*·ler
war movies	τα πολεμικά έργα	ta po·le·mi·*ka* *er*·gha

feelings

αισθήματα

Are you ...?	Είσαι ...;	*i*·se ...
I'm (not) ...	(Δεν) Είμαι ...	(then) *i*·me ...
annoyed	ενοχλημένος m	e·no·khli·*me*·nos
	ενοχλημένη f	e·no·khli·*me*·ni
disappointed	απογοητευμένος m	a·po·gho·i·tev·*me*·nos
	απογοητευμένη f	a·po·gho·i·tev·*me*·ni
embarrassed	αμήχανος m	a·*mi*·kha·nos
	αμήχανη f	a·*mi*·kha·ni
happy	ευτυχισμένος m	ef·ti·hiz·*me*·nos
	ευτυχισμένη f	ef·ti·hiz·*me*·ni
hot	ζεστός m	ze·*stos*
	ζεστή f	ze·*sti*
hungry	πεινασμένος m	pi·naz·*me*·nos
	πεινασμένη f	pi·naz·*me*·ni
in a hurry	βιαστικός m	via·sti·*kos*
	βιαστική f	via·sti·*ki*
sad	στενοχωρημένος m	ste·no·kho·ri·*me*·nos
	στενοχωρημένη f	ste·no·kho·ri·*me*·ni
surprised	έκπληκτος m	*ek*·plik·tos
	έκπληκτη f	*ek*·plik·ti
thirsty	διψασμένος m	ţhip·saz·*me*·nos
	διψασμένη f	ţhip·saz·*me*·ni
tired	κουρασμένος m	ku·raz·*me*·nos
	κουρασμένη f	ku·raz·*me*·ni
worried	ανύσυχος m	a·*ni*·si·khos
	ανύσυχη f	a·*ni*·si·hi

| I'm (not) cold. | (Δεν) Κρυώνω. | (then) kri·*o*·no |

If you're not feeling well, see **health**, page 195.

a little	λίγο	*li*·gho
I'm a little sad.	Είμαι λίγο στενοχωρημένος/ στενοχωρημένη. m/f	*i*·me *li*·gho ste·no·kho·ri·*me*·nos/ ste·no·kho·ri·*me*·ni
very	πολύ	po·*li*
I feel very lucky.	Αισθάνομαι πολύ τυχερός/τυχερή. m/f	es·*tha*·no·me po·*li* ti·he·*ros*/ti·he·*ri*
extremely	πάρα πολύ	*pa*·ra po·*li*
I'm extremely sorry.	Λυπάμαι πάρα πολύ.	li·*pa*·me *pa*·ra po·*li*

opinions

γνώμες

Did you like it?
Σου άρεσε; su *a*·re·se

What do you think of it?
Τι νομίζεις για αυτό; ti no·*mi*·zis yia af·*to*

I thought it was …	Νομίζω ήταν …	no·*mi*·zo *i*·tan …
It's …	Είναι …	*i*·ne …
awful	απαίσιο	a·*pe*·si·o
beautiful	όμορφο	o·*mor*·fo
boring	πληκτικό	plik·ti·*ko*
great	καταπληκτικό	ka·ta·plik·ti·*ko*
interesting	ενδιαφέρον	en·*thia*·*fe*·ron
OK	εντάξει	e·*dak*·si
strange	παράξενο	pa·*rak*·se·no
too expensive	πάρα πολύ ακριβό	*pa*·ra po·*li* a·kri·*vo*

politics & social issues

Who do you vote for?	Ποιον ψηφίζεις;	pion psi·fi·zis
I support the ... party.	Εγώ υποστηρίζω το κόμμα ...	e·gho i·po·sti·ri·zo to ko·ma ...
I'm a member of the ... party.	Είμαι μέλος του κόμματος ...	i·me me·los tu ko·ma·tos ...
coalition	συνασπισμός	si·nas·piz·mos
communist	κομμουνιστικό	ko·mu·ni·sti·ko
conservative	συντηρητικό	si·di·ri·ti·ko
democratic	δημοκρατικό	thi·mo·kra·ti·ko
green	οικολογικό	i·ko·lo·yi·ko
liberal	φιλελεύθεροι	fil·e·lef·the·ri
republican	ρεπουμπλικανικό	re·pu·bli·ka·ni·ko
social democratic	κοινωνικό δημοκρατικό	ki·no·ni·ko thi·mo·kra·ti·ko
socialist	σοσιαλιστικό	so·si·a·li·sti·ko

Did you hear about ...?
Άκουσες για ...;
a·ku·ses yia ...

Do you agree with it?
Συμφωνείς με αυτό ...;
sim·fo·*nis* me af·*to* ...

I (don't) agree with ...
(Δεν) Συμφωνώ με ...
(then) sim·fo·*no* me ...

How do people feel about ...?
Πώς αισθάνονται οι άνθρωποι για ...;
pos es·*tha*·no·de i *an*·thro·pi yia ...

How can we support ...?
Πώς μπορούμε να υποστηρίξουμε ...;
pos bo·*ru*·me na i·po·sti·*rik*·su·me ...

How can we protest against ...?
Πώς μπορούμε να διαμαρτυρηθούμε για ...;
pos bo·*ru*·me na thi·a·mar·ti·ri·*thu*·me yia ...

Although it may sound like 'no', remember that ναι ne really means 'yes'.

abortion	εκτρώσεις f	ek·*tro*·sis
animal rights	δικαιώματα	thi·ke·o·ma·ta
	των ζώων n	ton *zo*·on
civil servants	δημοσίους	tus thi·mo·*si*·us
	υπαλλήλους m	i·pa·*li*·lus
crime	έγκλημα n	*eng*·li·ma
democracy	δημοκρατία f	thi·mo·kra·*ti*·a
diaspora	διασπορά f	thi·a·spo·*ra*
discrimination	διακρίσεις f	thi·a·*kri*·sis
drugs	ναρκωτικά n	nar·ko·ti·*ka*
the economy	οικονομία f	i·ko·no·*mi*·a
education	εκπαίδευση f	ek·*pe*·thef·si
the environment	περιβάλλον n	pe·ri·*va*·lon
equal opportunity	ίσες ευκαιρίες f	*i*·ses ef·ke·*ri*·es
euthanasia	ευθανασία f	ef·tha·na·*si*·a
the European	Ευρωπαϊκή	ev·ro·pa·i·*ki*
Union	Ένωση f	*e*·no·si
gay rights	δικαιώματα	thi·ke·o·ma·ta
	των γκέι n	ton *ge*·i
globalisation	παγκοσμιοποίηση f	pa·goz·mi·o·*pi*·i·si
human rights	ανθρώπινα	an·*thro*·pi·na
	δικαιώματα n	thi·ke·o·ma·ta
immigration	μετανάστευση f	me·ta·*na*·stef·si
inequality	ανισότητα f	a·ni·*so*·ti·ta
inflation	πληθωρισμό m	pli·tho·riz·*mo*
the military junta	στρατιωτική	stra·ti·o·ti·*ki*
	χούντα f	*khu*·da
the Macedonian	Μακεδονικό	ma·ke·tho·ni·*ko*
question	ζήτημα n	*zi*·ti·ma
the monarchy	μοναρχία f	mo·nar·*hi*·a
NATO	NATO n	*na*·to
parliament	κοινοβούλιο n	ki·no·*vu*·li·o

the partition of Cyprus	διχοτόμηση της Κύπρου f	thi·kho·*to*·mi·si tis *ki*·pru
party politics	πολιτική του κόμματος f	po·li·ti·*ki* tu *ko*·ma·tos
privatisation	ιδιωτικοποίηση f	i·thi·o·ti·ko·*pi*·i·si
poverty	φτώχεια f	*fto*·hia
racism	ρατσισμό n	rat·siz·*mo*
refugees	πρόσφυγες m	*pros*·fi·yes
relations with Turkey	σχέσεις με την Τουρκία f	*she*·sis me tin tur·*ki*·a
sexism	σεξισμό m	sek·siz·*mo*
social welfare	κοινωνική πρόνοια f	ki·no·ni·*ki pro*·ni·a
strikes	απεργίες f	ap·er·*yi*·es
terrorism	τρομοκρατία f	tro·mo·kra·*ti*·a
traffic restrictions	περιορισμό της κυκλοφορίας m	pe·ri·o·riz·*mo* tis ki·klo·fo·*ri*·as
unemployment	ανεργία f	an·er·*yi*·a
US military bases	στρατιωτικές βάσεις των ΗΠΑ f	stra·ti·o·ti·*kes va*·sis ton *i*·pa
the war in (the Balkans)	πολέμους (στα Βαλκάνια) m	po·*le*·mus (sta val·*ka*·ni·a)

the environment

το περιβάλλον

Is there a … problem here?
Υπάρχει κάποιο πρόβλημα εδώ με …;   i·*par*·hi *ka*·pio *pro*·vli·ma e·*tho* me …

What should be done about …?
Τι θα πρέπει να γίνει με …;   ti tha *pre*·pi na *yi*·ni me …

beach cleaning	καθαρισμό	ka·tha·riz·*mo*
	των ακτών m	ton ak·*ton*
conservation	προστασία	pro·sta·*si*·a
	του περιβάλλοντος f	tu pe·ri·*va*·lo·dos
deforestation	αποδάσωση f	a·po·*ţha*·so·si
drought	ανομβρία f	a·nom·*vri*·a
earthquakes	σεισμούς m	siz·*mus*
ecosystem	οικοσύστημα n	i·ko·*si*·sti·ma
endangered	είδη υπό	*i*·ţhi i·*po*
species	εξαφάνιση n	ek·sa·*fa*·ni·si
erosion	διάβρωση f	ţhi·*av*·ro·si
forest fires	φωτιές στα δάση f	fo·*tyes* sta *ţha*·si
genetically	γενετικά	ye·ne·ti·*ka*
modified food	μεταλλαγμένο	me·ta·lagh·*me*·no
	φαγητό n	fa·yi·*to*
hunting	κυνήγι n	ki·*ni*·yi
hydroelectricity	υδροηλεκτρισμό m	i·ţhro·i·lek·triz·*mo*
irrigation	άρδευση f	*ar*·ţhef·si
marine	θαλάσσια	tha·*la*·si·a
reserves	διαφύλαξη f	ţhi·a·*fi*·lak·si
national parks	εθνικά πάρκα n	eth·ni·*ka par*·ka
nuclear energy	πυρηνική ενέργεια f	pi·ri·ni·*ki* e·*ner*·yi·a
nuclear testing	πυρηνικές δοκιμές f	pi·ri·ni·*kes* ţho·ki·*mes*
ozone layer	στρώμα του όζοντος n	*stro*·ma tu o·zo·dos
pesticides	φυτοφάρμακα n	fi·to·*far*·ma·ka
pollution	μόλυνση f	*mo*·lin·si
recycling	πρόγραμμα	*pro*·ghra·ma
program	ανακύκλωσης n	a·na·*ki*·klo·sis
smog	νέφος n	*ne*·fos
toxic waste	τοξικά απόβλητα n	tok·si·*ka* a·*pov*·li·ta
urban	αστική	a·sti·*ki*
encroachment	εξάπλωση f	ek·*sa*·plo·si
water supply	παροχή ύδατος f	pa·ro·*hi* i·*ţha*·tos
Is this a	Είναι αυτό	*i*·ne af·*to*
protected …?	προστατευόμενο …;	pro·sta·te·*vo*·me·no
forest	δάσος	*ţha*·sos
park	πάρκο	*par*·ko
species	είδος	*i*·ţhos

where to go

πού να πάμε

What's there to do in the evenings?

Τι μπορούμε να κάνουμε το βράδι;		ti bo·*ru*·me na *ka*·nu·me to *vra*·thi

English	Greek	Pronunciation
What's on ...?	Τι γίνεται ...;	ti *yi*·ne·te ...
locally	εδώ γύρω	e·*tho yi*·ro
this weekend	αυτό το Σαββατοκύριακο	af·*to* to sa·va·to·*ki*·ria·ko
today	σήμερα	*si*·me·ra
tonight	απόψε	a·*pop*·se
Where can I find ...?	Πού μπορώ να βρω ...;	pu bo·*ro* na vro ...
a *bouzouki* place (venue with live Greek music)	ταβέρνα με μπουζούκια	ta·*ver*·na me bu·*zu*·kia
clubs	κλαμπ	klab
gay venues	Χώρους συνάντησης για γκέη	*kho*·rus si·*na*·di·sis yia *ge*·i
an open-air cinema	θερινό κινηματογράφο	the·ri·*no* ki·ni·ma·to·*ghra*·fo
places to eat	εστιατόρια	e·sti·a·*to*·ri·a
pubs	μπυραρίες	bi·ra·*ri*·es
Is there a local ... guide?	Υπάρχει τοπικός οδηγός για ...;	i·*par*·hi to·pi·*kos* o·thi·*ghos* yia ...
entertainment	διασκεδάσεις	thias·ke·*tha*·sis
film	φιλμ	film
gay	γκέη	*ge*·i
music	μουσική	mu·si·*ki*

I feel like going to a ...	Έχω όρεξη να πάω σε ...	e·kho o·rek·si na pa·o se ...
ballet	μπαλέτο	ba·*le*·to
bar	μπαρ	bar
café	καφενείο	ka·fe·*ni*·o
concert	κονσέρτο	kon·*ser*·to
film	φιλμ	film
karaoke bar	καραόκι μπαρ	ka·ra·o·ki bar
nightclub	νυχτερινό κέντρο	nikh·te·ri·*no* ke·dro
party	πάρτυ	*par*·ti
performance	θέαμα	the·*a*·ma
play	έργο	er·gho
pub	μπυραρία	bi·ra·*ri*·a
rebetika club	κέντρο με ρεμπέτικα	*ke*·dro me re·*be*·ti·ka
restaurant	εστιατόριο	e·sti·a·*to*·ri·o
sports match	αθλητικό παιγνίδι	ath·li·ti·*ko* pegh·*ni*·thi

For more on bars and drinks, see **romance**, page 131, and **eating out**, pages 166–170.

invitations

προσκλήσεις

What are you doing ...?	Τι κάνεις ...;	ti *ka*·nis ...
now	τώρα	*to*·ra
this weekend	το Σαββατοκύριακο	to sa·va·to·*ki*·ria·ko
tonight	απόψε	a·*pop*·se

Do you know a good restaurant?

Ξέρεις κανένα καλό εστιατόριο; — *kse*·ris ka·*ne*·na ka·*lo* e·sti·a·*to*·ri·o

My round.

Η σειρά μου. — i si·*ra* mu

We're having a party.

Έχουμε πάρτι. — *e*·khu·me *par*·ti

Would you like to go (for a) ...?	Θα ήθελες να πας ...;	tha i·the·les na pas ...
coffee	για καφέ	yia ka·fe
dancing	για χορό	yia kho·ro
drink	για ποτό	yia po·to
meal	για φαγητό	yia fa·yi·to
out somewhere	κάπου έξω	ka·pu ek·so
walk	βόλτα	vol·ta

responding to invitations

Sure!		
Μάλιστα!		ma·li·sta
Yes, I'd love to.		
Ναι, θα ήθελα πολύ.		ne tha i·the·la po·li
That's very kind of you.		
Πολύ ευγενικό εκ μέρους σου.		po·li ev·ye·ni·ko ek me·rus su
No, I'm afraid I can't.		
Όχι, φοβάμαι πως δεν . μπορώ		o·hi fo·va·me pos then bo·ro
What about tomorrow?		
Τι θα έλεγες για αύριο;		ti tha e·le·yes yia av·ri·o
Where shall we go?		
Πού θα πάμε;		pu tha pa·me

arranging to meet

What time will we meet?		
Τι ώρα θα συναντηθούμε;		ti o·ra tha si·na·di·thu·me
Where will we meet?		
Πού θα συναντηθούμε;		pu tha si·na·di·thu·me

going out

129

Let's meet at … | Ας συναντηθούμε … | as si·na·di·*thu*·me …
(eight) o'clock | στις (οχτώ) | stis (okh·*to*)
the entrance | στην είσοδο | stin *i*·so·ţho

I'll pick you up.
Θα σε πάρω εγώ. | tha se *pa*·ro e·*gho*

Are you ready?
Είσαι έτοιμος/έτοιμη; m/f | *i*·se e·ti·mos/e·ti·mi

I'm ready.
Είμαι έτοιμος/έτοιμη. m/f | *i*·me e·ti·mos/e·ti·mi

Where will you be?
Πού θα είσαι; | pu tha *i*·se

If I'm not there by (nine), don't wait for me.
Αν δεν είμαι εκεί μέχρι | an ţhen *i*·me e·*ki* me·khri
(τις εννέα), μή με περιμένεις. | (tis e·*ne*·a) mi me pe·ri·*me*·mis

I'm looking forward to it.
Το περιμένω πώς και πώς. | to pe·ri·*me*·no pos ke pos

OK! | Εντάξει! | e·*dak*·si
I'll see you then. | Θα σε δω τότε. | tha se ţho *to*·te
Sorry I'm late. | Συγνώμη που | sigh·*no*·mi pu
| άργησα. | *ar*·yi·sa

drugs

Do you have a light?
Έχεις φωτιά; | e·his fo·*tia*

Do you want to have a smoke?
Θέλεις να καπνίσεις; | *the*·lis na kap·*ni*·sis

I don't take drugs.
Δεν παίρνω ναρκωτικά. | ţhen *per*·no nar·ko·ti·*ka*

I take … occasionally.
Παίρνω … καμιά φορά. | *per*·no … ka·*mia* fo·*ra*

asking someone out

ζητώντας να βγείτε έξω

Where would you like to go (tonight)?
Πού θα ήθελες να πάμε (απόψε);   pu tha *the*·lis na *pa*·me (a·*pop*·se)

Would you like to do something (tomorrow)?
Θα ήθελες να κάνουμε κάτι (αύριο);   tha i·*the*·les na *ka*·nu·me *ka*·ti (av·ri·o)

Yes, I'd love to.
Ναι, θα το ήθελα πολύ.   ne tha to i·*the*·la po·*li*

Sorry, I can't.
Συγνώμη, δεν μπορώ.   sigh·*no*·mi then bo·*ro*

pick-up lines

χώροι γνωριμίας

Would you like a drink?
Θα ήθελες ένα ποτό;   tha i·*the*·les e·na po·*to*

You look like someone I know. (to a man)
Μοιάζεις με κάποιον που ξέρω.   *mia*·zis me *ka*·pion pu *kse*·ro

You look like someone I know. (to a woman)
Μοιάζεις με κάποια που ξέρω.   *mia*·zis me *ka*·pia pu *kse*·ro

You're a fantastic dancer. (to a man)
Είσαι απίθανος χορευτής.   i·se a·*pi*·tha·nos kho·*ref*·tis

You're a fantastic dancer. (to a woman)
Είσαι απίθανη χορεύτρια.   i·se a·*pi*·tha·ni kho·*ref*·tria

Can I ...?	Μπορώ να ...;	bo·ro na ...
dance with	χορέψω	kho·rep·so
you	μαζί σου	ma·zi su
sit here	καθίσω εδώ	ka·thi·so e·tho
take you	σε πάρω	se pa·ro
home	στο σπίτι	sto spi·ti

rejections

No, thank you.
Όχι, ευχαριστώ.
o·hi ef·kha·ri·sto

I'd rather not.
Νομίζω όχι.
no·mi·zo o·hi

I'm here with my boyfriend.
Είμαι εδώ με τον φίλο μου.
i·me e·tho me ton fi·lo mu

I'm here with my girlfriend.
Είμαι εδώ με την φίλη μου.
i·me e·tho me tin fi·li mu

Excuse me, I have to go now.
Συγνώμη, πρέπει να
πηγαίνω τώρα.
sigh·no·mi pre·pi na
pi·ye·no to·ra

Leave me alone! (a man)
Άσε με ήσυχο!
a·se me i·si·kho

Leave me alone! (a woman)
Άσε με ήσυχη!
a·se me i·si·khi

Piss off!
Άντε από δω, ρε!
a·de a·po tho re

He's a babe.
Είναι κούκλος.   *i*·ne *ku*·klos

She's a babe.
Είναι κούκλα.   *i*·ne *ku*·kla

He's hot.
Είναι θερμός.   *i*·ne ther·*mos*

She's hot.
Είναι θερμή.   *i*·ne ther·*mi*

getting closer

πλησιάζοντας πιο κοντά

I like you very much.
Μου αρέσεις πολύ.   mu a·*re*·sis po·*li*

You're great.
Είσαι θαύμα.   *i*·se *thav*·ma

Can I kiss you?
Μπορώ να σε φιλήσω;   bo·*ro* na se fi·*li*·so

Do you want to come inside for a while?
Θέλεις να έρθεις μέσα,   *the*·lis na *er*·this *me*·sa
για λίγο;   yia *li*·gho

Do you want a massage?
Θέλεις ένα μασάζ;   *the*·lis e·na ma·*saz*

Can I stay over?
Μπορώ να μείνω τη νύχτα;   bo·*ro* na *mi*·no ti *nikh*·ta

Kiss me.	Φίλα με.	*fi*·la me
I want you.	Σε θέλω.	se *the*·lo
Touch me here.	Πιάσε με εδώ.	*pia*·se me e·*tho*
Let's go to bed.	Πάμε στο κρεβάτι.	*pa*·me sto kre·*va*·ti

Do you like this?
Σου αρέσει αυτό;   su a·*re*·si af·*to*

I (don't) like that.
(Δεν) Μου αρέσει αυτό.   (then) mu a·*re*·si af·*to*

I think we should stop now.
Νομίζω πως πρέπει να   no·*mi*·zo pos *pre*·pi na
σταματήσουμε τώρα.   sta·ma·*ti*·su·me *to*·ra

Do you have a condom?
Έχεις προφυλακτικό;   e·his pro·fi·lak·ti·*ko*

Let's use a condom.
Ας χρησιμοποιήσουμε   as khri·si·mo·pi·*i*·su·me
προφυλακτικό.   pro·fi·lak·ti·*ko*

I won't do it without protection.
Δεν το κάνω χωρίς   then to *ka*·no kho·*ris*
προφύλαξη.   pro·*fi*·lak·si

It's my first time.
Είναι η πρώτη μου φορά.   i·ne i *pro*·ti mu fo·*ra*

It helps to have a sense of humour.
Βοηθάει να έχεις την   vo·i·*tha*·i na e·his tin
αίσθηση του χιούμορ.   *es*·thi·si tu *hiu*·mor

Oh my god!
Ω, θεέ μου!   o the·*e* mu

That's great.
Είναι απίθανο.   i·ne a·*pi*·tha·no

Easy tiger! (to a man)
σιγά ρε γόη!   si·*gha* re *gho*·i

Easy tiger! (to a woman)
σιγά ρε γόισσα!   si·*gha* re *gho*·i·sa

That was …	Ήταν …	*i*·tan …
amazing	καταπληκτικό	ka·ta·plik·ti·*ko*
romantic	ρομαντικό	ro·ma·di·*ko*
wild	άγριο	*a*·ghri·o

love

αγάπη

I think we're good together.
Νομίζω ταιριάζουμε.   no·*mi*·zo te·*ria*·zu·me

I love you.
Σ'αγαπώ.   sa·gha·*po*

Will you …?	Θα …;	tha …
go out with me	έρθεις έξω	*er*·this ek·so
	μαζί μου	ma·*zi* mu
marry me	με παντρευτείς	me pa·dref·*tis*
meet my	συναντήσεις τους	si·na·*di*·sis tus
parents	γονείς μου	gho·*nis* mu

---

sweet talk

my baby	μωρό μου	mo·*ro* mu
my darling	μάνα μου	*ma*·na mu
my doll	κουκλί μου	ku·*kli* mu
my hunk	τζουτζούκο μου	tzu·*tzu*·ko mu
my soul	ψυχούλα μου	psi·*hu*·la mu
my treasure	χρυσό μου	khri·*so* mu
sweetheart	καρδούλα μου	kar·*thu*·la mu

romance

135

problems

Are you seeing someone else? (to a woman)
βλέπεις κάποιον άλλο; e·his ka·pion a·lon

Are you seeing someone else? (to a man)
βλέπεις κάποια άλλη; e·his ka·pia a·li

He/She is just a friend.
Είναι απλά φίλος/φίλη. i·ne a·pla fi·los/fi·li

You're just using me for sex.
Με θέλεις μόνο για το σεξ. me the·lis mo·no yia to seks

I never want to see you again.
Δεν θέλω να σε ξαναδώ. then the·lo na se ksa·na·tho

I don't think it's working out.
Δεν νομίζω ότι δουλεύει. then no·mi·zo o·ti thu·le·vi

We'll work it out.
Θα τα βρούμε. tha ta vru·me

leaving

I have to leave (tomorrow).
Πρέπει να φύγω (αύριο). pre·pi na fi·gho (av·ri·o)

I'll …	Θα …	tha …
keep in touch	βρίσκομαι σε επαφή	vris·ko·me se e·pa·fi
miss you	μου λείψεις	mu lip·sis
visit you	σε επισκεφτώ	se e·pis·kef·to

it's a tragedy

The poet Thespis (Θέσπις *thes*·pis) was one of the founders of the theatrical tragedy genre during the 6th century BC. His name survives in the English word 'Thespian', meaning 'dramatic' or 'relating to drama or theatre'.

religion

θρησκεία

What's your religion?
Ποια είναι η θρησκεία σου;   pia *i*·ne i thris·*ki*·a su

I'm not religious.
Δεν είμαι θρήσκος.   ţhen *i*·me *thris*·kos

I'm ...	Είμαι ...	*i*·me ...
agnostic	αγνωστικιστής m	agh·no·sti·ki·*stis*
	αγνωστικίστρια f	agh·no·sti·*ki*·stri·a
Buddhist	Βουδιστής m	vu·ţhi·*stis*
	Βουδίστρια f	vu·*ţhi*·stri·a
Catholic	Καθολικός m	ka·tho·li·*kos*
	Καθολική f	ka·tho·li·*ki*
Christian	Χριστιανός m	khri·stia·*nos*
	Χριστιανή f	khri·stia·*ni*
Hindu	Ινδουιστής m	in·ţhu·i·*stis*
	Ινδουίστρια f	in·ţhu·*i*·stri·a
Jewish	Ιουδαίος m	i·u·*the*·os
	Ιουδαία f	i·u·*the*·a
Muslim	Μουσουλμάνος m	mu·sul·*ma*·nos
	Μουσουλμάνα f	mu·sul·*ma*·na
Orthodox	Ορθόδοξος m	or·*tho*·thok·sos
	Ορθόδοξη f	or·*tho*·thok·si

I (don't) believe in ...	(Δεν) Πιστευω ...	(ţhen) pi·*ste*·vo ...
astrology	στην αστρολογία	stin a·stro·lo·*yi*·a
fate	στη μοίρα	sti *mi*·ra
God	στο Θεό	sto the·*o*

Can I ... here?	Μπορώ να ... εδώ;	bo·ro na ... e·tho
Where can I ...?	Πού μπορώ να ...;	pu bo·ro na ...
attend mass	παρακολουθήσω	pa·ra·ko·lu·thi·so
	τη λειτουργία	ti li·tur·yi·a
attend a	παρακολουθήσω	pa·ra·ko·lu·thi·so
service	την ακολουθία	tin a·ko·lu·thi·a
pray	προσευχηθώ	pro·sef·hi·tho
worship	προσκυνήσω	pros·ki·ni·so

cultural differences

Is this a local or national custom?
Είναι αυτό τοπικό ή   *i*·ne af·*to* to·pi·*ko* i
εθνικό έθιμο;   eth·ni·*ko* e·thi·mo

I'm not used to this.
Δεν είμαι συνηθισμένος   then *i*·me si·ni·thiz·*me*·nos
σ'αυτό.   saf·*to*

I'd rather not join in.
Θα προτιμούσα να μη   tha pro·ti·*mu*·sa na mi
λάβω μέρος.   *la*·vo *me*·ros

I'll try it.
Θα το δοκιμάσω.   tha to tho·ki·*ma*·so

I didn't mean to do anything wrong.
Δεν ήθελα να κάμω κάτι   then *i*·the·la na *ka*·mo *ka*·ti
που δεν έπρεπε.   pu then e·pre·pe

I didn't mean to say anything wrong.
Δεν ήθελα πω κάτι   then *i*·the·la po *ka*·ti
που δεν έπρεπε.   pu then e·pre·pe

I don't want to offend you.
Δεν θέλω να σε προσβάλω. then *the*·lo na se proz·*va*·lo

I'm sorry, it's   Συγνώμη, είναι   sigh·*no*·mi *i*·ne
against my ...   αντίθετο με ... μου. a·*di*·the·to me ... mu
beliefs   την πίστη   tin *pi*·sti
religion   τη θρησκεία   ti thris·*ki*·a

When's the museum open?
Πότε είναι ανοιχτό το μουσείο;   *po*·te *i*·ne a·nikh·*to* to mu·*si*·o

When's the gallery open?
Πότε είναι ανοιχτή   *po*·te *i*·ne a·nikh·*ti*
η πινακοθήκη;   i pi·na·ko·*thi*·ki

What kind of art are you interested in?
Τι είδους τέχνη σε ενδιαφέρει;   ti *i*·thus *tekh*·ni se en·thia·*fe*·ri

I'm interested in ...
Με ενδιαφέρει ...   me en·thia·*fe*·ri ...

What's in the collection?
Τι υπάρχει στη συλλογή;   ti i·*par*·hi sti si·lo·*yi*

It's an exhibition of ...
Είναι μια έκθεση ...   *i*·ne mia *ek*·the·si ...

Where are the exhibits from (Knossos)?
Πού είναι τα εκθέματα   pu *i*·ne ta ek·*the*·ma·ta
από την (Κνωσσό);   a·*po* tin (kno·*so*)

What style is this?
Τι στυλ είναι αυτό;   ti stil *i*·ne af·*to*

Is it an original or a copy?
Είναι αυθεντικό ή αντίγραφο;   *i*·ne af·the·di·*ko* i a·*di*·ghra·fo

What do you think of ...?
Πώς σου φαίνεται ...;   pos su *fe*·ne·te ...

I like the works of ...
Μου αρέσουν τα έργα ...   mu a·*re*·sun ta *er*·gha

It reminds me of ...
Μου θυμίζει ...   mu thi·*mi*·zi ...

Byzantine	Βυζαντινός	vi·za·di·*nos*
classical	κλασικός	kla·si·*kos*
Hellenistic	Ελληνιστικός	e·li·ni·sti·*kos*
modern	μοντέρνος	mo·*der*·nos
Roman	Ρωμαϊκός	ro·ma·i·*kos*

... civilisation	... πολιτισμός m	... po·li·tiz·mos
Cycladic	Κυκλαδικός	ki·kla·thi·kos
Minoan	Μινωικός	mi·no·i·kos
Mycenean	Μυκηναϊκός	mi·ki·ma·i·kos
... style	... ρυθμός m	... rith·mos
Corinthian	Κορινθιακός	ko·rin·thi·a·kos
Doric	Δωρικός	tho·ri·kos
Ionic	Ιωνικός	i·o·ni·kos
architecture	αρχιτεκτονική f	ar·hi·tek·to·ni·ki
artwork	καλλιτέχνημα n	ka·li·tekh·ni·ma
column	κολόνα f	ko·lo·na
curator	έφορος μουσείου m	e·fo·ros mu·si·u
decorative arts	διακοσμητικές τέχνες f pl	thi·a·koz·mi·ti·kes tekh·nes
etching	χαλκογραφία f	khal·ko·ghra·fi·a
exhibit	έκθεση f	ek·the·si
exhibition hall	αίθουσα έκθεσης f	e·thu·sa ek·the·sis
fresco	φρέσκο n	fres·ko
metalwork	μεταλλικά αντικείμενα n pl	me·ta·li·ka a·di·ki·me·na
mosaic	μωσαϊκό n	mo·sa·i·ko
painter	ζωγράφος m	zo·ghra·fos
painting (artwork)	πίνακας m	pi·na·kas
painting (the art)	ζωγραφική f	zo·ghra·fi·ki
period	περίοδος f	pe·ri·o·thos
permanent collection	μόνιμη συλλογή f	mo·ni·mi si·lo·yi
print	αντίγραφο n	a·di·ghra·fo
sculptor	γλύπτης m	ghlip·tis
sculpture	γλυπτική f	ghlip·ti·ki
shield	ασπίδα f	a·spi·tha
spear	δόρυ n	tho·ri
sword	σπαθί n	spa·thi
statue	άγαλμα n	a·ghal·ma
terracotta pot	αγγείο τερακότα n	a·gi·o te·ra·ko·ta
tunic	χιτώνας m	hi·to·nas
vessel	αγγείο n	a·gi·o

sporting interests

αθλητικά ενδιφέροντα

What sport do you follow/play?
 Τι σπορ ακολουθείς/παίζεις;　　ti spor a·ko·lu·*this*/*pe*·zis

I follow (basketball).
 Παρακολουθώ (μπάσκετ).　　pa·ra·ko·lu·*tho (ba*·sket)

I play (football).
 Παίζω (ποδόσφαιρο).　　*pe*·zo (po·*thos*·fe·ro)

I do …	Κάνω …	*ka*·no …
athletics	αθλήματα	ath·*li*·ma·ta
hiking	πεζοπορία	pe·zo·po·*ri*·a
sailing	ιστιοπλοΐα	i·sti·o·plo·*i*·a
scuba diving	υπόγειες	i·*po*·yi·es
	καταδύσεις	ka·ta·*thi*·sis
sailboarding	γουιντσέρφινγκ	ghu·id·*ser*·fing
water-skiing	θαλάσσιο σκι	tha·*la*·si·o ski

For more sports, see the **dictionary**.

top sport		
soccer	ποδόσφαιρο n	po·*thos*·fe·ro
	ευρωπαϊκό	ev·ro·pa·i·*ko*
basketball	μπάσκετ n	*bas*·ket
volleyball	βόλεϊ n	*vo*·le·i
gymnastics	κλασικός	kla·si·*kos*
	αθλητισμός m	ath·li·tiz·*mos*
swimming	κολύμπι n	ko·*lim*·bi

To exercise you brain, try Greece's favourite nonphysical pastime:

backgammon	τάβλι n	*tav*·li

I ...	Εγώ ...	e·gho ...
cycle	κάνω ποδήλατο	ka·no po·thi·la·to
run	τρέχω	tre·kho
walk	βαδίζω	va·thi·zo

Do you like (football)?
Σου αρέσει (το ποδόσφαιρο);   su a·re·si (to po·thos·fe·ro)

Yes, very much.
Ναι, πάρα πολύ.   ne pa·ra po·li

Not really.
Όχι.   o·hi

I like watching it.
Μου αρέσει να το κοιτάζω.   mu a·re·si na to ki·ta·zo

What's your favourite team?
Ποια ομάδα υποστηρίζεις;   pia o·ma·tha i·po·sti·ri·zis

Who's your favourite sportsperson?
Ποιος αθλητής σου αρέσει;   pios ath·li·tis su a·re·si

going to a game

πηγαίνοντας σε ένα παιγνίδι

Would you like to go to a game?
Θα ήθελες να πας σε   tha i·the·les na pas se
ένα παιγνίδι;   e·na pegh·ni·thi

Who are you supporting?
Ποιον υποστηρίζεις;   pion i·po·sti·ri·zis

Who's playing/winning?
Ποιος παίζει/κερδίζει;   pios pe·zi/ker·thi·zi

scoring		
What's the score?	Ποιο είναι το σκορ;	pio i·ne to skor
draw/even	ισοπαλία	i·so·pa·li·a
love/zero/nil	μηδέν	mi·then
match-point	πόντος για	po·dos yia
	παιγνίδι	pegh·ni·thi

What a …!	Τι …!	ti …
goal	γκολ	gol
hit	χτύπημα	*khti*·pi·ma
kick	κλωτσιά	klot·*sia*
pass	πάσα	*pa*·sa
performance	απόδοση	a·*po*·tho·si

That was a … game!	Ήταν … παιγνίδι!	i·tan … pegh·*ni*·thi
bad	άσχημο	*a*·shi·mo
boring	πληκτικό	plik·ti·*ko*
great	υπέροχο	i·*pe*·ro·kho

playing sport

παίζοντας σπορ

Do you want to play?
Θέλεις να παίξεις; *the*·lis na *pek*·sis

Can I join in?
Να παίξω και εγώ; na *pek*·so ke e·*gho*

That would be great.
Αυτό θα ήταν υπέροχο. af·*to* tha i·tan i·*pe*·ro·kho

I can't.
Δεν μπορώ. then bo·*ro*

I have an injury.
Έχω ένα τραύμα. *e*·kho *e*·na trav·ma

Your/My point.
Δικός σου/μου πόντος. thi·*kos* su/mu *po*·dos

Kick it to me!
κλώτσα την σε μένα!   *klot·sa tin se me·na*

Pass it to me!
ρίξ'την σε μένα!   *riks·tin se me·na*

You're a good player.
Είσαι καλός παίχτης.   *i·se ka·los pekh·tis*

Thanks for the game.
Ευχαριστώ για το παιγνίδι.   ef·kha·ri·*sto* yia to pegh·*ni*·ţhi

Where's a good place to …?	Πού είναι ένα καλό μέρος για να … κανείς;	pu *i*·ne *e*·na ka·*lo me*·ros yia na … ka·*nis*
fish	ψαρέψει	psa·*rep*·si
go horse riding	κάμει ιππασία	*ka*·mi i·pa·*si*·a
run	τρέξει	*trek*·si
snorkel	κάμει κατάδυση	*ka*·mi ka·*ta*·ţhi·si
surf	σερφάρει	ser·*fa*·ri

Where's the nearest ...?
Πού είναι το πιο κοντινό ...;
pu *i*·ne to pio ko·*di*·no ...

    golf course — γήπεδο του γκολφ — yi·pe·ṭho tu golf

    gym — γυμναστήριο — yim·na·*sti*·ri·o

    tennis court — γήπεδο του τένις — yi·pe·ṭho tu *te*·nis

Where's the nearest swimming pool?
Πού είναι η πιο κοντινή πισίνα;
pu *i*·ne i pio ko·di·*ni* pi·*si*·na

Do I have to be a member to attend?
Πρέπει να είμαι μέλος για να πάω;
pre·pi na *i*·me *me*·los yia na *pa*·o

Is there a women-only session?
Υπάρχει ορισμένη ώρα μόνο για γυναίκες;
i·*par*·hi o·riz·*me*·ni *o*·ra *mo*·no yia yi·*ne*·kes

Can I book a lesson?
Μπορώ να κλείσω ένα μάθημα;
bo·*ro* na *kli*·so *e*·na *ma*·thi·ma

Where are the changing rooms?
Πού είναι τα αποδυτήρια;
pu *i*·ne ta a·po·ṭhi·*ti*·ri·a

What's the charge per ...?
Πόσο κοστίζει ...;
po·so ko·*sti*·zi ...

    day — την ημέρα — tin i·*me*·ra

    game — το παινίδι — to pegh·*ni*·ṭhi

    hour — την ώρα — tin *o*·ra

    visit — την επίσκεψη — tin e·*pis*·kep·si

Can I hire a ...?
Μπορώ να νοικιάσω ...;
bo·*ro* na ni·*kia*·so ...

    ball — μια μπάλα — mia *ba*·la

    bicycle — ένα ποδήλατο — *e*·na po·*thi*·la·to

    court — το γήπεδο — to yi·pe·ṭho

    racquet — μια ρακέτα — mia ra·*ke*·ta

fishing

Where are the good spots?
Πού είναι τα καλά μέρη;   pu *i*·ne ta ka·*la* me·ri

Do I need a fishing permit?
Χρειάζομαι άδεια για   khri·*a*·zo·me *a*·thi·a yia
ψάρεμα;   *psa*·re·ma

Do you do fishing tours?
Κάνετε εκδρομές για   *ka*·ne·te ek·thro·*mes* yia
ψάρεμε;   *psa*·re·ma

What's the best bait?
Ποιο είναι το καλύτερο   pio *i*·ne to ka·*li*·te·ro
δόλωμα;   *tho*·lo·ma

Are they biting?
Τσιμπάει;   tsi·*ba*·i

What kind of fish are you landing?
Τι ψάρι βγάζεις;   ti *psa*·ri *vgha*·zis

How much does it weigh?
Πόσο ζυγίζει;   *po*·so zi·*yi*·zi

bait	δόλωμα n	*tho*·lo·ma
fishing line	πετονιά f	pe·to·*nia*
flare	φανάρι n	fa·*na*·ri
float	φελλός f	fe·*los*
hooks	αγκίστρια n pl	a·*gi*·stri·a
lifejacket	σωσίβιο n	so·*si*·vi·o
lure	δόλωμα n	*tho*·lo·ma
rod	καλάμι n	ka·*la*·mi
sinkers	βαρύδια n pl	va·*ri*·thia

not biting?

Fishing with dynamite used to be a popular pastime in Greece, but this 'sport' has been outlawed because of its environmental impact. Look out for signs warning Απαγορεύεται η χρήση δυναμίτη (No Dynamite).

horse riding

ιππασία

How much is a (one-)hour ride?
Πόσο κοστίζει η ιππασία
(την) ώρα;
*po·so kos·ti·zi i i·pa·si·a
(tin) o·ra*

How long is the ride?
πόση ώρα διαρκεί η
διαδρομή με το άλογο;
*po·si o·ra thi·ar·ki i
thi·a·thro·mi me to a·lo·gho*

I'm (not) an experienced rider.
(Δεν) Είμαι πεπειραμένος
αναβάτης.
*(then) i·me pe·pi·ra·me·nos
a·na·va·tis*

Can I rent a hat and boots?
Μπορώ να νοικιάσω ένα
καπέλο και μπότες;
*bo·ro na ni·kia·so e·na
ka·pe·lo ke bo·tes*

bit	στομίδα f	*sto·mi·tha*
bridle	χαλινάρι n	*kha·li·na·ri*
canter	τριποδισμός m	*tri·po·thiz·mos*
crop	μαστίγιο ιππασίας n	*mas·ti·yi·o i·pa·si·as*
gallop	καλπασμός m	*kal·paz·mos*
groom	ιπποκόμος m	*i·po·ko·mos*
horse	άλογο n	*a·lo·gho*
pony	πουλάρι n	*pu·la·ri*
race	κούρσα f	*kur·sa*
reins	γκέμια n pl	*ge·mia*
saddle	σέλλα f	*se·la*
stable	στάβλος m	*stav·los*
stirrup	σκάλα f	*ska·la*
trot	τροχασμός m	*tro·khaz·mos*
walk	βάδισμα n	*va·thiz·ma*

soccer/football

Who plays for (Iraklis)?
Ποιος παίζει στον (Ηρακλή);   pios *pe*·zi ston (i·ra·*kli*)

He's a great (player).
Είναι μεγάλος (παίχτης).   *i*·ne me·*gha*·los (*pekh*·tis)

He played brilliantly in the match against (Italy).
Έπαιξε υπέροχα στο ματς   *e*·pek·se i·*pe*·ro·kha sto mats
εναντίον (της Ιταλίας).   e·na·*di*·on (tis i·ta·*li*·as)

Which team is at the top of the league?
Ποια ομάδα είναι στην   pia o·*ma*·tha *i*·ne stin
κορυφή της πρώτης εθνικής;   ko·ri·*fi* tis *pro*·tis eth·ni·*kis*

What a great/terrible team!
Τι μεγάλη/κουρέλα ομάδα!   ti me·*gha*·li/ku·*re*·la o·*ma*·tha

ball	μπάλα f	*ba*·la
coach	προπονητής m	pro·po·ni·*tis*
corner (kick)	κόρνερ n	*kor*·ner
expulsion	αποβολή n	a·po·vo·*li*
fan	οπαδός n	o·pa·*thos*
foul	φάουλ n	*fa*·ul
free kick	φρίκικ n	*fri*·kik
goal (structure)	γκολπόστ n	gol·*post*
goalkeeper	γκολκήπερ m	gol·*ki*·per
manager	μάνατζερ m	*ma*·na·dzer
offside	οφσάιτ n	of·*sa*·it
penalty	πέναλτι n	*pe*·nal·ti
player	παίχτης m	*pekh*·tis
red card	κόκκινη κάρτα f	*ko*·ki·ni *kar*·ta
referee	διαιτητής m	ṭhi·e·ti·*tis*
throw in	αναπληρωματικός m	a·na·pli·ro·ma·ti·*kos*
yellow card	κίτρινη κάρτα n	*ki*·tri·ni *kar*·ta

tennis & table tennis

I'd like to …	Θα ήθελα να …	tha *i*·the·la na …
book a time	κλείσω ώρα να	*kli*·so *o*·ra na
to play	παίξω	*pek*·so
play table tennis	παίξω πινγκ πονγκ	*pek*·so ping pong
play tennis	παίξω τένις	*pek*·so *te*·nis

Can we play at night?
Μπορούμε να παίξουμε
τη νύχτα;
bo·*ru*·me na *pek*·su·me
ti *nikh*·ta

I need my racquet restrung.
Η ρακέτα μου χρειάζεται
επισκευή.
i ra·*ke*·ta mu khri·*a*·ze·te
e·pis·ke·*vi*

ace	άσος m	*a*·sos
advantage	πλεονέκτημα n	ple·o·*nek*·ti·ma
bat	ρακέτα f	ra·*ke*·ta
clay	πήλινη σφαίρα f	*pi*·li·ni *sfe*·ra
fault	φάουλ n	*fa*·ul
game, set, match	παιγνίδι, σετ, ματς n	pegh·*ni*·thi set mats
grass	γρασίδι n	ghra·*si*·thi
hard court	σκληρό γήπεδο n	skli·*ro* yi·pe·*tho*
net	δίχτυ n	*thikh*·ti
ping-pong ball	μπαλάκι του πινγκ πονγκ n	ba·*la*·ki tu ping pong
play doubles v	παίζουμε ζευγάρια	pe·zu·me zev·*gha*·ria
racket	ρακέτα f	ra·*ke*·ta
serve v	σερβ	serv
tennis ball	μπαλάκι του τένις	ba·*la*·ki tu *te*·nis
table-tennis table	τραπέζι του πινγκ πονγκ n	tra·*pe*·zi tu ping pong

water sports

Can I hire (a) …?	Μπορώ να	bo·ro na
	νοικιάσω …;	ni·kia·so …
boat	μια βάρκα	mia var·ka
canoe	ένα κανό	e·na ka·no
kayak	ένα καγιάκ	e·na ka·yiak
life jacket	ένα σωσίβιο	e·na so·si·vi·o
snorkelling	μια στολή	mia sto·li
gear	κατάδυσης	ka·ta·thi·sis
water-skis	θαλάσσια σκι	tha·la·si·a ski
wetsuit	αδιάβροχη στολή	a·thiav·ro·hi sto·li

Are there any …?	Υπάρχουν …;	i·par·khun …
reefs	ξέρες	kse·res
rips	δύνες	thi·nes
water	θαλάσσιοι	tha·la·si·i
hazards	κίνδυνοι	kin·thi·ni

guide	οδηγός m&f	o·thi·ghos
motorboat	βάρκα με μηχανή f	var·ka me mi·kha·ni
oars	κουπιά n pl	ku·pia
sailboarding	γουιντσέρφινγκ n	ghu·id·ser·fing
sailing boat	βάρκα με ιστία f	var·ka me i·sti·a
surfboard	σέρφμπορντ n	serf·bord
surfing	σέρφινγκ n	ser·fing
wave	κύμα n	ki·ma

---

diving in

During the summer months, ask around for diving classes:

Is there a diving school here?
Υπάρχει σχολή	i·par·hi skho·li
καταδύσεων εδώ;	ka·ta·thi·se·on e·tho

Do you offer diving lessons (in English)?
Προσφέρετε μαθήματα	pros·fe·re·te ma·thi·ma·ta
καταδύσεων	ka·ta·thi·se·on
(στα αγγλικά);	(sta ang·gli·ka)

hiking

πεζοπορία

Where can I ...?	Πού μπορώ να ...;	pu bo·*ro* na ...
buy supplies	αγοράσω προμήθειες	a·gho·*ra*·so pro·*mi*·thi·es
find someone	βρω κάποιον	vro *ka*·pion
who knows	που ξέρει αυτή	pu *kse*·ri af·*ti*
this area	την περιοχή	tin pe·ri·o·*hi*
get a map	πάρω ένα χάρτη	*pa*·ro e·na *khar*·ti
hire hiking	νοικιάσω	ni·*kia*·so
gear	εξοπλισμό για πεζοπορία	ek·so·pliz·*mo* yia pe·zo·po·*ri*·a
How ...?	Πόσο ...;	*po*·so ...
high is	ψηλό είναι το	psi·*lo* i·ne to
the climb	ανέβασμα	a·ne·vaz·ma
long is	μακρύ είναι το	ma·*kri* i·ne to
the trail	μονοπάτι	mo·no·*pa*·ti
Do we need to	Χρειάζεται να	khri·*a*·ze·te na
take ...?	πάρουμε ...;	*pa*·ru·me ...
bedding	σκεπάσματα	ske·*paz*·ma·ta
food	φαγητό	fa·yi·*to*
water	νερό	ne·*ro*

Do we need a guide?

Χρειαζόμαστε οδηγό;   khri·a·*zo*·ma·ste o·ţhi·*gho*

Are there guided treks?

Υπάρχουν μονοπάτια με σήματα;   i·*par*·khun mo·no·*pa*·tia me *si*·ma·ta

Is there a path to (Profitis Ilias)?

Υπάρχει μονοπάτι για (τον Προφήτη Ηλία);   i·*par*·hi mo·no·*pa*·ti yia (ton pro·*fi*·ti i·*li*·a)

Is it safe?
Είναι ασφαλές;   *i*·ne as·fa·*les*

Is it steep?
Είναι απόκρημνο;   *i*·ne a·*po*·krim·no

Are there any rockfalls?
Πέφτουν πουθενά πέτρες;   *pef*·tun pu·the·*na pet*·res

Is there a hut?
Υπάρχει κανένα καλύβι;   i·*par*·hi ka·*ne*·na ka·*li*·vi

When does it get dark?
Πότε σκοτεινιάζει;   *po*·te sko·ti·*nia*·zi

Is the track ...?	Είναι ο δρόμος ...;	*i*·ne o *thro*·mos ...
(well-)	σημαδεμένος	si·ma·*the*·*me*·nos
marked	(καλά)	(ka·*la*)
open	ανοιχτός	a·nikh·*tos*
scenic	γραφικός	ghra·fi·*kos*

Which is the ...	Ποια είναι η πιο	pia *i*·ne i pio
route?	... διαδρομή;	... *thi*·a·*thro*·*mi*
easiest	εύκολη	*ef*·ko·li
most interesting	ενδιαφέρουσα	en·*thia*·*fe*·ru·sa
shortest	κοντινή	ko·di·*ni*

Where can I	Πού μπορώ	pu bo·*ro*
find the ...?	να βρω το ...	na vro to ...
camping	χώρο του	*kho*·ro tu
ground	κάμπινγκ	*kam*·ping
nearest village	πιο κοντινό	pio ko·di·*no*
	χωριό	*kho*·*rio*
showers	ντουζ	duz
toilets	την τουαλέτα	tin tu·a·*le*·ta

Where have you come from?
Από πού ήρθες;   a·*po* pu *ir*·thes

How long did it take?
Πόση ώρα σου πήρε;   *po*·si o·ra su *pi*·re

Does this path go to ...?
Πηγαίνει αυτό το   pi·*ye*·ni af·*to* to
μονοπάτι στο ...;   mo·no·*pa*·ti sto ...

Can I go through here?
Μπορώ να πάω μέσα   bo·ro na pa·o me·sa
από εδώ;   a·po e·tho

Is the water OK to drink?
Είναι εντάξει το νερό   i·ne e·dak·si to ne·ro
για να πιω;   yia na pio

I'm lost.
Χάθηκα.   kha·thi·ka

beach

παραλία

Where's the …	Πού είναι η …	pu i·ne i …
beach?	παραλία;	pa·ra·li·a
best	καλύτερη	ka·li·te·ri
nearest	κοντινότερη	ko·di·no·te·ri
public	δημόσια	thi·mo·si·a

Where's the nudist beach?
Πού είναι η πλαζ γυμνιστών;   pu i·ne i plaz yim·ni·ston

Do we have to pay?
Πρέπει να πληρώσουμε;   pre·pi na pli·ro·su·me

What time is high/low tide?
Τι ώρα είναι η παλίρροια/   ti o·ra i·ne i pa·li·ri·a/
άμπωτις;   a·bo·tis

Is it safe to dive/swim here?
Είναι ασφαλές να κάμω   i·ne as·fa·les na ka·mo
βουτιές/κολυμπήσω εδώ;   vu·ties/ko·li·bi·so e·tho

---

listen for …

Είναι επικίνδυνο!
i·ne e·pi·kin·thi·no   **It's dangerous!**

Πρόσεχε το υπόγειο ρεύμα!
pro·se·he to i·po·yi·o rev·ma   **Be careful of the undertow!**

Απαγορεύεται το κολύμπι	a·pa·gho·*re*·ve·te to ko·*li*·bi	**No Swimming**
Απαγορεύονται οι βουτιές	a·pa·gho·*re*·vo·de i vu·*ties*	**No Diving**

Are there any …?	Υπάρχουν …;	i·*par*·khun …
currents	ρεύματα	*rev*·ma·ta
jelly fish	μέδουσες	*me*·thu·ses
rocks	βράχια	*vra*·hia
sea urchins	αχινοί	a·hi·*ni*

How much for a/an …?	Πόσο για μια …;	*po*·so yia mia …
chair	καρέκλα	ka·*re*·kla
hut	καλύβα	ka·*li*·va
umbrella	ομπρέλα	o·*bre*·la

weather

καιρός

What's the weather like?

Πώς είναι ο καιρός;   pos *i*·ne o ke·*ros*

What will the weather be like tomorrow?

Πώς θα είναι ο   pos tha *i*·ne o
καιρός αύριο;   ke·*ros* av·ri·o

It's …	Είναι …	*i*·ne …
cloudy	συννεφιά	si·ne·*fia*
dry	ξηρασία	ksi·ra·*si*·a
fine	καλός καιρός	ka·*los* ke·*ros*
freezing	παγωνιά	pa·gho·*nia*
humid	υγρασία	i·ghra·*si*·a
mild	μαλακός καιρός	ma·la·*kos* ke·*ros*
sunny	λιακάδα	lia·*ka*·ṭha

It's ...		
raining	Βρέχει.	*vre*·hi
snowing	Χιονίζει.	hio·*ni*·zi
windy	Φυσάει.	fi·*sa*·i
drizzling	Ψιχαλίζει.	psi·kha·*li*·zi

It's ...	Κάνει ...	*ka*·ni ...
cold	κρύο	*kri*·o
hot	πολλή ζέστη	po·*li ze*·sti
warm	ζέστη	*ze*·sti

Where can I	Πού μπορώ να	pu bo·*ro* na
buy a/an ...?	αγοράσω ...;	a·gho·*ra*·so ...
rain jacket	ένα αδιάβροχο	*e*·na a·*thiav*·ro·kho
umbrella	μια ομπρέλα	mia o·*bre*·la

weathering the local storms

heatwave	καύσωνας m	*kaf*·so·nas
strong northerly wind	μελτέμι n	mel·*te*·mi
strong cold wind	βαρδάρης m	var·*tha*·ris
thunderstorm	καταιγίδα f	ka·te·*yi*·tha

flora & fauna

χλωρίδα και πανίδα

What ... is that?	Τι ... είναι εκείνο;	ti ... *i*·ne e·*ki*·no
animal	ζώο	*zo*·o
flower	λουλούδι	lu·*lu*·thi
plant	φυτό	fi·*to*
tree	δέντρο	*the*·dro

What's it used for?
Σε τι χρησιμοποιείται;   se ti khri·si·mo·pi·*i*·te

Can you eat the fruit?
Μπορείς να φας τον καρπό;   bo·*ris* na fas ton kar·*po*

Is it ...?	Είναι ...;	i·ne ...
common	κοινό	ki·*no*
dangerous	επικίνδυνο	e·pi·*kin*·thi·no
endangered	υπό εξαφάνιση	i·*po* ek·sa·*fa*·ni·si
poisonous	δηλητηριώδες	thi·li·ti·ri·o·thes
protected	προστατευόμενο	pro·sta·te·*vo*·me·no

local plants & animals

basil	βασιλικός m	va·si·li·*kos*
carnation	γαρύφαλο n	gha·*ri*·fa·lo
carob	χαρούπι n	kha·*ru*·pi
Dalmatian	Δαλματικός	thal·ma·ti·*kos*
pelican	πελεκάνος m	pe·le·*ka*·nos
dolphin	δελφίνι n	thel·*fi*·ni
falcon	γεράκι n	ye·*ra*·ki
fig	σύκο n	*si*·ko
iris	κρίνος m	*kri*·nos
lizard	σαύρα f	*sav*·ra
monk seal	φώκια f	*fo*·kia
olive	ελιά f	e·*lia*
orchid	ορχιδέα f	or·hi·*the*·a
pine	πεύκο n	*pef*·ko
rose	τριαντάφυλλο n	tri·a·*da*·fi·lo
sea gull	γλάρος m	*gla*·ros
sea turtle	θαλάσσια	tha·*la*·si·a
	χελώνα f	khe·*lo*·na
snake	φίδι n	*fi*·thi
swallow	χελιδόνι n	he·li·*tho*·ni
wildflowers	αγριολούλουδα n pl	a·ghri·o·*lu*·lu·tha

basics

βασικά

breakfast	πρόγευμα n	pro·yev·ma
lunch	γεύμα n	yev·ma
dinner	δείπνο n	thip·no
snack	μεζεδάκι n	me·ze·tha·ki
eat v	τρώγω	tro·gho
drink v	πίνω	pi·no
I'd like …	Θα ήθελα …	tha i·the·la …
Please.	Παρακαλώ.	pa·ra·ka·lo
Thank you.	Ευχαριστώ.	ef·kha·ri·sto
I'm starving!	Πεινώ τρομερά!	pi·no tro·me·ra
Enjoy your meal.	Καλή όρεξη.	ka·li o·rek·si

For breakfast, Greeks usually have a hot cup of milk, tea or coffee with φρυγανιά fri·gha·nia (dry sweet toast). If eating out, a typical order is a τυρόπιτα ti·ro·pi·ta (cheese pie) or σπανακόπιτα spa·na·ko·pi·ta (spinach pie).

Lunch, the day's main meal, is an early afternoon affair, usually followed by a απογευματινός ύπνος a·po·yev·ma·ti·nos ip·nos (siesta). A typical lunch will be a meat dish with rice, pasta or potatoes, or fish with a side salad. Legume dishes such as φακές fa·kes (lentil broth) and φασολάδα fa·so·la·tha (bean broth) are especially popular in winter.

Dinner is a light meal eaten between eight and nine o'clock.

Dessert is rarely served. Instead, seasonal fresh fruit finishes off a meal.

eating out

157

finding a place to eat

Can you recommend a …?	Μπορείς να συστήσεις ένα …;	bo·*ris* na si·*sti*·sis e·na …
bar	μπαρ	bar
café	καφεστιατόριο	ka·fe·sti·a·*to*·ri·o
restaurant	ρεστωράν	re·sto·*ran*

Where would you go for (a) …?	Πού θα πήγαινες για …;	pu tha *pi*·ye·nes yia …
celebration	μια γιορτή	mia yior·*ti*
cheap meal	ένα φτηνό γεύμα	e·na fti·*no* *yev*·ma
local specialities	τοπικές λιχουδιές	to·pi·*kes* li·khu·*thies*

I'd like to reserve a table for …	Θα ήθελα να κρατήσω ένα τραπέζι για …	tha *i*·the·la na kra·*ti*·so e·na tra·*pe*·zi yia …
(two) people	(δύο) άτομα	(*thi*·o) *a*·to·ma
(eight) o'clock	τις (οχτώ)	stis (okh·*to*)

listen for …

Δεν υπάρχει άδειο τραπέζι. then i·*par*·hi *a*·thio tra·*pe*·zi	We're full.
Κλείσαμε. *kli*·sa·me	We're closed.
Μια στιγμή. mia stigh·*mi*	One moment.
Πού θα θέλατε να καθίσετε; pu tha *the*·la·te na ka·*thi*·se·te	Where would you like to sit?
Τι μπορώ να σας φέρω; ti bo·*ro* na sas *fe*·ro	What can I get for you?
Ορίστε! o·*ri*·ste	Here you go!

I'd like (a/the) ..., please.	Θα ήθελα ..., παρακαλώ.	tha *i*·thela ... pa·ra·ka·*lo*
children's menu	ένα μενού για παιδιά	*e*·na me·*nu* yia pe·*thia*
drink list	τον κατάλογο με τα ποτά	ton ka·*ta*·lo·gho me ta po·*ta*
half portion	μισή μερίδα	mi·*si* me·*ri*·τha
menu (in English)	ένα μενού (στα αγγλικά)	*e*·na me·*nu* (sta ang·gli·*ka*)
mixed plate	μια ποικιλία	mia pi·ki·*li*·a
nonsmoking	στους μη καπνίζοντες	stus mi kap·*ni*·zo·des
smoking	στους καπνίζοντες	stus kap·*ni*·zo·des
table for (five)	ένα τραπέζι για (πέντε)	*e*·na tra·*pe*·zi yia (*pe*·de)
table outside	ένα τραπέζι έξω	*e*·na tra·*pe*·zi ek·so

Are you still serving food?
Σερβίρετε ακόμη φαγητό;   ser·*vi*·re·te a·*ko*·mi fa·ghi·*to*

How long is the wait?
Πόση ώρα θα περιμένουμε;   *po*·si *o*·ra tha pe·ri·*me*·nu·me

eateries

Act like a local and order some μερικά παξιμάδια me·ri·*ka* pak·si·*ma*·τhia (dried bread) for dunking in your coffee or other hot drinks the next time you're at one of these eateries:

καφετηρία f	ka·fe·ti·*ri*·a	cafeteria
καφενείο n	ka·fe·*ni*·o	coffee shop
γλακτοπωλείο n	gha·lak·to·po·*li*·o	dairy shop
φαστφουντάδικο n	fast·fun·*da*·τhi·ko	fast-food eatery
ουζερί n	u·ze·*ri*	ouzeria
οινοπωλείο n	i·no·po·*li*·o	liquor shop
ταβέρνα f	ta·*ver*·na	taverna

at the restaurant

What would you recommend?
Τι θα συνιστούσες;   ti tha si·ni·*stu*·ses

What are you serving today?
Τι έχετε σήμερα;   ti *e*·he·te *si*·me·ra

What's that called?
Πώς το λένε αυτό;   pos to *le*·ne af·*to*

What's in that dish?
Τι περιέχει αυτό το φαγητό;   ti pe·ri·*e*·hi af·*to* to fa·ghi·*to*

I'll have that.
Θα πάρω αυτό.   tha *pa*·ro af·*to*

Πώς θα το θέλατε ψημένο;
  pos tha to *the*·la·te
  psi·*me*·no

How would you like that cooked?

Σας αρέσει ...;
  sas a·*re*·si ...

Do you like ...?

Συνιστώ ...
  si·ni·*sto* ...

I suggest the ...

Is it savoury or sweet?

Είναι πικάντικο ή γλυκό; *i*·ne pi·*ka*·di·ko i ghli·*ko*

I'd like it hot, please.

Θα το ήθελα ζεστό, tha to *i*·the·la ze·*sto*
παρακαλώ. pa·ra·ka·*lo*

Does it take long to prepare?

Θα αργήσει να ετοιμαστεί; tha ar·*ghi*·si na e·ti·ma·*sti*

Is it self-serve?

Είναι σελφ σέρβις; *i*·ne self *ser*·vis

Is there a cover charge?

Υπάρχει προσαύξηση τιμής; i·*par*·hi pro·*saf*·ksi·si ti·*mis*

Is service included in the bill?

Συμπεριλαμβάνεται si·be·ri·lam·*va*·ne·te
και η εξυπηρέτηση στο ke i ek·si·pi·*re*·ti·si sto
λογαριασμό; lo·gha·riaz·*mo*

Are these complimentary?

Είναι αυτά δωρεάν; *i*·ne af·*ta* tho·re·*an*

How much is that?

Πόσο κάνει αυτό; *po*·so *ka*·ni af·*to*

I'd like (a/the) ...	Θα ήθελα ...	tha *i*·the·la ...
chicken	το κοτόπουλο	to ko·*to*·pu·lo
local speciality	μια τοπική λιχουδιά	mia to·pi·*ki* li·khu·*thia*
meal fit for a king	ένα λουκούλλειο γεύμα	*e*·na lu·*ku*·li·o *yev*·ma
menu	το μενού	to me·*nu*
sandwich	ένα σάντουιτς	*e*·na *sa*·du·its
that dish	εκείνο το φαγητό	e·*ki*·no to fa·yi·*to*

look for ...

Ορεκτικά	o·rek·ti·*ka*	Appetisers
Σούπες	*su*·pes	Soups
Προδόρπια	pro·*thor*·pi·a	Entrees
Σαλάτες	sa·*la*·tes	Salads
Κύρια φαγητά	*ki*·ri·a fa·yi·ta	Main Courses
Ψητά της ώρας	psi·*ta* tis *o*·ras	Freshly Grilled Dishes
Μαγειρεμένα φαγητά	ma·yi·re·*me*·na fa·yi·*ta*	Precooked Dishes
Σαλάτες	sa·*la*·tes	Side Dishes
Μακαρόνια	ma·ka·*ro*·nia	Pasta
Ψάρια	*psa*·ria	Fish
Θαλασσινά	tha·la·si·*na*	Seafood
Επιδόρπια	e·pi·*thor*·pi·a	Desserts
Ποτά	po·*ta*	Drinks
Απεριτίφ	a·pe·ri·*tif*	Apéritifs
Αναψυκτικά	a·nap·sik·ti·*ka*	Soft Drinks
Οινοπνευματώδη ποτά	i·nop·nev·ma·*to*·thi po·*ta*	Spirits
Μπύρες	*bi*·res	Beers
Σαμπάνια	sam·*pa*·nia	Sparkling Wines
Άσπρο κρασί	*as*·pro kra·*si*	White Wines
Κόκκινο κρασί	*ko*·ki·no kra·*si*	Red Wines
Επιδόρπια κρασιά	e·pi·*thor*·pi·a kra·*sia*	Dessert Wines
Ρετσίνα	ret·*si*·na	Retsina
Χωνευτικά	kho·nef·ti·*ka*	Digestifs

If you've got the munchies, try one of these snacks:

κουλούρι n	ku·*lu*·ri	crisp sesame-coated bread rings
γύρος m	*yi*·ros	spit-roast lamb
πασατέμπο n	pa·sa·*tem*·po	pumpkin seeds
σουβλάκι n	suv·*la*·ki	skewered marinated meat
σπανακόπιτα f	spa·na·*ko*·pi·ta	spinach & cheese pie
τυρόπιτα f	ti·*ro*·pi·ta	cheese pie
ψημένα κάστανα n pl	psi·*me*·na *ka*·sta·ma	roasted chestnuts
ψημένο καλαμπόκι n	psi·*me*·no ka·la·*bo*·ki	roasted corn

I'd like it with/ without …	Θα το ήθελα με/ χωρίς …	tha to *i*·the·la me/ kho·*ris* …
cheese	τυρί	ti·*ri*
chilli	πιπεριά	pi·pe·*ria*
chilli sauce	σάλτσα πιπεριάς	*salt*·sa pi·pe·*rias*
garlic	σκόρδο	*skor*·tho
ketchup	σάλτσα	*salt*·sa
nuts	καρύδια	ka·*ri*·thia
oil	λάδι	*la*·thi
pepper	πιπέρι	pi·*pe*·ri
salt	αλάτι	a·*la*·ti
tomato sauce	σάλτσα ντομάτας	*salt*·sa do·*ma*·tas
vinegar	ξύδι	*ksi*·thi

For additional items, see the **menu decoder**, page 175.
For other specific meal requests, see **vegetarian & special meals**, page 173.

at the table

Please bring (a/the) ...	Παρακαλώ φέρε ...	pa·ra·ka·*lo* fe·re ...
bill	το λογαριασμό	to lo·gha·riaz·*mo*
cloth	ένα τραπεζομάντηλο	*e*·na tra·pe·zo·*ma*·di·lo
glass	ένα ποτήρι	*e*·na po·*ti*·ri
serviette	μια πετσέτα	mia pet·*se*·ta
wineglass	ένα ποτήρι κρασιού	*e*·na po·*ti*·ri kra·*siu*
This is ...	Αυτό είναι ...	af·*to* i·ne ...
(too) cold	(πολύ) κρύο	(po·*li*) kri·o
spicy	πιπεράτο	pi·pe·*ra*·to
superb	καταπληκτικό	ka·ta·plik·ti·*ko*

There's a mistake in the bill.

Υπάρχει κάποιο λάθος στο λογαριασμό.   i·*par*·hi *ka*·pio *la*·thos sto lo·gha·riaz·*mo*

ashtray
σταχτοθήκη f
stakh·to·*thi*·ki

spoon
κουτάλι n
ku·*ta*·li

fork
πιρούνι n
pi·*ru*·ni

plate
πιάτο n
pia·to

knife
μαχαίρι n
ma·*he*·ri

wineglass
κρασοπότηρο n
kra·so·*po*·ti·ro

glass
ποτήρι n
po·*ti*·ri

table
τραπέζι n
tra·*pe*·zi

talking food

I love this dish.
Μου αρέσει πολύ αυτό
το φαγητό.

mu a·*re*·si po·*li* af·*to*
to fa·yi·*to*

I love the local cuisine.
Μου αρέσει η τοπική κουζίνα.

mu a·*re*·si i to·pi·*ki* ku·*zi*·na

That was delicious!
Ήταν νοστιμότατο!

i·tan no·sti·*mo*·ta·to

My compliments to the chef.
Τα συγχαρητήριά μου στο σεφ.

ta sing·kha·ri·*ti*·ri·*a* mu sto sef

methods of preparation

I'd like it ...	Θα το ήθελα ...	tha to *i*·the·la ...
I don't want it ...	Δεν το θέλω ...	then to *the*·lo ...
boiled	βρασμένο	vraz·*me*·no
broiled	ψημένο στη σχάρα	psi·*me*·no sti *skha*·ra
deep-fried	τηγανισμένο σε καυτό λίπος	ti·gha·niz·*me*·no se kaf·*to li*·pos
fried	τηγανητό	ti·gha·ni·*to*
grilled	στα κάρβουνα	sta *kar*·vu·na
mashed	πουρέ	pu·*re*
reheated	ξαναζεσταμένο	ksa·na·ze·sta·*me*·no
steamed	βρασμένο στον ατμό	vraz·*me*·no ston at·*mo*

how would you like that?		
medium	ψημένο κανονικά	psi·*me*·no ka·no·ni·*ka*
rare	μισοψημένο	mi·sop·si·*me*·no
well-done	καλοψημένο	ka·lop·si·*me*·no

nonalcoholic drinks

... mineral water	... μεταλλικό νερό n	... me·ta·li·ko ne·ro
sparkling	γαζόζα	gha·zo·za
still	χωρίς ανθρακικό	kho·ris an·thra·ki·ko
(hot) water	(ζεστό) νερό n	(ze·sto) ne·ro
bottled water	εμφιαλωμένο νερό n	em·fi·a·lo·me·no ne·ro
tap water	νερό βρύσης n	ne·ro vri·sis
apple juice	χυμός μήλου m	hi·mos mi·lu
hot chocolate	ζεστό κακάο n	ze·sto ka·ka·o
herbal tea	τσάι από βότανα n	tsa·i a·po vo·ta·na
morello cherry juice	βισινάδα f	vi·si·na·tha
orange juice	χυμός πορτοκάλι m	hi·mos por·to·ka·li
soft drink	αναψυκτικό n	a·nap·sik·ti·ko
(cup of) tea	(ένα φλυτζάνι) τσάι n	(e·na fli·dza·ni) tsa·i
(cup of) coffee	(ένα φλυτζάνι) καφέ m	(e·na fli·dza·ni) ka·fe
with milk	με γάλα	me gha·la
with lemon	με λεμόνι	me le·mo·ni
sweetened	με ζάχαρη	me za·kha·ri
unsweetened	χωρίς ζάχαρη	kho·ris za·kha·ri

coffee time

black	χωρίς γάλα	kho·ris gha·la
decaffeinated	χωρίς καφεΐνη	kho·ris ka·fe·i·ni
Greek	ελληνικός	e·li·ni·kos
iced	φραπέ	fra·pe
instant	στιγμιαίος	stigh·mi·e·os
medium	μέτριος	me·tri·os
plain (no sugar)	σκέτος	ske·tos
strong	δυνατός	thi·na·tos
sweet	γλυκός	ghli·kos
weak	ελαφρύς	e·la·fris
white	με γάλα	me gha·la

κουμανταρία f	ku·ma·da·ri·a	traditional Cypriot wine
ζιβανία f	zi·va·ni·a	a clear Cypriot apéritif made from grapes
ούζο n	u·zo	spirit distilled from grapes with a strong aniseed flavour
ρετσίνα f	ret·si·na	pine-resinated wine, served chilled
τσίπουρο n	tsi·pu·ro	spirit made from grapes, high in alcohol
τσικουδιά f	tsi·ku·thia	Crete's version of τσίπουρο

alcoholic drinks

οινοπνευματώδη ποτά

To get drinks at a bar in Greece, you don't have to memorise numerous standard measurements – standard serves are ordered using 'one'. For example: μία μπύρα *mi·a bi·ra* (one beer) or ένα ούζο *e·na u·zo* (one ouzo). See also **numbers & amounts**, page 35.

beer	μπύρα f	*bi·ra*
brandy	μπράντι n	*bran·di*
champagne	σαμπάνια f	*sam·pa·nia*
cocktail	κοκτέηλ n	*kok·te·il*
a shot of …	ένα … m	*e·na …*
gin	τζιν	dzin
rum	ρούμι	*ru·mi*
whisky	ουίσκι	u·i·ski

eating out

a shot of ...	μία ... f	mia ...
tequila	τεκίλα	te·*ki*·la
vodka	βότκα	*vot*·ka

a bottle/glass of ... wine	ένα μπουκάλι/ ποτήρι ... κρασί n	*e*·na bu·*ka*·li/ po·*ti*·ri ... kra·*si*
dessert	επιδόρπιο	e·pi·*thor*·pi·o
dry	ξηρό	ksi·*ro*
red	κόκκινο	*ko*·ki·no
rosé	ροζέ	ro·*ze*
sparkling	σαμπάνια	sam·*pa*·nia
sweet	γλυκό	ghli·*ko*
white	άσπρο	*a*·spro

a ... of beer	ένα ... μπύρα n	*e*·na ... *bi*·ra
glass	ποτήρι	po·*ti*·ri
pint	μεγάλο ποτήρι	me·*gha*·lo po·*ti*·ri
small bottle	μικρό μπουκάλι	mi·*kro* bu·*ka*·li
large bottle	μεγάλο μπουκάλι	me·*gha*·lo bu·*ka*·li

a ... of beer	μια ... μπύρα f	mia ... *bi*·ra
carafe	καράφα	ka·*ra*·fa
jug	κανάτα	ka·*na*·ta

give it a go

Try more traditional Greek delicacies from these eateries:

αρτοποιείο n	ar·to·pi·*i*·o	bakery
ζαχαροπλαστείο n	za·kha·ro·pla·*sti*·o	patisserie or sweet shop
φαστφουντάδικο n	fast·fu·*da*·thi·ko	fast-food eatery
καντίνα f	kan·*ti*·na	canteen or food van
πιτσαρία f	pit·sa·*ri*·a	barbecue-style eatery
σουβλατζίδικο n	suv·lat·*zi*·thi·ko	kebab and souvlaki shop
τυροπωλείο n	ti·ro·po·*li*·o	cheese shop
ψαροταβέρνα f	psa·ro·ta·*ver*·na	taverna serving fish
ψησταριά f	psi·sta·*ria*	eatery serving spit-roasted meats

in the bar

Excuse me!
Συγνώμη!   sigh·*no*·mi

I'm next.
Είναι η δική μου σειρά.   i·ne i thi·*ki* mu si·*ra*

I'll have …
Θα πάρω …   tha *pa*·ro …

Same again, please.
Από τα ίδια, παρακαλώ.   a·*po* ta i·thia pa·ra·ka·*lo*

No ice, thanks.
Όχι πάγο, ευχαριστώ.   *o*·hi *pa*·gho ef·kha·ri·*sto*

I'll buy you a drink.
Θα σε κεράσω εγώ.   tha se ke·*ra*·so e·*gho*

What would you like?
Τι θα ήθελες;   ti tha *i*·the·les

I don't drink alcohol.
Δεν πίνω αλκοόλ.   then *pi*·no al·ko·*ol*

It's my round.
Είναι η σειρά μου.   *i*·ne i si·*ra* mu

How much is that?
Πόσο κάνει αυτό;   *po*·so *ka*·ni af·*to*

Do you serve meals here?
Σερβίρετε φαγητό εδώ;   ser·*vi*·re·te fa·yi·*to* e·*tho*

---

listen for …

Τι θα πάρεις;
   ti tha *pa*·ris   **What are you having?**

Νομίζω ήπιες αρκετά.
   no·*mi*·zo *i*·pies ar·ke·*ta*   **I think you've had enough.**

Τελευταίες παραγγελίες.
   te·lef·*te*·es pa·ra·ghe·*li*·es   **Last orders.**

Τα ποτά τα κερνάει το κατάστημα.
   ta po·*ta* ta ker·*na*·i
   to ka·*ta*·sti·ma   **Drinks are on the house.**

eating out

drinking up

Cheers!
Εις υγείαν!   is i·*yi*·an

I feel fantastic!
Είμαι στα κέφια μου!   *i*·me sta *ke*·fia mu

I think I've had one too many.
Νομίζω ήπια παραπάνω.   no·*mi*·zo *i*·pia pa·ra·*pa*·no

I'm feeling drunk.
Μέθυσα.   *me*·thi·sa

I feel ill.
Δεν αισθάνομαι καλά.   ţhen es·*tha*·no·me ka·*la*

Where's the toilet?
Πού είναι η τουαλέτα;   pu *i*·ne i tu·a·*le*·ta

I'm tired, I'd better go home.
Είμαι κουρασμένος/   *i*·me ku·raz·*me*·nos/
κουρασμένη, καλύτερα   ku·raz·*me*·ni ka·*li*·te·ra
να πάω σπίτι. m/f   na *pa*·o *spi*·ti

Can you call a taxi for me?
Μπορείς να μου καλέσεις   bo·*ris* na mu ka·*le*·sis
ένα ταξί;   *e*·na tak·*si*

I don't think you should drive.
Νομίζω ότι δεν πρέπει να   no·*mi*·zo *o*·ti ţhen *pre*·pi na
οδηγήσεις.   o·ţhi·*yi*·sis

---

pot plant

When you're in Greece, make sure that you don't eat the decoration – βασιλικός va·si·li·*kos* (basil) is favoured as an ornamental plant and is rarely used in cooking.

What's the local speciality?
Ποιες είναι οι τοπικές
λιχουδιές;
pies *i*·ne i to·pi·*kes*
li·khu·*thies*

What's that?
Τι είναι εκείνο;
ti *i*·ne e·*ki*·no

Can I taste it?
Μπορώ να το δοκιμάσω;
bo·*ro* na to tho·ki·*ma*·so

Can I have a bag, please?
Μπορώ να έχω μια
σακούλα, παρακαλώ;
bo·*ro* na *e*·kho mia
sa·*ku*·la pa·ra·ka·*lo*

How much is (a kilo of cheese)?
Πόσο κάνει (ένα κιλό τυρί);
po·so *ka*·ni (*e*·na ki·*lo* ti·*ri*)

I'd like ... | Θα ήθελα ... | tha *i*·the·la ...
(three) pieces | (τρία) κομμάτια | (*tri*·a) ko·*ma*·tia
(six) slices | (έξι) φέτες | (*ek*·si) *fe*·tes
that one | εκείνο | e·*ki*·no
this one | αυτό | af·*to*

Less. | Πιο λίγο. | pio *li*·gho
A bit more. | Λιγάκι πιο πολύ. | li·*gha*·ki pio po·*li*
Enough. | Αρκετά. | ar·ke·*ta*

For more on quantities, see **numbers & amounts**, page 35.

listen for ...

Δεν υπάρχει άλλο.
then i·*par*·hi *a*·lo | **There isn't any.**

Μπορώ να σας βοηθήσω;
bo·*ro* na sas vo·i·*thi*·so | **Can I help you?**

Τι θα θέλατε;
ti tha *the*·la·te | **What would you like?**

Τίποτε άλλο;
ti·po·te *a*·lo | **Anything else?**

food stuff

cooked	μαγειρεμένο	ma·yi·re·*me*·no
cured	παστό	pa·*sto*
dried	ξηρό	ksi·*ro*
fresh	φρέσκο	*fre*·sko
frozen	κατεψυγμένο	ka·tep·sigh·*me*·no
grilled	στα κάρβουνα	sta *kar*·vu·na
raw	ωμό	o·*mo*
roasted	ψητό	psi·*to*
savoury	πικάντικο	pi·*ka*·di·ko
smoked	καπνιστό	kap·ni·*sto*
sweet	γλυκό	ghli·*ko*

Do you have ...?	Έχετε κάτι ...;	e·he·te *ka*·ti ...
anything cheaper	πιο φτηνό	pio fti·*no*
other kinds	διαφορετικό	thia·fo·re·ti·*ko*

Where can I find the ... section?	Πού μπορώ να βρω το μέρος με ...;	pu bo·*ro* na vro to *me*·ros me ...
bread	το ψωμί	to pso·*mi*
dairy	τα γαλακτικά	ta gha·lak·ti·*ka*
fish	τα ψάρια	ta *psa*·ria
frozen goods	τα κατεψυγμένα	ta ka·tep·sigh·*me*·na
fruit and vegetable	τα φρούτα και τα λαχανικά	ta *fru*·ta ke ta la·kha·ni·*ka*
meat	το κρέας	to *kre*·as
poultry	τα πουλερικά	ta pu·le·ri·*ka*
seafood	τα θαλασσινά	ta tha·la·si·*na*

Could I please borrow a ...?	Μπορώ παρακαλώ να δανειστώ ...;	bo·*ro* pa·ra·ka·*lo* na tha·ni·*sto* ...
I need a ...	Χρειάζομαι ...	khri·*a*·zo·me ...
chopping board	μια σανίδα κοπής	mia sa·*ni*·tha ko·*pis*
frying pan	ένα τηγάνι	e·na ti·*gha*·ni
knife	ένα μαχαίρι	e·na ma·*he*·ri
saucepan	μια κατσαρόλα	mia kat·sa·*ro*·la

For more cooking implements, see the **dictionary** (p207).

ordering food

παραγγέλλοντας φαγητό

Do you have ... food?	Έχετε φαγητό ...;	e·he·te fa·yi·to ...
halal	χαλάλ	kha·lal
kosher	κόσια	ko·si·a
Lent	Σαρακοστιανό	sa·ra·ko·stia·no
pulse-based	με όσπρια	me os·pri·a
vegetarian	για χορτοφάγους	yia khor·to·fa·ghus

Is there a ... restaurant near here?

Υπάρχει ένα εστιατόριο ... εδώ κοντά;	i·par·hi e·na e·sti·a·to·ri·o ... e·tho ko·da

Is it cooked in/with ...?

Είναι μαγειρεμένο σε/με ...;	i·ne ma·yi·re·me·no se/me ...

Could you prepare a meal without ...?

Μπορείτε να κάνετε φαγητό χωρίς ...;	bo·ri·te na ka·ne·te fa·yi·to kho·ris ...

I don't eat ...	Δεν τρώγω ...	then tro·gho ...
butter	βούτυρο	vu·ti·ro
eggs	αβγά	av·gha
fish	ψάρι	psa·ri
fish stock	ζουμί από ψάρι	zu·mi a·po psa·ri
lamb	αρνί	ar·ni
(red) meat	(κόκκινο) κρέας	(ko·ki·no) kre·as
meat stock	ζουμί από κρέας	zu·mi a·po kre·as
oil	λάδι	la·thi
olives	ελιές	e·lies
pork	χοιρινό	hi·ri·no
poultry	πουλερικά	pu·le·ri·ka

Is this ...?	Είναι αυτό ...;	*i*·ne af·*to* ...
decaffeinated	χωρίς καφεΐνη	kho·*ris* ka·fe·*i*·ni
gluten-free	χωρίς γλουτένη	kho·*ris* ghlu·*te*·ni
low in fat	χαμηλό σε λίπος	kha·mi·*lo* se *li*·pos
low in sugar	χαμηλό σε	kha·mi·*lo* se
	ζάχαρη	*za*·kha·ri
organic	οργανικό	or·gha·ni·*ko*
salt-free	χωρίς αλάτι	kho·*ris* a·*la*·ti

special diets & allergies

I'm on a special diet.

Κάνω ειδική δίαιτα.   *ka*·no i·*thi*·ki *thi*·e·ta

I'm allergic to ...	Είμαι αλλεργικός/	*i*·me a·ler·yi·*kos*
	αλλεργική ... m/f	a·ler·yi·*ki* ...
dairy produce	στα γαλακτικά	sta gha·lak·ti·*ka*
eggs	στα αβγά	sta av·*gha*
gluten	στη γλουτένη	sti ghlu·*te*·ni
honey	στο μέλι	sto *me*·li
MSG	στο MSG	sto em si dzi
nuts	στους ξηρούς	stus ksi·*rus*
	καρπούς	kar·*pus*
seafood	στα θαλασσινά	sta tha·la·si·*na*
shellfish	στα οστρακοειδή	sta os·tra·ko·i·*thi*

I'm (a) ...	Είμαι ...	*i*·me ...
Buddhist	Βουδιστής m	vu·*thi*·stis
	Βουδίστρια f	vu·*thi*·stri·a
Hindu	Ινδουιστής m	in·*thu*·i·stis
	Ινδουίστρια f	in·*thu*·i·stri·a
Jewish	Ιουδαίος m	i·u·*the*·os
	Ιουδαία f	i·u·*the*·a
Muslim	Μουσουλμάνος m	mu·sul·*ma*·nos
	Μουσουλμάνα f	mu·sul·*ma*·na
vegan	βέγκαν m&f	*ve*·gan
vegetarian	χορτοφάγος m&f	khor·to·*fa*·ghos

This miniguide lists dishes and ingredients used in Greek cuisine. It's designed to help you get the most out of your gastronomic experience by providing you with food terms that you may see on menus. For certain dishes we've marked the region or city where they're most popular.

The **menu decoder** has been ordered according to the Greek alphabet:

Αα	Ββ	Γγ	Δδ	Εε	Ζζ	Ηη	Θθ	Ιι	Κκ	Λλ	Μμ
Νν	Ξξ	Οο	Ππ	Ρρ	Σσ/ς	Ττ	Υυ	Φφ	Χχ	Ψψ	Ωω

Α α

αβγολέμονο ⓝ av-gho-*le*-mo-no *egg and lemon sauce added to meat, chicken or fish soup and other dishes*

αβγοτάραχο ⓝ av-gho-*ta*-ra-kho *dried & salted grey mullet roe, coated in beeswax*

αγγινάρες ① pl av-gi-*na*-res *globe artichokes*

— **αλαπολίτα** a-la-po-*li*-ta *'Constantinople-style artichokes' – artichokes, carrots & potatoes in dill-spiked chicken stock*

— **καλογρές** ka-lo-*ghres* *'nuns' – artichoke hearts braised in creamy onion broth (Crete)*

αγγουροντομάτα σαλάτα ①
ang-gu-ro-do-*ma*-ta sa-*la*-ta *cucumber slices, tomato wedges & parsley with oil, lemon juice, salt & pepper*

αγγουροσαλάτα ① ang-gu-ro-sa-*la*-ta *sliced cucumbers sprinkled with salt & served with oil & vinegar*

άγρια χόρτα pl *a*-ghri-a *khor*-ta *seasonal wild greens*

άγρια σπαράγγια ① pl *a*-ghri-a spa-*rang*-gi-a *wild asparagus*

άγριες αγγινάρες ① pl *a*-ghri-es ang-gi-*na*-res *small prickly artichokes, eaten raw with salt & lemon juice*

αμπελοπούλια ⓝ pl am-be-lo-*pu*-lia *tiny birds preserved in vinegar & wine, eaten whole (Cyprus)*

αμελέτητα ⓝ pl a-me-*le*-ti-ta *lamb testicles*

αμπελοφάσουλα ⓝ pl am-be-lo-*fa*-su-la *green beans*

αμπερόριζα ① am-be-o-*ri*-za *rose geranium (leaves are used as a flavouring for cakes, pastries & preserved fruits)*

αμύγδαλα ⓝ pl *migh*-tha-la *almonds*

αμυγδαλωτά ⓝ pl a-migh-tha-lo-*ta* *almond shortbread sprinkled with icing sugar & chopped almonds*

αμυγδαλωτό γλύκισμα ⓝ
a-migh-tha-lo-to *ghli*-kiz-ma *nougat*

αναρή ① a-na-*ri* *soft ricotta-like cheese from goat's or sheep's milk (Cyprus)*

αρακάς ⓜ a-ra-*kas* *fresh peas*

— **λαδερός** la-*the*-ros *peas stewed with carrots, garlic bulbs & herbs in oil & paprika (Corfu)*

αρνάκι ⓝ ar-*na*-ki *milk-lamb (very young lamb)*

— **γεμιστό** ye-mi-*sto* *Easter dish of stuffed roast lamb (Dodecanese Islands)*

αρνί ⓝ ar-*ni* *lamb*

— **βραστό** vra-*sto* *slow-boiled mutton served with mutton-stock soup (Crete)*

— **γιαχνί** yiakh-*ni* *lamb stewed with tomatoes, onions, carrots & celery*

— **γιουβέτσι με κριθαράκι** yiu-*vet*-si me kri-tha-*ra*-ki *lamb baked with tomatoes & barley-shaped pasta in an earthenware pot*

— **εξοχικό** ek-so-hi-*ko* *'country-style lamb' – baked filo parcels of lamb, potato, feta & **κεφαλοτύρι***

— φρικασέ με μαρούλι
fri·ka·se me ma·ru·li poached lamb with
shredded lettuce, egg & lemon sauce
— κεφαλάκι ριγανάτο
ke·fa·la·ki ri·gha·na·to lamb's head (gen-
erally roasted) complete with tongue,
cheek, brains & eyes
— κοκκινιστό ko·ki·ni·sto lamb braised
in white wine with onions & bay leaves
— οφτό of·to roast lamb on the spit
— στη σούβλα sti suv·la spit-roast
lamb basted with olive oil, lemon juice &
garlic – a traditional Easter dish
— στο φούρνο sto fur·no
roasted leg or shoulder of lamb
αρνίσια παϊδάκια ® pl ar·ni·sia
pa·i·tha·kia marinated & chargrilled
lamb cutlets
αστακός a·sta·kos ®
lobster, usually boiled or chargrilled
αφέλια ® pl a·fe·lia meat braised with
potato & mushrooms in red wine
αχηβάδα ① a·hi·va·tha clam
αχινοί ® pl a·hi·ni sea urchins
— σαλάτα sa·la·ta sea urchin salad
— γεμιστοί ye·mi·sti sea urchin stuffed
with rice, onions & tomatoes

B β

βασιλόπιτα ① va·si·lo·pi·ta New Year loaf
decorated with almonds – whoever finds
the coin in the bread gets good luck
βατόμουρο ® va·to·mu·ro
blackberry · raspberry
βατραχοπόδαρα τηγανητά ® pl
va·tra·kho·po·tha·ra ti·gha·ni·ta
fried frog's legs (Western Greece)
βυσσινάδα ① vi·si·na·tha
syrup of morello cherries – mixed with
cold water for summer-time cordials
βύσσινο ® vi·si·no
morello cherry · sour black cherry
— γλυκό ghli·ko morello cherry preserve
βλίτο ® vli·to amaranth – its sweet nutty
flavour & soft texture make it popular for
warm salads
βοδινό ® vo·thi·no beef
— καπαμά ka·pa·ma beef stewed with
tomatoes, red wine, cinnamon & cloves

— με λαχανικά me la·kha·ni·ka beef
braised with carrots, potatoes & celery
βολβοί ® pl vol·vi grape hyacinth bulbs
— βραστοί vra·sti bulbs boiled, dressed
with dill vinaigrette & accompanied by
σκορδαλιά
βρούβα ① vru·va charlock · field green
with sharp peppery taste

Γ γ

γαϊδουρελιά ① gha·i·thu·re·lia 'donkey
olive' – named so because of its large size
γαλακτομπούρεκο ® gha·lak·to·bu·re·ko
baked custard-cream filo pie sprinkled
with a lemony syrup
γαλοπούλα ① gha·lo·pu·la turkey
— γεμιστή ye·mi·sti stuffed roast turkey
γαλύπες ① pl gha·li·pes a sea anemone
— τηγανητές ti·gha·ni·tes
lightly battered & fried sea anemone
γαλυποκεφτέδες ® pl
gha·li·po·kef·te·thes sea anemone rissoles
γαρδούμια ® pl ghar·thu·mia small offal
rolls made from strips of lamb's stomach,
bound with intestines then roasted
γαρίδες ① pl gha·ri·thes prawns · shrimps
— σαγανάκι sa·gha·na·ki
prawns fried with tomatoes & red wine,
topped with feta & baked
— τηγανητές ti·gha·ni·tes fried prawns
— βραστές vra·stes boiled prawns
accompanied by λαδολέμονο
— γιουβετσάκι yiu·vet·sa·ki prawns
with tomatoes, parsley, oregano & feta
chunks baked in earthenware pots
γαριδοσαλάτα ① gha·ri·tho·sa·la·ta
prawn salad
γαύρος ® ghav·ros fresh anchovy
γεμιστά ® pl ye·mi·sta stuffed vegetables
γεμιστός ye·mi·stos method of stuffing
meat, fish or vegetables prior to cooking
γιαούρτι ® yia·ur·ti thick, heavy yogurt
with a tangy bite, made from sheep's,
goat's or cow's milk
— αγελάδος a·ye·la·thos
cow's milk yogurt
— φρούτων fru·ton fruit yogurt
— με μέλι me·li yogurt with honey
— πρόβειο pro·vio sheep's milk yoghurt

γιαουρτογλού ① yia·ur·to·*ghlu*
pie cooked with finely sliced grilled meat,
topped with a yogurt sauce

γιαουρτόπιτα ① yia·ur·to·*pi*·ta
light moist cake made with yogurt,
sugar, lemon rind & lots of eggs

γίδα βραστή ① *yi*·tha vra·*sti*
aromatic dish of boiled goat

γύρος *yi*·ros 'to spin' – seasoned lamb
packed onto a spit & rotisseried upright,
carved for meat platters or served in
πίτα with tomatoes, onions & τζατζίκι

γιορτή ① yior·*ti* small pieces of pork & goat
boiled with corn, topped with melted
butter, cinnamon & pepper (Samos)

γιουβαρλάκια ⓝ pl yiu·var·*la*·kia egg-
shaped rissoles of minced beef or lamb
simmered in a light stock

γιουβέτσι ⓝ yiu·*vet*·si casserole of meat &
seafood with tomatoes & barley pasta
— **με θαλασσινά** me tha·la·si·*na*
casserole of seafood, barley pasta, tomatoes & chicken stock (Ionian Islands)

γιουσλεμέδες ⓜ pl yiuz·le·*me*·thes golden
pies filled with eggs & κεφαλοτύρι,
deep-fried then served with grated cheese
(Lesvos)

γλιστρίδα ① ghli·*stri*·tha purslane –
small-leafed plant with lemony flavour &
crisp texture used mainly in salads
— **με κανναρόφυλλα σαλάτα**
me ka·pa·ro·fi·la sa·*la*·ta purslane leaves,
sliced tomatoes, black olives & caper
leaves with oil & lemon dressing
— **με γιαούρτι** me yia·ur·ti
chopped purslane beaten with strained
yogurt, garlic, lemon, salt & oil (Crete)

γλυκά κουταλιού ⓝ pl ghli·ka ku·ta·*liu*
'spoon sweets' – preserved fruits

γλυκάνισο ⓝ ghli·ka·ni·so aniseed

γλυκά ταψιού ⓝ pl ghli·ka tap·*siu*
sweets made with filo pastry

γλύκισμα ⓝ pl ghli·kiz·ma
sweet pastry • cake

γλυκοκολοκύθα ① ghli·ko·lo·lo·*ki*·tha
marrow • pumpkin • squash

γλώσσα ① *ghlo*·sa tongue (fish) • generic
name for any flat fish

— **μοσχαρίσια κρασάτη**
mo·sha·ri·si·a kra·*sa*·ti tongue (fish) fried
in butter, then poached in white wine

γουρουνάκι (του γάλακτος) ⓝ
ghu·ru·*na*·ki (tu gha·lak·tos)
piglet • suckling pig
— **στη σούβλα** sti *suv*·la whole suckling
pig spit-roasted until tender
— **γεμιστό με φέτα** ye·mi·*sto* me *fe*·ta
suckling pig stuffed with feta & roasted

γυαλιστερές ① pl yia·li·ste·*res*
shellfish eaten alive with a squeeze of
lemon juice (Dodecanese Islands)

Δ δ

δάχτυλα ⓝ pl *thakh*·ti·la 'fingers' – deep-
fried, nut-filled pastries (Cyprus)

δίπλες ① pl *thi*·ples sweet pastry, deep-
fried & drizzled with honey & sesame seeds
— **Δράμας** *thra*·mas
yogurt pie with vine leaves

δρύλιοι αλευρολέμονο ⓝ pl *thri*·li
a·lev·ro·le·mo·no wild greens in lemon

Ε ε

ελαιόλαδο ⓝ e·le·o·la·*tho* olive oil

ελαιόπιτες ① pl e·le·o·pi·tes
small olive & leek pies (Cyprus)

ελαιότη ① e·le·o·ti bread with a layer of
chopped black olives & onions (Cyprus)

ελαιόψωμο ⓝ e·le·op·so·mo olive bread

ελιές ① pl e·*lies* olives
— **Αμφίσσης** am·fi·sis large blue-black
olives with nutty flavour
— **Αταλάντης** a·ta·*lan*·dis big fruity
greenish-purple or purple olives
— **χαμούρες** ha·*mu*·res
dried newly fallen olives
— **Ιονίων πράσινες** i·o·ni·on pra·si·nes
mild green olives (Ionian Islands)
— **Καλαμάτας** ka·la·*ma*·tas large black
olives with pungent flavour
— **μαύρες** *mav*·res black olives
— **Ναυπλίου** naf·*pli*·u
nutty flavoured green olives (Nafplio)
— **παστές** pa·*stes* dried salted olives
— **πελτέ** pel·*te* olive paste
— **πράσινες** pra·si·nes green olives

— τσακιστές tsa-ki-*stes* *cracked green olives marinated in oil, lemon & herbs*
— τουρσί tur-*si* *pickled olives*
ελίτσες ⓘ ple-*lit*-ses *tiny sweet black olives*
εντόσθια ⓝ plen-*do*-sthi-a *offal • innards (usually lamb)*
— κοκκινιστά ko-ki-ni-*sta* *chicken giblets in a rich gravy*
— πουλιών pu-*lion* *giblets*

Ζ ζ

ζαχαροπούλια ⓝ plza-kha-ro-*pu*-lia *marzipan sweets (Lesvos)*
ζαχαρωτό με αμύγδαλο ⓝ za-kha-ro-*to* me a-*migh*-tha-lo *marzipan*
ζαμπόν ⓝ zam-*bon* *ham*
ζαργάνα ⓘ zar-*gha*-na *garfish*
ζύμη ⓘ *zi*-mi *pastry*
— με γιαούρτι me yia-*ur*-ti *baked pasta dish consisting of homemade macaroni, strained yogurt & onions (Kos)*

Θ θ

θαλασσινά ⓝ pltha-la-si-*na* *seafood*
— του Αιγαίου tu *ye*-e-u *paella-style rice dish cooked with seafood (Hydra)*
θρούμπες ⓘ pl*thru*-mbes *ripe black olives*
θυμάρι ⓝ thi-*ma*-ri *thyme*

Ι ι

ιμάμ-μπαϊλντί ⓝ i-*mam*-ba-il-*di* *Turkish-inspired dish of eggplant stuffed with eggplant pulp, tomato, garlic, onion, parsley, then baked*

Κ κ

καβούρι ⓝ ka-*vu*-ri *crab*
— βραστό vra-*sto* *crab boiled & dressed with* λαδολέμονο
καϊμάκι ⓝ to ka-i-*ma*-ki *froth that forms on top of Greek coffee while it brews*
— πηγμένο pigh-*me*-no *clotted cream*
κακαβιά ⓘ ka-ka-*via* *saltwater fish soup*
καλαμαράκια ⓝ plka-la-ma-*ra*-kia *baby squid*

καλαμάρι ⓝ ka-la-*ma*-ri *squid*
— γεμιστό ye-mi-*sto* *squid stuffed with rice & baked in a lemony broth*
— Λεβριανά lev-ria-*na* *squid stewed in dry red wine with green olives, tomatoes, onions & parsley*
— με ρύζι me ri-zi *fried squid with onions simmered with water, crushed tomatoes, rice & cinnamon*
— τηγανητό ti-gha-ni-*to* *squid cut in rings or strips, lightly battered & fried*
καλιτσούνια ⓝ plka-lit-*su*-nia *small cheese pies*
καπαμάς ⓝ ka-pa-*mas* *method of stewing meat with tomatoes, wine, cinnamon & sometimes red capsicum & cloves*
κάππαρη ⓘ *ka*-pa-ri *capers, usually pickled & eaten as an appetiser*
κάπρος ⓝ *ka*-pros *wild boar*
καραμέλα ⓘ ka-ra-*me*-la *candy • caramel*
καραβίδα ⓘ ka-ra-*vi*-tha *crayfish*
καρύδια ⓝ plka-*ri*-thia *walnuts*
— γεμιστά ye-mi-*sta* *walnuts & roasted almonds preserved in syrup (Cyprus)*
καρυδόπιτα ⓘ ka-ri-*tho*-pi-ta *rich moist walnut cake*
κάσιου ⓝ *ka*-siu *cashews*
καταΐφι ⓝ ka-ta-*i*-fi *'angel hair' pastry – syrupy nest-like nut-filled rolls*
κατσικάκι ⓝ kat-si-*ka*-ki *goat • kid*
— πατούδο pa-*tu*-tho *roast kid stuffed with liver, rice, bread-crumbs, feta & raisins or* κεφαλοτύρι, *bacon, rice & dill (Cyclades)*
— ψητό psi-*to* *roast kid, sometimes served with a spicy red wine sauce*
καφές ⓝ ka-*fes* *coffee*
— ελληνικός e-li-ni-*kos* *freshly brewed Greek coffee*
— γλυκός ghli-*kos* *sweet coffee*
— μέτριος *me*-tri-os *medium-strength coffee with a little sugar*
— πολλά βαρύς po-*la* va-*ris* *strong coffee*
— σκέτος *ske*-tos *sugarless coffee*
— βαρύγλυκος va-*ri*-ghli-kos *strong & sweet coffee*
κεφαλάκι ⓝ ke-fa-*la*-ki *head – usually refers specifically to lamb's head*

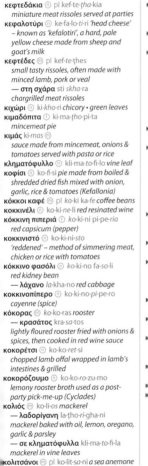

κεφτεδάκια ⓝ pl kef·te·*tha*·kia
miniature meat rissoles served at parties

κεφαλοτύρι ⓝ ke·fa·lo·*ti*·ri 'head cheese'
– known as 'kefalotiri', a hard, pale
yellow cheese made from sheep and
goat's milk

κεφτέδες ⓜ pl kef·*te*·thes
small tasty rissoles, often made with
minced lamb, pork or veal
— **στη σχάρα** sti *skha*·ra
chargrilled meat rissoles

κιχώρι ⓝ ki·*kho*·ri chicory • green leaves

κιμαδόπιτα ⓕ ki·ma·*tho*·pi·ta
mincemeat pie

κιμάς ki·*mas* ⓜ
sauce made from mincemeat, onions &
tomatoes served with pasta or rice

κληματόφυλλο ⓝ kli·ma·to·fi·lo vine leaf

κοφίσι ⓝ ko·*fi*·si pie made from boiled &
shredded fish mixed with onion,
garlic, rice & tomatoes (Kefallonia)

κόκκοι καφέ ⓜ pl *ko*·ki ka·*fe* coffee beans

κοκκινέλι ⓝ ko·ki·*ne*·li red resinated wine

κόκκινη πιπεριά ⓕ *ko*·ki·ni pi·pe·*ria*
red capsicum (pepper)

κοκκινιστό ⓝ ko·ki·ni·*sto*
'reddened' – method of simmering meat,
chicken or rice with tomatoes

κόκκινο φασόλι ⓝ *ko*·ki·no fa·*so*·li
red kidney bean
— **λάχανο** *la*·kha·no red cabbage

κοκκινοπίπερο ⓝ ko·ki·no·*pi*·pe·ro
cayenne (spice)

κόκορας ⓜ *ko*·ko·ras rooster
— **κρασάτος** kra·*sa*·tos
lightly floured rooster fried with onions &
spices, then cooked in red wine sauce

κοκορέτσι ⓝ ko·ko·*ret*·si
chopped lamb offal wrapped in lamb's
intestines & grilled

κοκορόζουμο ⓝ ko·ko·ro·*zu*·mo
lemony rooster broth used as a post-
party pick-me-up (Cyclades)

κολιός ⓜ ko·li·os mackerel
— **λαδορίγανη** la·tho·*ri*·gha·ni
mackerel baked with oil, lemon, oregano,
garlic & parsley
— **σε κληματόφυλλα** kli·ma·to·fi·la
mackerel in vine leaves

κολιτσάνοι ⓝ pl ko·lit·*sa*·ni a sea anemone

κολοκέτα ⓕ ko·lo·*ke*·ta
pastries stuffed with red pumpkin,
raisins & cracked wheat (Cyprus)

κολοκύθα ⓕ ko·lo·*ki*·tha
marrow • pumpkin • squash

κολοκυθάκια ⓝ pl ko·lo·ki·*tha*·kia zucchini
— **με αβγά** me av·*gha*
zucchini & egg omelette
— **τηγανητά** ti·gha·ni·*ta*
zucchini battered & deep-fried, served
with lemon & **σκορδαλιά**
— **βραστά** vra·*sta* boiled baby zucchini
with oil & lemon dressing

κολοκύθι ⓝ ko·lo·*ki*·thi
marrow • pumpkin • squash

κολοκυθάνθοι ⓝ pl ko·lo·ki·*tho*·an·thi
zucchini flowers
— **τηγανητοί** ti·gha·ni·*ti*
zucchini flowers & cheese fritters (Andros)
— **γεμιστοί** ye·mi·*sti* zucchini flower
ντολμάδες stuffed with rice, tomato &
parsley & simmered until tender

κολοκυθοκεφτέδες
ko·lo·ki·tho·kef·*te*·thes rissoles of puréed
zucchini, parsley, onion, mint & garlic

κολοκυθόπιτα ⓕ ko·lo·ki·*tho*·pi·ta
zucchini pie

κόλυβα ⓝ pl *ko*·li·va wheat mixed with
fruit, pomegranate seeds, sugar & nuts –
eaten after the death of a family member
& on the anniversary of their death

κομπόστα ⓕ ko·*bo*·sta
compote • stewed fruit

κονσερβολιά ⓕ kon·ser·vo·*lia* common
type of olive from the central mainland

κοντοσούβλι ⓝ kon·do·*suv*·li
spit-roast pieces of lamb or pork seasoned
with onions, oregano, salt & pepper

κορωναϊκη ⓕ ko·ro·ne·*i*·ki a smaller, oil-
bearing variety of the kalamata olive

κοτόπιτα ⓕ ko·to·pi·ta chicken filo pastry

κοτόπουλο ⓝ ko·to·pu·lo chicken
— **χυλοπίτες** hi·lo·*pi*·tes whole chicken &
noodles simmered in tomato, onion &
cinnamon broth until liquid is absorbed
— **λεμονάτο** le·mo·*na*·to roast chicken
basted with butter & lemon juice
— **με μπάμιες** me *ba*·mies chicken &
okra braised in tomato & onion gravy

menu decoder

179

κοτόσουπα ① ko·to·su·pa
soup made from boiled whole chicken

κρασί ⓝ kra·si wine
— **άσπρο** a·spro white wine
— **κόκκινο** ko·ki·no red wine
— **λευκό** lef·ko white wine
— **ροζέ** ro·ze rosé wine

κρέας ⓝ kre·as meat
— **ελαφιού** e·la·fiu venison
— **στη στάμνα** sti stam·na
meat cooked in a pot
— **στο φούρνο με πατάτες** sto fur·no
me pa·ta·tes roast meat with potatoes

κρεατικά ⓝ pl kre·a·ti·ka
meat dishes, mostly stewed or roasted

κρεατόπιτα ① kre·a·to·pi·ta
lamb or veal pie, usually with cinnamon
— **Κεφαλλονίτικη** ke·fa·lo·ni·ti·ki
meat pie cooked with onions, eggs, rice,
potatoes, tomatoes & spices (Kefallonia)
— **της Κρήτης** tis kri·tis
pie of alternating layers of cubed lamb
(or goat) & **μυζήθρα** covered in butter &
baked in shortcrust pastry (Crete)

κρεατόσουπα ① kre·a·to·su·pa nourish-
ing broth made from boiled meat –
sometimes thickened with rice &
αβγολέμονο

κρεμμυδόπιτα ① kre·mi·tho·pi·ta
pie with a filling of **μυζήθρα**, grated
onion, eggs & dill (Mykonos)

Κρητική κρεατόπιτα ①
kri·ti·ki kre·a·to·pi·ta
see **κρεατόπιτα της Κρήτης**

κριθαράκι ⓝ kri·tha·ra·ki
tiny spindle-shaped barley pasta used
for pasta dishes, soups & casseroles
— **με βούτυρο και τυρί** me vu·ti·ro
ke ti·ri pasta baked with brown butter,
cheese, lemon juice & herbs

κουκουβάγια ① ku·ku·va·yia
see **παξιμάδια σαλάτα**

κουκιά ⓝ pl ku·kia broad beans
— **ξερά βραστά** kse·ra vra·sta broad
beans boiled in water & lemon juice &
served with oil, dill & onion rings
— **με αγριαγκινάρες**
me a·ghri·ang·gi·na·res
broad beans with artichokes

κουλουκόψωμο ⓝ ku·lu·kop·so·mo
see **παξιμάδια με ντομάτες και φέτα**

κουλουράκια ⓝ pl ku·lu·ra·kia
cookies · biscuits · buns
— **με πετιμέζι** me pe·ti·me·zi
sweet buns made with syrup, cinnamon
& spices

κουλούρι ⓝ ku·lu·ri crisp sesame-coated
bread rings sold on streets & outside
church after Sunday mass · generic
name for circular rolls, buns & biscuits

κουλούρια αστυπαλίτικα ⓝ pl ku·lu·ri·a
a·sti·pa·li·ti·ka saffron biscuits (Astypalea)

κουμκουάτ ⓝ kum·ku·at cumquat
— **λικέρ** li·ker cumquat liqueur (Corfu)

Κουμανταρία ① ku·man·da·ri·a
heavy dessert wine originally made
during the Crusades by the Knights of
the Order of St John (Cyprus)

κουνέλι ⓝ ku·ne·li rabbit
— **κρασάτο** kra·sa·to rabbit casserole
with red wine, garlic & bay leaves
— **με καρύδι** me ka·ri·thi marinated
rabbit, fried & simmered in white wine
infused with coarsely ground walnuts
— **με γιαούρτι** me yia·ur·ti
rabbit marinated in lemon juice & black
pepper, then baked with a creamy egg &
yogurt sauce
— **στιφάδο** sti·fa·tho rabbit ragout
spiced with cloves, cinnamon & cumin

κουπέπια ⓝ pl ku·pe·pia **ντολμάδες**
made with minced lamb & veal, served
hot with **αβγολέμονο** sauce (Cyprus)

κούπες ① pl ku·pes deep-fried pastries of
mincemeat, onion & spices (Cyprus)

κουραμπιέδες ⓝ pl ku·ra·bie·thes
buttery almond shortbread

κυδώνι ⓝ ki·tho·ni quince
— **μπελτές** bel·tes quince jelly
— **γλυκό** ghli·ko quince preserve
flavoured with rose geranium
— **στο φούρνο** sto fur·no buttered
quince baked in a water & sugar solution
until liquid has caramelised
— **γεμιστό** ye·mi·sto
large quince stuffed with minced beef,
rice, onions, raisins, cloves & nutmeg

κυδωνόπαστο ⓝ ki·tho·no·pa·sto
dark-red quince paste dried until firm, cut
in small diamonds & dusted with sugar

Λ λ

λαβράκι ⓝ lav·ra·ki sea bass
— **στο αλάτι** sto a·la·ti whole sea bass
buried in salt & baked – the salt-encrusted
skin is slit & the flesh is eaten from the
bone with an oil & lemon dressing

λαγάνα ⓕ la·gha·na bread sprinkled with
sesame seeds baked on the first day of Lent

λαγός ⓜ la·ghos hare
— **στιφάδο** sti·fa·tho hare ragout
spiced with cumin & cloves, usually
marinated in vinegar prior to cooking

λαγωτό ⓝ la·gho·to hare ragout (Kefallonia)

λαδόξιδο ⓝ la·thok·si·tho vinaigrette of
oil, vinegar, parsley, salt & pepper

λαδολέμονο ⓝ la·tho·le·mo·no
thick dressing of oil beaten with lemon
juice, salt & pepper

λάχανα ⓝ pl la·kha·na seasonal wild greens
— **με λαρδί** me lar·thi casserole of seasonal greens & fatty bacon (Mykonos)

λαχανικά ⓝ pl la·kha·ni·ka vegetables
— **της θάλασσας** tis tha·la·sas
sea vegetables

λάχανο ⓝ la·kha·no cabbage
— **κοκκινιστό** ko·ki·ni·sto
cabbage stewed with tomatoes, onions,
parsley, dill & paprika (Corfu)
— **με κιμά** me ki·ma cabbage braised
with onions, mincemeat & tomatoes,
finished with fresh butter (Chios)

λαχανοσαλάτα ⓕ la·kha·no·sa·la·ta
shredded white cabbage sprinkled with
oil, lemon juice & salt

λεμονάτος ⓜ le·mo·na·tos
method of cooking with oil & lemon juice

λιθρίνι ⓝ li·thri·ni sea bream

λουκάνικα ⓝ pl lu·ka·ni·ka pork sausages
seasoned with coriander & orange peel •
generic word for sausages & frankfurters

λουκανόπιτες ⓕ pl lu·ka·no·pi·tes
filo-wrapped sausages

λουκουμάδες ⓜ pl lu·ku·ma·thes
rosette-shaped, light-as-air doughnuts
served hot with honey & cinnamon

λουκούμι ⓝ lu·ku·mi Turkish delight

λουκούμια ⓝ pl lu·ku·mia
wedding shortbread (Cyprus)

λούντζα ⓕ lun·dza spicy ham made from
cured smoked pork fillet (Cyprus, Cyclades)
— **με χαλούμι** me kha·lu·mi grilled ham
topped with melted χαλούμι (Cyprus)

λουβιά ⓝ pl lu·via black-eyed peas
— **με λάχανα** me la·kha·na warm salad
of black-eyed peas & seasonal greens
with oil & lemon dressing (Cyprus)

λουζές ⓜ lu·zes salted fillet of pork stuffed
into thick pig's intestine & sun-dried
(Mykonos)

λιαστός ⓜ lia·stos sun-dried

Μ μ

μαγειρίτσα ⓕ ma·yi·rit·sa lamb's offal
soup thickened with rice & **αβγολέμονο**,
eaten to celebrate the end of Lent

μακαρόνια ⓝ pl ma·ka·ro·nia
macaroni • spaghetti
— **με κιμά** me ki·ma pasta with a sauce of
mincemeat, tomatoes, onions & red wine
— **με σάλτσα** me sal·tsa pasta with
tomato, onion & oregano sauce
— **με βούτυρο και τυρί** me vu·ti·ro ke
ti·ri pasta with butter sauce & cheese
— **στο φούρνο** sto fur·no pasta baked
in cheese & butter sauce

μαντί ⓝ man·di small pasta pockets filled
with mincemeat, cooked in meat broth
seasoned with capsicum & served with a
yogurt & garlic sauce (Northern Greece)

μάραθο ⓝ ma·ra·tho fennel
— **με ούζο σούπα** me u·zo su·pa
ouzo & fennel soup

μαχαλεπί ⓝ ma·kha·le·pi creamy custard
pudding in rose-water syrup (Cyprus)

μαχλέπι ⓝ ma·khle·pi
pungent bitter-sweet black cherry pips
used for spicing breads & stuffings

μαρίδα πικάντικη ⓕ ma·ri·tha
pi·kan·di·ki whitebait, tomato & mint
fritters (Rhodes)

μαρίδες ⓕ pl ma·ri·thes whitebait
— **λιαστές** lia·stes whitebait seasoned
with oregano & strung out to dry then
chargrilled & served with oil & lemon juice

— τηγανητές ti·gha·ni·tes whitebait rolled in flour & deep fried until crisp, served with lemon wedges

μαστίχα ① ma·sti·kha mastic • crystallised resin from the mastic bush, eaten as chewing gum & used as a flavouring (Chios)

μαυρομάτικα φασόλια ⑩ pl mav·ro·ma·ti·ka fa·so·lia black-eyed peas
— με χόρτα me khor·ta black-eyed peas stewed with greens, onions, tomatoes, parsley, mint & garlic (Crete)

μεγαρίτικη ① me·gha·ri·ti·ki olives grown in Attica, near Athens, named after the city of Megara

μελανούρι ⑩ me·la·nu·ri sea bream

μεζές ⑩ me·zes snack

μεζεδάκι ⑩ me·ze·tha·ki tasty morsels served with ouzo • favourites include olives, salted cucumber slices, feta, salted anchovies, mackerel & mini-meat rissoles

μέλι ⑩ me·li honey
— με ξηρούς καρπούς me ksi·rus kar·pus honey poured over walnuts or almonds

μελιτζάνες ① pl me·li·dza·nes eggplant
— στο φούρνο sto fur·no sliced eggplant fried with potatoes, & baked with tomatoes, cumin, parsley & feta
— τηγανητές ti·gha·ni·tes see κολοκυθάκια τηγανητά

μελιτζανοσαλάτα ① me·li·dza·no·sa·la·ta smoky purée of grilled mashed eggplant, onion, garlic, oil & lemon

μελιτίνι ⑩ me·li·ti·ni golden pastry tarts filled with fresh cheese, eggs & sugar, traditionally eaten at Easter

μελόπιτα ① me·lo·pi·ta cheesecake made with μυζήθρα & clear honey

μηλοπιτάκια ① pl mi·lo·pi·ta·kia crescent-shaped apple & walnut pies

μοσχάρι ⑩ mo·sha·ri veal
— κατσαρόλας με αρακά kat·sa·ro·las me a·ra·ka veal stewed with fresh peas in white wine & thyme
— κοκκινιστό με μακαρόνια ko·ki·ni·sto me ma·ka·ro·nia veal stewed with tomatoes, served with spaghetti
— ψητό psi·to rolled veal rubbed with lemon juice, pepper & salt, pot-roasted with onion, tomatoes & wine

— στιφάδο sti·fa·tho veal ragout with garlic, peppercorns & bay leaves

μουσακάς ⑩ mu·sa·kas thick-sliced eggplant & mincemeat arranged in layers, topped with béchamel & baked
— με αγγινάρες me ang·gi·na·res alternating layers of minced veal & artichoke hearts

μουσταλευριά ① mu·sta·lev·ri·a dark gelatinous pudding made from boiled grape must, thickened with flour & sprinkled with cinnamon, seeds & nuts

μούστος ⑩ mu·stos grape must collected from crushed wine grapes
— κουλούρα ku·lu·ra hard, turban-shaped grape must buns

μπακαλιάρος ⑩ ba·ka·lia·ros dried salt cod soaked for several hours prior to cooking

μπουρδέτο ⑩ bur·the·to salt cod stew
— κροκετάκια kro·ke·ta·kia deep-fried salt cod mashed with potato & nutmeg
— πλακί pla·ki salt cod simmered with onions, potatoes, celery, carrots & garlic in a tomato-based sauce
— τηγανητός ti·gha·ni·tos salt cod fried in crisp, golden batter, traditionally accompanied with σκορδαλιά

μπακλαβάς ⑩ pl ba·kla·vas nut-filled layers of filo bathed in honey syrup

μπάμιες ① pl ba·mies okra
— λαδερές la·the·res okra stewed in oil
— γιαχνί yia·khni okra braised with pulped tomatoes & onions

μπαρμπούνια ⑩ pl bar·bu·nia small, sweet-fleshed sea red mullet
— ψητά στον άνιθο psi·ta ston a·ni·tho red mullet on a bed of dill
— στη σκάρα sti ska·ra red mullet basted with oil & lemon & chargrilled
— τηγανητά ti·gha·ni·ta red mullet rolled in seasoned flour & fried

μπεκάτσα ① be·kat·sa woodcock
— κρασάτη kra·sa·ti woodcock casserole with dry red wine, tomatoes & spices, served on fried bread

μπεκρή μεζέ be·kri me·ze 'drunken μεζέ' – meat cooked in tomato & wine sauce

καμπομπότα ① bo·*bo*·ta
sweet corn bread studded with raisins,
walnuts, cloves & flavoured with cinnamon & orange juice (Zakynthos)

μπισκότα ⑩ pl bi·*sko*·ta biscuits • cookies

μπιζελόσουπα ① bi·ze·*lo*·su·pa
fragrant pea soup loaded with dill

μπόλια bo·li·a ①
lacy caul of fat encasing lamb's stomach

μπριάμι ⑪ bri·*a*·mi casserole of sliced
potatoes, zucchini, capsicums, tomatoes
& herbs • roast vegetables

μπριζόλες ① pl bri·*zo*·les chops • steak

μπουγάτσα ① bu·*ghat*·sa creamy semolina pudding wrapped in pastry & baked

μπουρδέτο ⑩ bur·*the*·to
hot fish casserole spiked with paprika

μπουρεκάκια ⑩ pl bu·re·*ka*·kia little filo
pies in cigar, cigarette & envelope shapes

μπουρέκια ⑩ pl bu·*re*·kia filo pies shaped
into thin long rolls, batons & pinwheels
— **με ανερί** me a·ne·*ri* deep-fried pastry
pouches stuffed with cheese (Cyprus)

μυαλά ⑩ pl mia·*la* brains
— **αρνίσια λαδολέμονο** ar·*ni*·si·a
la·*tho*·le·mo·no poached lamb's brains
— **τηγανητά** ti·gha·ni·*ta* fried brains

μύδια ⑩ pl mi·thia mussels
— **κρασάτα** kra·*sa*·ta
poached mussels in a white wine sauce
— **τηγανητά** ti·gha·ni·*ta* mussels
shucked, lightly battered, fried in hot oil &
served with a garlic yogurt sauce
— **γεμιστά** ye·mi·*sta* mussels stuffed with
rice, onions & parsley, slow-simmered in
fish stock, tomato purée & white wine

μυζήθρα ① mi·*zi*·thra
soft mild ricotta-like cheese made from
sheep's or goat's milk (sweet or savoury)

μυζηθρόπιτες ① pl mi·zi·thro·*pi*·tes delicate deep-fried pies with **μυζήθρα** (Crete)

N ν

νεγκόσκα ① ne·*go*·ska variety of red grape

νεραντζάκι γλυκό ⑩ ne·ran·*dza*·ki ghli·*ko*
preserved small bitter green oranges

νεράτη ① ne·*ra*·ti
variety of cheese pie (Crete)

νουμπουλό ⑩ num·bu·*lo*
bacon-flavoured sausage (Corfu)

ντολμάδες dol·*ma*·thes ⑩ pl
dolmades – parcels of rice-wrapped
leaves (usually vine leaves) & cooked in
water, oil & lemon juice
— **φυλλιανές** fi·li·a·*nes* Christmas & New
Year dish of onion sleeves stuffed with
minced veal, pork & rice (Lesvos)
— **με αυγολέμονο** me av·gho·*le*·mo·no
dolmades with rice, minced lamb,
tomatoes, mint & cumin, served hot with
αλευρολέμονο
— **με κουκιά** me ku·*kia*
dolmades with boiled & sliced broad
beans & dried ox meat, cooked on a bed
of beef bones (Northern Greece)
— **με λαχανόφυλλα** me la·kha·*no*·fi·la
stuffed cabbage leaves, served hot with
αβγολέμονο
— **γιαλαντζί** yia·lan·*dzi*
'fraud' – stuffed meatless dolmades
— **Σμυρναίικα** zmir·*ne*·i·ka
dolmades stuffed with sautéed onions,
rice, eggplant, oregano, dill, garlic &
cooked in tomato broth

ντομάτες ① pl do·*ma*·tes tomatoes
— **λιαστές** lia·*stes* sun-dried tomatoes
— **γεμιστές** ye·mi·*stes*
large tomatoes stuffed with rice, tomato
pulp, onion, garlic & herbs

ντοματοκεφτέδες ⑩ pl
do·ma·to·kef·*te*·thes
deep-fried tomato rissoles

ντοματομπελτές ⑩ do·ma·to·pel·*tes*
tomato paste

ντοματόσουπα ① do·ma·*to*·su·pa soup
made with tomatoes & sometimes pasta

νυχάκι ① ni·*kha*·ki kalamata table olive
(Messenia & Laconia)

Ξ ξ

ξεροτήγανα ⑩ pl kse·ro·*ti*·gha·na see
δίπλες

ξινόχοντρος ⑩ ksi·*no*·khon·dros ground
wheat cooked in sour milk & dried

ξινομυζήθρα ① ksi·no·mi·*zi*·thra
savoury **μυζήθρα**

O o

οινοπνευματώδη ⓝ pl
i·nop·nev·ma·*to*·thi *alcoholic spirits*

οστρακοειδή ⓝ pl o·stra·ko·i·*thi shellfish*

ούζο ⓝ *u·*zo *clear spirit distilled from grape seeds, stems & skins with a strong aniseed flavour*

οφτή σαλάτα ⓕ of·ti sa·*la·*ta *grilled salad of potatoes, onions & σταφιδολιές, foil-wrapped & chargrilled (Crete)*

οφτό ⓝ of·to *sausage made from pig's intestines, rice, walnuts, pistachios, raisins, cinnamon & orange peel (Crete)*

ουρά βοδιού ⓕ u·*ra* vo·*thiu oxtail*

Π π

παϊδάκια ⓝ pl pa·i·*tha*·kia *chops • cutlets*

παξιμάδια ⓝ pl pak·si·*ma·*thia
hard wheat or barley rusks eaten slightly moistened with water at meal times (both wheat & barley varieties are common)

— **με ντομάτες και φέτα** me do·*ma*·tes ke fe·ta **παξιμάδια** *moistened with water or tomato juice & topped with sliced tomatoes, feta, oregano, oil, salt & pepper – very popular snack or light lunch*

— **σαλάτα** sa·*la·*ta **παξιμάδια** *broken into pieces, moistened with water & sprinkled with diced tomatoes, crumbled feta or oregano, oil, salt & pepper*

παλαμίδα ⓕ pa·la·*mi·*tha
bonito • tunny fish (a variety of tuna)

— **ψητή με χόρτα** psi·*ti* me *khor*·ta *marinated bonito steaks*

παλικάρια ⓝ pl pa·li·ka·ri·a
mix of legumes & grains boiled & tossed with oil, onions & dill

πανέ pa·ne *crumbed & fried*

παντρεμένοι ⓝ pl pan·dre·*me*·ni *beans with other foods (rice, meat, tomatoes)*

παντζάρι ⓝ pan·*dza·*ri *beetroot*

— **σαλάτα** sa·*la·*ta *boiled thickly sliced beetroot dressed with vinaigrette & served with σκορδαλιά*

παντσέττα ⓕ pan·*tse·*ta *pancetta*

— **γεμιστή στο φούρνο**
ye·mi·*sti* sto *fur*·no *pig's stomach stuffed with parmesan, garlic, onions & oregano basted with oil, wine & lemon juice & baked with potatoes (Zakynthos)*

πάπια ⓕ *pa·*pia *duck*

— **με σάλτσα ροδιού** me *sal*·tsa ro·*thiu* fried duck breast served with sauce made from pomegranate seeds, lemon juice, duck stock & walnuts (Northern Greece)*

— **σαλμί** sal·*mi whole duck seared in oil then tendered & cooked in its own juices, wine, orange juice & onions*

πάπρικα ⓕ *pa·*pri·ka *paprika*

παπουτσάκι ⓝ pa·put·*sa*·ki *'little shoe' – stuffed baby eggplant topped with béchamel sauce & baked*

παρμεζάνα ⓕ par·me·*za*·na *parmesan*

πασατέμπος ⓜ pa·sa·*te*·bos
'pass the time' – roasted pumpkin seeds sold as a snack

πάστα ⓕ *pa*·sta *gateau*

παστέλι ⓝ pa·*ste*·li
sweet honey & sesame seed wafers

παστιτσάδα ⓕ pa·stit·*sa*·tha *pot-roasted veal with tomato, red wine, cloves, cinnamon & paprika (Corfu)*

παστίτσιο ⓝ pa·*stit*·si·o *baked layers of buttery macaroni & minced lamb topped with white sauce & grated κεφαλοτύρι*

παστός pa·*stos salted & dried*

παστουρμάς ⓜ pa·stur·*mas*
spicy dried ox meat

πατάτες ⓕ pl pa·*ta*·tes *potatoes*

— **γιαχνί** yia·khni *potatoes stewed with tomatoes, onions & oregano*

— **κεφτέδες** kef·*te*·thes
fried potato, feta & parsley rissoles

— **λεμονάτες** le·mo·*na*·tes
potatoes roasted with oil, lemon juice, oregano, salt & pepper

— **πουρέ** pu·*re mashed potatoes*

— **στο φούρνο** sto *fur*·no *potatoes baked or roasted with oil, salt & oregano*

— **τηγανιτές** ti·gha·ni·tes
fried potato slices

πατατοσαλάτα ⓕ pa·ta·to·sa·*la*·ta *potato salad*

πατατού ⓕ pa·ta·tu
baked mashed potato pie (Cyclades)

τατσάς pat-*sas* ⓜ *tripe • rich-textured & surprisingly delicate-flavoured soup made with the stomach of a young lamb & finished with αβγολέμονο*

τατούδα ① pa-*tu*-tha *pastries filled with walnuts, almonds & cinnamon, baked, sprinkled with orange flower water & dredged in icing sugar (Crete)*

τεϊνιρλί ⓝ pe-i-nir-*li savoury pastries with a variety of fillings such as mincemeat, feta, ham & egg, & dried ox meat*

τέρδικες ① pl *per*-thi-kes *partridges*
— **με ελιές και σέλινο** e-*lies* ke *se*-li-no *partridges browned in butter & simmered in their own juices with green olives, sliced celery & tomatoes*

τέρκα ① *per*-ka *sea perch*

τέστροφα ① pe-stro-fa *trout*

τεταλίδες ① pl pe-ta-*li*-thes *limpets*
— **με θαλασσινούς χοχλιούς** me tha-la-si-*nus* kho-khli-*us limpets & sea snails stewed with ripe tomatoes, onions & black pepper (Lesvos)*

τετιμέζι ① pe-ti-*me*-zi *syrup made from unfermented grape juice, used to flavour rolls, cakes & sweets – when mixed with cold water makes a refreshing drink*

τιλάφι ① pi-*la*-fi *pilau – rice & stock cooked to a creamy consistency – served to complement boiled meat or chicken*
— **με ντομάτες** me do-*ma*-tes *pilau with the addition of tomatoes, meat stock, garlic, parsley, salt & pepper*
— **με γαρίδες** me gha-*ri*-thes *pilau with prawns, onions & oregano*
— **με μύδια** me *mi*-thia *pilau with fresh mussels, onions & white wine*
— **με περδίκια** me per-*thi*-ki-a *pilau with partridge, tomato & cloves (Kefallonia)*

τιπέρι ① pi-*pe*-ri *black pepper*

τροσκί ⓝ pi-ro-*ski deep-fried, dough-wrapped sausage roll*

τίτα ① *pi*-ta *pie – filo is the most common pastry used • flat doughy circular bread seared on grill until golden, mainly used for wrapping σουβλάκι & γύρος*

τιτσούνια ⓝ pl pit-*su*-nia *squab • love-bird • any tiny bird used for cooking*

— **κρασάτα** kra-*sa*-ta *baby squabs doused in red wine, tomato pulp, cinnamon & cloves then braised*
— **με κουκουνάρια** me ku-ku-*na*-ria *squab ignited with brandy, splashed with retsina & dressed with a garlic cream sauce (Northern Greece)*
— **με κουκιά** me ku-*kia stewed squab & fresh broad beans cooked in chicken stock, white wine, dill, garlic & lots of black pepper*

πλακί pla-*ki method of baking or braising with tomatoes, onion, garlic & parsley*

ποδαράκια ⓝ pl po-tha-*ra*-kia *trotters*
— **αρνίσια** ar-*ni*-si-a *boiled lamb's trotters browned in butter & garlic, roasted, then finished with egg & lemon sauce*

πόρτο ⓝ *por*-to *port*

πορτοκάλι ⓝ por-to-*ka*-li *orange*
— **γλυκό** ghli-*ko preserved orange*

ποτό ⓝ po-*to drinks • spirits (on menus)*

πράσα ⓝ pl *pra*-sa *leeks*
— **αλευρολέμονο** a-lev-ro-*le*-mo-no *braised leeks in lemony sauce*
— **με δαμάσκηνα** me tha-*ma*-ski-na *leeks & prunes sprinkled with cinnamon & nutmeg*
— **με ρύζι** me *ri*-zi *leeks & celery simmered with rice & crushed tomatoes*

πρασάκια με πατάτες ⓝ pl pra-*sa*-ki-a me pa-*ta*-tes *leeks & sliced potatoes cooked in butter, chicken stock, onions, oregano & parsley*

πρασόπιτα ① pra-so-*pi*-ta *pie made with braised leeks, feta, μυζήθρα & skim milk (Western Greece)*

Ρ ρ

ραβιόλες ① pl ra-vi-*o*-les *pasta envelopes stuffed with a mixture of cheese & mint, served with melted butter & grated cheese (Cyprus)*

ραδίκι ① ra-*thi*-ki *chicory • term used for common varieties of χόρτα*
— **σαλάτα** sa-*la*-ta *spring salad of young dandelion leaves splashed with oil & lemon*

ρακί ⓝ ra·*ki* fiery village spirit made from grapes, like ouzo but without the aniseed taste, high in alcohol

ραφιόλια ⓟ pl ra·fi·*o*·li·a sweet half-moon filo pastries stuffed with cheese, eggs, cinnamon, orange rind & ouzo (Cyclades)

ρεβανί ⓝ re·va·*ni* very sweet semolina sponge, flavoured with vanilla & orange juice & smothered with honey syrup

ρεβίθια ⓟ pl re·*vi*·thia chickpeas
— **αλευρολέμονο** a·lev·ro·*le*·mo·no chickpeas simmered in a rich lemony broth
— **στο φούρνο** sto *fur*·no casserole of chickpeas, onions, garlic & bay leaves – favourite fasting food during Lent
— **σούπα** *su*·pa chickpea soup

ρεβιθοκεφτέδες ⓟ pl re·vi·tho·kef·*te*·thes rissoles of mashed chickpeas, potatoes, onion, parsley & black pepper

ρέγγα ⓕ *reng*·ga smoked herrings, eaten plain or grilled with oil & lemon

ρέσι ⓝ *re*·si pilau made with burghul & lamb (including the tail) & served at weddings (Cyprus)

ρετσίνα ⓕ ret·*si*·na retsina – pine-resinated wine, often served chilled

ριγανάτος ⓜ ri·gha·*na*·tos seasoned with oregano, salt & pepper

ρίγανη ⓕ *ri*·gha·ni pungent Greek oregano

ριζάδα ⓕ ri·*za*·tha thick soup made with rice & shellfish or tiny game birds (Corfu)

ριζόγαλο ⓝ ri·*zo*·gha·lo vanilla-flavoured rice pudding sprinkled with cinnamon

ρόδι ⓝ *ro*·thi pomegranate – used to flavour sweets, syrups, cakes & salads

ροδόνερο ⓝ ro·*tho*·ne·ro fragrant rose-water used to flavour cakes, pies & sweets

ροφός ⓜ ro·*fos* grouper • blackfish

ρολό από κιμά ⓝ ro·*lo* a·po ki·*ma* baked mincemeat roll with hard-boiled eggs cuddled in the middle

ρύζι ⓝ *ri*·zi rice

Σ σ

σαλάχι ⓝ sa·*la*·hi ray fish • skate
— **σαλάτα** sa·*la*·ta boiled ray fish salad dressed with λαδολέμονο

σαλιγκάρια ⓟ pl sa·ling·*ga*·ri·a snails – cooked in the shell & eaten with a fork
— **φρικασέ** fri·ka·*se* large snails sautéed in oil & stewed with zucchini, onions, fresh dill & finished with αβγολέμονο
— **με σάλτσα** me *sal*·tsa snails cooked with crushed tomatoes, tomato paste, onions & oregano
— **συμπεθεριό** sim·be·the·*rio* 'in-laws' – snails cooked with sliced eggplant, tomato pulp & ξινόχοντρος
— **στα κάρβουνα** sta *kar*·vu·na live snails chargrilled & doused with λαδολέμονο & bay leaves (Cyclades)
— **στιφάδο** sti·*fa*·tho snail ragout with bay leaves (Crete)

σαλμί ⓝ sal·*mi* method of casseroling game with red wine, vegetables & herbs

σάλτσα ⓕ *sal*·tsa sauce • generic term for tomato sauce
— **από ζωμό κρέατος** a·po zo·mo kre·a·tos gravy
— **άσπρη** *a*·spri béchamel sauce with eg
— **άσπρη ξινή** *a*·spri ksi·ni 'sharp white sauce' – made with butter, flour, meat stock, eggs & lemon
— **αυγολέμονο** av·gho·*le*·mo·no see αβγολέμονο
— **ντομάτα** do·*ma*·ta tomato sauce with bay leaves
— **ντομάτα με κιμά** do·*ma*·ta me ki·*m* tomato & mincemeat sauce
— **μαρινάτα** ma·ri·*na*·ta marinade
— **μουστάρδα** mu·*star*·tha mustard & garlic beaten with lemon juice
— **ταρτάρ** tar·*tar* tartare sauce

Σάμος *sa*·mos rich golden dessert wine (Samos)

σαρακοστιανά ⓟ pl sa·ra·ko·sti·a·na see νηστήσιμα

σαρδέλες ⓕ pl sar·*the*·les sardines
— **παστές** pa·*stes* salted sardines
— **στο φούρνο** sto *fur*·no sardines baked with oil, lemon, garlic & oregano

σαρμάς ⓜ sar·*mas* pie-like offal dish (Northern Greece)

σβίγγοι ⓟ pl zving·gi deep-fried fritters served with honey, cinnamon & cognac syrup

σελινόριζα ① se·li·no·ri·za *celeriac*
— **με αυγολέμονο** me av·gho·*le*·mo·no *creamy dish of celeriac in chicken stock & finished with egg & lemon sauce*
— **με πράσα** me *pra*·sa *braised celeriac wedges & leek strips thickened with αβγολέμονο*

σέσκουλο ⑩ *se*·sku·lo *swiss chard, type of* χόρτα
— **με κιμά** me ki·*ma silverbeet sautéed with chopped onion in butter & cooked with minced lamb, rice, dill, lemon juice & salt*

σεσκουλόρυζο ⑩ se·sku·lo·ri·zo *see* σπανακόρυζο

σεφταλιά ① sef·ta·*lia pork rissoles wrapped in sheep's caul & chargrilled (Cyprus)*

σκαλτσοτσέτα ⑩ pl skal·tsot·se·ta *paper-thin slices of fillet steak skewered & simmered in oil, water & tomatoes*

σκορδαλιά ① skor·*tha*·lia *thick paste of walnuts, bread, potatoes, olive oil, lemon & garlic*

σκόρδο ⑩ *skor*·tho *garlic*
— **στούμπι** *stu*·bi *vinegar bottled with a garlic bulb, used for dressing vegetable dishes & salads (Ionian Islands)*
— **τσιγαριστά** tsi·gha·ri·*sta fried whole garlic bulbs • peeled & sliced garlic cloves fried & simmered in white wine, tomato paste, salt & pepper (Ithaca)*

σκουμπρί ⑩ sku·*bri mackerel*

σνακς ⑩ pl *snaks snacks*

σοφρίτο ⑩ so·*fri*·to *fried veal slices braised in a sauce of crushed garlic, wine vinegar, parsley, mint & brandy (Corfu)*

σοκολάτα ① so·ko·*la*·ta *chocolate*
— **γάλα** *gha*·la *hot chocolate*

σουσάμι ⑩ su·*sa*·mi *sesame seed*

σούβλα ① *suv*·la *spit-roasted • skewers • method of chargrilling meat or fish*

σουβλάκι ⑩ suv·*la*·ki *souvlaki • tender chunks of seasoned or marinated meat (or fish) skewered & chargrilled*
— **με πίτα** me *pi*·ta *souvlaki with* πίτα

σούγλι ⑩ *sugh*·li *sun-dried baby bogue fish coated in batter & fried (Cyclades)*

σούπα ① *su*·pa *soup*
— **ξιδάτη** ksi·*tha*·ti *sour soup of lentils, parsley & vinegar*

— **με τσουκνίδες** me tsuk·*ni*·thes *electric-green soup of stinging nettles & diced potatoes cooked in chicken stock & thickened with milk*

σουπιές ① pl su·*pies cuttlefish*
— **κρασάτες** kra·*sa*·tes *cuttlefish cooked in wine*
— **με σάλτσα μελάνης** me *sal*·tsa me·*la*·nis *cuttlefish cooked in a rich sauce made from its own black ink & wine (Crete)*
— **με σπανάκι** me spa·*na*·ki *cuttlefish cooked with spinach, onions, dill & mint*

σουτζουκάκια ① pl su·dzu·*ka*·kia *rissoles of minced lamb, veal or pork braised in a very spicy tomato gravy*

σουτζούκι ① su·*dzu*·ki *strings of almonds dipped in syrup & sun-dried*

σπάλα ① *spa*·la *shoulder of meat*
— **μοσχαρίσια** mos·kha·*ri*·si·a *silverside*

σπανακόπιτα ① spa·na·*ko*·pi·ta *spinach filo pie, often includes feta or* κεφαλοτύρι, *eggs & herbs*

σπανακόρυζο ① spa·na·ko·ri·zo *sautéed spinach, rice, spring onions & dill simmered in water until liquid is absorbed*

σπετζοφάι ① spe·dzo·*fa*·i *sliced pork sausages stewed with sweet green peppers, eggplant, tomatoes & oregano*

σπλήνα ① *spli*·na *spleen*
— **γεμιστή** ye·mi·*sti calf's spleen stuffed with chopped sautéed liver, onion, garlic & herbs, then roasted*

σπληνάντερο ⑩ spli·*nan*·de·ro *spit-roast sausage made from intestine stuffed with sliced spleen & garlic*

σταφίδες ① pl sta·*fi*·thes *raisins • currants*

σταφιδολιές ① pl sta·fi·tho·*lies type of olive sun-dried until wrinkled, lightly salted & packed, or immersed in oil*

σταφιδωτά ⑩ pl sta·fi·*tho*·ta *oval shortbread biscuits with chewy raisin centres*

σταφύλια ⑩ pl sta·*fi*·li·a *grapes*

στάκα ① *sta*·ka *creamy butter made from fresh goat's or sheep's milk, used to flavour pies, stuffed vegetables & pilau*
— **με αβγά** me av·*gha omelette with* στάκα *(Crete)*

στάμνα ① *stam·na* method of cooking meat & potatoes in a pot sealed with wet clay & baked in charcoal embers

στιφάδο ① *sti·fa·tho* meat, game or seafood ragout

στραγάλια ① pl *stra·gha·lia* roasted chickpeas for snacking

σύκο ① *si·ko* fig
— **αποστολιάτικο** *a·po·sto·lia·ti·ko* young green fig
— **γλυκό** *ghli·ko* green fig preserve
— **στο φούρνο** *sto fur·no* figs baked in a syrup of honey, vanilla, orange juice & orange flower water

συκόπιτα ① *si·ko·pi·ta* fig cake (Corfu)

συκόψωμο ① *si·kop·so·mo* heavy aromatic fig cake • dried green figs minced & mixed with ouzo shaped into balls, flattened, dried & wrapped in vine leaves

συκωταριά ① *si·ko·ta·ria* innards • offal

συκώτι ① *si·ko·ti* liver
— **κρασάτα** *kra·sa·ta* chopped liver marinated in red wine
— **λαδορίγανη** *la·tho·ri·gha·ni* grilled liver with oil, lemon & oregano
— **μαρινάτα** *ma·ri·na·ta* thinly sliced livers fried & finished with vinegar, white wine & rosemary
— **με κρεμμυδάκια** *me kre·mi·tha·kia* livers fried with spring onions & cloves in a sauce of white wine & tomato juice

σφακιανόπιτες ① pl *sfa·kia·no·pi·tes* cheese pies consisting of balls of cheese wrapped in dough, then fried & served with a dollop of honey

σφουγγάτο ⓝ *sfung·ga·to* Spanish-style omelette made with more vegetables than eggs, fried or baked (Rhodes)

T τ

ταβάς ⓜ *ta·vas* casserole of seasoned beef or lamb, fried onions, diced tomatoes, oil, vinegar & cinnamon

ταλαττούρι ① *ta·la·tu·ri* τζατζίκι flavoured with mint (Cyprus)

ταραμάς ⓜ *ta·ra·mas* salted pressed roe of the grey mullet or cod

ταράξακο ⓝ *ta·rak·sa·ko* dandelion

ταχίνι ⓝ *ta·hi·ni* sesame seed paste

ταχινόσουπα ① *ta·hi·no·su·pa* creamy lemony soup made from sesame paste (popular during Lent)

τελεμές ⓜ *te·le·mes* heavily salted feta-style cheese

τηγανόψωμο ⓝ *ti·gha·nop·so·mo* fried tomato & spring onion bread (Santorini)

τίλιο ⓝ *ti·li·o* infusion of lime leaves

τζατζίκι ⓝ *dza·dzi·ki* refreshing purée of grated cucumber, yogurt & garlic

τσόχος ⓜ *tso·khos* milk thistle – mild sweet-tasting green used in warm salads, pies & stews • type of χόρτα

της ώρας *tis o·ras* dishes cooked to order, such as steaks or chops

τσουρέκι ⓝ *tot·su·re·ki* braided Easter bread spiced with lemon rind & cherry pips, sprinkled with almonds & crushed μαστίχα

τραχανόσουπα ① *tra·kha·no·su·pa* thick gruel of granulated pasta cooked in chicken broth with butter, lemon juice

τριανταφυλλο γλυκό ⓝ *tri·an·da·fi·lo ghli·ko* delicate soft jam made from dark red rose petals

τσικουδιά ① *tsi·ku·thia* see ρακί

τσιπούρα ① *tsi·pu·ra* gilt head bream • snapper

τσίπουρο ⓝ *tsi·pu·ro* see ρακί

τσίρος ⓜ *tsi·ros* small dried mackerel

τσουκνίδες ⓝ pl *tsu·kni·thes* stinging nettles used in salads & soups

τουρσί ⓝ *tur·si* pickles • pickled

τούρτα ① *tur·ta* cake • gateau • tart

τυρί ⓝ *ti·ri* cheese
— **μπλε** *ble* blue cheese
— **ημίσκληρο** *i·mi·skli·ro* semi-firm cheese
— **κατσικίσιο** *kat·si·ki·si·o* goat's cheese
— **κρεμώδες** *kre·mo·thes* cream cheese
— **μαλακή μυζήθρα** *ma·la·ki mi·zi·thra* cottage cheese
— **μαλακό** *ma·la·ko* soft cheese
— **σαγανάκι** *sa·gha·na·ki* sharp, hard cheese fried until crispy on the outside & soft in the centre, served with a squeeze of lemon juice
— **σκληρό** *skli·ro* hard cheese

τυρόπηγμα ⓝ *ti·ro·pigh·ma* curd

τυρόπιτα ⓕ ti-ro-pi-ta *cheese pies, the classic mixture is feta &* **κεφαλοτύρι** *wrapped in flaky filo pastry & baked*

τυροβολιά ⓕ ti-ro-vo-*lia* *cheese variety*

Φ φ

φάβα ⓕ *fa*-va *yellow split pea purée served with raw onion rings*
— **παντρεμένη** pan-dre-*me*-ni *'married' – leftover* **φάβα** *served as a hot dish with the addition of tomatoes & cumin*

φαγρί ⓝ fa-*ghri sea bream*

φακές ⓕ fa-*kes lentils*
— **με μακαρόνια** me ma-ka-*ro*-nia *lentils simmered in water & vinegar with mint, garlic & pearl pasta (Astypalea)*
— **σούπα** su-pa *lentil soup*

Φανουρόπιτα ⓕ fa-nu-ro-pi-ta *cake spiced with dried fruit, brandy & cinnamon – served on Saint Fanourios Day*

φασκόμηλο ⓝ fa-*sko*-mi-lo *sage*

φασολάδα ⓕ fa-so-*la*-tha *thick fragrant soup of beans, tomatoes, tomato paste, carrots, celery, garlic & parsley*

φασολάκια ⓝ pl fa-so-*la*-kia *green beans*
— **λαδερά** la-the-*ra green beans cooked in oil with tomatoes & onions*
— **σαλάτα** sa-*la*-ta *boiled fresh green beans with* **λαδολέμονο** *or* **λαδόξιδο**

φασόλια ⓝ pl fa-so-li-a *dried beans – usually refers to white haricot/lima beans*
— **μάραθο** *ma*-ra-tho
dried beans browned in oil & onions, simmered with tomato pulp & fennel leaves
— **σαλάτα** sa-*la*-ta *bean salad*

φέτα ⓕ *fe*-ta
feta – white, crumbly, salty cheese
— **σχάρας** *skha*-ras *grilled feta*

φέτες ψαριού με ντομάτα και σταφίδες ⓕ pl *fe*-tes psa-*riu* me do-*ma*-ta ke sta-fi-thes *fish with tomato & currants*

φιλέτο ⓝ fi-*le*-to *fillet • steak*

φιρίκια ⓝ pl fi-ri-ki-a
small crisp apples (Northern Greece)
— **με αμύγδαλα** me a-*migh*-tha-la *baked* **φιρίκια** *stuffed with almonds*
— **γεμιστά** ye-mi-*sta* **φιρίκια** *stuffed with minced veal, coriander & cumin*

φιστίκια ⓝ pl fi-*sti*-kia *peanuts*
— **Αιγίνης** e-*yi*-nis *pistachios*

φλαούνες ⓕ pl fla-*u*-nes *baked savoury tarts (Cyprus)*

φοινίκια ⓝ pl fi-*ni*-ki-a *honey-dipped shortbread sprinkled with cinnamon & marked with a criss-cross design*

φρικασέ ⓝ fri-ka-se *meat or vegetable stew thickened & flavoured with* **αβγολέμονο**

φρουταλιά ⓕ fru-ta-*lia* *omelette-type dish consisting of eggs, potatoes, parsley & sliced smoked pork sausages (Andros)*

φρυγαδέλια ⓝ pl fri-gha-*the*.lia *liver parcels in lamb's caul, fried or skewered & chargrilled (Northern Greece, Thessaly)*

φύλλο ⓝ fi-lo *flaky tissue-thin pastry used for pies & sweet pastries*

Χ χ

χαβιάρι ⓝ kha-*via*-ri *caviar*

χαλβάς ⓜ khal-*vas*
rich creamy sweet made from sesame seeds & honey, flavoured with pistachio, chocolate or almonds
— **σιμιγδαλένιος** si-migh-tha-*le*-nios *moist cake of semolina & honey, decorated with almonds & cinnamon*
— **της Ρίνας** tis *ri*-nas *baked semolina & almond cake served hot with sugar syrup*

χαλορίνι ⓝ kha-lo-ri-ni *pouch-shaped cheese filled with crushed coriander (Cyprus)*

χαλούμι ⓝ kha-*lu*-mi *firm, white, sheep's milk cheese with elastic texture & salty taste (Cyprus)*

χαλουμπίτες ⓕ pl kha-lu-*mo*-pi-tes *savoury cake made with* **χαλούμι**, *eggs, mint, sultanas &* **μαστίχα** *(Cyprus)*

χαλουμόψωμο ⓝ kha-lu-*mop*-so-mo *bread baked with chunks of* **χαλούμι** *(Cyprus)*

χαμομήλι ⓝ kha-mo-*mi*-li *chamomile*

χαμψιά ⓕ kham-*psia fresh anchovy*

χαμψοπίλαφο ⓝ kham-pso-pi-la-fo *onion & anchovy pilau seasoned with oregano*

χείλη της χανούμισσας ⓕ pl hi-li tis kha-*nu*-mi-sas *'the Turkish lady's lips' – crunchy honey cakes (Rhodes)*

χέλι ⓝ he-li *eel*
— **πλακί** pla-*ki eel baked with tomatoes, onions, potatoes & herbs (Corfu)*

χοιρινές ① pl hi·ri·nes *pork chops*

— **κρασάτες** kra·sa·tes *pork chops simmered in red wine*

— **στη σχάρα** sti skha·ra *pork chops chargrilled with salt, pepper & lemon juice*

— **τηγανητές** ti·gha·ni·tes *fried pork chops*

χοιρινό ① hi·ri·no *pork*

— **με κυδώνια** me ki·tho·nia *pork & quinces simmered in red wine spiced with orange peel & cinnamon*

— **με πράσα** me pra·sa *pork & leek casserole*

— **με σέλινο αυγολέμενο** me se·li·no av·gho·le·mo·no *pork & celery in egg & lemon sauce*

— **μπούτι ψητό** bu·ti psi·to *crispy, roast leg of pork*

— **παστό** pa·sto *salted pork*

χοιρομέρι ① hi·ro·me·ri *cured leg of ham (Cyprus, Zakynthos)*

χόντρος ⑩ khon·dros *hand-milled wheat used in soups, dolmades, snail dishes & stews (see also ξινόχοντρος)*

χόρτα ① pl khor·ta *wild or cultivated greens used in salads, pie fillings, casseroles or boiled & served hot with an oil & lemon dressing*

— **τσιγάρι** tsi·gha·ri *lightly fried wild greens*

χορτόπιτα ① khor·to·pi·ta *pies made from seasonal greens*

χορτοσαλάτα ① khor·to·sa·la·ta *warm salad of greens dressed with salt, oil & lemon*

χορτόσουπα ① khor·to·su·pa *vegetable soup*

χουρμάδες ⑩ pl khur·ma·thes *dates*

χοχλιοί ⑩ pl kho·khli·i *snails*

— **μπουμπουριστοί** bu·bu·ri·sti *'upside-down' – live snails deep-fried & doused with vinegar & rosemary*

χριστόψωμο ① khri·stop·so·mo *sweet Christmas bread baked in the shape of a cross*

χταπόδι ① khta·po·thi *octopus*

— **βραστό** vra·sto *boiled octopus coated with oil & lemon sauce*

— **κεφτέδες** kef·te·thes *rissoles of minced octopus, onion, mint & cheese*

— **κρασάτο** kra·sa·to *octopus cooked in red wine sauce*

— **λιαστό** lia·sto *sun-dried, chargrilled octopus sprinkled with oil & lemon juice*

— **με μακαρόνι κοφτό** me ma·ka·ro·ni kof·to *casserole of octopus, tomatoes, macaroni & red wine*

— **στα κάρβουνα** sta kar·vu·na *grilled octopus*

— **στιφάδο** sti·fa·tho *octopus ragout*

— **τουρσί** tur·si *pickled octopus*

χυλόφτα ① pl hi·lof·ta *macaroni served with hot butter & grated cheese (Crete)*

χωριάτικη σαλάτα ① kho·ria·ti·ki sa·la·t *'village salad' – salad of tomatoes, cucumber, olives & feta (known outside Greece as 'Greek salad')*

Ψ ψ

ψάρι ① psa·ri *fish*

— **μαρινάτο** ma·ri·na·to *fish fried until golden, served with a piquant sauce of garlic, rosemary & vinegar (also called ψάρι σαβόρι)*

— **πλακί** pla·ki *whole fish basted with oil, lemon & parsley, baked on a bed of chopped tomatoes & onions*

— **σαβόρι** sa·vo·ri *see ψάρι μαρινάτο*

— **Σπετσιώτο** spet·si·o·to *fish baked with bread crumbs & white wine (Spetses)*

— **στη σχάρα** sti skha·ra *chargrilled fis.*

— **στο φούρνο λαδορίγανη** sto fur·no la·tho·ri·gha·ni *sliced fish & potato wedges baked in a broth of oil, water & lemon juice*

— **τηγανητό** ti·gha·ni·to *battered fish*

— **βραστό με λαχανικά** vra·sto me la·kha·ni·ka *poached fish with vegetables – the broth is often strained, thickened with αβγολέμονο*

ψαροκεφτέδες ⑩ pl psa·ro·kef·te·thes *fried fish rissoles*

ψαρονέφρι ① psa·ro·ne·fri *pork fillet steak*

ψαρόσουπα ① psa·ro·su·pa *fish soup thickened with rice & αβγολέμονο*

ψητός psi·tos *an all-purpose term for grilling, baking & barbecueing*

ψωμί με ανάλυφες διακοσμήσεις ⑩ pl pso·mia me a·na·ghli·fes thi·a·koz·mi·sis *decorated bread (usually made with doughs of different colours) eaten at festivals, baptisms & weddings*

emergencies

έκτακτη ανάγκη

Help!	Βοήθεια!	vo·i·thia
Stop!	Σταμάτα!	sta·ma·ta
Go away!	Φύγε!	fi·ye
Thief!	Κλέφτης!	klef·tis
Fire!	Φωτιά!	fo·tia
Watch out!	Πρόσεχε!	pro·se·he

Call an ambulance!
Κάλεσε το ασθενοφόρο.　　ka·le·se to as·the·no·fo·ro

Call the doctor!
Κάλεσε ένα γιατρό.　　ka·le·se e·na yia·tro

Call the police!
Κάλεσε την αστυνομία.　　ka·le·se tin a·sti·no·mi·a

It's an emergency.
Είναι μια έκτακτη ανάγκη.　　i·ne mia ek·tak·ti a·na·gi

There's been an accident.
Έγινε ατύχημα.　　e·yi·ne a·ti·hi·ma

Could you please help?
Μπορείς να βοηθήσεις,　　bo·ris na vo·i·thi·sis
παρακαλώ;　　pa·ra·ka·lo

signs

Αστυνομία	a·sti·no·mi·a	Police
Αστυνομικός Σταθμός	a·sti·no·mi·kos stath·mos	Police Station
Νοσοκομείο	no·so·ko·mi·o	Hospital
Σταθμός Πρώτων Βοηθειών	stath·mos pro·ton vo·i·thi·on	Emergency Department

Is it safe …?	Είναι ασφαλές …;	*i*·ne as·fa·*les* …
at night	τη νύχτα	ti *nikh*·ta
for gay people	για γκέι	yia *ge*·i
for travellers	για ταξιδιώτες	yia tak·si·*thio*·tes
for women	για γυναίκες	yia yi·*ne*·kes
on your own	χωρίς παρέα	kho·*ris* pa·*re*·a

I'm lost.
Έχω χαθεί.   *e*·kho kha·*thi*

Where are the toilets?
Πού είναι η τουαλέτα;   pu *i*·ne i tu·a·*le*·ta

Is that a UN zone?
Είναι αυτή η ζώνη του ΟΗΕ;   *i*·ne af·*ti* i *zo*·ni tu o·i·*e*

Where's the demarcation line?
Πού είναι η διαχωριστική   pu *i*·ne i thi·a·kho·ri·sti·*ki*
γραμμή;   ghra·*mi*

Are there military bases in this region?
Υπάρχουν στρατιωτικές   i·*par*·khun stra·ti·o·ti·*kes*
βάσεις σ' αυτή την περιοχή;   *va*·sis saf·*ti* tin pe·ri·o·*hi*

police

Where's the police station?
Πού είναι ο αστυνομικός   pu *i*·ne o a·sti·no·mi·*kos*
σταθμός;   stath·*mos*

Please telephone the Tourist Police.
Παρακαλώ τηλεφωνα την   pa·ra·ka·*lo* ti·le·*fo*·na tin
τουριστική αστυνομία.   tu·ri·sti·*ki* a·sti·no·*mi*·a

I want to report an offence.
Θέλω να αναφέρω   *the*·lo na a·na·*fe*·ro
μια παρανομία.   mia pa·ra·no·*mi*·a

It was him/her.
Ήταν αυτός/αυτή.   *i*·tan af·*tos*/af·*ti*

I have insurance.
Έχω ασφάλεια.   *e*·kho as·*fa*·li·a

SAFE TRAVEL

I've been ...	Με έχουν ...	me e·khun ...
He/She has been ...	Τον/Την έχουν ...	ton/tin e·khun ...
assaulted	κακοποιήσει	ka·ko·pi·í·si
raped	βιάσει	vi·a·si
robbed	ληστέψει	li·step·si

the police may say ...

Κατηγορείσαι για ...
ka·ti·gho·ri·se yia ... **You're charged with ...**

Αυτός κατηγορείται για ...
af·ti ka·ti·gho·ri·te yia ... **He's charged with ...**

Αυτή κατηγορείται για ...
af·ti ka·ti·gho·ri·te yia ... **She's charged with ...**

διατάραξη ησυχίας	thi·a·ta·rak·si i·si·hi·as	disturbing the peace
εξαγωγή αρχαιοτήτων χωρίς άδεια	ek·sa·gho·yi ar·he·o·ti·ton kho·ris a·thi·a	exporting antiquities without a permit
κακοποίηση	ka·ko·pi·í·si	assault
κλοπή από κατάστημα	klo·pi a·po ka·ta·sti·ma	shoplifting
κλοπή	klo·pi	theft
μετακίνηση αρχαιοτήτων	me·ta·ki·ni·si ar·he·o·ti·ton	removing antiquities
μη κατοχή βίζας	mi ka·to·hi vi·zas	not having a visa
κατοχή (παράνομων ουσιών)	ka·to·hi (pa·ra·no·mon u·si·on)	possession (of illegal substances)
υπέρβαση της βίζας	i·per·va·si tis vi·zas	overstaying a visa

Είναι πρόστιμο για ...	i·ne pro·sti·mo yia ...	It's a ... fine.
πάρκινγκ	par·king	parking
ταχύτητα	ta·hi·ti·ta	speeding

essentials

193

I've lost my ...	Έχασα ... μου.	e·kha·sa ... mu
My ... was/were stolen.	Έκλεψαν ... μου.	e·klep·san ... mu
bags	τις βαλίτσες	tis va·lit·se
money	τα χρήματά	ta khri·ma·ta
passport	το διαβατήριό	to thia·va·ti·rio

What am I accused of?

Για τι πράγμα
κατηγορούμαι;

yia ti pra·ghma
ka·ti·gho·ru·me

I didn't realise I was doing anything wrong.

Δεν κατάλαβα ότι έκαμα
κάτι λάθος.

then ka·ta·la·va o·ti e·ka·ma
ka·ti la·thos

I didn't do it.

Δεν το έκαμα.

then to e·ka·ma

I'm sorry.

Συγνώμη.

sigh·no·mi

Can I pay an on-the-spot fine?

Μπορώ να πληρώσω ένα
πρόστιμο επί τόπου;

bo·ro na pli·ro·so e·na
pro·sti·mo e·pi to·pu

I want to contact my embassy.

Θέλω να έρθω σε επαφή
με την πρεσβεία μου.

the·lo na er·tho se e·pa·fi
me tin prez·vi·a mu

Can I make a phone call?

Μπορώ να κάμω ένα
τηλεφώνημα;

bo·ro na ka·mo e·na
ti·le·fo·ni·ma

Can I have a lawyer (who speaks English)?

Μπορώ να έχω ένα
δικηγόρο (που να
μιλάει αγγλικά);

bo·ro na e·kho e·na
thi·ki·gho·ro (pu na
mi·la·i ang·gli·ka)

This drug is for personal use.

Αυτό το φάρμακο είναι
για προσωπική χρήση.

af·to to far·ma·ko i·ne
yia pro·so·pi·ki hri·si

I have a prescription for this drug.

Έχω συνταγή για αυτό
το φάρμακο.

e·kho si·da·yi yia af·to
to far·ma·ko

I (don't) understand.

(Δεν) καταλαβαίνω.

(then) ka·ta·la·ve·no

doctor

γιατρός

Where's the nearest …?	Πού είναι το πιο κοντινό…;	pu *i*·ne to pio ko·di·*no* …
emergency department	πρώτων βοηθειών	*pro*·ton vo·i·thi·*on*
hospital	νοσοκομείο	no·so·ko·*mi*·o
medical centre	ιατρικό κέντρο	i·a·tri·*ko ke*·dro
(night)	(νυχτερινό)	(nikh·te·ri·*no*)
pharmacy	φαρμακείο	far·ma·*ki*·o
Where's the nearest …?	Πού είναι ο πιο κοντινός …;	pu *i*·ne o pio ko·di·*nos* …
dentist	οδοντίατρος	o·tho·di·a·*tros*
doctor	γιατρός	yia·*tros*
optometrist	οφθαλμίατρος	of·thal·*mi*·a·tros

I need a doctor (who speaks English).
Χρειάζομαι ένα γιατρό
(που να μιλάει αγγλικά).
khri·*a*·zo·me *e*·na yia·*tro*
(pu na mi·*la*·i ang·gli·*ka*)

Could I see a female doctor?
Μπορώ να δω μια γυναίκα
γιατρό;
bo·*ro* na tho mia yi·*ne*·ka
yia·*tro*

Could the doctor come here?
Μπορεί ο γιατρός να
έρθει εδώ;
bo·*ri* o yia·*tros* na
er·thi e·*tho*

Is there an after-hours emergency number?
Υπάρχει τηλεφωνικός
αριθμός για επείγουσες
ανάγκες τη νύχτα;
i·*par*·hi ti·le·fo·ni·*kos*
a·rith·*mos* yia e·*pi*·ghu·ses
a·*na*·ges ti *nikh*·ta

I've run out of my medication.
Μου έχουν τελειώσει τα
φάρμακά μου.
mu *e*·khun te·li·*o*·si ta
far·ma·*ka* mu

This is my usual medicine.

Αυτά είναι τα συνηθισμένα
μου φάρμακα.

af·*ta i*·ne ta si·ni·thiz·*me*·na
mu *far*·ma·ka

What's the correct dosage?

Ποια είναι η σωστή δόση;

pia *i*·ne i so·*sti tho*·si

I don't want a blood transfusion.

Δεν θέλω μετάγγιση
αίματος.

then *the*·lo me·*ta*·gi·si
e·ma·tos

Please use a new syringe.

Παρακαλώ χρησιμοποίησε
καινούργια σύριγγα.

pa·ra·ka·*lo* khri·si·mo·*pi*·i·se
ke·*nur*·yia *si*·ri·ga

I have my own syringe.

Έχω δική μου σύριγγα.

e·kho thi·*ki* mu *si*·ri·ga

I've been vaccinated against …

Έχω κάμει εμβόλιο για …

e·kho *ka*·mi em·*vo*·li·o yia

He/She has been vaccinated against …	Αυτός/Αυτή έχει κάμει εμβόλιο για …	af·*tos*/af·*ti e*·khi *ka*·mi em·*vo*·li·o yia …
hepatitis A/B/C	ηπατίτιδα A/B/C	i·pa·*ti*·ti·tha e·i/bi/si
tetanus	τέτανο	*te*·ta·no
typhoid	τύφο	*ti*·fo

I need new …	Χρειάζομα …	khri·*a*·zo·me …
contact lenses	καινούργιους φακούς επαφής	ke·*nur*·yius fa·*kus* e·pa·*fis*
glasses	καινούργια γιαλιά	ke·*nur*·yia yia·*lia*

My prescription is …

Η συνταγή μου είναι …

i si·da·*yi* mu *i*·ne …

How much will it cost?

Πόσο θα κοστίσει;

po·so tha ko·*sti*·si

Can I have a receipt for my insurance?

Μπορώ να έχω μια
απόδειξη για την
ασφάλειά μου;

bo·*ro* na *e*·kho mia
a·*po*·thik·si yia tin
as·*fa*·li·a mu

Ποιο είναι το πρόβλημα;
pio *i*·ne to *prov*·li·ma — What's the problem?

Πού πονάει;
pu po·*na*·i — Where does it hurt?

Έχετε πυρετό;
e·he·te pi·re·*to* — Do you have a temperature?

Πόσον καιρό είστε έτσι;
po·son ke·*ro i*·ste et·si — How long have you been like this?

Το είχατε αυτό πριν;
to *i*·kha·te af·*po* prin — Have you had this before?

Έχετε σεξουαλικές σχέσεις;
e·he·te sek·su·a·li·*kes* she·sis — Are you sexually active?

Μήπως είχατε σεξ χωρίς προφύλαξη;
mi·pos *i*·kha·te seks kho·*ris* pro·*fi*·lak·si — Have you had unprotected sex?

Πίνετε;/Καπνίζετε;
pi·ne·te/ka·*pni*·ze·te — Do you drink/smoke?

Παίρνετε ναρκωτικά;
per·ne·te nar·ko·ti·*ka* — Do you take drugs?

Είστε αλλεργικός σε κάτι;
i·ste a·ler·yi·*kos* se *ka*·ti — Are you allergic to anything?

Παίρνετε φάρμακα;
per·ne·te *far*·ma·ka — Are you on medication?

Πόσον καιρό ταξιδεύετε;
po·son ke·*ro* tak·si·*the*·ve·te — How long are you travelling for?

Πρέπει να μπείτε στο νοσοκομείο.
pre·pi na *bi*·te sto no·so·ko·*mi*·o — You need to be admitted to hospital.

Πρέπει να το ελέγξετε όταν επιστρέψετε στη χώρα σας.
pre·pi na to e·*leng*·kse·te *o*·tan e·pi·*strep*·se·te sti *kho*·ra sas — You should have it checked when you go home.

the doctor may say ...

Πρέπει να επιστρέψετε στη
χώρα σας για θεραπεία.
pre·pi na e·pi·strep·se·te sti
kho·ra sas yia the·ra·pi·a
You should return home for treatment.

Είστε υποχονδριακός/υποχονδριακή. m/f
i·ste i·po·khon·thri·a·kos/
po·khon·thri·a·ki
You're a hypochondriac.

symptoms & conditions

συμπτώματα και καταστάσεις

I'm sick.
Είμαι άρρωστος. *i·me a·ro·stos*

My friend is (very) sick. (about a man)
Ο φίλος μου είναι *o fi·los mu i·ne*
(πολύ) άρρωστος. *(po·li) a·ro·stos*

My friend is (very) sick. (about a woman)
Η φίλη μου είναι *i fi·li mu i·ne*
(πολύ) άρρωστη. *(po·li) a·ro·sti*

My child is (very) sick.
Το παιδί μου *to pe·thi mu*
είναι (πολύ) άρρωστο. *i·ne (po·li) a·ro·sto*

He/She is having a/an ...	Αυτός/Αυτή έχει ...	*af·tos/af·ti e·hi ...*
allergic reaction	αλλεργική αντίδραση	*a·ler·yi·ki a·di·thra·si*
asthma attack	προσβολή από άσθμα	*proz·vo·li a·po as·thma*
epileptic fit	επιληπτική κρίση	*e·pi·lip·ti·ki kri·si*
heart attack	καρδιακή προσβολή	*kar·thi·a·ki pros·vo·li*

He/She has been ...	Αυτός/Αυτή ...	*af·tos/af·ti ...*
injured	έχει τραυματιστεί	*e·hi trav·ma·ti·sti*
vomiting	κάνει εμετό	*ka·ni e·me·to*

I've been ...

injured	Έχω τραυματιστεί.	*e*·kho trav·ma·ti·*sti*
vomiting	Κάνω εμετό.	*ka*·no e·me·*to*

I've been bitten/ stung by a ...

	Με έχει δαγκώσει/ τσιμπήσει ...	me *e*·hi ṭha·*go*·si/ tsi·*bi*·si ...
bee	μέλισσα	*me*·li·sa
jellyfish	μέδουσα	*me*·ṭhu·sa
sea urchin	αχινός	a·hi·*nos*
snake	φίδι	*fi*·ṭhi
wasp	σφήκα	*sfi*·ka
weever fish	δράκαινα	*ṭhra*·ke·na

I feel ...

	Αισθάνομαι ...	es·*tha*·no·me ...
anxious	ανυπόμονος/η m/f	a·ni·*po*·mo·nos/i
better	καλύτερα m&f	ka·*li*·te·ra
depressed	θλιμμένος/η m/f	thli·*me*·nos/i
dizzy	ζαλάδα m&f	za·*la*·ṭha
hot and cold	ζέστη και κρύο m&f	*ze*·sti ke *kri*·o
nauseous	ναυτία m&f	naf·*ti*·a
shivery	ρίγος m&f	*ri*·ghos
strange	παράξενα m&f	pa·*rak*·se·na
weak	αδύνατος/η m/f	a·*thi*·na·tos/i
worse	χειρότερα m&f	hi·*ro*·te·ra

It hurts here.

Πονάει εδώ.   po·*na*·i e·ṭho

I can't sleep.

Δεν μπορώ να κοιμηθώ.   ṭhen bo·*ro* na ki·mi·*tho*

I think it's the medication I'm on.

Νομίζω είναι τα φάρμακα   no·*mi*·zo *i*·ne ta *far*·ma·ka
που παίρνω.   pu *per*·no

I'm on medication for ...

Παίρνω φάρμακα για ...   *per*·no *far*·ma·ka yia ...

He/She is on medication for ...

Αυτός/αυτή παίρνει   af·*tos*/af·*ti per*·ni
φάρμακα για ...   *far*·ma·ka yia ...

I have (a/an) …
Έχω …   *e·*kho …

He/She has (a/an) …
Αυτός/αυτή έχει …   af·*tos*/af·*ti* e·hi …

I've recently had (a/an) …
Είχα πρόσφατα …   *i·*kha pros·fa·ta …

He/She has recently had (a/an) …
Αυτός/αυτή είχε πρόσφατα …   af·*tos*/af·*ti* i·he pros·fa·ta …

AIDS	Έηντς n	*e·*idz
asthma	άσθμα n	*as·*thma
burn	έγκαυμα n	*e·*gav·ma
cold	κρύωμα n	*kri·*o·ma
constipation	δυσκοιλιότητα f	*this·*ki·li·o·ti·ta
cough	βήχα m	*vi·*kha
dehydration	αφυδάτωση f	a·fi·*tha·*to·si
diabetes	διαβήτη m	thia·*vi·*ti
diarrhoea	διάρροια f	thi·*a·*ri·a
encephalitis	εγκεφαλίτιδα f	e·ge·fa·*li·*ti·tha
fever	πυρετό m	pi·re·*to*
headache	πονοκέφαλο m	po·no·*ke·*fa·lo
heatstroke	ηλιακή συμφόρηση f	i·lia·*ki* sim·*fo·*ri·si
indigestion	δυσπεψία f	this·pep·*si·*a
(fungal) infection	(μυκητώδη) μόλυνση f	(mi·ki·*to·*thi) *mo·*lin·si
insect bite	τσίμπημα από έντομο n	*tsi·*bi·ma a·*po* *e·*do·mo
Lyme disease	νόσο του lyme f	*no·*so tu *la·*im
nausea	ναυτία f	naf·*ti·*a
pain	πόνο m	*po·*no
rabies	λύσσα f	*li·*sa
rash	εξάνθημα n	ek·*san·*thi·ma
sea sickness	ναυτία f	naf·*ti·*a
sore throat	πονόλαιμο m	po·*no·*le·mo
sprain	στραμπούλισμα n	stra·*bu·*liz·ma
stomachache	στομαχόπονο m	sto·ma·*kho·*po·no
sunburn	ηλιακό έγκαυμα n	i·li·a·*ko* *e·*gav·ma
tick typhus	τσιμπούρι τύφου n	tsi·*bu·*ri *ti·*fu

women's health

(I think) I'm pregnant.
(Νομίζω) Είμαι έγγυος.   (no·*mi*·zo) *i*·me *e*·gi·os

I'm on the pill.
Παίρνω το Χάπι.   *per*·no to *kha*·pi

I haven't had my period for (six) weeks.
Δεν έχω περίοδο για (έξι)   *then e*·kho pe·*ri*·o·*t*ho yia (*ek*·si)
εβδομάδες.   ev·*t*ho·*ma*·*t*hes

I've noticed a lump here.
Παρατήρησα ένα   pa·ra·*ti*·ri·sa *e*·na
εξόγκωμα εδώ.   ek·*so*·go·ma *e*·*t*ho

Do you have something for (period pain)?
Έχετε κάτι για (πόνο για   *e*·he·te *ka*·ti yia (*po*·no yia
την περίοδο);   tin pe·*ri*·o·*t*ho)

I have a …	Έχω …	*e*·kho …
urinary tract infection	μόλυνση στον ουρικό σωλήνα	*mo*·lin·si ston u·ri·*ko* so·*li*·na
yeast infection	μυκωτική μόλυνση	mi·ko·ti·*ki mo*·lin·si

---

the doctor may say …

Χρησιμοποιείτε αντισυλληπτικά; khri·si·mo·pi·*i*·te a·di·si·lip·ti·*ka*	**Are you using contraception?**
Έχετε περίοδο; *e*·he·te pe·*ri*·o·*t*ho	**Are you menstruating?**
Είστε έγγυος; *i*·ste *e*·gi·os	**Are you pregnant?**
Πότε είχατε περίοδο τελευταία; *po*·te *i*·kha·te pe·*ri*·o·*t*ho te·lef·*te*·a	**When did you last have your period?**
Είστε έγγυος. *i*·ste *e*·gi·os	**You're pregnant.**

I need (a/the) …	Χρειάζομαι …	khri·*a*·zo·me …
contraception	αντισυλληπτικό	a·di·si·lip·ti·*ko*
morning-after	το χάπι του	to *kha*·pi tu
pill	επόμενου πρωινού	e·*po*·me·nu pro·i·*nu*
pregnancy test	τεστ εγγυμοσύνης	test e·gi·mo·*si*·nis

allergies

αλλεργίες

I have a skin allergy.
  Έχω αλλεργία στο δέρμα.   *e*·kho a·ler·yi·a sto *ther*·ma

I'm allergic to …	Είμαι αλλεργικός/	*i*·me a·ler·yi·*kos*
	αλλεργική … m/f	a·ler·yi·*ki*
He's allergic to …	Αυτός είναι	af·*tos* i·ne
	αλλεργικός …	a·ler·yi·*kos* …
She's allergic to …	Αυτή είναι	af·*ti* i·ne
	αλλεργική …	a·ler·yi·*ki* …
antibiotics	στα αντιβιωτικά	sta a·di·vi·o·ti·*ka*
anti-	στα	sta
inflammatories	αντιφλεγμονώδη	a·di·flegh·mo·*no*·thi
aspirin	στην ασπιρίνη	stin as·pi·*ri*·ni
bees	στις μέλισσες	stis *me*·li·ses
codeine	στην κωδεΐνη	stin ko·the·*i*·ni
penicillin	στην πενικιλλίνη	stin pe·ni·ki·*li*·ni
pollen	στη γύρη	sti *yi*·ri
sulphur-based	στα φάρμακα με	sta *far*·ma·ka me
drugs	θείο	*thi*·o
wasps	στις σφήκες	stis *sfi*·kes

inhaler	αναπνευστήρας m	a·nap·nef·*sti*·ras
injection	ένεση f	*e*·ne·si
antihistamines	αντιισταμίνες f	a·di·i·sta·*mi*·nes

For food-related allergies, see **vegetarian & special meals**, page 173.

parts of the body

μέρη του σώματος

My ... hurts.
Πονάει ...
po·*na*·i ...

I can't move my ...
Δεν μπορώ να κουνήσω ...
ţhen bo·*ro* na ku·*ni*·so ...

I have a cramp in my ...
Έχω κράμπα ...
e·kho *kra*·ba ...

My ... is swollen.
Είναι πρησμένο ...
i·ne priz·*me*·no ...

It hurts when you touch it.
Πονάει όταν το αγγίζεις.
po·*ne* o·tan to a·*gi*·zis

eye
μάτι n
ma·ti

nose
μύτη f
mi·ti

ear
αφτί n
af·*ti*

mouth
στόμα n
sto·ma

head
κεφάλι n
ke·*fa*·li

hand
χέρι n
he·ri

arm
μπράτσο n
brat·so

chest
στήθος n
sti·thos

stomach
στομάχι n
sto·*ma*·hi

bum
πισινός m
pi·si·*nos*

leg
σκέλος n
ske·los

foot
πόδι n
po·*ţhi*

alternative treatments

I don't use (Western medicine).
Δεν χρησιμοποιώ   ţhen khri·si·mo·pi·*o*
(συμβατική ιατρική).   (sim·va·ti·*ki* i·a·tri·*ki*)

I prefer ...	Προτιμώ ...	pro·ti·*mo* ...
Can I see someone	Μπορώ να δω	bo·*ro* na ţho
who practises ...?	κάποιον που	*ka*·pion pu
	ασκεί ...;	a·*ski* ...
acupuncture	βελονισμό	ve·lo·niz·*mo*
naturopathy	φυσική θεραπεία	fi·si·*ki* the·ra·*pi*·a
reflexology	αντανακλαστική	a·da·na·kla·sti·*ki*

pharmacist

I need something for (a headache).
Χρειάζομαι   khri·*a*·zo·me
κάτι για (πονοκέφαλο).   *ka*·ti yia (po·no·*ke*·fa·lo)

Do I need a prescription for (antihistamines)?
Χρειάζομαι συνταγή για   khri·*a*·zo·me si·da·*yi* yia
(αντισταμίνες);   (a·di·i·sta·*mi*·nes)

I have a prescription.
Έχω συνταγή.   *e*·kho si·da·*yi*

come again?

If you need something repeated in a consultation or conversation, say Ορίστε; o·*ris*·te (Sorry?). Use Συγνώμη sigh·*no*·mi (Sorry) when you need to apologise.

How many times a day?
Πόσες φορές την ημέρα;   *po·ses fo·res tin i·me·ra*

Will it make me drowsy?
Θα με κάμει να νυστάζω;   *tha me ka·mi na ni·sta·zo*

antiseptic	αντισηπτικό n	a·di·sip·ti·ko
condoms	προφυλακτικά n pl	pro·fi·lakh·ti·ka
contraceptives	αντισυλληπτικά n pl	a·di·si·lip·ti·ka
insect repellent	εντομοαπωθητικό n	e·do·mo·a·po·thi·ti·ko
laxative	καθαρτικό n	ka·thar·ti·ko
painkillers	παυσίπονα	paf·si·po·na
(for infants)	(για μωρά) n pl	(yia mo·ra)
rehydration	ενυδρωτικά	en·i·thro·ti·ka
salts	άλατα n pl	a·la·ta
spray for insect	σπρέι για	spre·i yia
bites	τσιμπήματα	tsi·bi·ma·ta
	κουνουπιών n	ku·nu·pion
sunburn lotion	λοσιόν για ηλιακό	lo·sion yia i·li·a·ko
	έγκαυμα n	e·gav·ma
sunscreen	αντιηλιακό n	a·di·i·li·a·ko
talcum powder	ταλκ n	talk
thermometer	θερμόμετρο n	ther·mo·me·tro
zinc cream	ψευδαργυρούχος	psev·thar·yi·ru·khos
	αλοιφή f	a·li·fi

---

the pharmacist may say ...

Δυο φορές την ημέρα (με φαγητό).
     thio fo·res tin i·me·ra   **Twice a day (with food).**
     (me fa·yi·to)

Το έχετε ξαναπάρει;
     to e·he·te ksa·na·pa·ri   **Have you taken this before?**

Πρέπει να τελειώσετε όλη τη σειρά.
     pre·pi na te·li·o·se·te   **You must complete the course.**
     o·li ti si·ra

dentist

I have a ...	Έχω ...	e·ho ...
broken tooth	ένα σπασμένο δόντι	e·na spaz·me·no tho·di
cavity	ένα κούφιο δόντι	e·na ku·fio tho·di
toothache	πονόδοντο	po·no·tho·do

I've lost a filling.
Έχασα ένα σφράγισμα.　　　　e·kha·sa e·na sfra·yiz·ma

My dentures are broken.
Οι μασέλες μου έσπασαν.　　　i ma·se·les mu e·spa·san

My gums hurt.
Πονούν τα ούλα μου.　　　　 po·nun ta u·la mu

I need an anaesthetic/a filling.
Χρειάζομαι αναισθητικό/　　　khri·a·zo·me a·nes·thi·ti·ko/
σφράγισμα.　　　　　　　　 sfra·yiz·ma

I don't want it extracted.
Δεν θέλω να το βγάλω.　　　 then the·lo na to vgha·lo

Ouch!
Όου!　　　　　　　　　　　 o·u

---

the dentist may say ...

Ανοίξτε το στόμα πολύ a·nik·ste to sto·ma po·li.	Open wide.
Δεν θα πονέσει καθόλου. then tha po·ne·si ka·tho·lu	This won't hurt a bit.
Δαγκώστε αυτό. tha·go·ste af·to	Bite down on this.
Μην κινείστε. min ki·ni·ste	Don't move.
Ξεβγάλτε! ksev·ghal·te	Rinse!
Γυρίστε πίσω, δεν τελείωσα. yi·ri·ste pi·so then te·li·o·sa	Come back, I haven't finished.

Greek nouns in the **dictionary** have their gender indicated by ⓜ masculine, ⓕ feminine or ⓝ neuter. If it's a plural noun you'll also see pl. When a word that could be either a noun or a verb has no gender indicated, it's a verb. Adjectives are given in the masculine form only – see **adjectives & adverbs** in the **phrasebuilder** for more on how to form feminine and neuter adjectives. Both nouns and adjectives are provided in the nominative case only – refer to the **phrasebuilder** for more information on **case**. Note that we've also added the abbreviations a adjective and v verb for added clarity where required.

A

aboard (επάνω στο) κατάστρωμα
(e-*pa*-no sto) ka-*tas*-tro-ma
abortion έκτρωση ⓕ *ek*-tro-si
about περίπου pe-*ri*-pu
above από πάνω a-*po pa*-no
abroad στο εξωτερικό sto ek-so-te-ri-*ko*
accident ατύχημα ⓝ a-*ti*-hi-ma
accommodation κατάλυμα ⓝ ka-*ta*-li-ma
account λογαριασμός ⓜ lo-gha-riaz-*mos*
across απέναντι a-*pe*-na-di
activist ακτιβιστής/ακτιβίστρια ⓜ/ⓕ
a-kti-vi-*stis*/a-kti-*vi*-stri-a
actor ηθοποιός ⓜ&ⓕ i-tho-pi-*os*
acupuncture βελονισμός ⓜ ve-lo-niz-*mos*
adaptor μετασχηματιστής ⓜ
me-ta-shi-ma-ti-*stis*
addiction εθισμός ⓜ e-thiz-*mos*
address διεύθυνση ⓕ thi-*ef*-thin-si
administration διοίκηση ⓕ thi-*i*-ki-si
admission (price) τιμή εισόδου ⓕ
ti-*mi* i-so-thu
admit δέχομαι *the*-kho-me
adult ενήλικος/ενήλικη ⓜ/ⓕ
e-*ni*-li-kos/e-*ni*-li-ki
advertisement διαφήμιση ⓕ thi-a-*fi*-mi-si
advice συμβουλή ⓕ sim-vu-*li*
Aegean Αιγαίο ⓝ e-*ye*-o
aerobics αερόμπικς ⓝ pl a-e-ro-biks
aeroplane αεροπλάνο ⓝ a-e-ro-*pla*-no
Africa Αφρική ⓕ a-fri-*ki*
after μετά me-*ta*
(this) afternoon (αυτό το) απόγευμα ⓝ
(af-*to* to) a-*po*-yev-ma

aftershave κολόνια ξυρίσματος ⓕ
ko-*lo*-ni-a ksi-*riz*-ma-tos
again πάλι *pa*-li
age ηλικία ⓕ i-li-*ki*-a
(three days) ago (τρεις μέρες) πριν
(tris *me*-res) prin
agree συμφωνώ sim-fo-*no*
agriculture γεωργία ⓕ ye-or-*yi*-a
ahead εμπρός e-*bros*
AIDS Έηντς ⓝ e-idz
air αέρας ⓜ a-*e*-ras
air-conditioned με ερκοντίσιον
me er-kon-*di*-si-on
air conditioning έρκοντίσιον ⓝ
er kon-*di*-si-on
airline αερογραμμή ⓕ a-e-ro-ghra-*mi*
airmail αεροπορικό ταχυδρομείο ⓝ
a-e-ro-po-ri-*ko* ta-hi-*thro*-mi-o
airplane αεροπλάνο ⓝ a-e-ro-*pla*-no
airport αεροδρόμιο ⓝ a-e-ro-*thro*-mi-o
airport tax δασμός αεροδρομίου ⓜ
thaz-mos a-e-ro-*thro*-mi-u
aisle (on plane) διάδρομος (αεροπλάνου)
ⓜ thi-*a*-thro-mos (a-e-ro-*pla*-nu)
alarm clock ξυπνητήρι ⓝ ksi-pni-*ti*-ri
Albania Αλβανία ⓕ al-va-*ni*-a
alcohol αλκοόλ ⓝ al-ko-*ol*
all όλοι ⓜ *o*-li
allergy αλλεργία ⓕ a-ler-*yi*-a
almond αμύγδαλο ⓝ a-*migh*-tha-lo
almost σχεδόν she-*thon*
alone μόνος *mo*-nos
already ήδη *i*-thi
also επίσης e-*pi*-sis

altar βωμός ⓜ vo·mos
altitude ύψος ⓝ ip·sos
always πάντα pa·da
ambassador πρέσβης/πρέσβειρα ⓜ/①
prez·vis/prez·vi·ra
ambulance νοσοκομειακό ⓝ
no·so·ko·mi·a·ko
America Αμερική ① a·me·ri·ki
American football
Αμερικανικό ποδόσφαιρο ⓝ
a·me·ri·ka·ni·ko po·thos·fe·ro
amphitheatre αμφιθέατρο ⓝ
am·fi·the·a·tro
anaemia αναιμία ① a·ne·mi·a
anarchist αναρχικός/αναρχική ⓜ/①
a·nar·hi·kos/a·nar·hi·ki
ancient a αρχαίος ar·he·os
and και ke
angry θυμωμένος thi·mo·me·nos
animal ζώο ⓝ zo·o
ankle αστράγαλος ⓜ a·stra·gha·los
another ένας άλλος e·nas a·los
answer ① απάντηση ① a·pa·di·si
ant μυρμήγκι ⓝ mir·mi·gi
antibiotics αντιβιοτικά ⓝ pl a·di·vi·o·ti·ka
antinuclear αντιπυρηνικό ⓝ
a·di·pi·ri·ni·ko
antique αντίκα ① an·ti·ka
antiseptic αντισηπτικό ⓝ a·di·si·lip·ti·ko
any καθόλου ka·tho·lu
anxious ανυπόμονος/ανυπόμονη ⓜ/①
a·ni·po·mo·nos/a·ni·po·mo·ni
apartment διαμέρισμα ⓝ thi·a·me·riz·ma
appendix (body) σκωληκοειδίτης ⓜ
sko·li·ko·i·thi·tis
apple μήλο ⓝ mi·lo
appointment ραντεβού ⓝ ra·de·vu
apricot βερύκοκο ⓝ ve·ri·ko·ko
April Απρίλιος ⓜ a·pri·li·os
archaic αρχαϊκός ar·kha·i·kos
archaeological αρχαιολογικός
ar·he·o·lo·yi·kos
architect αρχιτέκτονας ⓜ&①
ar·hi·tek·to·nas
architecture αρχιτεκτονική ①
ar·hi·tek·to·ni·ki
argue συζητώ si·zi·to
arm χέρι ⓝ he·ri
aromatherapy αρωμοθεραπεία ①
a·ro·mo·the·ra·pi·a

arrest v συλλαμβάνω si·lam·va·no
arrivals αφίξεις ① pl a·fik·sis
arrive φτάνω fta·no
art τέχνη ① tekh·ni
art gallery πινακοθήκη ① pi·na·ko·thi·ki
artist καλλιτέχνης/καλλιτέχνιδα ⓜ/①
ka·li·tekh·nis/ka·li·tekh·ni·tha
ashtray σταχτοθήκη ① stakh·to·thi·ki
Asia Ασία ① a·si·a
ask (a question) ρωτάω ro·ta·o
ask (for something) ζητάω zi·ta·o
asparagus σπαράγγι ① spa·ra·gi
aspirin ασπιρίνη ① a·spi·ri·ni
asthma άσθμα ⓝ asth·ma
astrology αστρολογία ① a·stro·lo·yi·a
at σε se
athletics αθλητικά ⓝ pl a·thli·ti·ka
atmosphere ατμόσφαιρα ① at·mos·fe·ra
aubergine μελιτζάνα ① me·li·dza·na
August Αύγουστος ⓜ av·ghu·stos
aunt θεία ① thi·a
Australia Αυστραλία ① af·stra·li·a
Australian Rules Football
Αυστραλέζικο ποδόσφαιρο ⓝ
af·stra·le·zi·ko po·thos·fe·ro
automated teller machine (ATM)
αυτόματη μηχανή χρημάτων ①
af·to·ma·ti mi·kha·ni khri·ma·ton
autumn φθινόπωρο ⓝ fthi·no·po·ro
avenue λεωφόρος ① le·o·fo·ros
avocado αβοκάντο ⓝ a·vo·ka·do
awful απαίσιος a·pe·si·os

B

B&W (film) μαυρόασπρο (φιλμ) ⓝ
mav·ro·a·spro (film)
baby μωρό ⓝ mo·ro
baby food φαγητό για μωρά ⓝ
fa·yi·to yia mo·ra
baby powder ταλκ ⓝ talk
babysitter μπέιμπι σίτερ ① be·i·bi si·ter
back (body) πλάτη ① pla·ti
back (position) πίσω pi·so
backgammon τάβλι ⓝ tav·li
backpack σακίδιο ⓝ sa·ki·thi·o
bacon μπέικον ⓝ be·i·kon
bad κακός ka·kos
bag σάκος ⓜ sa·kos

baggage αποσκευές ① pl a·po·ske·*ves*

baggage allowance επιτρεπόμενες αποσκευές ① pl e·pi·tre·*po*·me·nes a·po·ske·*ves*

baggage claim παραλαβή αποσκευών ① pa·ra·la·*vi* a·po·ske·*von*

bakery φούρνος ⓜ *fur*·nos

balance (account) υπόλοιπο (λογαριασμού) ① i·*po*·li·po (lo·gha·riaz·*mu*)

Balcans Βαλκάνια ⓝ pl val·*ka*·ni·a

balcony μπαλκόνι ⓝ bal·*ko*·ni

ball (sport) μπάλα ① *ba*·la

ballet μπαλέτο ⓝ ba·*le*·to

banana μπανάνα ① ba·*na*·na

band (music) μπάντα ① *ba*·da

bandage επίδεσμος ⓜ e·*pi*·thez·mos

Band-Aid τσιρότο ⓝ tsi·*ro*·to

bank τράπεζα ① *tra*·pe·za

bank account τραπεζικός λογαριασμός ⓜ tra·pe·zi·kos lo·gha·riaz·*mos*

banknote χαρτονόμισμα ⓝ khar·to·*no*·miz·ma

baptism βάπτιση ① *vap*·ti·si

bar μπαρ ⓝ bar

barber κουρέας ⓜ ku·*re*·as

bar work δουλειά σε μπαρ ① thu·*lia* se bar

baseball μπέιζμπολ ⓝ *be*·iz·bol

basket καλάθι ⓝ ka·*la*·thi

basketball μπάσκετ ⓝ *ba*·sket

bath μπάνιο ⓝ *ba*·nio

bathing suit μαγιό ⓝ ma·*yio*

bathroom μπάνιο ⓝ *ba*·nio

battery μπαταρία ① ba·ta·*ri*·a

be είμαι *i*·me

beach παραλία ① pa·ra·*li*·a

beach volleyball βόλεϊ παραλίας ⓝ vo·le·i pa·ra·*li*·as

bean φασόλι ⓝ fa·*so*·li

beansprouts φύτρα φασολιών ① *fit*·ra fa·so·*lion*

beautiful όμορφος o·*mor*·fos

beauty salon ινστιτούτο αισθητικής ⓝ in·sti·*tu*·to es·thi·ti·*kis*

because διότι thi·o·ti

bed κρεβάτι ⓝ kre·*va*·ti

bedding σκεπάσματα ⓝ pl ske·*paz*·ma·ta

bed linen σεντόνια ⓝ pl se·*do*·nia

bedroom υπνοδωμάτιο ⓝ ip·no·tho·*ma*·ti·o

bee μέλισσα ① *me*·li·sa

beef βοδινό ⓝ vo·thi·*no*

beer μπύρα ① *bi*·ra

beetroot πατζάρι ⓝ pat·*za*·ri

before πριν prin

beggar ζητιάνος/ζητιάνα ⓜ/① zi·*tia*·nos/zi·*tia*·na

behind πίσω *pi*·so

Belgium Βέλγιο ⓝ vel·yi·o

below κάτω *ka*·to

beside δίπλα *thi*·pla

best α ο καλύτερο ο ka·*li*·te·ros

bet στοίχημα ⓝ *sti*·hi·ma

better καλύτερος/καλύτερη ⓜ/① ka·*li*·te·ros/ka·*li*·te·ri

between ανάμεσα a·*na*·me·sa

bible Βίβλος ① *viv*·los

bicycle ποδήλατο ⓝ po·*thi*·la·to

big μεγάλος me·*gha*·los

bigger μεγαλύτερος me·gha·*li*·te·ros

biggest ο μεγαλύτερος ο me·gha·*li*·te·ros

bike ποδήλατο ⓝ po·*thi*·la·to

bike chain αλυσίδα ποδηλάτου ① a·li·*si*·tha po·thi·*la*·tu

bike lock κλειδαριά ποδηλάτου ① kli·tha·*ria* po·thi·*la*·tu

bike path δρόμος ποδηλάτου ⓜ *thro*·mos po·thi·*la*·tu

bike shop κατάστημα ποδηλάτου ⓝ ka·*ta*·sti·ma po·thi·*la*·tu

bill (restaurant etc) λογαριασμός ⓜ lo·gha·riaz·*mos*

billiards μπιλιάρδο ⓝ bi·*liar*·tho

binoculars κιάλια ⓝ pl *kia*·lia

bird πουλί ⓝ pu·*li*

birthday γενέθλια ⓝ pl ye·*ne*·thli·a

birth certificate πιστοποιητικό γεννήσεως ⓝ pi·sto·pi·i·ti·ko ye·*ni*·se·os

biscuit μπισκότο ⓝ bi·*sko*·to

bite (dog) δαγκωματιά ① tha·go·ma·*tia*

bite (insect) τσίμπημα ⓝ *tsi*·bi·ma

bitter πικρός pi·*kros*

black α μαύρος *mav*·ros

bladder κύστη ① *ki*·sti

blanket κουβέρτα ① ku·*ver*·ta

blind α τυφλός ti·*flos*

blister φουσκάλα ① fu·*ska*·la

blocked μπλοκαρισμένος blo·ka·riz·*me*·nos

blood αίμα ⓝ *e*·ma

blood group ομάδα αίματος ① o·*ma*·tha *e*·ma·tos

blood pressure πίεση αίματος ①
pi·e·si e·ma·tos

blood test εξέταση αίματος ①
ek·se·ta·si e·ma·tos

blue a μπλε ble

board (transport) v ανεβαίνω a·ne·ve·no

boarding house πανσιόν ① pan·sion

boarding pass κάρτα επιβίβασης ①
kar·ta e·pi·vi·va·sis

boat βάρκα ① var·ka

body σώμα ⑩ so·ma

boiled βρασμένος vraz·me·nos

bone κόκαλο ⑩ ko·ka·lo

book βιβλίο ⑩ viv·li·o

book (reserve) v κλείνω θέση kli·no the·si

booked out πλήρες pli·res

bookshop βιβλιοπωλείο ⑩ viv·li·o·po·li·o

boot (footwear) μπότα ① bo·ta

boots (footwear) μπότες ① pl bo·tes

border σύνορο ⑩ si·no·ro

bored βαριεστημένος va·ri·e·sti·me·nos

boring ανιαρός a·ni·a·ros

borrow δανείζομαι tha·ni·zo·me

botanical garden βοτανικός κήπος ⑩
vo·ta·ni·kos ki·pos

both και οι δύο ke i thi·o

bottle μπουκάλι ⑩ bu·ka·li

bottle opener ανοιχτήρι ⑩ a·nikh·ti·ri

bottle shop κάβα ① ka·va

bottom (body) πισινός ⑩ pi·si·nos

bottom (position) κάτω ka·to

bouzouki (traditional music)
μπουζούκι ⑩ bu·zu·ki

bouzouki place μπουζουκτσίδικο ⑩
bu·zuk·tsi·thi·ko

bowl μπωλ ⑩ bol

box κουτί ⑩ ku·ti

boxer shorts σλιπάκι ⑩ sli·pa·ki

boxing μποξ ⑩ boks

boy αγόρι ⑩ a·gho·ri

boyfriend φίλος ⑩ fi·los

bra σουτιέν ⑩ su·ti·en

brakes φρένα ⑩ pl fre·na

brandy κονιάκ ⑩ ko·niak

brave γενναίος ye·ne·os

bread ψωμί ⑩ pso·mi

bread rolls ψωμάκια ⑩ pl pso·ma·kia

break v σπάω spa·o

break down χαλάω ha·la·o

breakfast πρόγευμα ⑩ pro·yev·ma

breast (body) στήθος ⑩ sti·thos

breathe αναπνέω a·nap·ne·o

bribe v δωροδοκώ tho·ro·tho·ko

bridge γεφύρι ① ye·fi·ri

briefcase ⑩ χαρτοφύλακας khar·to·fi·la·kas

brilliant λαμπρός la·bros

bring φέρνω fer·no

broccoli μπρόκολο ⑩ bro·ko·lo

brochure μπροσούρα ① bro·su·ra

broken σπασμένος spaz·me·nos

broken down χαλασμένος
kha·laz·me·nos

bronchitis βρογχίτιδα ① vro·hi·ti·tha

bronze μπρούτζος ⑩ bru·dzos

brother αδερφός ⑩ a·ther·fos

brown καφέ ka·fe

bruise σημάδι από χτύπημα ⑩
si·ma·thi a·po khti·pi·ma

brush βούρτσα ① vur·tsa

bucket κουβάς ⑩ ku·vas

Buddhist Βουδιστής/Βουδίστρια
vu·thi·stis/vu·thi·stri·a ⑩/①

budget προϋπολογισμός ⑩
pro·i·po·lo·yiz·mos

buffet μπουφές ⑩ bu·fes

bug κοριός ⑩ ko·rios

build v χτίζω khti·zo

builder χτίστης ⑩ khti·stis

building κτίριο ⑩ kti·ri·o

Bulgaria Βουλγαρία ① vul·gha·ri·a

bumbag πορτοφόλι μέσης ⑩
por·to·fo·li me·sis

burn έγκαυμα ⑩ e·gav·ma

burnt καμένος ka·me·nos

bus (city) αστικό λεωφορείο ⑩
a·sti·ko le·o·fo·ri·o

bus (intercity) υπεραστικό λεωφορείο ⑩
i·per·a·sti·ko le·o·fo·ri·o

bus station σταθμός λεωφορείου ⑩
stath·mos le·o·fo·ri·u

bus stop στάση λεωφορείου ①
sta·si le·o·fo·ri·u

business επιχείρηση ① e·pi·hi·ri·si

business class μπίζνες κλασ biz·nes klas

businessperson επιχειρηματίας ⑩&①
e·pi·hi·ri·ma·ti·as

business trip ταξίδι εργασίας ⑩
tak·si·thi er·gha·si·as

busker περιοδεύτης τραγουδιστής ⑩
pe·ri·o·the·von tra·ghu·thi·stis
περιοδεύουσα τραγουδίστρια ①
pe·ri·o·the·vu·sa tra·ghu·thi·stri·a

busy απασχολημένος a-pa-skho-li-me-nos
but αλλά a-la
butcher χασάπης ⓜ kha-sa-pis
butcher's shop κρεοπωλείο ⓝ kre-o-po-li-o
butter βούτυρο ⓝ vu-ti-ro
butterfly πεταλούδα ⓕ pe-ta-lu-tha
button κουμπί ⓝ ku-bi
buy v αγοράζω a-gho-ra-zo
Byzantine Βυζαντινός vi-za-di-nos

C

cabin καμπίνα ⓕ ka-bi-na
cabbage μάπα ⓕ ma-pa
cable car τελεφερίκ ⓝ te-le-fe-rik
café καφεστιατόριο ⓝ ka-fe-sti-a-to-ri-o
cafeteria καφετηρία ⓕ ka-fe-ti-ri-a
cake γλυκό ⓝ ghli-ko
cake shop ζαχαροπλαστείο ⓝ za-kha-ro-pla-sti-o
calculator αριθμομηχανή ⓕ a-rith-mo-mi-kha-ni
calendar ημερολόγιο ⓝ i-me-ro-lo-yi-o
call v καλώ ka-lo
camera φωτογραφική μηχανή ⓕ fo-to-ghra-fi-ki mi-kha-ni
camera shop κατάστημα φωτογραφικών ειδών ⓝ ka-ta-sti-ma fo-to-ghra-fi-kon i-thon
camp v κατασκηνώνω ka-ta-ski-no-no
camping ground χώρος για κάμπινγκ ⓜ kho-ros yia kam-ping
camping store
  κατάστημα ειδών κατασκήνωσης ⓝ ka-ta-sti-ma i-thon ka-ta-ski-no-sis
campsite χώρος για κάμπινγκ ⓜ kho-ros yia kam-ping
can (be able) v μπορώ bo-ro
can (tin) κουτί ⓝ ku-ti
can opener ανοιχτήρι ⓝ a-nikh-ti-ri
Canada Καναδάς ⓜ ka-na-thas
cancel ακυρώνω a-ki-ro-no
cancer καρκίνος ⓜ kar-ki-nos
candle κερί ⓝ ke-ri
candy καραμέλα ⓕ ka-ra-me-la
cantaloupe πεπόνι ⓝ pe-po-ni
capsicum πιπεριά ⓕ pi-pe-ria
car αυτοκίνητο ⓝ af-to-ki-ni-to
caravan τροχόσπιτο ⓝ tro-kho-spi-to
cardiac arrest καρδιακή προσβολή ⓕ kar-thi-a-ki proz-vo-li

cards (playing) χαρτιά ⓝ pl khar-tia
care (for someone) φροντίζω fro-di-zo
car hire ενοικίαση αυτοκινήτου ⓕ e-ni-ki-a-si af-to-ki-ni-tu
carob χαρούπι ⓝ kha-ru-pi
car owner's title
  τίτλος κατόχου αυτοκινήτου ⓜ tit-los ka-to-khu af-to-ki-ni-tu
car park χώρος στάθμευσης αυτικινήτων ⓜ kho-ros stath-mef-sis af-to-ki-ni-tu
carpenter μαραγκός ⓜ ma-ra-gos
car registration
  άδεια κυκλοφορίας αυτοκινήτου ⓕ a-thia ki-klo-fo-ri-as af-to-ki-ni-tu
carrot καρότο ⓝ ka-ro-to
carry μεταφέρω me-ta-fe-ro
carton χαρτοκιβώτιο ⓝ khar-to-ki-vo-ti-o
cash μετρητά ⓝ pl me-tri-ta
cash (a cheque) v εξαργυρώνω ek-sar-yi-ro-no
cash register ταμείο ⓝ ta-mi-o
cashew κάσιου ⓝ ka-si-u
cashier ταμίας ⓜ&ⓕ ta-mi-as
casino καζίνο ⓝ ka-zi-no
cassette κασέτα ⓕ ka-se-ta
castle κάστρο ⓝ ka-stro
casual work ημερομίσθια εργασία ⓕ i-me-ro-mi-sthi-a er-gha-si-a
cat γάτα ⓕ gha-ta
catamaran καταμαράν ⓜ ka-ta-ma-ran
cathedral μητρόπολη ⓕ mi-tro-po-li
Catholic Καθολικός/Καθολική ⓜ/ⓕ ka-tho-li-kos/ka-tho-li-ki
cauliflower κουνουπίδι ⓝ ku-nu-pi-thi
cave σπηλιά ⓕ spi-lia
CD οι ντι si di
celebration γιορτή ⓕ yior-ti
cellphone κινητό ⓝ ki-ni-to
cemetery κοιμητήριο ⓝ ki-mi-ti-ri-o
cent σεντ ⓝ sent
centimetre εκατοστόμετρο ⓝ e-ka-to-sto-me-tro
centre κέντρο ⓝ ke-dro
ceramics κεραμικά ⓝ pl ke-ra-mi-ka
cereal δημητριακά ⓝ pl thi-mi-tri-a-ka
certificate πιστοποιητικό ⓝ pi-sto-pi-i-ti-ko
chain αλυσίδα ⓕ a-li-si-tha
chair καρέκλα ⓕ ka-re-kla
chairlift (skiing) τελεφερίκ ⓝ te-le-fe-rik
champagne σαμπάνια ⓕ sam-pa-nia

championships αγώνες πρωταθλήματος ⑩ a-*gho*-nes pro-ta-*thli*-ma-tos

chance πιθανότητα ① pi-tha-*no*-ti-ta

change αλλαγή ① a-la-*yi*

change (coins) ψιλά ⑩ pl psi-*la*

change (from sale) ρέστα ⑩ pl *re*-sta

change (money) v αλλάζω a-*la*-zo

changing room (in shop) δοκιμαστήριο ρούχων ⑩ tho-ki-ma-*sti*-ri-o *ru*-khon

charming χαριτωμένος kha-ri-to-*me*-nos

charter flight πτήση τσάρτερ ① *pti*-si *tsar*-ter

chat up (somebody) v ψήνω *psi*-no

cheap φτηνός fti-*nos*

cheat απατεώνας/απατεώνισσα ⑩/① a-pa-te-o-nas/a-pa-te-o-ni-sa

check v ελέγχω e-*leng*-kho

check (banking) προσωπική επιταγή ① pro-so-pi-*ki* e-pi-ta-*yi*

check (bill) λογαριασμός ⑩ lo-gha-riaz-*mos*

check-in (desk) ρεσεψιόν ① re-sep-*sion*

checkpoint σημείο ελέγχου ⑩ si-*mi*-o e-*leng*-khu

cheese τυρί ⑩ ti-*ri*

cheese shop τυροπωλείο ⑩ ti-ro-po-*li*-o

chef ⑩ σεφ sef

chemist (shop) φαρμακείο ⑩ far-ma-*ki*-o

chemist (pharmacist) φαρμακοποιός ⑩&① far-ma-ko-pi-*os*

cheque προσωπική επιταγή ① pro-so-pi-*ki* e-pi-ta-*yi*

cherry κεράσι ① ke-*ra*-si

chess σκάκι ⑩ *ska*-ki

chessboard σκακιέρα ① ska-*kie*-ra

chest (body) στήθος ⑩ *sti*-thos

chestnut κάστανο ⑩ *ka*-sta-no

chewing gum μαστίχα ① ma-*sti*-kha

chicken κοτόπουλο ⑩ ko-*to*-pu-lo

chicken pox ανεμοβλογιά ① a-ne-mov-lo-*yia*

chickpea στραγάλι ⑩ stra-*gha*-li

child παιδί ⑩ pe-*thi*

childminding επιτήρηση παιδιών ① e-pi-*ti*-ri-si pe-*thion*

children παιδιά ⑩ pl pe-*thia*

child seat παιδικό κάθισμα ⑩ pe-*thi*-ko *ka*-thiz-ma

chilli πιπεριά ① pi-pe-*ria*

chilli sauce σάλτσα πιπεριάς ① *sal*-tsa pi-pe-*rias*

chipura τσίπουρο ⑩ *tsi*-pu-ro

chiropractor χειροπράκτωρ ⑩&① hi-ro-*prak*-stor

chocolate σοκολάτα ① so-ko-*la*-ta

choose διαλέγω thia-*le*-gho

chopping board σανίδα κοπής ① sa-*ni*-tha ko-*pis*

chopsticks τσοπ στικς ⑩ pl tsop stiks

Christian Χριστιανός/Χριστιανή ⑩/① khri-sti-a-*nos*/khri-sti-a-*ni*

Christian name μικρό όνομα ⑩ mi-*kro* o-no-ma

Christmas Χριστούγεννα ⑩ pl khri-*stu*-ye-na

Christmas Day ημέρα Χριστουγέννων ① i-*me*-ra khri-stu-*ye*-non

Christmas Eve παραμονή Χριστουγέννων ① pa-ra-mo-*ni* khri-stu-*ye*-non

church εκκλησία ① e-kli-*si*-a

cider κρασί από μήλο ⑩ kra-*si* a-po *mi*-lo

cigar πούρο ⑩ *pu*-ro

cigarette τσιγάρο ⑩ tsi-*gha*-ro

cigarette lighter αναπτήρας ⑩ a-nap-*ti*-ra

cinema σινεμά ⑩ si-ne-*ma*

circus τσίρκο ⑩ *tsir*-ko

citizenship ιθαγένεια ① i-tha-*ye*-ni-a

city πόλη ① *po*-li

city centre κέντρο της πόλης ⑩ *ke*-dro tis *po*-lis

civil rights πολιτικά δικαιώματα ⑩ pl po-li-ti-*ka* thi-ke-o-ma-ta

civil servant δημόσιος υπάλληλος ⑩&① thi-mo-si-os i-*pa*-li-los

class (category) τάξη ① *tak*-si

classical κλασσικός kla-si-*kos*

class system ταξικό σύστημα ⑩ tak-si-*ko* si-sti-ma

clean a καθαρός ka-tha-*ros*

clean v καθαρίζω ka-tha-*ri*-zo

cleaning καθάρισμα ① ka-*tha*-riz-ma

client πελάτης/πελάτισσα ⑩/① pe-*la*-tis/pe-*la*-ti-sa

cliff γκρεμός ⑩ gre-*mos*

climb v αναρριχούμαι a-na-ri-*khu*-me

cloakroom ιματιοφυλάκιο ⑩ i-ma-ti-o-fi-*la*-ki-o

clock ρολόι ⑩ ro-*lo*-i

close a κοντινός ko-di-*nos*

close v κλείνω *kli*-no

closed κλεισμένος kliz-*me*-nos

clothesline μύλος (για ρούχα) ⓜ
mi·los (yia ru·kha)
clothing ρούχα ⓝ pl ru·kha
clothing store κατάστημα ρούχων ⓝ
ka·ta·sti·ma ru·khon
cloud σύννεφο ⓝ si·ne·fo
cloudy συννεφιασμένος si·ne·fiaz·me·nos
clutch (car) συμπλέκτης ⓜ si·ble·ktis
coach (sport) προπονητής/προπονήτρια
ⓜ/ⓕ pro·po·ni·tis/pro·po·ni·tri·a
coalition συνασπισμός ⓜ sin·as·piz·mos
coast ακτή ⓕ ak·ti
coat παλτό ⓝ pal·to
cocaine κοκαΐνη ⓕ ko·ka·i·ni
cockroach κοριός ⓜ ko·rios
cocktail κοκτέιλ ⓝ kok·te·il
cocoa κακάο ⓝ ka·ka·o
coconut ινδική καρύδα ⓕ in·thi·ki ka·ri·tha
coffee καφές ⓜ ka·fes
coffee shop καφενείο ⓝ ka·fe·ni·o
coins κέρματα ⓝ pl ker·ma·ta
cold κρύο ⓝ kri·o
cold a κρωμμένος kri·o·me·nos
colleague συνάδελφος/συναδέλφισσα
ⓜ/ⓕ si·na·thel·fos/si·na·thel·fi·sa
collect call
κλήση με αντιστροφή της επιβάρυνσης
ⓕ kli·si me a·dis·tro·fi tis e·pi·va·rin·sis
college κολλέγιο ⓝ ko·le·yi·o
colour χρώμα ⓝ khro·ma
column κολώνα ⓕ ko·lo·na
comb χτένα ⓕ khte·na
come έρχομαι er·kho·me
comedy κωμωδία ⓕ ko·mo·thi·a
comfortable άνετος a·ne·tos
commission προμήθεια ⓕ pro·mi·thi·a
communications (profession)
επικοινωνίες ⓕ pl e·pi·ki·no·ni·es
communist κομμουνιστής/κομμουνίστρια
ⓜ/ⓕ ko·mu·ni·stis/ko·mu·ni·stri·a
companion σύντροφος/συντρόφισσα
ⓜ/ⓕ si·dro·fos/si·dro·fi·sa
company (firm) εταιρεία ⓕ e·te·ri·a
company (friends) συντροφιά ⓕ si·dro·fya
compass πυξίδα ⓕ pik·si·tha
complain παραπονούμαι pa·ra·po·nu·me
complaint παράπονο ⓝ pa·ra·po·no
complimentary (free) δωρεάν tho·re·an
computer κομπιούτερ ⓝ kom·piu·ter

computer game παιγνίδι στο κομπιούτερ
ⓝ pegh·ni·thi sto kom·piu·ter
concert κονσέρτο ⓝ kon·ser·to
concussion κλονισμός ⓜ klo·niz·mos
conditioner (hair) κοντίσιονερ ⓝ
kon·di·si·o·ner
condom προφυλακτικό ⓝ pro·fi·lak·ti·ko
conference (big) συνέδριο ⓝ si·ne·thri·o
conference (small) σεμινάριο ⓝ
se·mi·na·ri·o
confession εξομολόγηση ⓕ
ek·so·mo·lo·ghi·si
confirm (a booking) επικυρώνω
e·pi·ki·ro·no
conjunctivitis επιπεφυκίτις ⓜ
e·pi·pe·fi·ki·tis
connection σύνδεσμος ⓜ sin·thez·mos
conservative a συντηρητικός si·di·ri·ti·kos
constipation δυσκοιλία ⓕ this·ki·li·a
consulate προξενείο ⓝ prok·se·ni·o
contact lenses φακοί επαφής ⓜ pl
fa·ki e·pa·fis
contact lens solution υγρό φακών
επαφής ⓝ i·ghro fa·kon e·pa·fis
contraceptives αντισυλληπτικά ⓝ pl
a·di·si·lip·ti·ka
contract συμβόλαιο ⓝ sim·vo·le·o
convenience store σούπερ μάρκετ ⓝ
su·per mar·ket
convent μοναστήρι γυναικών ⓝ
mo·na·sti·ri yi·ne·kon
cook (temperature) δροσερό thro·se·ro
copper χαλκός ⓜ khal·kos
copy αντίγραφο ⓝ a·di·ghra·fo
Corinthian Κορινθιακός ko·rin·thi·a·kos
corkscrew ανοιχτήρι ⓝ a·nikh·ti·ri
corn καλαμπόκι ⓝ ka·la·bo·ki
corner γωνία ⓕ gho·ni·a
cornflakes κορν φλέικς ⓝ pl korn fle·iks
corrupt διεφθαρμένος thi·ef·thar·me·nos
cost v κοστίζω ko·sti·zo
cotton βαμβάκι ⓝ va·ba·ki
cotton balls μπαλάκια από βαμβάκι ⓝ pl
ba·la·kia a·po va·ba·ki
cotton buds ξιλάκι με βαμβάκι ⓝ
ksi·la·ki me va·ba·ki

cook (temperature) δροσερό thro·se·ro
cook μάγειρας/μαγείρισσα ⓜ/ⓕ
ma·yi·ras/ma·yi·ri·sa
cook v μαγειρεύω ma·yi·re·vo
cookie μπισκότο ⓝ bis·ko·to
cooking μαγείρεμα ⓝ ma·yi·re·ma

english–greek

C

213

cough v βήχω *vi*·kho

cough medicine φάρμακο για το βήχα ⓝ *far*·ma·ko yia to *vi*·kha

count v μετράω me·*tra*·o

counter (at bar) πάγκος ⓜ *pa*·gos

country χώρα ⓕ *kho*·ra

countryside εξοχή ⓕ ek·so·*hi*

coupon κουπόνι ⓝ ku·*po*·ni

courgette κολοκυθάκι ⓝ ko·lo·ki·*tha*·ki

court (legal) δικαστήριο ⓝ thi·ka·*sti*·ri·o

court (tennis) γήπεδο ⓝ *yi*·pe·tho

couscous κουσκούς ⓝ kus·*kus*

cover charge προσαύξηση τιμής ⓕ pro·*saf*·ksi·si ti·*mis*

cow γελάδα ⓕ ye·*la*·tha

cracker (biscuit) γαλέτα ⓕ gha·*le*·ta

craft τέχνη ⓕ *tekh*·ni

crash ⓜ κρότος *kro*·tos

crazy τρελός tre·*los*

cream κρέμα ⓕ *kre*·ma

crèche παιδικός σταθμός ⓜ pe·thi·*kos* stath·*mos*

credit πίστωση ⓕ *pi*·sto·si

credit card πιστωτική κάρτα ⓕ pi·sto·ti·*ki* *kar*·ta

cricket (sport) κρίκετ ⓝ *kri*·ket

crop σοδειά ⓕ so·*thia*

cross (religious) σταυρός ⓜ stav·*ros*

crowded γεμάτο (κόσμο) ye·*ma*·to (*koz*·mo)

cruise κρουαζέρα ⓕ kru·a·*ze*·ra

cucumber αγγούρι ⓝ a·*gu*·ri

cup φλυτζάνι ⓝ fli·*dza*·ni

cupboard ντουλάπι ⓝ du·*la*·pi

currency exchange τιμή συναλλάγματος ⓕ ti·*mi* si·na·*lagh*·ma·tos

current (electricity) ρεύμα ⓝ *rev*·ma

current affairs επίκαιρα θέματα ⓝ pl e·*pi*·ke·ra *the*·ma·ta

curry κάρι ⓝ *ka*·ri

cushion cover μαξιλαροθήκη ⓕ mak·si·la·ro·*thi*·ki

custom έθιμο ⓝ *e*·thi·mo

customs τελωνείο ⓝ te·lo·*ni*·o

cut v κόβω *ko*·vo

cutlery μαχαιροπήρουνα ⓝ pl ma·he·ro·*pi*·ru·na

CV βιογραφικό σημείωμα ⓝ vi·o·ghra·fi·*ko* si·*mi*·o·ma

Cycladic Κυκλαδικός ki·kla·thi·*kos*

cycle v κάνω ποδήλατο *ka*·no po·*thi*·la·to

cycling ποδηλασία ⓕ po·thi·la·*si*·a

cyclist ποδηλάτης/ποδηλάτισσα ⓜ/ⓕ po·thi·*la*·tis/po·thi·*la*·ti·sa

Cypriot (person) Κύπριος/Κύπρια ⓜ/ⓕ *ki*·pri·os/*ki*·pri·a

Cypriot (wine etc) κυπριακός/κυπριακή ⓜ/ⓕ ki·pri·a·*kos*/ki·pri·a·*ki*

Cyprus Κύπρος ⓕ *ki*·pros

cystitis κύστη ⓕ *ki*·sti

D

dad μπαμπάς ⓜ ba·*bas*

daily καθημερινός ka·thi·me·ri·*nos*

dairy shop γαλακτοπωλείο ⓝ gha·lak·to·po·*li*·o

dance v χορεύω kho·*re*·vo

dancing χορός kho·*ros*

dangerous επικίνδυνος e·pi·*kin*·thi·nos

dark (night) a σκοτεινός sko·ti·*nos*

dark (colour) a σκούρος *sku*·ros

date (a person) v βγαίνω (με κάποιον) *vye*·no (me *ka*·pion)

date (appointment) ραντεβού ⓝ ra·de·*vu*

date (day) ημερομηνία ⓕ i·me·ro·mi·*ni*·a

date (fruit) χουρμάς ⓜ khur·*mas*

date of birth ημερομηνία γεννήσεως ⓕ i·me·ro·mi·*ni*·a ye·*ni*·se·os

daughter κόρη ⓕ *ko*·ri

dawn αυγή ⓕ av·*yi*

day ημέρα ⓕ i·*me*·ra

day after tomorrow μεθαύριο me·*thav*·ri·o

day before yesterday προχθές prokh·*tes*

dead a νεκρός ne·*kros*

deaf a κουφός ku·*fos*

deal (cards) μοιράζω (χαρτιά) mi·ra·zo (khar·*tia*)

December Δεκέμβριος ⓜ de·*kem*·vri·os

decide αποφασίζω a·po·fa·*si*·zo

deck κατάστρωμα ⓝ ka·ta·stro·ma

deep βαθύς va·*this*

deforestation αποδάσωση ⓕ a·po·*tha*·so·si

degrees (temperature) βαθμοί ⓜ pl vath·*mi*

dehydration αφυδάτωση ① a·fi·*tha*·to·si

delay καθυστέρηση ① ka·thi·*ste*·ri·si

delicatessen ντελικατέσεν ① de·li·ka·te·sen

delineation line διαχωριστική γραμμή ① thi·a·kho·ri·sti·ki ghra·*mi*

deliver παραδίνω pa·ra·*thi*·no

democracy δημοκρατία ① thi·mo·kra·*ti*·a

demonstration διαδήλωση ① thi·a·*thi*·lo·si

Denmark Δανία ① tha·*ni*·a

dental floss οδοντιατρική κλωστή ① o·tho·di·a·tri·*ki* klo·*sti*

dentist οδοντίατρος ⑩&① o·tho·*di*·a·tros

deodorant αποσμητικό ⑩ a·poz·mi·ti·*ko*

depart (leave) αναχωρώ a·na·kho·*ro*

department store κατάστημα ⑩ ka·*ta*·sti·ma

departure αναχώρηση ① a·na·*kho*·ri·si

departure gate θύρα αναχώρησης ① *thi*·ra a·na·*kho*·ri·sis

deposit (bank) κατάθεση ① ka·*ta*·the·si

deposit (on house etc) προκαταβολή ① pro·ka·ta·vo·*li*

depressed θλιμμένος/θλιμμένη ⑩/① thli·*me*·nos/thli·*me*·ni

derailleur εκτροχιασμός ⑩ ek·tro·hi·az·*mos*

descendent απόγονος ⑩ a·*po*·gho·nos

desert έρημος ① *e*·ri·mos

design σχέδιο ⑩ *skhe*·thi·o

dessert επιδόρπιο ⑩ e·pi·*thor*·pi·o

destination προορισμός ⑩ pro·o·riz·*mos*

details λεπτομέρειες ① pl lep·to·*me*·ri·es

diabetes διαβήτης ⑩ thi·a·*vi*·tis

dial tone ήχος κλήσης ⑩ *i*·khos *kli*·sis

diaper πάνα ① *pa*·na

diaphragm διάφραγμα ⑩ thi·*a*·ghra·ma

diarrhoea διάρροια ① thi·*a*·ri·a

diary ημερολόγιο ⑩ i·me·ro·*lo*·yi·o

diaspora διασπορά ① thi·a·spo·*ra*

dice ζάρια ⑩ pl *za*·ria

dictionary λεξικό ⑩ lek·si·*ko*

die v πεθαίνω pe·*the*·no

different διαφορετικός thia·fo·re·ti·*kos*

difficult δύσκολος *thi*·sko·los

digital a ψηφιακός psi·fi·a·*kos*

dining car βαγόνι φαγητού ⑩ va·*gho*·ni fa·yi·*tu*

dinner δείπνο ⑩ *thip*·no

direct a άμεσος *a*·me·sos

direct-dial κατ' ευθείαν γραμμή ① ka·tef·*thi*·an gra·*mi*

direction κατεύθυνση ① ka·*tef*·thin·si

director διευθυντής/διευθύντρια ⑩/① thi·ef·thi·*dis*/thi·ef·*thi*·dri·a

dirty a βρώμικος *vro*·mi·kos

disabled a ανάπηρος a·*na*·pi·ros

disco ντισκοτέκ ① di·sko·*tek*

discount έκπτωση ① *ek*·pto·si

discrimination διάκριση ① thi·*a*·kri·si

disease ασθένεια ① a·*sthe*·ni·a

dish πιάτο ⑩ *pia*·to

disk (CD-ROM) σι ντι ρομ ⑩ si di rom

disk (floppy) δισκέτα ① *thi*·ske·ta

diving βουτιά ① vu·*tia*

diving equipment εξαρτήματα βουτηχτή ⑩ pl ek·sar·*ti*·ma·ta vu·tikh·*ti*

divorced ① διαζευγμένος/διαζευγμένη ⑩/① thi·a·zev·*ghme*·nos/thi·a·zev·*ghme*·ni

dizzy ζαλισμένος/ζαλισμένη ⑩/① za·liz·*me*·nos/za·liz·*me*·ni

do v κάνω *ka*·no

doctor γιατρός ⑩&① yia·*tros*

documentary ντοκυμαντέρ ⑩ do·ki·man·*ter*

dog σκυλί ⑩ ski·*li*

dole επίδομα ανεργίας ⑩ e·*pi*·tho·ma an·er·*yi*·as

doll κούκλα ① *ku*·kla

dollar δολλάριο ⑩ tho·*la*·ri·o

dolphin δελφίνι ⑩ thel·*fi*·ni

dhomatia (room for rent) δωμάτια (για νοίκιασμα) ⑩ pl tho·*ma*·ti·a (yia *ni*·kiaz·ma)

dominoes ντόμινο ⑩ *do*·mi·no

door πόρτα ① *por*·ta

dope (drugs) ναρκωτικά ⑩ pl nar·ko·ti·*ka*

Doric Δωρικός tho·ri·*kos*

double a διπλός *thi*·plos

double bed διπλό κρεβάτι ⑩ *thi*·plo kre·*va*·ti

double room διπλό δωμάτιο ⑩ *thi*·plo tho·*ma*·ti·o

down κάτω *ka*·to

downhill κατηφορικά ka·ti·fo·ri·*ka*

dozen ντουζίνα ① du·*zi*·na

drama δράμα ⑩ *thra*·ma

dream όνειρο ⑩ o·*ni*·ro

dress ⑩ φόρεμα ① *fo*·re·ma

dried ξηρός ksi·*ros*
dried fruit ξηρά φρούτα ⓝ pl ksi·*ra* fru·ta
drink ποτό ⓝ po·*to*
drink v πίνω *pi*·no
drink (alcoholic) ποτό (αλκοολικό) ⓝ
  po·*to* (al·ko·o·li·*ko*)
drive v οδηγώ o·thi·*gho*
drivers licence άδεια οδήγησης ⓕ
  a·thi·a o·*thi*·yi·sis
drizzle ψιχάλα ⓕ psi·*kha*·la
drug (illegal) ναρκωτικό ⓝ nar·ko·ti·*ko*
drug addiction εθισμός στα ναρκωτικά
  ⓜ e·thiz·*mos* sta nar·ko·ti·*ka*
drug dealer έμπορος ναρκωτικών ⓜ&ⓕ
  e·bo·ros nar·ko·ti·*kon*
drug trafficking κυκλοφορία ναρκωτικών
  ⓕ ki·klo·fo·*ri*·a nar·ko·ti·*kon*
drug user ναρκομανής ⓜ&ⓕ
  nar·ko·ma·*nis*
drugs (illicit) ναρκωτικά ⓝ pl nar·ko·ti·*ka*
drum τύμπανο ⓝ *ti*·ba·no
drunk μεθυσμένος me·thiz·*me*·nos
dry a στεγνός stegh·*nos*
dry v στεγνώνω stegh·*no*·no
duck πάπια ⓕ *pa*·pia
dummy (pacifier) πιπίλα ⓕ pi·*pi*·la
DVD Ντι-Βι-Ντί ⓝ di·vi·*di*

E

each καθένας ka·*the*·nas
ear αφτί ⓝ af·*ti*
early νωρίς no·*ris*
earn κερδίζω ker·*thi*·zo
earplugs ωτοασπίδες ⓕ pl o·to·a·*spi*·thes
earrings σκουλαρίκια ⓝ pl sku·la·*ri*·kia
Earth Γη ⓕ yi
earthquake σεισμός ⓜ siz·*mos*
east ανατολή ⓕ a·na·to·*li*
Easter Πάσχα ⓝ *pas*·kha
easy εύκολο *ef*·ko·lo
eat τρώγω *tro*·gho
economy class τουριστική θέση ⓕ
  tu·ri·sti·*ki the*·si
ecstasy (drug) έκσταση ⓕ *ek*·sta·si
eczema έκζεμα ⓝ *ek*·ze·ma
education εκπαίδευση ⓕ ek·*pe*·thef·si
egg αβγό ⓝ av·*gho*
eggplant μελιτζάνα ⓕ me·li·*dza*·na

election εκλογή ⓕ ek·lo·*yi*
electrical store κατάστημα ηλεκτρικών
  ειδών ⓝ ka·ta·sti·ma i·lek·tri·*kon* i·*thon*
electricity ηλεκτρισμός ⓜ i·lek·triz·*mos*
elevator ασανσέρ ⓝ a·san·*ser*
email ημέιλ ⓝ i·me·il
embarrassed αμήχανος a·*mi*·kha·nos
embassy πρεσβεία ⓕ pre·zvi·a
embroidery κέντημα ⓝ *ke*·di·ma
emergency έκτακτη ανάγκη ⓕ
  ek·tak·ti a·*na*·gi
emotional συναισθηματικός
  si·ne·sthi·ma·ti·*kos*
employee υπάλληλος ⓜ&ⓕ i·*pa*·li·los
employer εργοδότης/εργοδότρια ⓜ/ⓕ
  er·gho·*tho*·tis/er·gho·*tho*·tri·a
empty a άδειο *a*·thi·o
end τέλος ⓝ *te*·los
endangered species είδη υπό εξαφάνισ[η]
  ⓝ pl *i*·thi i·po ek·sa·*fa*·ni·si
engaged (to marry)
  αρραβωνιασμένος/αρραβωνιασμένη
  ⓜ/ⓕ a·ra·vo·niaz·*me*·nos/
  a·ra·vo·niaz·*me*·ni
engagement (undertaking) υποχρέωση
  ⓕ i·po·*khre*·o·si
engine μηχανή ⓕ mi·kha·*ni*
engineer μηχανικός ⓜ&ⓕ mi·kha·ni·*kos*
engineering μηχανική ⓕ mi·kha·ni·*ki*
England Αγγλία ⓕ ang·*gli*·a
English (language) Αγγλικά ⓝ ang·gli·*ka*
enjoy oneself απολαμβάνω a·po·lam·*va*·no[ι]
enough αρκετά ar·ke·*ta*
enter μπαίνω *be*·no
entertainment guide οδηγός διασκέδαση[ς]
  ⓜ o·thi·*ghos* thia·ske·tha·sis
entry είσοδος ⓕ *i*·so·thos
envelope φάκελος ⓜ *fa*·ke·los
environment περιβάλλον ⓝ pe·ri·*va*·lon
epilepsy επιληψία ⓕ e·pi·lip·*si*·a
erosion διάβρωση ⓕ *thi*·av·ro·si
equal opportunity ίσες ευκαιρίες ⓕ pl
  i·ses ef·ke·*ri*·es
equality ισότητα ⓕ i·*so*·ti·ta
equipment εξοπλισμός ⓜ ek·so·pliz·*mos*
escalator κυλιόμενες σκάλες ⓕ pl
  ki·li·o·me·nes *ska*·les
estate agency κτηματομεσιτικό γραφείο
  ⓝ kti·ma·to·me·si·ti·*ko* ghra·*fi*·o
euro ευρώ ⓝ ev·*ro*

Europe Ευρώπη ① ev·ro·pi
European Union Ευρωπαϊκή Ένωση ①
ev·ro·pa·i·ki e·no·si
euthanasia ευθανασία ① ef·tha·na·si·a
evening βράδι ⓝ vra·thi
every κάθε ka·the
everyone καθένας ⓜ ka·the·nas
everything καθετί ⓝ ka·the·ti
exactly ακριβώς a·kri·vos
example παράδειγμα ⓝ pa·ra·thigh·ma
excavation ανασκαφή ① a·na·ska·fi
excellent εξαιρετικός ek·se·re·ti·kos
excess (baggage) υπέρβαρο (φορτίο) ⓝ
i·per·va·ro (for·ti·o)
exchange συνάλλαγμα ⓝ si·na·lagh·ma
exchange v ανταλλάσσω a·da·la·so
exchange rate τιμή συναλλάγματος ①
ti·mi si·na·lagh·ma·tos
excluded εξαιρούμενος ek·se·ru·me·nos
exhaust (car) εξάτμιση ① ek·sat·mi·si
exhibition έκθεση ① ek·the·si
exhibit έκθεμα ⓝ ek·the·ma
exit έξοδος ① ek·so·thos
expensive ακριβός a·kri·vos
experience εμπειρία ① e·bi·ri·a
exploitation εκμετάλλευση ①
ek·me·ta·lef·si
export permit άδεια εξαγωγής ①
a·thi·a ek·sa·gho·yis
(by) express mail επείγον (ταχυδρομείο)
ⓝ e·pi·ghon (ta·hi·thro·mi·o)
extension (visa) παράταση ① pa·ra·ta·si
eye μάτι ⓝ ma·ti
eye drops σταγόνες ματιών ① pl
sta·gho·nes ma·ti·on
eyes μάτια ⓝ pl ma·tia

F

fabric ύφασμα ⓝ i·faz·ma
face πρόσωπο ⓝ pro·so·po
face cloth πετσέτα προσώπου ①
pet·se·ta pro·so·pu
factory εργοστάσιο ⓝ er·gho·sta·si·o
factory worker εργάτης εργοστασίου ⓜ
er·gha·tis er·gho·sta·si·u
εργάτρια εργοστασίου ①
er·gha·tri·a er·gho·sta·si·u
falcon γεράκι ⓝ ye·ra·ki

fall (autumn) φθινόπωρο ⓝ fthi·no·po·ro
fall (down) πτώση ① pto·si
family οικογένεια ① i·ko·ye·ni·a
family name επώνυμο ⓝ e·po·ni·mo
famous a φημισμένος fi·miz·me·nos
fan (machine) ανεμιστήρας ⓜ
a·ne·mi·sti·ras
fan (of sport) οπαδός ⓜ o·pa·thos
fanbelt λουρί ⓝ lu·ri
far μακριά ma·kri·a
fare εισιτήριο ① i·si·ti·ri·o
farm φάρμα ① far·ma
farmer γεωργός ⓜ&① ye·or·ghos
fashion μόδα ① mo·tha
fast a γρήγορος ghri·gho·ros
fat a παχύς pa·his
father πατέρας ⓜ pa·te·ras
father-in-law πεθερός ⓜ pe·the·ros
faucet βρύση ① vri·si
fault (someone's) λάθος ⓝ la·thos
faulty ελαττωματικός e·la·to·ma·ti·kos
fax machine μηχανή φαξ ① mi·kha·ni faks
February Φεβρουάριος ⓜ fev·ru·a·ri·os
feed v ταΐζω ta·i·zo
feel (touch) v αγγίζω a·gi·zo
feeling (physical) αφή ① a·fi
feelings αισθήματα ⓝ pl es·thi·ma·ta
female a θηλυκός thi·li·kos
fence φράχτης ⓜ frakh·tis
fencing (sport) ξιφομαχία ① ksi·fo·ma·hi·a
ferry φέρυ ⓝ fe·ri
festival φεστιβάλ ⓝ fe·sti·val
fever πυρετός ⓜ pi·re·tos
few λίγοι li·yi
fiancé αρραβωνιαστικός ⓜ
a·ra·vo·nia·sti·kos
fiancée αρραβωνιαστικιά ①
a·ra·vo·nia·sti·kia
fiction μυθοπλασία ① mi·tho·pla·si·a
fig σύκο ⓝ si·ko
fight πάλη ① pa·li
filigree (jewellery) φιλιγκράν ⓝ fi·li·gran
fill γεμίζω ye·mi·zo
fillet φιλέτο ⓝ fi·le·to
film (camera/cinema) φιλμ ⓝ film
film speed ταχύτητα φιλμ ① ta·hi·ti·ta film
filtered φιλτραρισμένος fil·tra·riz·me·nos
find βρίσκω vri·sko
fine (penalty) πρόστιμο ⓝ pros·ti·mo
fine (weather) a ωραίος o·re·os

finger δάκτυλο ⓝ *thak*·ti·lo
finish τελείωμα ⓝ te·*li*·o·ma
finish v τελειώνω te·li·*o*·no
Finland Φιλανδία ① fi·lan·*thi*·a
fire φωτιά ① fo·*tia*
firewood καυσόξυλα ⓝ pl kaf·*sok*·si·la
first a πρώτος *pro*·tos
first class πρώτη τάξη ① *pro*·ti *tak*·si
first-aid kit κυτίο πρώτων βοηθειών ⓝ ki·*ti*·o *pro*·ton vo·i·*thi*·on
first name μικρό όνομα ⓝ mi·*kro* o·no·na·ma
fish ψάρι ⓝ *psa*·ri
fishing ψάρεμα ⓝ *psa*·re·ma
fish monger ιχθυοπώλης/ιχθυοπώλισσα ⓜ/① ikh·thi·o·*po*·lis/ikh·thi·o·*po*·li·sa
fish shop ιχθυοπωλείο ⓝ ikh·thi·o·po·*li*·o
flag σημαία ① si·*me*·a
flannel φανέλλα (ύφασμα) ① fa·*ne*·la (*i*·faz·ma)
flashlight φλας ⓝ flas
flat a επίπεδος e·*pi*·pe·thos
flat (apartment) διαμέρισμα ⓝ thi·a·*me*·riz·ma
flea ψύλος ⓜ *psi*·los
fleamarket παζάρι ⓝ pa·*za*·ri
flight πτήση ① *pti*·si
flood πλημμύρα ① pli·*mi*·ra
floor πάτωμα ⓝ *pa*·to·ma
floor (storey) όροφος ⓜ *o*·ro·fos
florist ανθοπώλης/ανθοπώλισσα ⓜ/① an·tho·*po*·lis/an·tho·*po*·li·sa
flour αλεύρι ⓝ a·*lev*·ri
flower λουλούδι ⓝ lu·*lu*·thi
flu γρίπη ① *ghri*·pi
fly πετάω v pe·*ta*·o
foggy ομιχλώδης o·mi·*khlo*·this
folk (art) λαϊκός la·i·*kos*
food φαγητό ⓝ fa·yi·*to*
food supplies προμήθειες φαγητού ① pl pro·*mi*·thi·es fa·yi·*tu*
foot πόδι ⓝ *po*·thi
football (soccer) ποδόσφαιρο ⓝ po·*thos*·fe·ro
footpath πεζοδρόμιο ⓝ pe·zo·*thro*·mi·o
foreign ξένος *kse*·nos
forest δάσος ⓝ *tha*·sos
forever πάντα *pa*·da
forget ξεχνώ ksekh·*no*
forgive συγχωρώ sing·kho·*ro*
fork πιρούνι ⓝ pi·*ru*·ni

fortnight δεκαπενθήμερο ⓝ da·ka·pen·*thi*·me·ro
fortune teller μάντης/μάντισσα ⓜ/① *ma*·dis/*ma*·di·sa
foul φάουλ ⓝ *fa*·ul
foyer φουαγιέ ⓝ fu·a·*ye*
fragile εύθραυστος ef·*thraf*·stos
France Γαλλία ① gha·*li*·a
free (available) διαθέσιμος thi·a·*the*·si·mos
free (gratis) δωρεάν tho·re·*an*
free (not bound) ελεύθερος e·*lef*·the·ros
freeze παγώνω pa·*gho*·no
fresco φρέσκο ⓝ *fre*·sko
fresh φρέσκος *fre*·skos
Friday Παρασκευή ① pa·ra·ske·*vi*
fridge ψυγείο ⓝ psi·*yi*·o
fried τηγανισμένος ti·gha·niz·*me*·nos
friend φίλος/φίλη ⓜ/① *fi*·los/*fi*·li
from από a·*po*
frost παγωνιά ① pa·gho·*nia*
frozen παγωμένος pa·gho·*me*·nos
fruit φρούτα ⓝ pl *fru*·ta
fruit picking μάζεμα φρούτων ⓝ *ma*·ze·ma *fru*·ton
fry v τηγανίζω ti·gha·*ni*·zo
frying pan τηγάνι ⓝ ti·*gha*·ni
full γεμάτο ye·*ma*·to
full-time πλήρους απασχόλησης *pli*·rus a·pa·*skho*·li·sis
fun ο διασκεδαστικό thia·ske·tha·sti·*ko*
funeral κηδεία ① ki·*thi*·a
funny αστείος a·*sti*·os
furniture έπιπλα ⓝ pl *e*·pi·pla
future μέλλον ⓝ *me*·lon

G

game (football) ματς ⓝ mats
game (sport) παιγνίδι ⓝ pegh·*ni*·thi
garage γκαράζ ⓝ ga·*raz*
garbage σκουπίδια ⓝ pl sku·*pi*·thia
garbage can σκουπιδοτενεκές ⓜ sku·pi·tho·te·ne·*kes*
garden κήπος ⓜ *ki*·pos
gardener κηπουρός ⓜ&① ki·pu·*ros*
gardening κηπουρική ① ki·pu·ri·*ki*
garlic σκόρδο ⓝ *skor*·tho
gas (for cooking) πετρογκάζ ⓝ pe·tro·*ga*
gas (petrol) βενζίνα ① ven·*zi*·na

gas cartridge μπουκάλα γκαζιού ①
bu·ka·la ga·zi·u

gastroenteritis γαστροεντερίτιδα ①
gha·stro·e·de·ri·ti·tha

gate (airport etc) θύρα ① thi·ra

gauze αραχνούφαντος ⑩
a·rakh·no·i·fa·dos

gay γκέι ge·i

gelatine ζελατίνη ① ze·la·ti·ni

Germany Γερμανία ① yer·ma·ni·a

get παίρνω per·no

get off (transport) κατεβαίνω ka·te·ve·no

gift δώρο ⑩ tho·ro

gig παράσταση ① pa·ra·sta·si

gin τζιν ⑩ dzin

girl κορίτσι ⑩ ko·rit·si

girlfriend φιλενάδα ① fi·le·na·tha

give δίνω thi·no

given name μικρό όνομα ⑩
mi·kro o·no·ma

glandular fever αδενώδης πυρετός ⑩
a·the·no·this pi·re·tos

glass (drinking) ποτήρι ⑩ po·ti·ri

glasses (spectacles) γιαλιά ⑩ pl yia·lia

glove γάντι ⑩ ghan·ti

gloves γάντια ⑩ pl ghan·tia

glue κόλα ① ko·la

go πηγαίνω pi·ye·no

go out βγαίνω vye·no

go out with (a male) βγαίνω με κάποιον
vye·no me ka·pi·on

go out with (a female) βγαίνω με κάποια
vye·no me ka·pia

go shopping πάω για ψώνια
pa·o yia pso·nia

goal (score/point) γκολ ⑩ gol

goalkeeper τερματοφύλακας ⑩&①
ter·ma·to·fi·la·kas

goat κατοίκα ① kat·si·ka

god (general) θεός ⑩ the·os

goddess θεά ① the·a

goggles προστατευτικά γιαλιά ⑩ pl
pro·sta·tef·ti·ka yia·lia

goggles (swimming)
προστατευτικά γιαλιά για κολύμπι
⑩ pl pro·sta·tef·ti·ka yia·lia yia ko·li·bi

gold χρυσάφι ⑩ khri·sa·fi

golf ball μπαλάκι του γκολφ ⑩
ba·la·ki tu golf

golf course γήπεδο του γκολφ ⑩
yi·pe·tho tu golf

good καλός ka·los

government κυβέρνηση ① ki·ver·ni·si

gram γραμμάριο ⑩ ghra·ma·ri·o

granddaughter εγγονή ① e·go·ni

grandfather παπούς ⑩ pa·pus

grandmother γιαγιά ① yia·yia

grandson εγγονός ⑩ e·go·nos

grapefruit γκρέιπ φρούτ ⑩ gre·ip frut

grapes σταφύλια ⑩ pl sta·fi·lia

grass γρασίδι ⑩ ghra·si·thi

grateful ευγνώμων ev·ghno·mon

grave τάφος ⑩ ta·fos

gray γκρίζος gri·zos

great (fantastic) απίθανος a·pi·tha·nos

Greece Ελλάδα ① e·la·tha

Greek (language) Ελληνικά ⑩ pl
e·li·ni·ka

Greek (people) Έλληνες ⑩ pl e·li·nes

green πράσινος pra·si·nos

greengrocer
οπωροπώλης/οπωροπώλισσα ⑩/①
o·po·ro·po·lis/o·po·ro·po·li·sa

grey γκρίζος gri·zos

grilled ψημένο στη σχάρα
psi·me·no sti skha·ra

grocery οπωροπωλείο ⑩ o·po·ro·po·li·o

groundnut φυστίκι ⑩ fi·sti·ki

grow μεγαλώνω me·ga·lo·no

guaranteed εγγυημένος e·ghi·i·me·nos

guess v μαντεύω ma·de·vo

guesthouse ξενώνας ⑩ kse·no·nas

guide (audio) μαγνητοφωνημένες
οδηγίες ① pl magh·ni·to·fo·ni·me·nes
o·dhi·yi·es

guide (person) οδηγός ⑩&① o·thi·ghos

guidebook τουριστικός οδηγός ⑩
tu·ri·sti·kos o·thi·ghos

guide dog σκυλί οδηγός ⑩ ski·li o·thi·ghos

guided tour περιήγηση με οδηγό ①
pe·ri·i·yi·si me o·thi·gho

guilty a ένοχος e·no·khos

guitar κιθάρα ① ki·tha·ra

gum μαστίχα ① ma·sti·kha

gun όπλο ⑩ o·plo

gym (fitness) γυμναστήριο ⑩
yim·na·sti·ri·o

gymnastics γυμναστική ① yim·na·sti·ki

gynaecologist γυναικολόγος ⑩&①
yi·ne·ko·lo·ghos

gyros γύρος ⑩ yi·ros

H

hair μαλλιά ⓝ pl ma·*lia*

hairbrush βούρτσα μαλλιών ⓕ
vur·tsa ma·*lion*

haircut κούρεμα ⓝ *ku*·re·ma

hairdresser κομμωτής/κομμώτρια ⓜ/ⓕ
ko·mo·*tis*/ko·mo·tri·a

halal χαλάλ kha·*lal*

half μισό mi·*so*

hallucination παραίσθηση ⓕ pa·*res*·thi·si

ham ζαμπόν ⓝ za·*bon*

hammer ⓝ σφυρί sfi·*ri*

hammock αιώρα ⓕ e·*o*·ra

hand χέρι ⓝ *he*·ri

handbag τσάντα ⓕ *tsa*·da

handball χάντμπολ ⓝ *khand*·bol

handicrafts εργόχειρα ⓝ pl er·*gho*·hi·ra

handkerchief μαντήλι ⓝ ma·*di*·li

handlebars χειρολαβή ⓕ hi·ro·la·*vi*

handmade a χειροποίητο hi·ro·*pi*·i·to

handsome όμορφος *o*·mor·fos

happy ευτυχισμένος ef·ti·hiz·*me*·nos

harassment παρενόχληση ⓕ
pa·re·*no*·khli·si

harbour λιμάνι ⓝ li·*ma*·ni

hard (not soft) σκληρός skli·*ros*

hard-boiled σφιχτός sfikh·*tos*

hardware store κατάστημα σιδερικών ⓝ
ka·*ta*·sti·ma si·*the*·ri·*kon*

hash τουρλού ⓝ tur·*lu*

hat καπέλο ⓝ ka·*pe*·lo

have έχω e·*kho*

have a cold έχω κρύωμα e·kho kri·o·ma

have fun διασκεδάζω thia·ske·*tha*·zo

hay fever ρινική αλλεργία ⓕ
ri·ni·*ki* a·ler·*yi*·a

hazelnut φουντούκι ⓝ fu·*du*·ki

he αυτός ⓝ af·*tos*

head κεφάλι ⓝ ke·*fa*·li

headache πονοκέφαλος ⓜ po·no·*ke*·fa·los

headlights μεγάλα φώτα αυτοκινήτου
ⓝ pl me·*gha*·la *fo*·ta af·to·ki·*ni*·tu

health υγεία ⓕ i·*yi*·a

hear ακούω a·*ku*·o

hearing aid ακουστικά ⓝ pl a·ku·sti·*ka*

heart καρδιά ⓕ kar·*thia*

heart attack καρδιακή προσβολή ⓕ
kar·thi·a·*ki* proz·vo·*li*

heart condition καρδιακή κατάσταση ⓕ
kar·thi·a·*ki* ka·ta·sta·si

heat ζέστη ⓕ *ze*·sti

heated ζεσταμένος ze·sta·*me*·nos

heater σόμπα ⓕ *so*·ba

heating θέρμανση ⓕ *ther*·man·si

heatstroke θερμοπληξία ⓕ
ther·mo·plik·*si*·a

heatwave καύσωνας ⓜ *kaf*·so·nas

heavy βαρύς va·*ris*

Hellenistic Ελληνιστικός e·li·ni·sti·*kos*

helmet περικεφαλαία ⓕ pe·ri·ke·fa·*le*·a

help βοήθεια ⓕ vo·*i*·thi·a

help v βοηθώ vo·i·*tho*

hepatitis ηπατίτιδα ⓕ i·pa·*ti*·ti·tha

her (ownership/direct object) της tis

herb βότανο ⓝ *vo*·ta·no

herbalist βοτανολόγος ⓜ&ⓕ
vo·ta·no·*lo*·ghos

here εδώ e·*tho*

heroin ηρωίνη ⓕ i·ro·*i*·ni

herring ρέγκα ⓕ *re*·ga

high ψηλός psi·*los*

highchair καρέκλα για μωρά ⓕ
ka·*re*·kla yia mo·*ro*

high school γυμνάσιο ⓝ yim·*na*·si·o

highway δημόσιος δρόμος ⓜ
thi·mo·si·os *thro*·mos

hike v πεζοπορώ pe·zo·po·*ro*

hiking πεζοπορία ⓕ pe·zo·po·*ri*·a

hiking boots μπότες πεζοπορίας ⓕ pl
bo·tes pe·zo·po·*ri*·as

hiking route δρόμος πεζοπορίας ⓜ
thro·mos pe·zo·po·*ri*·as

hill λόφος ⓜ *lo*·fos

Hindu Ινδουιστής/Ινδουίστρια ⓜ/ⓕ
in·thu·i·*stis*/in·thu·i·stri·a

hire v ενοικιάζω e·ni·ki·*a*·zo

his (ownership/direct object) του tu

historical ιστορικός i·sto·ri·*kos*

history ιστορία ⓕ i·sto·*ri*·a

hitchhike v ταξιδεύω με ωτοστόπ
tak·si·*the*·vo me o·to·*stop*

HIV έιτς άι βι ⓝ e·idz a·i vi

hockey χόκι ⓝ *kho*·ki

holiday αργεία ⓕ ar·*yi*·a

holidays διακοπές ⓕ pl thi·a·ko·*pes*

home σπίτι ⓝ *spi*·ti

homeless άστεγος a·ste·ghos

homemaker νοικοκύρης/νοικοκυρά
ⓜ/ⓕ ni·ko·*ki*·ris/ni·ko·ki·*ra*

omeopathy ομοιοπαθητική ① o·mi·o·pa·thi·ti·ki
omosexual ομοφυλόφιλος ⓜ o·mo·fi·lo·fi·los
oney μέλι ⓝ me·li
oneymoon ταξίδι του μέλιτος ⓝ tak·si·thi tu me·li·tos
oroscope ωροσκόπιο ⓝ o·ro·sko·pi·o
orse άλογο ⓝ a·lo·gho
orse riding ιππασία ① i·pa·si·a
ospital νοσοκομείο ⓝ no·so·ki·mi·o
ospitality φιλοξενία ① fi·lok·se·ni·a
ot ζεστός ze·stos
otel ξενοδοχείο ⓝ kse·no·tho·hi·o
ot water ζεστό νερό ⓝ ze·sto ne·ro
our ώρα ① o·ra
ouse σπίτι ⓝ spi·ti
ousework νοικοκυριό ⓝ ni·ko·ki·rio
ow πώς pos
ow much πόσο po·so
ug ν αγκαλιάζω a·ga·lia·zo
uge πελώριος pe·lo·ri·os
umanities ανθρωπιστικές σπουδές ① pl an·thro·pi·sti·kes spu·thes
uman resources ανθρώπινο δυναμικό ⓝ an·thro·pi·no thi·na·mi·ko
uman rights ανθρώπινα δικαιώματα ⓝ pl an·thro·pi·na thi·ke·o·ma·ta
undred εκατό e·ka·to
ungry (be) ν πεινώ pi·no
unting κυνήγι ⓝ ki·ni·yi
urt ν πληγώνω pli·gho·no
usband σύζυγος ⓜ si·zi·ghos
ydrofoil ιπτάμενο φελφίνι ⓝ ip·ta·me·no thel·fi·ni

eγώ e·gho
e πάγος ⓜ pa·ghos
e cream παγωτό ⓝ pa·gho·to
e-cream parlour παγωπατζίδικο ⓝ pagho·ta·dzi·thi·ko
e hockey άις χόκεϊ ⓝ a·is kho·ke·i
con εικόνα ① i·ko·na
dentification (ID) ταυτότητα ① taf·to·ti·ta
diot βλάκας ⓜ vla·kas
— **av** an
ι άρρωστος a·ro·stos

---

immigration μετανάστευση ① ma·ta·na·stef·si
important σπουδαίος spu·the·os
impossible αδύνατος a·thi·na·tos
in μέσα me·sa
in a hurry βιαστικός via·sti·kos
in front of μπροστά bro·sta
included συμπεριλαμβανομένου si·ber·i·lam·va·no·me·nu
income tax φόρος εισοδήματος ⓜ fo·ros i·so·thi·ma·tos
India Ινδίες ① pl in·thi·es
indicator δείχτης ⓜ thikh·tis
indigestion δυσπεψία ① this·pep·si·a
indoor εσωτερικός e·so·te·ri·kos
industry βιομηχανία ① vi·o·mi·kha·ni·a
infection μόλυνση ① mo·lin·si
inflammation φλεγμονή ① flegh·mo·ni
inflation πληθωρισμός ⓜ pli·tho·riz·mos
influenza γρίπη ① ghri·pi
information πληροφορία ① pli·ro·fo·ri·a
ingredient συστατικό ⓝ si·sta·ti·ko
inject ν κάνω ένεση ka·no e·ne·si
injection ένεση ① e·ne·si
injured πληγωμένος pli·gho·me·nos
injury πληγή ① pli·yi
inner tube (bicycle) εσωτερική σαμπρέλλα ① e·so·te·ri·ki sa·bre·la
innocent a αθώος a·tho·os
insect έντομο ⓝ e·do·mo
inside μέσα me·sa
instructor δάσκαλος/δασκάλα ⓜ/① tha·ska·los/tha·ska·la
insurance ασφάλεια ① as·fa·li·a
interest (hobby) ενδιαφέρον ⓝ en·thia·fe·ron
interesting ενδιαφέρων en·thia·fe·ron
intermission διάλειμμα ⓝ thia·li·ma
international διεθνής thi·eth·nis
Internet διαδίκτυο ⓝ thi·a·thik·ti·o
Internet café καφενείο διαδικτύου ⓝ ka·fe·ni·o thi·a·thik·ti·u
interpreter διερμηνέας ⓜ&① thi·er·mi·ne·as
interview συνέντευξη ① si·ne·def·ksi
invite προσκαλώ pros·ka·lo
Ionian ιωνικός i·o·ni·kos
Ireland Ιρλανδία ① ir·lan·thi·a
iron (for clothes) σίδερο ⓝ si·the·ro
iris (eye) ίρις ① i·ris
island νησί ⓝ ni·si

Israel Ισραήλ ⓝ iz·ra·*il*
it αυτό af·*to*
IT πληροφορική ① pli·ro·fo·ri·*ki*
Italy Ιταλία ① i·ta·*li*·a
itch φαγούρα ① fa·*ghu*·ra
itemize αναλυτικός a·na·li·ti·*kos*
itinerary κατάλογος ⓜ ka·*ta*·lo·ghos
IUD (contraceptive)
ενδομήτριο αντισυλληπτικό ⓝ
en·tho·*mi*·tri·o a·di·si·lip·ti·*ko*

J

jacket ζακέτα ① za·*ke*·ta
jail φυλακή ① fi·la·*ki*
jam μαρμελάδα ① mar·me·*la*·tha
January Ιανουάριος ⓜ i·a·nu·*a*·ri·os
Japan Ιαπωνία ① i·a·po·*ni*·a
jar βάζο ⓝ *va*·zo
jaw σαγόνι ⓝ sa·*gho*·ni
jealous ζηλιάρης zi·*lia*·ris
jeans τζιν ⓝ dzin
jeep τζιπ ⓝ dzip
jellyfish μέδουσα ① *me*·thu·sa
jet lag τζετ λαγκ ⓝ dzet lag
jewellery κοσμήματα ⓝ pl koz·*mi*·ma·ta
Jewish Ιουδαϊκός/Ιουδαϊκή ⓜ/①
i·u·tha·i·*kos*/i·u·tha·i·*ki*
job δουλειά ① du·*lia*
jogging τρέξιμο ⓝ *trek*·si·mo
joke αστείο ⓝ a·*sti*·o
journalist δημοσιογράφος ⓜ&①
thi·mo·si·o·*ghra*·fos
journey ταξίδι ⓝ tak·si·*thi*
judge δικαστής ⓜ&① thi·ka·*stis*
jug κανάτα ① ka·*na*·ta
juice χυμός ⓜ hi·*mos*
July Ιούλιος ⓜ i·*u*·li·os
junta χούντα ① *khu*·da
jump v πηδώ pi·*tho*
jumper (sweater) πουλόβερ ⓝ pu·*lo*·ver
jumper leads καλώδια μπαταρίας ⓝ pl
ka·*lo*·thi·a ba·ta·*ri*·as
June Ιούνιος ⓜ i·*u*·ni·os

K

kebab shop σουβλατζίδικο ⓝ
suv·la·*tzi*·thi·ko
ketchup σάλτσα ① *salt*·sa

key κλειδί ⓝ kli·*thi*
keyboard πληκτρολόγιο ⓝ plik·tro·*lo*·yi
kick v κλωτσάω klot·*sa*·o
kidney νεφρό ⓝ ne·*fro*
kilo κιλό ⓝ ki·*lo*
kilogram χιλιόγραμμο ⓝ hi·*lio*·gra·mo
kilometre χιλιόμετρο ⓝ hi·*lio*·me·tro
kind (nice) καλός ka·*los*
kindergarten νηπιαγωγείο ⓝ
ni·pi·a·gho·*yi*·o
king βασιλιάς ⓜ va·si·*lias*
kiosk περίπτερο ⓝ pe·*rip*·te·ro
kiss φιλί ⓝ fi·*li*
kiss v φιλώ fi·*lo*
kitchen κουζίνα ① ku·*zi*·na
kiwifruit ακτινίδιο ⓝ ak·ti·*ni*·thi·o
knee γόνατο ⓝ *gho*·na·to
knife μαχαίρι ⓝ ma·*he*·ri
know v ξέρω *kse*·ro
kosher a κόσια *ko*·si·a

L

labourer εργάτης/εργάτρια ⓜ/①
er·*gha*·tis/er·*gha*·tri·a
labyrinth λαβύρινθος ⓜ la·*vi*·rin·thos
lace δαντέλα ① tha·*de*·la
lake λίμνη ① *li*·mni
lamb αρνί ⓝ ar·*ni*
land ξηρά ① ksi·*ra*
landlady νοικοκυρά ① ni·ko·ki·*ra*
landlord ιδιοκτήτης ⓜ i·thi·ok·*ti*·tis
language γλώσσα ① *ghlo*·sa
laptop λάπτοπ ⓝ *lap*·top
large μεγάλος me·*gha*·los
last (previous) προηγούμενος
pro·i·*ghu*·me·nos
last week περασμένη εβδομάδα
pe·raz·*me*·ni ev·tho·*ma*·tha
late καθυστερημένος ka·thi·ste·ri·*me*·no
later αργότερα ar·*gho*·te·ra
laugh v γελάω ye·*la*·o
launderette πλυντήριο ⓝ pli·*di*·ri·o
laundry (place) πλυντήριο ⓝ pli·*di*·ri·o
law νόμος ⓜ *no*·mos
law (study, profession) νομικά ⓝ no·mi·*ka*
lawyer δικηγόρος ⓜ&① thi·ki·*gho*·ros
laxative καθαρτικό ⓝ ka·thar·ti·*ko*
lazy τεμπέλης te·*be*·lis

ader αρχηγός ⓜ&ⓕ ar·hi·*ghos*
af φύλλο ⓝ *fi*·lo
arn μαθαίνω ma·*the*·no
ather δέρμα ⓝ *ther*·ma
cturer λέκτορας ⓜ&ⓕ *lek*·to·ras
dge ξέρες ⓕ pl *kse*·res
ek πράσο ⓝ *pra*·so
ft (direction) αριστερός ⓜ a·ri·ste·*ros*
ft-luggage (office) (γραφείο) φύλαξη αποσκευών ⓝ (gra·*fi*·o) *fi*·lak·si a·po·ske·*von*
ft-wing αριστερά ⓕ a·ri·ste·*ra*
g πόδι ⓝ *po*·thi
gal νόμιμος *no*·mi·mos
gislation νομοθεσία ⓕ no·mo·the·*si*·a
gume όσπρια ⓝ pl os·pri·a
mon λεμόνι ⓝ le·*mo*·ni
monade λεμονάδα ⓕ le·mo·*na*·tha
ns φακός ⓜ fa·*kos*
ent Σαρακοστή ⓕ sa·ra·ko·*sti*
ntil φακές ⓕ pl fa·*kes*
sbian λεσβία ⓕ les·*vi*·a
ss λιγότερο li·*gho*·te·ro
etter (mail) γράμμα ⓝ *ghra*·ma
ttuce μαρούλι ⓝ ma·*ru*·li
ar ψεύτης/ψεύτρα ⓜ/ⓕ *psef*·tis/*psef*·tra
brary βιβλιοθήκη ⓕ viv·li·o·*thi*·ki
cence άδεια ⓕ *a*·thi·a
cense plate number αριθμός κυκλοφορίας ⓜ a·rith·*mos* ki·klo·fo·ri·as
e (not stand) κείτομαι *ki*·to·me
fe ζωή ⓕ zo·*i*
fe jacket σωσίβιο ⓝ so·*si*·vi·o
ft (elevator) ασανσέρ ⓝ a·san·*ser*
ght φως ⓝ fos
ght (colour) a ανοιχτός a·nikh·*tos*
ght (weight) a ελαφρύς e·la·*fris*
ght bulb λάμπα ⓕ *lam*·pa
ght meter μετρητής ρεύματος ⓜ me·tri·*tis* rev·ma·tos
ghter αναπτήρας ⓜ a·nap·*ti*·ras
ke v μου αρέσει mu a·*re*·si
me (fruit) κιτρολέμονο ⓝ ki·tro·le·mo·no
nen (material) λινό ⓝ li·*no*
nen (sheets) σεντόνια ⓝ pl se·*do*·nia
p balm αλοιφή για τα χείλη ⓕ a·li·*fi* yia ta *hi*·li
ps χείλη ⓝ pl *hi*·li
pstick κραγιόν ⓝ kra·*yion*
quor store κάβα ⓕ *ka*·va

listen (to) ακούω a·*ku*·o
little (quantity) λίγο *li*·gho
little (size) μικρός mi·*kros*
live (somewhere) v μένω *me*·no
liver συκώτι ⓝ si·*ko*·ti
lizard σαύρα ⓕ *sav*·ra
local a τοπικός to·pi·*kos*
lock κλειδαριά ⓕ kli·tha·*ria*
lock v κλειδώνω kli·*tho*·no
locked κλειδωμένος kli·tho·*me*·nos
lollies καραμέλες ⓕ pl ka·ra·*me*·les
long a μακρύς ma·*kris*
look v κοιτάζω ki·*ta*·zo
look after προσέχω pro·*se*·kho
look for ψάχνω psakh·no
lookout παρατηρητήριο ⓝ pa·ra·ti·ri·*ti*·ri·o
loose a χαλαρός kha·la·*ros*
loose change ψιλά ⓝ pl psi·*la*
lose χάνω kha·no
lost a χαμένος kha·*me*·nos
lost property office γραφείο απωλεσθέντων αντικειμένων ⓝ gra·*fi*·o a·po·les·*the*·don a·di·ki·*me*·non
(a) lot πολύ po·*li*
lotion λοσιόν ⓝ lo·*sion*
loud δυνατός thi·na·tos
love αγάπη ⓕ a·*gha*·pi
love v αγαπώ a·gha·po
lover εραστής/ερωμένη ⓜ/ⓕ e·ra·*stis*/e·ro·*me*·ni
low a χαμηλός kha·mi·*los*
lubricant λιπαντικό ⓝ li·pa·di·*ko*
luck τύχη ⓕ *ti*·hi
lucky a τυχερός ti·he·*ros*
luggage αποσκευές ⓕ pl a·po·ske·*ves*
luggage lockers φύλαξη αποσκευών ⓕ *fi*·lak·si a·po·ske·*von*
luggage tag ταμπέλα αποσκευών ⓕ ta·*be*·la a·po·ske·*von*
lump εξόγκωμα ⓝ ek·so·gho·ma
lunch μεσημεριανό φαγητό ⓝ me·si·me·ria·no fa·yi·to
lung πνευμόνι ⓝ pnev·*mo*·ni
luxury πολυτέλεια ⓕ po·li·te·li·a

M

Macedonia Μακεδονία ⓕ ma·ke·tho·*ni*·a
machine μηχανή ⓕ mi·kha·*ni*
magazine περιοδικό ⓝ pe·ri·o·thi·*ko*

M

english–greek

223

mail (letters) αλληλογραφία ⓕ
a·li·lo·ghra·fi·a

mail (postal system) ταχυδρομείο ⓝ
ta·hi·thro·mi·o

mailbox ταχυδρομικό κουτί ⓝ
ta·hi·thro·mi·ko ku·ti

main κύριος ki·ri·os

main road κύριος δρόμος ⓜ
ki·ri·os thro·mos

make v κάνω ka·no

make-up καλλυντικά ⓝ pl ka·li·di·ka

mammogram μαμογράφημα ⓝ
ma·mo·ghra·fi·ma

man (male) άντρας ⓜ a·dras

manager διευθυντής/διευθύντρια ⓜ/ⓕ
thi·ef·thi·dis/thi·ef·thi·dri·a

mandarin μανταρίνι ⓝ ma·da·ri·ni

mango μάνγκο ⓝ man·go

manual work χειρωνακτική εργασία ⓕ
hi·ro·nak·ti·ki er·gha·si·a

many πολλοί po·li

map χάρτης ⓜ khar·tis

March Μάρτιος ⓜ mar·ti·os

margarine μαργαρίνη ⓕ mar·gha·ri·ni

marijuana μαριχουάνα ⓕ ma·ri·khu·a·na

marine reserve θαλάσσια αποθέματα
ⓝ pl tha·la·si·a a·po·the·ma·ta

marital status γαμήλια κατάσταση ⓕ
gha·mi·li·a ka·ta·sta·si

market αγορά ⓕ a·gho·ra

marmalade μαρμελάδα ⓕ mar·me·la·tha

marriage γάμος ⓜ gha·mos

married a παντρεμένος/παντρεμένη
ⓜ/ⓕ pa·dre·me·nos/pa·dre·me·ni

marry παντρεύομαι pa·dre·vo·me

martial arts πολεμική τέχνη ⓕ
po·le·mi·ki tekh·ni

mass (Catholic) λειτουργία ⓕ li·tur·yi·a

massage μασάζ ⓝ ma·saz

masseur μασέρ ⓜ ma·ser

masseuse μασέζ ⓕ ma·sez

mat χαλί ⓝ kha·li

match (sports) ματς ⓝ mats

matches (for lighting) σπίρτα ⓝ pl spir·ta

mattress στρώμα ⓝ stro·ma

May Μάιος ⓜ ma·i·os

maybe ίσως i·sos

mayonnaise μαγιονέζα ⓕ ma·yi·o·ne·za

mayor δήμαρχος ⓜ&ⓕ thi·mar·khos

me εγώ e·gho

meal γεύμα ⓝ yev·ma

measles ιλαρά ⓕ i·la·ra

meat κρέας ⓝ kre·as

mechanic μηχανικός ⓜ mi·kha·ni·kos

media μέσα ενημέρωσης ⓝ pl
me·sa e·ni·me·ro·sis

medicine (medication) φάρμακο ⓝ
far·ma·ko

medicine (study, profession) Ιατρική ⓕ
i·a·tri·ki

meditation αυτοσυγκέντρωση ⓕ
af·to·si·ge·dro·si

Mediterranean Μεσογειακός ⓜ
me·so·yi·a·kos

meet v συναντώ si·na·do

melon πεπόνι ⓝ pe·po·ni

member μέλος ⓝ me·los

menstruation περίοδος ⓕ pe·ri·o·thos

menu μενού ⓝ me·nu

message μήνυμα ⓝ mi·ni·ma

metal μέταλλο ⓝ me·ta·lo

metre μέτρο ⓝ me·tro

metro (train) μετρό ⓝ me·tro

metro station σταθμός μετρό ⓜ
stath·mos me·tro

microwave (oven)
φούρνος μικροκυμάτων ⓜ
fur·nos mi·kro·ki·ma·ton

midday (noon) μεσημέρι ⓝ me·si·me·ri

midnight μεσάνυχτα ⓝ pl me·sa·nikh·ta

migraine ημικρανία ⓕ i·mi·kra·ni·a

mild μαλακός ma·la·kos

military a στρατιωτικός stra·ti·o·ti·kos

military base στρατιωτική βάση ⓕ
stra·ti·o·ti·ki va·si

military service στρατιωτική θητεία ⓕ
stra·ti·o·ti·ki thi·ti·a

milk γάλα ⓝ gha·la

millimetre χιλιοστόμετρο ⓝ
hi·li·o·sto·me·tro

million εκατομμύριο ⓝ e·ka·to·mi·ri·o

mince κιμάς ⓜ ki·mas

mineral water μεταλλικό νερό ⓝ
me·ta·li·ko ne·ro

Minoan Μινωικός mi·no·i·kos

minute λεπτό ⓝ lep·to

mirror καθρέφτης ⓜ ka·thref·tis

miscarriage αποβολή ⓕ a·po·vo·li

Miss Δις ⓕ the·spi·nis

miss (feel absence of) μου λείπει mu li·

mistake λάθος ⓝ *la*·thos

nix v ανακατώνω a·na·ka·*to*·no

mixed plate ποικιλία ⓕ pi·ki·*li*·a

mobile phone κινητό ⓝ ki·ni·*to*

modem μόντεμ ⓝ *mo*·dem

modern μοντέρνος mo·*der*·nos

moisturiser υγραντική κρέμα ⓕ
i·ghra·di·*ki kre*·ma

monarchy μοναρχία ⓕ mo·nar·*hi*·a

monastery μοναστήρι ⓝ mo·na·*sti*·ri

Monday Δευτέρα ⓕ def·*te*·ra

money χρήματα ⓝ pl khri·*ma*·ta

monk καλόγερος ⓜ ka·*lo*·ye·ros

monk seal φώκια ⓕ *fo*·ki·a

month μήνας ⓜ *mi*·nas

monument μνημείο ⓝ mni·*mi*·o

moon φεγγάρι ⓝ fe·*ga*·ri

more περισσότερος pe·ri·*so*·te·ros

morning πρωί ⓝ pro·*i*

morning sickness πρωινή αδιαθεσία ⓕ
pro·i·*ni* a·thi·a·the·*si*·a

mosaic μωσαϊκό ⓝ mo·sa·i·*ko*

mosque τζαμί ⓝ dza·*mi*

mosquito κουνούπι ⓝ ku·*nu*·pi

mosquito coil φιδάκι για κουνούπια ⓝ
fi·*dha*·ki yia ku·*nu*·pia

mosquito net κουνουπιέρα ⓕ ku·nu·pi·*e*·ra

motel μοτέλ ⓝ mo·*tel*

mother μητέρα ⓕ mi·*te*·ra

mother-in-law πεθερά ⓕ pe·the·*ra*

motorbike μηχανάκι ⓝ mi·kha·*na*·ki

motorboat βενζινάκατος ⓕ
ven·zi·*na*·ka·tos

motorcycle μοτοσυκλέτα ⓕ mo·to·si·*kle*·ta

motorway (tollway) αυτοκινητόδρομος ⓜ
af·to·ki·ni·*to*·thro·mos

mountain βουνό ⓝ vu·*no*

mountain bike ποδήλατο για βουνό ⓝ
po·*thi*·la·to yia vu·*no*

mountain path μονοπάτι ⓝ mo·no·*pa*·ti

mountain range οροσειρά ⓕ o·ro·si·*ra*

mountaineering ορειβασία ⓕ o·ri·va·*si*·a

mouse ποντικός ⓜ po·di·*kos*

mouth στόμα ⓝ *sto*·ma

movie φιλμ ⓝ film

Mr Κος ⓜ *khi*·ri·os

Mrs Κα ⓕ *khi*·ri·a

Ms Δις the·spi·*nis*

mud λάσπη ⓕ *la*·spi

muesli δημητριακά ⓝ pl thi·mi·tri·a·*ka*

mum μαμά ⓕ ma·*ma*

mumps μαγουλάδες ⓜ pl ma·ghu·*la*·thes

murder δολοφονία ⓕ tho·lo·fo·*ni*·a

murder v δολοφονώ tho·lo·fo·*no*

muscle μυς ⓜ mis

museum μουσείο ⓝ mu·*si*·o

mushroom μανιτάρι ⓝ ma·ni·*ta*·ri

music μουσική ⓕ mu·si·*ki*

music shop κατάστημα μουσικών ειδών
ⓝ ka·*ta*·sti·ma mu·si·*kon* i·*thon*

musician μουσικός ⓜ&ⓕ mu·si·*kos*

Muslim Μουσουλμάνος/Μουσουλμάνα
ⓜ/ⓕ mu·sul·*ma*·nos/mu·sul·*ma*·na

mussel μύδι ⓝ *mi*·thi

mustard μουστάρδα ⓕ mus·*tar*·tha

mute a βουβός vu·*vos*

my μου mu

Mycenean Μυκηναϊκός ⓜ mi·ki·na·i·*kos*

mythological μυθολογικός
mi·tho·lo·yi·*kos*

N

nail clippers νυχοκόπτης ⓜ ni·kho·*kop*·tis

name όνομα ⓝ o·no·ma

napkin πετσετάκι ⓝ pet·se·*ta*·ki

nappy πάνα ⓕ *pa*·na

nappy rash ερεθισμός από πάνα ⓜ
e·re·thiz·*mos* a·po *pa*·na

national park εθνικό πάρκο ⓝ
eth·ni·*ko par*·ko

nationality εθνικότητα ⓕ eth·ni·*ko*·ti·ta

NATO NATO ⓝ *na*·to

nature φύση ⓕ *fi*·si

naturopathy φυσιοθεραπευτική ⓕ
fi·si·o·the·ra·pef·ti·*ki*

nausea ναυτία ⓕ naf·*ti*·a

near(by) κοντά ko·*da*

nearest το πιο κοντινό το pio ko·di·*no*

necessary αναγκαίο a·na·*ge*·o

neck λαιμός ⓜ le·*mos*

necklace κολιέ ⓝ ko·li·*e*

nectarine νεκταρίνι ⓝ nek·ta·*ri*·ni

need v χρειάζομαι khri·*a*·zo·me

needle (sewing) βελόνα ⓕ ve·*lo*·na

needle (syringe) σύριγκα ⓕ *si*·ri·ga

negative a αρνητικός ar·ni·ti·*kos*

neither κανένα από τα δύο
ka·*ne*·na a·po ta *thi*·o

net δίκτι ⓝ *thik*·ti

Netherlands Ολλανδία ⓕ o·lan·*thi*·a

never ποτέ po·*te*
new νέος *ne*·os
New Year's Day Πρωτοχρονιά ⓕ
pro·to·khro·*nia*
New Year's Eve Παραμονή Πρωτοχρονιάς
ⓕ pa·ra·mo·*ni* pro·to·khro·*nias*
New Zealand Νέα Ζηλανδία ⓕ
ne·a zi·lan·*thi*·a
news νέα ⓝ pl *ne*·a
newsagency πρακτορείο εφημερίδων ⓝ
prak·to·*ri*·o e·fi·me·*ri*·thon
newspaper εφημερίδα ⓕ e·fi·me·*ri*·tha
newsstand περίπτερο ⓝ pe·*rip*·te·ro
next a επόμενος e·*po*·me·nos
next to δίπλα *thi*·pla
nice ωραίος o·*re*·os
nickname παρατσούκλι ⓝ pa·rat·*su*·kli
night νύχτα ⓕ *nikh*·ta
night out ξενύχτι ⓝ kse·*nikh*·ti
nightclub νάιτ κλαμπ ⓝ *na*·it klab
no όχι o·hi
noisy θορυβώδης tho·ri·*vo*·this
none κανένας ka·*ne*·nas
nonsmoking μη καπνίζοντες
mi kap·*ni*·zo·des
noodles λαζάνια ⓝ pl la·*za*·nia
noon μεσημέρι ⓝ me·si·*me*·ri
north βοράς ⓝ vo·*ras*
Norway Νορβηγία ⓕ nor·vi·*yi*·a
nose μύτη ⓕ *mi*·ti
not όχι o·hi
notebook σημειωματάριο ⓝ
si·mi·o·ma·*ta*·ri·o
nothing τίποτε *ti*·po·te
November Νοέμβριος ⓜ no·*em*·vri·os
now τώρα *to*·ra
nuclear energy πυρηνική ενέργεια ⓕ
pi·ri·ni·*ki* e·*ner*·yi·a
nuclear testing πυρηνικές δοκιμές ⓕ pl
pi·ri·ni·*kes* tho·ki·*mes*
nuclear waste πυρηνικά απόβλητα ⓝ pl
pi·ri·ni·*ka* a·*pov*·li·ta
number αριθμός ⓜ a·rith·*mos*
numberplate αριθμός κυκλοφορίας ⓜ
a·rith·*mos* ki·klo·fo·*ri*·as
nun καλόγρια ⓕ ka·*lo*·ghri·a
nurse νοσοκόμος/νοσοκόμα ⓜ/ⓕ
no·so·*ko*·mos/no·so·*ko*·ma
nut καρύδι ⓝ ka·*ri*·thi

O

oats βρώμη ⓕ *vro*·mi
ocean ωκεανός ⓜ o·ke·a·*nos*
October Οκτώβριος ⓜ ok·*tov*·ri·os
off (food) μπαγιάτικος ba·*yia*·ti·kos
office γραφείο ⓝ ghra·*fi*·o
often συχνά sikh·*na*
oil (cooking) λάδι ⓝ *la*·thi
oil (car) λάδι αυτοκινήτου ⓝ
la·thi af·to·ki·*ni*·tu
old παλιός pa·*lios*
olive ελιά ⓕ e·*lia*
olive oil λάδι ελιάς ⓝ *la*·thi e·*lias*
Olympic Games Ολυμπιακοί Αγώνες ⓜ
o·li·bi·a·*ki* a·*gho*·nes
omelette ομελέτα ⓕ o·me·*le*·ta
on πάνω *pa*·no
on time στην ώρα stin o·ra
once μια φορά mia fo·*ra*
one ένα e·na
one-way (ticket) απλό εισιτήριο ⓝ
a·*plo* i·si·*ti*·ri·o
onion κρεμμύδι ⓝ kre·*mi*·thi
only μόνο *mo*·no
open a ανοιχτός a·nikh·*tos*
open v ανοίγω a·*ni*·gho
opening hours ώρες λειτουργίας ⓕ pl
o·res li·tur·*yi*·as
opera (house) όπερα ⓕ *o*·pe·ra
operation (medical) εγχείρηση ⓕ
eng·*hi*·ri·si
operator χειριστής/χειρίστρια ⓜ/ⓕ
hi·ri·*stis*/hi·*ri*·stri·a
opinion γνώμη ⓕ *ghno*·mi
opposite απέναντι a·*pe*·na·di
optometrist οφθαλμίατρος ⓜ&ⓕ
of·thal·*mi*·a·tros
or ή i
oracle χρησμός ⓜ khriz·*mos*
orange (fruit) πορτοκάλι ⓝ por·to·*ka*·li
orange (colour) a πορτοκαλής
por·to·ka·*lis*
orange juice χυμός πορτοκάλι ⓝ
hi·*mos* por·to·*ka*·li
orchestra ορχήστρα ⓕ or·*hi*·stra
orchid ορχιδέα ⓕ or·hi·*the*·a
order σειρά ⓕ si·*ra*
order v διατάζω thia·*ta*·zo

rdinary συνηθισμένος si·ni·thiz·*me*·nos
rgasm οργασμός or·*ghaz*·mos
riginal αρχικός ar·hi·kos
Orthodox Ορθόδοξος/Ορθόδοξη or·*tho*·thok·sos/or·*tho*·thok·si
ther άλλος *a*·los
Ottoman a Οθωμανικός o·tho·ma·ni·kos
ur μας mas
utside έξω ek·so
uzo ούζο *u*·zo
uzeria ουζερί u·ze·ri
varian cyst ωοθηκική κύστη o·o·thi·ti·ki *ki*·sti
vary ωοθήκη o·o·*thi*·ki
ven φούρνος *fur*·nos
vercoat πανωφόρι pa·no·*fo*·ri
verdose υπερβολική δόση i·per·vo·li·ki *tho*·si
vernight ολονυχτίς o·lo·nikh·*tis*
verseas εξωτερικό ek·so·te·ri·*ko*
we οφείλω o·*fi*·lo
wner κάτοχος *ka*·to·khos
xygen οξυγόνο ok·si·*gho*·no
yster στρείδι *stri*·thi
zone layer στρώμα όζοντος *stro*·ma o·zo·dos

acemaker βηματοδότης vi·ma·to·*tho*·tis
acifier (dummy) πιπίλα pi·*pi*·la
ackage πακέτο pa·*ke*·to
acket πακέτο pa·*ke*·to
adlock κλειδαριά kli·tha·*ria*
age σελίδα *se*·li·tha
ain πόνος *po*·nos
ainful οδυνηρός o·thi·ni·*ros*
ainkiller παυσίπονο paf·*si*·po·no
ainter ζωγράφος @&@ zo·*ghra*·fos
ainting (a work) πίνακας *pi*·na·kas
ainting (the art) ζωγραφική zo·ghra·fi·*ki*
air (couple) ζευγάρι zev·*gha*·ri
alace παλάτι pa·*la*·ti
an κατσαρόλα kat·sa·*ro*·la
ants (trousers) παντελόνι pa·de·*lo*·ni
anty liners πετσετάκι υγείας pet·se·*ta*·ki i·*yi*·as

pantyhose καλτσόν kal·*tson*
paper χαρτί khar·*ti*
papers (documents) πιστοποιητικά pl pi·sto·pi·i·ti·*ka*
paperwork προετοιμασία εγγράφων pro·e·ti·ma·*si*·a e·*gra*·fon
paprika πάπρικα *pa*·pri·ka
pap smear τεστ παπ test pap
paraplegic παραπληγικός pa·ra·pli·*yi*·kos
parcel δέμα *the*·ma
parents γονείς pl gho·*nis*
park πάρκο *par*·ko
park (a car) παρκάρω par·*ka*·ro
parliament Βουλή vu·*li*
part (component) εξάρτημα ek·*sar*·ti·ma
part-time μερική απασχόληση me·ri·*ki* a·pas·*kho*·li·si
party (night out) πάρτυ *par*·ti
party (politics) κόμμα *ko*·ma
pass v περνάω per·*na*·o
passenger επιβάτης/επιβάτισσα e·pi·*va*·tis/e·pi·*va*·ti·sa
passionfruit πάσιον φρουτ *pa*·si·on frut
passport διαβατήριο thia·va·*ti*·ri·o
passport number αριθμός διαβατηρίου a·rith·*mos* thia·va·*ti*·ri·u
past παρελθόν pa·rel·*thon*
pasta ζυμαρικά pl zi·ma·*ri*·ka
pastry φύλλο *fi*·lo
path μονοπάτι mo·no·*pa*·ti
patisserie ζαχαροπλαστείο za·kha·ro·pla·*sti*·o
pay v πληρώνω pli·*ro*·no
payment πληρωμή pli·ro·*mi*
pea αρακάς a·ra·*kas*
peace ειρήνη i·*ri*·ni
peach ροδάκινο ro·*tha*·ki·no
peak (mountain) κορυφή ko·ri·*fi*
peanut φυστίκι fi·*sti*·ki
pear αχλάδι a·*khla*·thi
pedal πετάλι pe·*ta*·li
pedestrian πεζός pe·*zos*
pelican πελεκάνος pe·le·*ka*·nos
pen (ballpoint) στυλό sti·*lo*
pencil μολύβι mo·*li*·vi
penis πέος *pe*·os
penknife σουγιάς su·*yias*
pension σύνταξη *si*·dak·si

pensioner συνταξιούχος/συνταξιούχα ⑩/① si·dak·si·*u*·khos/si·dak·si·*u*·kha
people κόσμος ⑩ *koz*·mos
pepper πιπέρι ⑪ pi·*pe*·ri
pepper (bell) πιπεριέρα ① pi·pe·*rie*·ra
per κάθε *ka*·the
per cent τοις εκατό tis e·ka·*to*
perfect a τέλειος *te*·li·os
performance απόδοση ① a·*po*·tho·si
perfume άρωμα ⑩ *a*·ro·ma
period pain πόνος περιόδου ⑩ *po*·nos pe·ri·*o*·thu
permission άδεια ① a·*thi*·a
permit άδεια ① a·*thi*·a
person πρόσωπο ⑪ *pro*·so·po
petition συλλογή υπογραφών ① si·lo·*yi* i·po·ghra·*fon*
petrol πετρέλαιο ⑪ pe·*tre*·le·o
petrol station πρατήριο βενζίνας ⑩ pra·*ti*·ri·o ven·*zi*·nas
pharmacist φαρμακοποιός ⑩&① far·ma·ko·pi·*os*
pharmacy φαρμακείο ⑪ far·ma·*ki*·o
phone book τηλεφωνικός κατάλογος ⑩ ti·le·fo·ni·kos ka·*ta*·lo·ghos
phone box δημόσιο τηλέφωνο ⑪ *thi*·mo·si·o ti·*le*·fo·no
phonecard τηλεκάρτα ① ti·le·*kar*·ta
photo φωτογραφία ① fo·to·gra·*fi*·a
photographer φωτογράφος ⑩&① fo·to·*ghra*·fos
photography φωτογραφική ① fo·to·ghra·fi·*ki*
phrasebook βιβλίο φράσεων ① viv·*li*·o *fra*·se·on
pickaxe τσεκούρι ⑪ tse·*ku*·ri
pickles τουρσί ⑪ tur·*si*
picnic πίκνικ ⑪ pik·*nik*
pie πίτα ① *pi*·ta
piece κομμάτι ⑪ ko·*ma*·ti
pig γουρούνι ⑪ ghu·*ru*·ni
pill χάπι ⑪ *kha*·pi
the pill το Χάπι ⑩ to *kha*·pi
pillow μαξιλάρι ⑪ mak·si·*la*·ri
pillowcase μαξιλαροθήκη ① mak·si·la·ro·*thi*·ki
pine πεύκο ⑪ *pef*·ko
pineapple ανανάς ⑩ a·na·*nas*
pink a ροζ roz
pistachio φυστίκι ⑪ fi·*sti*·ki

place θέση ① *the*·si
place of birth τόπος γεννήσεως ⑩ *to*·pos ye·*ni*·se·os
plane αεροπλάνο ⑪ a·e·ro·*pla*·no
planet πλανήτης ⑩ pla·*ni*·tis
plant φυτό ⑪ fi·*to*
plastic a πλαστικός pla·sti·kos
plate πιάτο ⑪ *pia*·to
plateau πλατό ⑪ pla·*to*
platform πλατφόρμα ① plat·*for*·ma
play (theatre) θεατρικό έργο ⑪ the·a·tri·ko *er*·gho
play cards v παίζω χαρτιά pe·zo khar·*tia*
play guitar v παίζω κιθάρα pe·zo ki·*tha*·ra
plug (bath) βούλωμα ⑪ *vu*·lo·ma
plug (electricity) βύσμα ⑪ *viz*·ma
plum δαμάσκηνο ⑪ tha·*ma*·ski·no
poached ποσέ po·*se*
pocket τσέπη ① *tse*·pi
pocket knife σουγιάς ⑩ su·*yias*
poetry ποίηση ① pi·*i*·si
point σημείο ⑪ si·*mi*·o
point v δείχνω *thi*·khno
poisonous δηλητηριώδης thi·li·ti·ri·*o*·this
police αστυνομία ① a·sti·no·*mi*·a
police officer (in city) αστυφύλακας/αστυφυλακίνα ⑩/① a·sti·*fi*·la·kas/a·sti·fi·la·*ki*·na
police officer (in country) χωροφύλακας/χωροφυλακίνα ⑩/① kho·ro·*fi*·la·kas/kho·ro·fi·la·*ki*·na
police station αστυνομικός σταθμός ⑩ a·sti·no·mi·kos stath·*mos*
policy πολιτική ① po·li·ti·*ki*
politician πολιτικός ⑩&① po·li·ti·*kos*
politics πολιτικά ⑩ pl po·li·ti·*ka*
pollen γύρη ① *yi*·ri
pollution ρύπανση ① *ri*·pan·si
pool (game) μπιλιάρδο ⑪ bi·*liar*·tho
pool (swimming) πισίνα ① pi·*si*·na
poor a φτωχός fto·khos
popular δημοφιλής thi·mo·fi·*lis*
pork χοιρινό ⑪ hi·ri·no
pork sausage χοιρινό λουκάνικο ⑪ hi·*ri*·no lu·*ka*·ni·ko
port (sea) λιμάνι ⑪ li·*ma*·ni
positive a θετικός the·ti·kos
possible δυνατός thi·na·tos
post v ταχυδρομώ ta·hi·*thro*·mo
postage ταχυδρομικά τέλη ⑪ pl ta·hi·*thro*·mi·*ka* te·li

postcard κάρτα ① kar·ta
postcode ταχυδρομικός τομέας ⓜ
ta·hi·thro·mi·kos to·me·as
post office ταχυδρομείο ⓝ
ta·hi·thro·mi·o
poster πόστερ ⓝ po·ster
pot (ceramics) κεραμικό ⓝ ke·ra·mi·ko
pot (dope) μαριχουάνα ① ma·ri·khu·a·na
potato πατάτα ① pa·ta·ta
pottery αγγειοπλαστική ① a·gi·o·pla·sti·ki
pound (money) λίρα ① li·ra
pound (weight) λίτρα ① li·tra
poverty φτώχεια ① fto·hia
powder πούδρα ① pu·thra
power δύναμη ① thi·na·mi
prawn γαρίδα ① gha·ri·tha
prayer προσευχή ① pro·sef·hi
prayer book βιβλίο προσευχών ⓝ
viv·li·o pro·sef·khon
prefer προτιμώ pro·ti·mo
pregnancy test kit τεστ εγκυμοσύνης ⓝ
test e·gi·mo·si·nis
pregnant a έγκυος e·gi·os
prehistoric προϊστορικός pro·i·sto·ri·kos
premenstrual tension ένταση πριν την
περίοδο ① e·da·si pri tin pe·ri·o·tho
prepare προετοιμάζω pro·e·ti·ma·zo
prescription συνταγή ① si·da·yi
present (gift) δώρο ⓝ tho·ro
present (time) παρόν ⓝ pa·ron
president πρόεδρος ⓜ&① pro·e·thros
pressure πίεση ① pi·e·si
pretty όμορφος o·mor·fos
price τιμή ① ti·mi
priest παπάς ⓜ pa·pas
prime minister πρωθυπουργός ⓜ&①
pro·thi·pur·ghos
printer (computer) εκτυπωτής ⓜ
ek·ti·po·tis
prison φυλακή ① fi·la·ki
prisoner φυλακισμένος ⓜ fi·la·kiz·me·nos
private a ιδιωτικός i·thi·o·ti·kos
problem πρόβλημα ⓝ pro·vli·ma
produce v παράγω pa·ra·gho
profit κέρδος ⓝ ker·thos
program πρόγραμμα ⓝ pro·gra·ma
projector προβολέας ⓜ pro·vo·le·as
promise v υπόσχομαι i·pos·kho·me
prostitute πόρνη ① por·ni
protect προστατεύω pro·sta·te·vo

protected (species) προστατευόμενα
(είδη) ⓝ pl pro·sta·te·vo·me·na (i·thi)
protest διαμαρτυρία ① thi·a·mar·ti·ri·a
protest v διαμαρτύρομαι
thi·a·mar·ti·ro·me
provisions προμήθειες ① pl pro·mi·thi·es
prune (dried fruit) ξηρό δαμάσκηνο ⓝ
ksi·ro tha·ma·ski·no
pub (bar) μπυραρία ① bi·ra·ri·a
public gardens εθνικός κήπος ⓜ
eth·ni·kos ki·pos
public relations δημόσιες σχέσεις ① pl
thi·mo·si·es she·sis
public telephone δημόσιο τηλέφωνο ⓝ
thi·mo·si·o ti·le·fo·no
public toilet δημόσια αποχωρητήρια ⓝ pl
thi·mo·si·a a·po·kho·ri·ti·ria
pulse σφυγμός ⓜ sfigh·mos
pull v τραβάω tra·va·o
pump τρόμπα ① tro·ba
pumpkin κολοκύθι ⓝ ko·lo·ki·thi
puncture τρύπα ρόδας ① tri·pa ro·thas
punch (ticket) v ακυρώνω a·ki·ro·no
pure a καθαρός ka·tha·ros
purple μαβής ma·vis
purse πορτοφόλι ⓝ por·to·fo·li
push v σπρώχνω sprokh·no
put βάζω va·zo

Q

quadriplegic παραπληγικός ⓜ
pa·ra·pli·yi·kos
qualifications προσόντα ⓝ pl pro·so·da
quality ποιότητα ① pi·o·ti·ta
quarantine καραντίνα ① ka·ra·di·na
quarter τέταρτο ⓝ te·tar·to
queen βασίλισσα ① va·si·li·sa
question ερώτηση ① e·ro·ti·si
queue ουρά ① u·ra
quick a γρήγορος ghri·gho·ros
quiet a ήσυχος i·si·khos
quit v παραιτούμαι pa·re·tu·me

R

rabies λύσσα ① li·sa
rabbit κουνέλι ⓝ ku·ne·li
race (sport) ιπποδρομία ① i·po·thro·mi·a

racetrack ιππόδρομος ⓜ i-po-thro-mos
racing bike ποδήλατο κούρσας ⓝ po-thi-la-to kur-sas
racism ρατσισμός ⓜ rat-sis-mos
racquet ρακέτα ⓕ ra-ke-ta
radiator ψυγείο αυτοκινήτου ⓝ psi-yi-o af-to-ki-ni-tu
radio ράδιο ⓝ ra-thi-o
radish ραπάνι ⓝ ra-pa-ni
railway station σιδηροδρομικός σταθμός ⓜ si-thi-ro-thro-mi-kos stath-mos
rain ⓕ βροχή vro-hi
raincoat αδιάβροχο ⓐ a-thi-av-ro-ho
raisin σταφίδα ⓕ sta-fi-tha
rally ράλι ⓝ ra-li
rape βιασμός ⓜ vi-az-mos
rape v βιάζω vi-a-zo
rare (uncommon) σπάνιος spa-ni-os
rare (food) μισοψημένο ⓝ mi-so-psi-me-no
rash εξάνθημα ⓝ ek-san-thi-ma
raspberry βατόμουρο ⓝ va-to-mu-ro
rat ποντίκι ⓝ po-di-ki
raw ωμός o-mos
razor ξυριστική μηχανή ⓕ ksi-ri-sti-ki mi-kha-ni
razor blade ξυράφι ⓝ ksi-ra-fi
read διαβάζω v thia-va-zo
reading διάβασμα ⓝ thia-vaz-ma
ready έτοιμος e-ti-mos
real estate agent κτηματομεσίτης/κτηματομεσίτρια ⓜ/ⓕ kti-ma-to-me-si-tis/kti-ma-to-me-si-tri-a
realistic ρεαλιστικός re-a-li-sti-kos
rear (seat etc) οπίσθιος o-pi-sthi-os
reason αιτία ⓕ e-ti-a
receipt απόδειξη ⓕ a-po-thik-si
recently πρόσφατα pros-fa-ta
recommend συνιστώ si-ni-sto
record v καταγράφω ka-ta-ghra-fo
recording καταγραφή ⓕ ka-ta-ghra-fi
recyclable ανακυκλώσιμο a-na-ki-klo-si-mo
recycle ανακυκλώνω a-na-ki-klo-no
red κόκκινο ko-ki-no
referee διαιτητής/διαιτήτρια ⓜ/ⓕ thi-e-ti-tis/thi-e-ti-tri-a
reference (letter) συστατική επιστολή ⓕ si-sta-ti-ki e-pi-sto-li
reflexology αντανακλαστική ⓕ a-da-na-kla-sti-ki
refrigerator ψυγείο ⓝ psi-yi-o

refugee πρόσφυγας ⓜ&ⓕ pros-fi-ghas
refund ⓕ επιστροφή χρημάτων e-pi-stro-fi khri-ma-ton
refuse v αρνούμαι ar-nu-me
regional τοπικός to-pi-kos
(by) registered mail συστημένο sis-ti-me-no
rehydration salts υδρωτικά άλατα ⓝ pl i-thro-ti-ka a-la-ta
relationship σχέση ⓕ she-si
relax v χαλαρώνω kha-la-ro-no
relic κειμήλιο ⓝ ki-mi-li-o
religion θρησκεία ⓕ thri-ski-a
religious a θρήσκος thri-skos
remote a απόμακρος a-po-mak-ros
remote control τηλεκατεύθυνση ⓕ ti-le-ka-tef-thin-si
rent v ενοικιάζω e-ni-ki-a-zo
repair v επισκευάζω e-pi-ske-va-zo
republic δημοκρατία ⓕ thi-mo-kra-ti-a
reservation (booking) κράτηση ⓕ kra-ti-si
residency permit άδεια παραμονής ⓕ a-thi-a pa-ra-mo-nis
rest v ξεκουράζομαι kse-ku-ra-zo-me
restaurant εστιατόριο ⓝ e-sti-a-to-ri-o
restriction περιορισμός ⓜ pe-ri-o-riz-mos
résumé (CV) βιογραφικό σημείωμα ⓝ vi-o-ghra-fi-ko si-mi-o-ma
retired συνταξιούχος si-dak-si-u-khos
retsina (drink) ρετσίνα ⓕ ret-si-na
return (come back) v επιστρέφω e-pi-stre-fo
return (ticket) εισιτήριο μετ' επιστροφής ⓝ i-si-ti-ri-o me-te-pi-stro-fis
review αναθεώρηση ⓕ a-na-the-o-ri-si
rhythm ρυθμός ⓜ rith-mos
rib πλευρό ⓝ plev-ro
rice ρύζι ⓝ ri-zi
rich (wealthy) πλούσιος plu-si-os
ride (horse) ιππασία ⓕ i-pa-si-a
ride (horse) v ιππεύω i-pe-vo
right (correct) a σωστός so-stos
right (direction) δεξιός thek-si-os
right-wing δεξιά ⓕ thek-si-a
ring (jewellery) δαχτυλίδι ⓝ thakh-ti-li-thi
ring (phone) v τηλεφωνώ ti-le-fo-na-o
rip-off γδάρσιμο ⓝ gthar-si-mo
risk ρίσκο ⓝ ri-sko
river ποτάμι ⓝ po-ta-mi
road δρόμος ⓜ thro-mos

road map οδικός χάρτης ⓜ o·thi·kos khar·tis

roasted ψημένος psi·me·nos

rob ληστεύω li·ste·vo

rock βράχος ⓜ vra·khos

rock climbing αναρρίχηση ⓕ a·na·ri·hi·si

rock music μουσική ροκ ⓕ mu·si·ki rok

rockfalls κατολίσθηση ⓕ ka·to·lis·thi·si

rock group μπάντα ροκ ⓕ ba·da rok

rockmelon πεπόνι ⓝ pe·po·ni

roll (bread) ψωμάκι ⓝ pso·ma·ki

rollerblading τροχοπέδιλο ⓝ tro·kho·pe·thi·lo

Roman Ρωμαϊκός ro·ma·i·kos

romantic ρομαντικός ro·ma·di·kos

room δωμάτιο ⓝ tho·ma·ti·o

room number αριθμός δωματίου ⓜ a·rith·mos tho·ma·ti·u

rope σκοινί ⓝ ski·ni

round a στρογγυλός stro·gi·los

roundabout κυκλική διασταύρωση ⓕ ki·kli·ki thi·a·stav·ro·si

route δρόμος ⓜ thro·mos

rowing κωπηλασία ⓕ ko·pi·la·si·a

rubbish σκουπίδια ⓝ pl sku·pi·thia

rubella ερυθρά ⓕ e·ri·thra

rug χαλί ⓝ kha·li

rugby ράγκμπυ ⓝ rag·bi

ruins ερρίπια ⓝ pl e·ri·pi·a

rule κανόνας ka·no·nas

rum ρούμι ⓝ ru·mi

run v τρέχω tre·kho

running τρέξιμο ⓝ trek·si·mo

runny nose τρέξιμο μύτης ⓝ trek·si·mo mi·tis

S

sad λυπημένος li·pi·me·nos

saddle σέλλα ⓕ se·la

safe ασφάλεια ⓕ as·fa·li·a

safe a ασφαλής as·fa·lis

safe sex ασφαλές σεξ ⓝ as·fa·les seks

saint άγιος/αγία ⓜ/ⓕ a·yi·os/a·yi·a

sailing ιστίο ⓝ i·sti·o

salad σαλάτα ⓕ sa·la·ta

salami σαλάμι ⓝ sa·la·mi

salary μισθός ⓜ mis·thos

sale πώληση ⓕ po·li·si

sales tax φόρος πώλησης ⓜ fo·ros po·li·sis

salmon σολομός ⓜ so·lo·mos

salt αλάτι ⓝ a·la·ti

same ίδιος i·thi·os

sand άμμος a·mos

sandal σανταλι ⓝ sa·da·li

sanitary napkin πετσετάκι υγείας ⓝ pet·se·ta·ki i·yi·as

sardine σαρδέλα ⓕ sar·the·la

Saturday Σάββατο ⓝ sa·va·to

sauce σάλτσα ⓕ sal·tsa

saucepan κατσαρόλα ⓕ kat·sa·ro·la

sauna σάουνα ⓕ sa·u·na

sausage λουκάνικο ⓝ lu·ka·ni·ko

savoury πικάντικος pi·ka·di·kos

say v λέγω le·gho

scalp κρανίο ⓝ kra·ni·o

scarf κασκόλ ⓝ ka·skol

school σχολείο ⓝ skho·li·o

science επιστήμη ⓕ e·pi·sti·mi

scientist επιστήμονας ⓜ&ⓕ e·pi·sti·mo·nas

scissors ψαλίδι ⓝ psa·li·thi

score v σκοράρω sko·ra·ro

scoreboard πίνακας σκορ ⓜ pi·na·kas skor

Scotland Σκωτία ⓕ sko·ti·a

scrambled χτυπητά (αβγά) khti·pi·ta (av·gha)

sculpture γλυπτική ⓕ ghlip·ti·ki

sea θάλασσα ⓕ tha·la·sa

seafood θαλασσινά ⓝ pl tha·la·si·na

(be) seasick πάσχει από ναυτία pa·shi a·po naf·ti·a

seasickness ναυτία ⓕ naf·ti·a

seaside παραλία ⓕ pa·ra·li·a

season εποχή ⓕ e·po·hi

seat (place) θέση ⓕ the·si

seatbelt ζώνη καθίσματος ⓕ zo·ni ka·thiz·ma·tos

sea turtle θαλάσσια χελώνα ⓕ tha·la·si·a he·lo·na

sea urchin αχινός ⓜ a·hi·nos

second δευτερόλεπτο ⓝ thef·te·ro·lep·to

second a δεύτερος thef·te·ros

second class δεύτερη τάξη ⓕ thef·te·ri tak·si

second-hand a μεταχειρισμένος me·ta·hi·riz·me·nos

second-hand shop παλαιοπωλείο ⓝ pa·le·o·po·li·o

secretary γραμματέας ⓜ&ⓕ ghra·ma·te·as

see βλέπω *vle·po*

self-employed a ιδιωτικός υπάλληλος i·thi·o·ti·kos i·pa·li·los

selfish ατομιστής a·to·mi·stis

self-service ⓝ σελφ σέρβις self *ser·*vis

sell v πουλάω pu·*la·o*

seminar σεμινάριο ⓝ se·mi·*na·*ri·o

send στέλνω *stel·*no

sensible συνετός si·ne·*tos*

sensual αισθησιακός e·sthi·si·a·*kos*

separate a χωριστός kho·ri·*stos*

September Σεπτέμβριος ⓜ sep·*tem·*vri·os

serious σοβαρός so·va·*ros*

service υπηρεσία ⓕ i·pi·re·*si·*a

service charge τιμή εξυπηρέτησης ⓕ ti·*mi* ek·si·pi·re·ti·sis

service station βενζινάδικο ⓝ ven·zi·*na·*thi·ko

serviette πετσέτα φαγητού ⓕ pet·*se·*ta fa·yi·*tu*

several a μερικοί me·ri·*ki*

sew v ράβω *ra·*vo

sex (intercourse) σεξ ⓝ seks

sexism σεξισμός ⓜ sek·siz·*mos*

sexy σέξυ *sek·*si

shade σκιά ⓕ ski·*a*

shadow σκιά ⓕ ski·*a*

shampoo σαμπουάν ⓝ sam·pu·*an*

shape σχήμα ⓝ *shi·*ma

share (with) μοιράζομαι mi·*ra·*zo·me

shave v ξυρίζω ksi·*ri·*zo

she αυτή af·*ti*

sheep πρόβατο ⓝ *pro·*va·to

sheet (bed) σεντόνι ⓝ se·*do·*ni

shelf ράφι ⓝ *ra·*fi

shiatsu σιάτσου ⓝ si·*at·*su

shield ασπίδα ⓕ as·*pi·*tha

shingles (illness) έρπης ⓜ *er·*pis

ship πλοίο ⓝ *pli·*o

shirt πουκάμισο ⓝ pu·*ka·*mi·so

shoe παπούτσι ⓝ pa·*put·*si

shoes παπούτσια ⓝ pl pa·*put·*si·a

shoe shop υποδηματοποιείο ⓝ i·po·thi·ma·to·pi·*i·*o

shoot v πυροβολώ pi·ro·vo·*lo*

shop μαγαζί ⓝ ma·gha·*zi*

shop v ψωνίζω pso·*ni·*zo

shopping ψώνια ⓝ pl pso·nia

shopping centre αγορά ⓕ a·gho·*ra*

short (height) κοντός ko·*dos*

shortage έλλειψη ⓕ *e·*lip·si

shorts σορτς ⓝ sorts

shoulder ώμος ⓜ *o·*mos

shout v φωνάζω fo·*na·*zo

show επίδειξη ⓕ e·*pi·*thik·si

show v δείχνω *thikh·*no

shower ντους ⓝ duz

shrine βωμός ⓜ vo·*mos*

shut a κλειστός kli·*stos*

shy a ντροπαλός dro·pa·*los*

sick a άρρωστος *a·*ro·stos

side πλευρά ⓕ plev·*ra*

siesta μεσημεριανή ανάπαυση ⓕ me·si·me·ria·*ni* a·*na*·paf·si

sign πινακίδα ⓕ pi·na·*ki·*tha

signature υπογραφή ⓕ i·po·ghra·*fi*

silk μετάξι ⓝ me·*tak·*si

silver ασήμι ⓝ a·*si·*mi

similar παρόμοιος pa·*ro·*mi·os

simple απλός a·*plos*

since (May) από (το Μάη) a·*po* (to *ma·*i)

sing v τραγουδώ tra·ghu·*tho*

Singapore Σιγγαπούρη ⓕ sing·ga·*pu·*ri

singer τραγουδιστής/τραγουδίστρια ⓜ/ⓕ tra·ghu·thi·*stis*/tra·ghu·*thi·*stri·a

single (person) a εργένης/εργένισσα ⓜ/ⓕ er·*ye·*nis/er·*ye·*ni·sa

single room μονό δωμάτιο ⓝ mo·*no* tho·*ma·*tio

singlet φανελάκι ⓝ fa·ne·*la·*ki

sister αδερφή ⓕ a·ther·*fi*

sit κάθομαι *ka·*tho·me

size μέγεθος ⓝ *me·*ye·thos

skate v παγοδρομώ pa·gho·thro·*mo*

skateboarding πατίνι ⓝ pa·*ti·*ni

ski v κάνω σκι *ka·*no ski

skiing σκι ⓝ ski

skim milk άπαχο γάλα ⓝ a·pa·kho *gha·*la

skin δέρμα ⓝ *ther·*ma

skirt φούστα ⓕ *fu·*sta

skull κρανίο ⓝ kra·*ni·*o

sky ουρανός ⓜ u·ra·*nos*

sleep v κοιμάμαι ki·*ma·*me

sleeping bag σλίπινγκ μπαγκ ⓝ *sli·*ping bag

sleeping berth κρεββατάκι ⓝ kre·va·*ta·*ki

sleeping car βαγκόν λι ⓝ va·gon li
sleeping pills υπνωτικά χάπια ⓝ pl ip·no·ti·ka kha·pia
sleepy νυσταγμένος nis·tagh·me·nos
slice φέτα ① fe·ta
slide (film) σλάιντ ⓝ sla·id
slow a αργός ar·ghos
slowly αργά ar·gha
small μικρός mi·kros
smaller μικρότερος mi·kro·te·ros
smallest ο μικρότερος o mi·kro·te·ros
smell μυρουδιά ① mi·ru·thia
smile v χαμογελώ kha·mo·ye·lo
smog νέφος ⓝ ne·fos
smoke v καπνίζω kap·ni·zo
snack μικρό γεύμα ⓝ mi·kro ghev·ma
snail σαλιγκάρι ⓝ sa·li·ga·ri
snake φίδι ⓝ fi·dhi
snorkelling υπόγεια κατάδυση ① i·po·yi·a ka·ta·thi·si
snow χιόνι ⓝ hio·ni
snowboarding σκι με χιονοσανίδα ⓝ ski me hio·no·sa·ni·tha
snow pea αρακάς ⓝ a·ra·kas
soap σαπούνι ⓝ sa·pu·ni
soap opera αισθηματικό σίριαλ ⓝ es·thi·ma·ti·ko si·ri·al
soccer ποδόσφαιρο ⓝ po·thos·fe·ro
social welfare κοινωνική πρόνοια ① ki·no·ni·ki pro·ni·a
socialist σοσιαλιστής/σοσιαλίστρια ⓜ/① so·si·a·li·stis/so·si·a·li·stri·a
sock κάλτσα ① kal·tsa
socks κάλτσες ① pl kal·tses
soft drink αναψυκτικό ⓝ a·nap·sik·ti·ko
soft-boiled μελάτο ⓝ me·la·to
soldier στρατιώτης ⓜ stra·ti·o·tis
some μερικοί me·ri·ki
someone κάποιος ka·pi·os
something κάτι ka·ti
sometimes μερικές φορές me·ri·kes fo·res
son γιος ⓜ yios
song τραγούδι ⓝ tra·ghu·thi
soon σύντομα si·do·ma
sore a πονεμένος po·ne·me·nos
soup σούπα ① su·pa
sour cream ξινή κρέμα ① ksi·ni kre·ma
south νότος ⓜ no·tos
souvenir σουβενίρ ⓝ su·ve·nir
souvenir shop κατάστημα για σουβενίρ ⓝ ka·ta·sti·ma yia su·ve·nir

souvlaki σουβλάκι ⓝ suv·la·ki
soy milk γάλα σόγια ① gha·la so·yi·a
soy sauce σάλτσα ① σόγια sal·tsa so·yi·a
space διάστημα ① thi·a·sti·ma
Spain Ισπανία ① i·spa·ni·a
sparkling wine σαμπάνια ① sam·pa·ni·a
speak μιλάω mi·la·o
special a ειδικός i·thi·kos
spear καμάκι ⓝ ka·ma·ki
specialist σπεσιαλίστας/σπεσιαλίστρια ⓜ/① spe·si·a·li·stas/spe·si·a·li·stri·a
speed (velocity) ταχύτητα ① ta·hi·ti·ta
speed limit όριο ταχύτητας ⓝ o·ri·o ta·hi·ti·tas
speedometer ταχύμετρο ⓝ ta·hi·me·tro
spider αράχνη ① a·rakh·ni
spinach σπανάκι ⓝ spa·na·ki
spoiled (food) χαλασμένος kha·laz·me·nos
spoke ακτίνα τροχού ⓝ ak·ti·na tro·khu
spoon κουτάλι ⓝ ku·ta·li
sport σπορ ⓝ spor
sportsman σπόρτσμαν ⓜ sports·man
sportswoman σπορτσγούμαν ① sports·ghu·man
sports store κατάστημα των σπορ ⓝ ka·ta·sti·ma ton spor
sprain στραμπούλισμα ⓝ stra·bu·liz·ma
spring (coil) ελατήριο ⓝ e·la·ti·ri·o
spring (season) άνοιξη ① a·nik·si
square (town) πλατεία ① pla·ti·a
spray σπρέι ⓝ spre·i
stadium στάδιο ⓝ sta·thi·o
stairway σκάλα ① ska·la
stale μπαγιάτικος ba·yia·ti·kos
stamp γραμματόσημο ⓝ ghra·ma·to·si·mo
stand-by ticket εισιτήριο σταντ μπάι ⓝ i·si·ti·ri·o stand ba·i
star (sky) αστέρι ⓝ a·ste·ri
start αρχή ① ar·hi
start v αρχίζω ar·hi·zo
station σταθμός ⓜ stath·mos
stationer's χαρτοπωλείο ⓝ khar·to·po·li·o
statue άγαλμα ① a·ghal·ma
stay μένω me·no
steak (beef) μπριζόλα ① bri·zo·la
steal κλέβω kle·vo
steep απόκρημνος a·po·krim·nos
step βήμα ⓝ vi·ma
stereo στέρεο ⓝ ste·re·o
still water νερό χωρίς ανθρακικό ⓝ ne·ro kho·ris an·thra·ki·ko

S

english–greek

233

sting v τσιμπάω tsi-*ba*-o
stock (food) ζουμί ⓝ zu-*mi*
stockings καλτσόν ⓝ kal-*tson*
stolen κλεμμένο kle-*me*-no
stomach στομάχι ⓝ sto-*ma*-hi
stomachache στομαχόπονος ⓜ sto-ma-*kho*-po-nos
stone πέτρα ⓕ *pe*-tra
stoned (drugged) μαστουρωμένος ma-stu-ro-*me*-nos
stop (bus etc) στάση ⓕ *sta*-si
stop (cease) v σταματάω sta-ma-*ta*-o
stop (prevent) v εμποδίζω e-bo-*thi*-zo
storm καταιγίδα ⓕ ka-te-*yi*-tha
story ιστορία ⓕ i-sto-*ri*-a
stove ηλεκτρική κουζίνα ⓕ i-lek-tri-*ki* ku-*zi*-na
straight ίσιος *i*-si-os
strange παράξενος pa-*rak*-se-nos
stranger (person) ξένος/ξένη ⓜ/ⓕ *kse*-nos/*kse*-ni
strawberry φράουλα ⓕ *fra*-u-la
stream ατμός ⓜ at-*mos*
street οδός ⓕ o-*thos*
street market λαϊκή ⓕ la-i-*ki*
strike απεργία ⓕ a-per-*yi*-a
string κλωστή ⓕ klo-*sti*
stroke (health) εγκεφαλικό ⓝ e-ge-fa-li-*ko*
stroller καροτσάκι ⓝ ka-rot-*sa*-ki
strong δυνατός thi-na-*tos*
stubborn ισχυρογνώμων is-hi-rog-*no*-mon
student σπουδαστής/σπουδάστρια ⓜ/ⓕ spu-*tha*-stis/spu-*tha*-stri-a
studio στούντιο ⓝ *stu*-di-o
stupid χαζός kha-*zos*
style στυλ ⓝ stil
subtitles υπότιτλοι ⓜ pl i-*po*-ti-tli
suburb προάστειο ⓝ pro-*a*-sti-o
subway a υπόγειος i-*po*-yi-os
subway (train) υπόγειος σιδηρόδρομος ⓜ i-*po*-yi-os si-thi-*ro*-thro-mos
sugar ζάχαρη ⓕ *za*-kha-ri
suitcase βαλίτσα ⓕ va-*lit*-sa
sultana σταφίδα ⓕ sta-*fi*-tha
summer καλοκαίρι ⓝ ka-lo-*ke*-ri
sun ήλιος ⓜ *i*-li-os
sunblock αντιηλιακό ⓝ a-di-i-li-a-*ko*
sunburn ηλιακό έγκαυμα ⓝ i-li-a-*ko* e-*gav*-ma
Sunday Κυριακή ⓕ ki-ria-*ki*

sunglasses γιαλιά ηλίου ⓝ pl yia-*lia* i-*li*-u
sunny ηλιόλουστος i-li-o-lu-stos
sunrise ανατολή ⓕ a-na-to-*li*
sunset δύση ⓕ *thi*-si
sunstroke ηλιοπληξία ⓕ i-li-o-plik-*si*-a
supermarket σουπερμάρκετ ⓝ su-per-*mar*-ket
superstition πρόληψη ⓕ *pro*-lip-si
supporter (politics, sport) οπαδός ⓜ&ⓕ o-pa-*thos*
surf σερφ ⓝ serf
surface mail (land) δια ξηράς thi-a ksi-*ras*
surface mail (sea) ατμοπλοϊκώς at-mo-plo-i-*kos*
surfboard σέρφμπορντ ⓝ serf-bord
surfing σέρφινγκ ⓝ *ser*-fing
surname επώνυμο ⓝ e-*po*-ni-mo
surprise έκπληξη ⓕ *ek*-plik-si
sweater ζακέτα ⓕ za-*ke*-ta
Sweden Σουηδία ⓕ su-i-*thi*-a
sweet a γλυκός ghli-*kos*
sweets γλυκά ⓝ pl ghli-*ka*
swelling πρήξιμο ⓝ *prik*-si-mo
swim v κολυμπώ ko-li-*bo*
swimming (sport) κολύμπι ⓝ ko-*li*-bi
swimming pool πισίνα ⓕ pi-*si*-na
swimsuit μαγιό ⓝ ma-*yio*
Switzerland Ελβετία ⓕ el-ve-*ti*-a
sword σπαθί ⓝ spa-*thi*
synagogue συναγωγή ⓕ si-na-gho-*yi*
synthetic a συνθετικός sin-the-ti-*kos*
syringe σύριγκα ⓕ *si*-ri-ga

T

table τραπέζι ⓝ tra-*pe*-zi
tablecloth τραπεζομάντηλο ⓝ tra-pe-zo-*ma*-di-lo
table tennis πινγκ πονγκ ⓝ ping pong
tail ουρά ⓕ u-*ra*
tailor ράφτης/ράφτρα ⓜ/ⓕ *raf*-tis/*raf*-tra
take παίρνω *per*-no
take a photo βγάλω φωτογραφία *vga*-zo fo-to-gra-*fi*-a
talk v μιλάω mi-*la*-o
tall ψηλός psi-*los*
tampon ταμπόν ⓝ ta-*bon*
tanning lotion λοσιόν για μαύρισμα ⓝ lo-*sion* yia *mav*-riz-ma

tap βρύση ① *vri*·si

tap water νερό βρύσης ① *ne*·ro vri·sis

tasty νόστιμος *no*·sti·mos

taverna ταβέρνα ① ta·*ver*·na

tax φόρος ⑩ *fo*·ros

taxi ταξί ⑪ tak·*si*

taxi stand στάση ταξί ① *sta*·si tak·*si*

tea τσάι ⑪ *tsa*·i

teacher δάσκαλος/δασκάλα ⑩/① *tha*·ska·los/*tha*·ska·la

team ομάδα ① o·*ma*·tha

teaspoon κουτάλι τσαγιού ⑩ ku·*ta*·li tsa·*yiu*

technique τεχνική ① tekh·ni·*ki*

teeth δόντια ⑪ *tho*·dia

telegram τηλεγράφημα ⑪ ti·le·*ghra*·fi·ma

telephone τηλέφωνο ⑪ ti·*le*·fo·no

telephone v τηλεφωνώ ti·le·fo·*no*

telephone box δημόσιο τηλέφωνο ⑪ *thi*·mo·si·o ti·*le*·fo·no

telephone centre τηλεφωνικό κέντρο ⑪ ti·le·fo·ni·*ko ke*·dro

telescope τηλεσκόπιο ⑪ ti·le·*sko*·pi·o

television τηλεόραση ① ti·le·o·ra·si

tell λέγω *le*·gho

temperature (fever) πυρετός ⑩ pi·re·*tos*

temperature (weather) θερμοκρασία ① ther·mo·kra·*si*·a

temple (church) ναός ⑩ na·*os*

tennis τένις ⑪ *te*·nis

tennis court γήπεδο του τένις ⑪ *yi*·pe·tho tu *te*·nis

tent τέντα ① *te*·da

tent peg πάσαλος τέντας ⑩ *pa*·sa·los *te*·das

terracotta pot αγγείο τερακότα ⑪ a·*gi*·o te·ra·*ko*·ta

terrible τρομερός tro·me·*ros*

test τεστ ⑩ test

thank ευχαριστώ ef·kha·ri·*sto*

that (one) εκείνο e·*ki*·no

theatre θέατρο ⑪ *the*·a·tro

their τους tus

there εκεί e·*ki*

they αυτοί af·*ti*

thick πυκνός pik·*nos*

thief κλέφτης ⑩ *klef*·tis

thin λεπτός lep·*tos*

think νομίζω no·*mi*·zo

third τρίτος *tri*·tos

thirsty διψασμένος thip·saz·*me*·nos

this (one) αυτός af·*tos*

thread κλωστή ① klo·*sti*

throat λαιμός ⑩ le·*mos*

thrush (health) μυκητώδης στοματίτις ⑩ mi·ki·to·*this* sto·ma·*ti*·tis

thunderstorm καταιγίδα ① ka·te·*yi*·tha

Thursday Πέμπτη ① *pem*·ti

tick τσιμπούρι ⑪ tsi·*bu*·ri

ticket εισιτήριο ⑪ i·si·*ti*·ri·o

ticket collector εισπράκτορας ⑩&① is·*prak*·to·ras

ticket machine μηχανή εισιτηρίων ① mi·kha·*ni* i·si·ti·*ri*·on

ticket office γραφείο εισιτηρίων ⑪ ghra·*fi*·o i·si·ti·*ri*·on

tide παλίρροια ① pa·*li*·ri·a

tight σφιχτός sfikh·*tos*

time ώρα ① o·ra

time difference διαφορά ώρας ① thia·fo·*ra* o·ras

timetable πρόγραμμα ⑪ *pro*·ghra·ma

tin (can) κουτί ⑪ ku·*ti*

tin opener ανοιχτήρι ⑪ a·nikh·*ti*·ri

tiny μικροσκοπικός mi·kro·sko·pi·*kos*

tip (gratuity) φιλοδώρημα ⑪ fi·lo·*tho*·ri·ma

tire λάστιχο ⑪ *la*·sti·kho

tired κουρασμένος ku·raz·*me*·nos

tissues χαρτομάντηλα ⑪ pl khar·to·*ma*·di·la

to σε se

toast τοστ ⑩ tost

toaster τοστιέρα ① to·sti·*e*·ra

tobacco καπνός ⑩ kap·*nos*

tobacconist καπνοπώλης/καπνοπώλισσα ⑩/① ka·pno·*po*·lis/ka·pno·*po*·li·sa

today σήμερα *si*·me·ra

toe δάχτυλο ποδιού ⑪ *thakh*·ti·lo po·*thiu*

tofu τόφου ⑪ *to*·fu

together μαζί ma·*zi*

toilet τουαλέτα ① tu·a·*le*·ta

toilet paper χαρτί υγείας ⑪ khar·*ti* i·*yi*·as

tomato ντομάτα ① do·*ma*·ta

tomato sauce σάλτσα ① *sal*·tsa

tomb μνήμα ⑪ *mni*·ma

tomorrow αύριο *av*·ri·o

tomorrow afternoon αύριο το απόγευμα *av*·ri·o to a·*po*·yev·ma

tomorrow evening αύριο το βράδι
av·ri·o το vra·*thi*
tomorrow morning αύριο το πρωί
av·ri·o το pro·*i*
tonight απόψε a·*pop*·se
too (excess) πάρα πολύ *pa*·ra po·*li*
tooth δόντι ⓝ *tho*·di
toothache πονόδοντος ⓜ po·*no*·tho·dos
toothbrush οδοντόβουρτσα ⓕ
o·*tho*·do·vur·tsa
toothpaste οδοντόπαστα ⓕ
o·*tho*·do·pa·sta
toothpick οδοντογλυφίδα ⓕ
o·*tho*·do·ghli·*fi*·tha
torch (flashlight) φακός ⓜ fa·*kos*
touch v αγγίζω a·*gi*·zo
tour περιήγηση ⓕ pe·ri·*i*·yi·si
tourist τουρίστας/τουρίστρια ⓜ/ⓕ
tu·*ri*·stas/tu·*ri*·stri·a
tourist office τουριστικό γραφείο ⓝ
tu·ri·sti·*ko* ghra·*fi*·o
towards προς pros
towel πετσέτα ⓕ pet·se·ta
tower πύργος ⓜ *pir*·ghos
toxic waste τοξικά απόβλητα ⓝ pl
tok·si·*ka* a·*pov*·li·ta
toy shop κατάστημα παιγνιδιών ⓝ
ka·*ta*·sti·ma pegh·ni·*thion*
track (path) μονοπάτι ⓝ mo·no·*pa*·ti
track (sport) στίβος ⓜ *sti*·vos
trade εμπόριο ⓝ e·*bo*·ri·o
tradesperson έμπορος ⓜ&ⓕ e·bo·ros
traffic κυκλοφορία ⓕ ki·klo·fo·*ri*·a
traffic light φανάρι ⓝ fa·*na*·ri
trail μονοπάτι ⓝ mo·no·*pa*·ti
train τρένο ⓝ *tre*·no
train station σταθμός τρένου ⓜ
stath·*mos* *tre*·nu
tram τραμ ⓝ tram
transit lounge αίθουσα τράνζιτ ⓕ
e·thu·sa *tran*·zit
translate μεταφράζω me·ta·*fra*·zo
transport μεταφορά ⓕ me·ta·fo·*ra*
travel v ταξιδεύω tak·si·*the*·vo
travel agency ταξιδιωτικό γραφείο ⓝ
tak·si·thi·o·ti·*ko* ghra·*fi*·o
travel sickness ναυτία ⓕ naf·*ti*·a
travellers cheque ταξιδιωτική επιταγή ⓕ
tak·si·thi·o·ti·*ki* e·pi·ta·*yi*
tree δέντρο ⓝ *the*·dro

trip (journey) ταξίδι ⓝ tak·*si*·thi
trolley καροτσάκι ⓝ ka·rot·sa·ki
trolley bus τρόλεϊ ⓝ *tro*·le·i
trousers παντελόνι ⓝ pa·de·*lo*·ni
truck φορτηγό ⓝ for·ti·*gho*
trust v εμπιστεύομαι e·bi·*ste*·vo·me
try (attempt) προσπαθώ pros·pa·*tho*
T-shirt μπλουζάκι ⓝ blu·*za*·ki
tube (tyre) σαμπρέλα ⓕ sa·*bre*·la
Tuesday Τρίτη ⓕ *tri*·ti
tumour όγκος ⓜ o·gos
tuna τόνος ⓜ *to*·nos
tune σκοπός ⓜ sko·*pos*
tunic χιτώνας ⓜ hi·*to*·nas
Turkey Τουρκία ⓕ tur·*ki*·a
turkey γαλοπούλα ⓕ gha·lo·*pu*·la
Turkish (language) Τουρκικά tur·ki·*ka*
Turkish (people) Τούρκοι ⓜ pl *tur*·ki
turn v γυρίζω yi·*ri*·zo
TV τηλεόραση ⓕ ti·le·o·ra·si
tweezers τσιμπιδάκι ⓝ tsi·bi·*tha*·ki
twice δυο φορές *thio* fo·*res*
twin beds δίκλινο δωμάτιο ⓝ
thi·kli·no tho·*ma*·ti·o
twins δίδυμα ⓝ pl *thi*·thi·ma
two δύο *thi*·o
type τύπος ⓜ *ti*·pos
typhus τύφος ⓜ *ti*·fos
typical τυπικός ti·pi·*kos*
tyre λάστιχο ⓝ la·sti·kho

U

ultrasound υπερηχητικό κύμα ⓝ
i·pe·ri·hi·ti·*ko* *ki*·ma
umbrella ομπρέλα ⓕ o·*bre*·la
uncomfortable άβολος a·vo·los
understand καταλαβαίνω ka·ta·la·ve·no
underwear εσώρουχα ⓝ pl e·so·ru·kha
unemployed a άνεργος/άνεργη ⓜ/ⓕ
a·ner·ghos/*a*·ner·yi
unfair άδικος a·thi·kos
uniform στολή ⓕ sto·*li*
universe σύμπαν ⓝ *si*·ban
university πανεπιστήμιο ⓝ
pa·ne·pi·*sti*·mi·o
unleaded (petrol) αμόλυβδος ⓕ
a·*mo*·liv·thos
unsafe ανασφαλής a·nas·fa·*lis*

until μέχρι *me*·khri

unusual ασυνήθιστος a·si·*ni*·thi·stos

UN zone ζώνη των Ηνωμένων Εθνών ① *zo*·ni ton i·no·*me*·non e·*thnon*

up πάνω *pa*·no

uphill ανηφορικά a·ni·fo·ri·*ka*

urgent επείγον e·*pi*·ghon

urinary infection ουρική μόλυνση ① u·ri·*ki* mo·lin·si

USA ΗΠΑ ① *i*·pa

useful χρήσιμος *khri*·si·mos

V

vacancy κενή θέση ① ke·*ni the*·si

vacant ελεύθερος e·*lef*·the·ros

vacation διακοπές ① pl thia·ko·*pes*

vaccination εμβόλιο ① em·*vo*·li·o

vagina κόλπος γυναίκας ① *kol*·pos yi·*ne*·kas

validate επικυρώνω e·pi·ki·*ro*·no

valley κοιλάδα ① ki·*la*·tha

valuable πολύτιμος po·*li*·ti·mos

value (price) αξία ① ak·*si*·a

van φορτηγάκι ① for·ti·*gha*·ki

VAT (Value Added Tax) Φ.Π.Α. ① fpa

veal μοσχάρι ⓝ mos·*kha*·ri

vegan βέγκαν ⓜ&① ve·gan

vegetable λαχανικά ⓝ pl la·kha·ni·*ka*

vegetarian a χορτοφάγος ⓜ&① khor·to·*fa*·ghos

vein φλέβα ① *fle*·va

venereal disease αφροδισιακό νόσημα ⓝ a·fro·thi·si·a·*ko* no·si·ma

venue χώρος ⓜ *kho*·ros

very πολύς po·*lis*

vessel σκάφος ⓝ *ska*·fos

video recorder βίντεο ρεκόρντερ ⓝ *vi*·de·o re·*kor*·der

video tape βιντεοταινία ① vi·de·o·te·*ni*·a

view θέα ① *the*·a

village χωριό ⓝ kho·*rio*

vine κλήμα ① *kli*·ma

vinegar ξύδι ⓝ *ksi*·thi

vineyard αμπέλι ① a·*be*·li

virus ιός ⓜ i·os

visa βίζα ① *vi*·za

visit επίσκεψη ① e·*pi*·skep·si

visit v επισκέπτομαι e·pi·*ske*·pto·me

vitamins βιταμίνες ① pl vi·ta·*mi*·nes

vodka βότκα ① *vot*·ka

voice φωνή ① fo·*ni*

volleyball ⓝ βόλεϊ *vo*·le·i

vote v ψηφίζω psi·*fi*·zo

W

wage μισθός ⓜ mis·*thos*

wait (for) περιμένω pe·ri·*me*·no

waiter γκαρσόν ⓝ gar·*son*

waiting room αίθουσα αναμονής ① e·thu·sa a·na·mo·*nis*

waitress σερβιτόρα ① ser·vi·*to*·ra

wake (someone) up ξυπνάω ksip·*na*·o

walk v περπατάω per·pa·*ta*·o

wall (outer) τείχος ⓝ *ti*·khos

wallet πορτοφόλι ⓝ por·to·*fo*·li

want θέλω *the*·lo

war πόλεμος ⓜ *po*·le·mos

wardrobe ντουλάπα ① du·*la*·pa

warm a ζεστός ze·*stos*

warn ζεσταίνω ze·ste·no

wash (oneself) v πλένομαι ple·no·me

wash (something) v πλένω ple·no

wash cloth (flannel) σφουγγάρι ⓝ sfu·*ga*·ri

washing machine πλυντήριο ⓝ pli·*di*·ri·o

wasp σφήκα ① *sfi*·ka

watch v κοιτάζω ki·*ta*·zo

watch ρολόι ⓝ ro·*lo*·i

water νερό ⓝ ne·ro

water bottle μπουκάλι νερού ⓝ bu·*ka*·li ne·*ru*

water bottle (hot) θερμοφόρα ① ther·mo·*fo*·ra

waterfall καταράχτης ⓜ ka·ta·*rakh*·tis

watermelon καρπούζι ⓝ kar·*pu*·zi

waterproof a αδιάβροχος a·thi·*av*·ro·khos

waterskiing θαλάσσιο σκι ⓝ tha·*la*·si·o ski

wave κύμα ⓝ *ki*·ma

way δρόμος ⓜ *thro*·mos

we εμείς e·*mis*

weak a αδύνατος a·*thi*·na·tos

wealthy πλούσιος ⓜ *plu*·si·os

wear v φοράω fo·*ra*·o

weather καιρός ⓜ ke·ros

weaving υφαντό ⓝ i·fa·*do*

wedding γάμος ⓜ *gha*·mos

wedding cake γαμήλια τούρτα ①
gha·*mi*·li·a tur·ta

wedding present γαμήλιο δώρο ⓝ
gha·*mi*·li·o *tho*·ro

Wednesday Τετάρτη ① te·*tar*·ti

week εβδομάδα ① ev·tho·*ma*·tha

weekend Σαββατοκύριακο ⓝ
sa·va·to·*ki*·ria·ko

weigh ζυγίζω zi·*yi*·zo

weight βάρος ⓝ *va*·ros

weights βάρη ⓝ pl va·ri

welcome v καλωσορίζω ka·lo·so·*ri*·zo

welfare πρόνοια ① *pro*·ni·a

well (health) καλά ka·*la*

west δύση ① *thi*·si

wet a βρεγμένος vregh·*me*·nos

what τι ti

wheel τροχός ⓜ tro·*khos*

wheelchair αναπηρική καρέκλα ①
a·na·pi·ri·*ki* ka·*re*·kla

when όταν o·tan

where πού pu

which ποιος pios

whisky ουίσκυ ⓝ u·*i*·ski

white άσπρος *as*·pros

who ποιος pios

wholemeal bread ψωμί ολικής αλέσεως
ⓝ pso·*mi* o·li·*kis* a·*le*·se·os

why γιατί yia·*ti*

wide πλατύς pla·*tis*

wife σύζυγος ① *si*·zi·ghos

wildflowers αγριολούλουδα ⓝ pl
a·ghri·o·*lu*·lu·tha

win v κερδίζω ker·*thi*·zo

wind άνεμος ⓜ *a*·ne·mos

window παράθυρο ⓝ pa·*ra*·thi·ro

windscreen παμπρίζ ⓝ pa·*briz*

windsurfing γουιντσέρφινγκ ⓝ
ghu·id·*ser*·fing

wine κρασί ⓝ kra·*si*

wings φτερούγες ① pl fte·ru·*ghes*

winner νικητής ⓜ ni·ki·*tis*

winter χειμώνας ⓜ hi·*mo*·nas

wire καλώδιο ⓝ ka·*lo*·thi·o

wish v εύχομαι *ef*·kho·me

with με me

within (an hour) εντός e·*dos*

without χωρίς kho·*ris*

wok γουόκ ⓝ ghu·*ok*

woman γυναίκα ① yi·*ne*·ka

wonderful θαυμάσιος thav·*ma*·si·os

wood δάσος ⓝ *tha*·sos

wool μαλλί ⓝ ma·*li*

word λέξη ① *lek*·si

work δουλειά ① thu·*lia*

work v δουλεύω thu·*le*·vo

work experience πείρα εργασίας ①
pi·ra er·gha·*si*·as

workout εξάσκηση ① ek·*sa*·ski·si

work permit άδεια εργασίας ①
a·thi·a er·gha·*si*·as

workshop εργαστήρι ⓝ er·gha·*sti*·ri

world κόσμος ⓜ *koz*·mos

World Cup Παγκόσμιο Κύπελο ⓝ
pa·*goz*·mi·o *ki*·pe·lo

worm σκουλίκι ⓝ sku·*li*·ki

worried ανήσυχος a·*ni*·si·khos

worship v λατρεύω la·*tre*·vo

wrist καρπός ⓜ kar·*pos*

write γράφω *ghra*·fo

writer συγγραφέας ⓜ&① si·gra·*fe*·as

wrong a λανθασμένος lan·thaz·*me*·nos

Y

year χρόνος ⓜ *khro*·nos

(this) year (αυτό το) χρόνο
(af·*to* to) *khro*·no

yellow a κίτρινος *ki*·tri·nos

yes ναι ne

yesterday χτες khtes

(not) yet (όχι) ακόμη (*o*·hi) a·*ko*·mi

yoga γιόγκα ① *yiog*·ka

yogurt γιαούρτι ⓝ yia·*ur*·ti

you sg inf εσύ e·*si*

you sg pol & pl inf&pol εσείς e·*sis*

young νέος *ne*·os

your sg pol & pl inf&pol σας sas

your sg inf σου su

youth hostel γιουθ χόστελ ⓝ yuth *kho*·stel

Z

zip/zipper φερμουάρ ⓝ fer·mu·*ar*

zodiac ζωδιακός ⓜ zo·thi·a·*kos*

zoo ζωολογικός κήπος ⓜ
zo·o·lo·yi·*kos* *ki*·pos

zucchini κολοκυθάκι ⓝ ko·lo·ki·*tha*·ki

Greek nouns in the **dictionary** have their gender indicated by ⓜ masculine, ⓕ feminine or ⓝ neuter. If it's a plural noun you'll also see pl. When a word that could be either a noun or a verb has no gender indicated, it's a verb. Adjectives are given in the masculine form only – see **adjectives & adverbs** in the **phrasebuilder** for more on how to form feminine and neuter adjectives. Both nouns and adjectives are provided in the nominative case only – refer to the **phrasebuilder** for more information on **case**. You'll also find the English words marked as a adjective and v verb, sg singular, pl plural, inf informal, and pol polite where necessary.

The **greek–english dictionary** has been ordered according to the Greek alphabet:

| Αα | Ββ | Γγ | Δδ | Εε | Ζζ | Ηη | Θθ | Ιι | Κκ | Λλ | Μμ |
| Νν | Ξξ | Οο | Ππ | Ρρ | Σσ/ς | Ττ | Υυ | Φφ | Χχ | Ψψ | Ωω |

Α α

άβολος a·vo·los uncomfortable
αγάπη a·gha·pi ⓕ love
αγαπώ a·gha·po love
Αγγλία ⓕ ang·gli·a England
Αγγλικά ⓝ pl ang·gli·ka English (language)
αγορά ⓕ a·gho·ra market • shopping centre
αγοράζω a·gho·ra·zo buy ⓥ
αγόρι ⓝ a·gho·ri boy
άδειο a·thi·o empty a
αδερφή ⓕ a·ther·fi sister
αδερφός ⓜ a·ther·fos brother
αδιάβροχο a·thi·av·ro·ho ⓝ raincoat
αδύνατος a·thi·na·tos impossible a
αερογραμμή ⓕ a·e·ro·ghra·mi airline
αεροδρόμιο a·e·ro·thro·mi·o ⓝ airport
αεροπλάνο a·e·ro·pla·no ⓝ airplane
αίθουσα αναμονής
  e·thu·sa a·na·mo·nis ⓕ waiting room
αίθουσα τράνζιτ ⓕ e·thu·sa tran·zit
  transit lounge
αίμα e·ma ⓝ blood
ακριβός a·kri·vos expensive
ακριβώς a·kri·vos exactly
ακυρώνω a·ki·ro·no cancel
αλλαγή a·la·yi ⓕ change
αλλεργία a·ler·yi·a ⓕ allergy
αλληλογραφία a·li·lo·ghra·fi·a ⓕ mail
άλλος a·los other
άμεσος a·me·sos direct a
αναπηρική καρέκλα
  a·na·pi·ri·ki ka·re·kla ⓕ wheelchair

ανάπηρος a·na·pi·ros disabled a
αναπτήρας ⓜ a·nap·ti·ras cigarette lighter
ανατολή ⓕ a·na·to·li east • sunrise
αναχώρηση ⓕ a·na·kho·ri·si departure
αναχωρώ a·na·kho·ro depart ⓥ • leave ⓥ
ανεβαίνω a·ne·ve·no board (transport) ⓥ
ανεμιστήρας ⓜ a·ne·mi·sti·ras
  fan (machine)
άνετος a·ne·tos comfortable
ανθοπώλης ⓜ an·tho·po·lis florist
ανθοπώλισσα ⓕ an·tho·po·li·sa florist
ανιαρός a·ni·a·ros boring
άνοιξη ⓕ a·nik·si spring (season)
ανοιχτήρι ⓝ a·nikh·ti·ri bottle opener •
  can opener • corkscrew
ανοιχτός a·nikh·tos light (colour) • open a
ανταλλάσσω a·da·la·so exchange ⓥ
αντιβιοτικά ⓝ pl a·di·vi·o·ti·ka antibiotics
αντίγραφο ⓝ a·di·ghra·fo copy
αντιηλιακό ⓝ a·di·i·li·a·ko sunblock
αντισηπτικό ⓝ a·di·si·lip·ti·ko antiseptic
άντρας ⓜ a·dras man
απαίσιος a·pe·si·os awful
απασχολημένος a·pa·skho·li·me·nos busy
απεργία ⓕ a·per·yi·a strike
απίθανος a·pi·tha·nos fantastic • great
απλό εισιτήριο ⓝ a·plo i·si·ti·ri·o
  one-way (ticket)
απόγευμα ⓝ a·po·yev·ma afternoon
απόδειξη ⓕ a·po·thik·si receipt
αποσκευές ⓕ pl a·po·ske·ves baggage
αποσμητικό ⓝ a·poz·mi·ti·ko deodorant
απόψε a·pop·se tonight

αργά ar-*gha slowly*
αργότερα ar-*gho-*te-ra *later*
αριθμομηχανή ⓕ a-rith-mo-mi-kha-*ni calculator*
αριθμός ⓜ a-rith-*mos number*
αριθμός διαβατηρίου ⓜ a-rith-*mos* thia-va-ti-*ri-*u *passport number*
αριθμός δωματίου ⓜ a-rith-*mos* tho-ma-ti-u *room number*
αριθμός κυκλοφορίας αυτοκινήτου ⓜ a-rith-*mos* ki-klo-fo-*ri-*as af-to-ki-*ni-*tu *car registration*
αριθμός οδήγησης ⓕ a-rith-*mos* o-thi-yi-sis *drivers licence*
αριστερός a-ri-ste-*ros left (direction)* a
αρκετά ar-ke-*ta enough*
αρραβωνιασμένη ⓕ a-ra-vo-niaz-*me-*ni *engaged (to marry)*
αρραβωνιασμένος ⓜ a-ra-vo-niaz-*me-*nos *engaged (to marry)*
αρραβωνιαστικιά ⓕ a-ra-vo-nia-sti-*kia fiancée*
αρραβωνιαστικός ⓜ a-ra-vo-nia-sti-*kos fiancé*
άρρωστος a-ro-stos *ill • sick*
αρχιτέκτονας ⓜ&ⓕ ar-hi-*tek-*to-nas *architect*
αρχιτεκτονική ⓕ ar-hi-tek-to-ni-*ki architecture*
άρωμα ⓝ a-ro-ma *perfume*
ασανσέρ ⓝ a-san-*ser elevator • lift*
ασήμι ⓝ a-*si-*mi *silver*
άσπρος as-pros *white*
αστείος a-sti-os *funny*
αστικό λεωφορείο ⓝ a-sti-ko le-o-fo-*ri-*o *bus*
αστράγαλος ⓜ a-stra-gha-los *ankle*
αστυνομία ⓕ a-sti-no-*mi-*a *police*
αστυνομικός σταθμός ⓜ a-sti-no-mi-*kos* stath-*mos police station*
αστυφύλακας ⓜ a-sti-*fi-*la-kas *police officer*
αστυφυλακίνα ⓕ a-sti-fi-la-*ki-*na *police officer*
ασφάλεια ⓕ as-*fa-*li-a *insurance*
ασφαλές σεξ ⓝ as-fa-*les* seks *safe sex*
ατύχημα ⓝ a-*ti-*hi-ma *accident*
αυγή ⓕ av-*yi dawn*
αύριο av-ri-o *tomorrow*
αυτοκίνητο ⓝ af-to-*ki-*ni-to *car*
αυτοκινητόδρομος ⓜ af-to-ki-ni-to-thro-mos *motorway • tollway*
αυτόματη μηχανή χρημάτων ⓕ af-to-ma-ti mi-kha-*ni* khri-*ma-*ton *ATM*

αυτός ⓜ af-*tos he • this (one)*
αφή ⓕ a-*fi feeling (physical)*
αφίξεις ⓕ pl a-*fik-*sis *arrivals*
αφτί ⓝ af-*ti ear*

Β β

βαγκόν λι ⓝ va-*gon* li *sleeping car*
βαγόνι φαγητού ⓝ va-*gho-*ni fa-yi-*tu dining car*
βαλίτσα ⓕ va-*lit-*sa *suitcase*
βαμπάκι ⓝ va-ba-ki *cotton*
βάρκα ⓕ var-ka *boat*
βαρύς va-ris *heavy*
βγάζω φωτογραφία vga-zo fo-to-gra-*fi-*a *take a photo*
βγαίνω vye-no *go out*
βελόνα ⓕ ve-lo-na *needle (sewing)*
βενζίνα ⓕ ven-*zi-*na *gas • petrol*
βενζινάδικο ⓝ ven-zi-*na-*thi-ko *service station*
βήχω *vi-*kho *cough*
βιαστικός via-sti-*kos in a hurry*
βιβλίο viv-*li-*o *book* ⓝ
βιβλιοθήκη ⓕ viv-li-o-*thi-*ki *library*
βιβλιοπωλείο ⓝ viv-li-o-po-*li-*o *bookshop*
βιβλίο φράσεων ⓝ viv-*li-*o fra-se-on *phrasebook*
βίζα ⓕ *vi-*za *visa*
βιντεοταινία ⓕ vi-de-o-te-*ni-*a *video tape*
βοήθεια ⓕ vo-*i-*thi-a *help*
βοηθώ vo-i-tho *help*
βορράς ⓜ vo-ras *north*
βούλωμα ⓝ vu-lo-ma *plug (bath)*
βουνό ⓝ vu-no *mountain*
βούρτσα ⓕ vur-tsa *brush*
βράδι ⓝ vra-thi *evening*
βροχή ⓕ vro-hi *rain*
βρύση ⓕ *vri-*si *faucet • tap*
βρώμικος a vro-mi-kos *dirty*
βύσμα ⓝ viz-ma *plug (electricity)*

Γ γ

γάλα ⓝ *gha-*la *milk*
γαστροεντερίτιδα ⓕ gha-stro-e-de-*ri-*ti-tha *gastroenteritis*
γεμάτο ye-ma-to *full*
γενέθλια ⓝ pl ye-*ne-*thli-a *birthday*
Γερμανία ⓕ yer-ma-*ni-*a *Germany*
γεύμα ⓝ yev-ma *meal*
γεφύρι ⓝ ye-fi-ri *bridge*

η ① yi *Earth*

ήπεδο ① *yi*·pe·tho *court (tennis)*

— του γκολφ ① tu golf *golf course*

— του τένις ① tu *te*·nis *tennis court*

ιαγιά ① *yia*·*yia grandmother*

ιαλιά ① pl yia·*lia glasses · spectacles*

ιαλιά ηλίου ① pl yia·*lia i·li·u sunglasses*

ιατί yia·*ti why*

ιατρός ⓜ&① yia·*tros doctor*

ιος ⓜ *yios son*

ιουθ χόστελ ① yuth *kho·*stel *youth hostel*

καρσόν ① gar·*son waiter*

κέι *ge·*i *gay* a

κρίζος *gri·*zos gray · *grey* a

λυκός ghli·*kos sweet* a

λυπτική ① ghlip·ti·*ki sculpture*

λώσσα *ghlo·*sa *language*

όνατο ① *gho·*na·to *knee*

ονείς ⓜ pl gho·*nis parents*

ράμμα ① *ghra·*ma *letter (mail)*

ραμμάριο ① ghra·*ma·*ri·o *gram*

ραμματόσημο ① ghra·ma·*to·*si·mo *stamp*

ραφείο απολεσθέντων αντικειμένων ① gra·fi·o a·po·le·*sthe·*don a·di·ki·me·non *left-luggage office*

ραφείο εισιτηρίων ghra·fi·o i·si·ti·ri·on ① *ticket office*

ράφω *ghra·*fo *write*

ρήγορος a *ghri·*gho·ros *fast*

ρίπη ① *ghri·*pi influenza · *flu*

υμναστήριο ① yi·mna·*sti·*ri·o *gym (place)*

υναίκα ① yi·*ne·*ka *woman*

Δ δ

δάκτυλο ① *thak·*ti·lo *finger*

δασμός αεροδρομίου ⓜ thaz·mos a·e·ro·thro·*mi·u airport tax*

δάσος ① *tha·*sos *forest · wood*

δαχτυλίδι ① thakh·ti·*li·*thi *ring (on finger)*

δείπνο ① *thip·*no *dinner*

δείχνω *thi·*khno *point* ⓥ · *show* ⓥ

Δεκαπενθήμερο ① tha·ka·pen·*thi·*me·ro *fortnight*

δέμα ① *the·*ma *parcel*

δεξιός thek·si·os *right (direction)* a

δέρμα ① *ther·*ma *leather · skin*

Δεύτερη τάξη ① *thef·*te·ri tak·*si second class*

Δημόσια αποχωρητήρια ⓜ pl thi·*mo·*si·a a·po·kho·ri·*ti·*ria *public toilet*

δημόσιο τηλέφωνο ① thi·*mo·*si·o ti·*le·*fo·no *phone box · public telephone*

δημοσιογράφος ⓜ&① thi·mo·si·o·*ghra·*fos *journalist*

δημόσιος δρόμος ① thi·*mo·*si·os *thro·*mos *highway*

δια ξηράς *thi·a ksi·ras surface mail*

διαβατήριο ① thi·a·va·*ti·*ri·o *passport*

διαδίκτυο ① thi·a·*thik·*ti·o *Internet*

διάδρομος ① thi·a·*thro·*mos *aisle*

διαζευγμένη ① thi·a·zev·*ghme·*ni *divorced* a

διαζευγμένος ⓜ thi·a·zev·*ghme·*nos *divorced* a

διαθέσιμος thi·a·*the·*si·mos *free (available)* a

διακοπές ① pl thia·ko·*pes vacation*

διάλειμμα ① thia·*li·*ma *intermission*

διαμέρισμα ① thi·a·*me·*riz·ma *apartment*

διάρροια ① thi·*a·*ri·a *diarrhoea*

διαφορά ώρας ① thia·fo·*ra o·*ras *time difference*

διαφορετικός thia·fo·re·ti·*kos different*

διαχωριστική γραμμή ① thi·a·kho·ri·sti·*ki* ghra·*mi delineation line*

διερμηνέας ⓜ&① thi·er·mi·*ne·*as *interpreter*

διεύθυνση ① thi·*ef·*thin·si *address*

δικηγόρος ⓜ&① thi·ki·*gho·*ros *lawyer*

δίκλινο δωμάτιο ① *thi·*kli·no tho·*ma·*ti·o *twin beds*

δίπλα *thi·*pla *beside · next to*

διπλό δωμάτιο ① thi·*plo* tho·*ma·*ti·o *double room*

διπλό κρεβάτι ① thi·*plo* kre·*va·*ti *double bed*

Δις ① the·*spi·*nis *Ms · Miss*

δισκέτα ① thi·*ske·*ta *disk (floppy)*

διψασμένος thip·saz·*me·*nos *thirsty*

δοκιμάζω tho·ki·*ma·*zo *try* ⓥ

δοκιμαστήριο ρούχων ① tho·ki·ma·*sti·*ri·o *ru·*khon *changing room (in shop)*

δολλάριο ① tho·*la·*ri·o *dollar*

δουλειά ① thu·*lia job · work*

δρόμος ① *thro·*mos *road · route · way*

δροσερό thro·se·ro *cool (temperature)*

δυνατός thi·na·*tos loud · strong · possible*

δύο *thi·*o *two*

δύση *thi·*si *sunset · west*

δυσπεψία ① this·pep·*si·*a *indigestion*

δωμάτιο ① tho·*ma·*ti·o *room*

δωρεάν tho·re·*an complimentary · free*

δώρο ① *tho·*ro *gift · present*

Ε ε

εβδομάδα ① ev·tho·ma·tha week
εγγονή ① e·go·ni granddaughter
εγγονός ⑩ e·go·nos grandson
εγγυημένος e·ghi·i·me·nos guaranteed
έγκαυμα ⑪ e·gav·ma burn
έγκυος e·gi·os pregnant
εγώ e·gho me
εδώ e·tho here
έθιμο ⑪ e·thi·mo custom
εισιτήριο ① i·si·ti·ri·o fare • ticket
　— **μετ' επιστροφής** ⑪ me·te·pi·stro·fis
　return ticket
　— **σταντ μπάι** ⑪ stand ba·i stand-by
　ticket
είσοδος ① i·so·thos entry
εκατοστόμετρο ⑪ e·ka·to·sto·me·tro
centimetre
εκεί e·ki there
εκείνο e·ki·no that (one)
έκθεμα ⑪ ek·the·ma exhibit
έκθεση ① ek·the·si exhibition
εκκλησία ① e·kli·si·a church
έκπτωση ① ek·pto·si discount
έκτακτη ανάγκη ① ek·tak·ti a·na·gi
emergency
εκτυπωτής ⑩ ek·ti·po·tis printer (computer)
ελαττωματικός e·la·to·ma·ti·kos faulty
ελαφρύ γεύμα ⑪ e·laf·ri ghev·ma snack
ελαφρύς e·la·fris light (weight)
ελεύθερος e·lef·the·ros vacant
Ελλάδα ① e·la·tha Greece
Έλληνες ⑪ pl e·li·nes Greek (people)
Ελληνικά ⑪ pl e·li·ni·ka Greek (language)
εμβόλιο ⑪ em·vo·li·o vaccination
ένα e·na one
ένας άλλος e·nas a·los another
ένεση ① e·ne·si injection
ενοικιάζω e·ni·ki·a·zo hire ⓥ • rent ⓥ
ενοικίαση αυτοκινήτου ①
　e·ni·ki·a·si af·to·ki·ni·tu car hire
εξαργυρώνω ⑩ ek·sar·yi·ro·no
　cash a cheque
έξοδος ① ek·so·thos exit
εξοχή ① ek·so·hi countryside
εξπρές eks·pres express mail a
έξω ek·so outside
εξωτερικό ek·so·te·ri·ko overseas
επάνω e·pa·no aboard
επείγον e·pi·ghon urgent
　— **ταχυδρομείο** ① ta·hi·thro·mi·o
　by express mail

επιβάτης ⑩ e·pi·va·tis passenger
επιβάτισσα ① e·pi·va·ti·sa passenger
επίδειξη ① e·pi·thik·si show
επίδεσμος ⑩ e·pi·thez·mos bandage
επιδόρπιο ⑪ e·pi·thor·pi·o dessert
επικίνδυνος e·pi·kin·thi·nos dangerous
επικυρώνω e·pi·ki·ro·no
　confirm (booking) • validate
έπιπλα ⑪ pl e·pi·pla furniture
επισκευάζω e·pi·ske·va·zo repair ⓥ
επιστήμη ① e·pi·sti·mi science
επιστήμονας ⑩&① e·pi·sti·mo·nas
scientist
επιστρέφω e·pi·stre·fo come back • return ⓥ
επιστροφή χρημάτων ①
　e·pi·stro·fi khri·ma·ton refund
επίτηρηση παιδιών ①
　e·pi·ti·ri·si pe·thion childminding
επιτρεπόμενες αποσκευές ① pl
　e·pi·tre·po·me·nes a·po·ske·ves
　baggage allowance
επιχείρηση ① e·pi·hi·ri·si business
επόμενος e·po·me·nos next a
εποχή ① e·po·hi season
επώνυμο ⑪ e·po·ni·mo surname
εργόχειρα ⑪ pl er·gho·hi·ra handicrafts
ερείπια ⑪ pl e·ri·pi·a ruins
εσείς e·sis you sg you pol & pl
εστιατόριο ⑪ e·sti·a·to·ri·o restaurant
εσύ e·si you sg inf
εσώρουχα ⑪ pl e·so·ru·kha underwear
εταιρεία ① e·te·ri·a company (firm)
ευγνώμων ev·ghno·mon grateful
εύθραυστος ef·thraf·stos fragile
ευτυχισμένος ef·ti·hiz·me·nos happy
εφημερίδα ① e·fi·me·ri·tha newspaper
έχω e·kho have

Ζ ζ

ζακέτα ① za·ke·ta jacket • sweater
ζαχαροπλαστείο ⑪ za·kha·ro·pla·sti·o
　cake shop
ζεστός ze·stos hot • warm a
ζωγραφική ① zo·ghra·fi·ki
　painting (the art)
ζωγράφος ⑩&① zo·ghra·fos painter
ζώνη καθίσματος ① zo·ni ka·thiz·ma·tos
　seatbelt
ζωολογικός κήπος ⑩
　zo·o·lo·yi·kos ki·pos zoo

H η

ηθοποιός ⑩&① i·tho·pi·os actor
ηλεκτρισμός ⑩ i·lek·triz·mos electricity
ηλιακό έγκαυμα ⑪ i·li·a·ko e·gav·ma sunburn
ήλιος ⑩ i·li·os sun
ημέρα ① i·me·ra day
ημερολόγιο ⑪ i·me·ro·lo·yi·o diary
ημερομηνία ① i·me·ro·mi·ni·a date (day)
— γεννήσεως ① ye·ni·se·os date of birth
ΗΠΑ ⑪ i·pa USA
ήσυχος i·si·khos quiet a
ήχος κλήσης ⑩ i·khos kli·sis dial tone

Θ θ

θάλασσα ① tha·la·sa sea
θέα ① the·a view
θεά ① the·a goddess
θεατρικό έργο ⑪ the·a·tri·ko er·gho play (theatre)
θέατρο ⑪ the·a·tro theatre
θεία ① thi·a aunt
θερμοκρασία ① ther·mo·kra·si·a temperature (weather)
θερμοπληξία ① ther·mo·plik·si·a heatstroke
θερμοφόρα ① ther·mo·fo·ra (hot) water bottle
θηλυκός a thi·li·kos female
θορυβώδης tho·ri·vo·this noisy
Φ.Π.Α. ⑩ fpa VAT (Value Added Tax)

I ι

ιατρική ① i·a·tri·ki medicine (job, study)
ιδιωτικός i·thi·o·ti·kos private a
ιματιοφυλάκιο ⑪ i·ma·ti·o·fi·la·ki·o cloakroom
ινστιτούτο αισθητικής ⑪ in·sti·tu·to es·thi·ti·kis beauty salon
ιππασία ① i·pa·si·a horse riding • ride
ιχθυοπωλείο ⑪ ikh·thi·o·po·li·o fish shop

K κ

κα ① khi·ri·a Mrs
καθαρίζω ka·tha·ri·zo clean ⑨
καθάρισμα ⑪ ka·tha·riz·ma cleaning
καθαρός ka·tha·ros clean a
καθαρτικό ⑪ ka·thar·ti·ko laxative
κάθε ka·the every • per
καθένας ka·the·nas each • everyone
καθετί ka·the·ti everything
καθημερινός ka·thi·me·ri·nos daily
καθρέφτης ⑩ ka·thref·tis mirror
καθυστερημένος ka·thi·ste·ri·me·nos late
καθυστέρηση ① ka·thi·ste·ri·si delay ⑨
και ke and
και οι δύο ke i thi·o both
κακός ka·kos bad
καλλιτέχνης ⑩ ka·li·tekh·nis artist
καλλιτέχνιδα ① ka·li·tekh·ni·tha artist
καλλυντικά ⑪ pl ka·li·di·ka make-up
καλοκαίρι ⑪ ka·lo·ke·ri summer
καλός ka·los good a • kind a
κάλτσες ① kal·tses socks
καλύτερος ka·li·te·ros better
καλώ ka·lo call ⑨
Καναδάς ⑩ ka·na·thas Canada
καπέλο ⑪ ka·pe·lo hat
καπνίζω kap·ni·zo smoke ⑨
καρδιά ① kar·thia heart
καρδιακή κατάσταση ① kar·dhi·a·ki ka·ta·sta·si heart condition
καρέκλα ① ka·re·kla chair
καροτσάκι ⑪ ka·rot·sa·ki stroller • trolley
κάρτα ① kar·ta postcard
— επιβίβασης ① e·pi·vi·va·sis boarding pass
— τηλεφώνου ① ti·le·fo·nu phonecard
κασέτα ① ka·se·ta cassette
κασκόλ ⑪ ka·skol scarf
κάστρο ⑪ ka·stro castle
κατ' ευθείαν γραμμή ① ka·tef·thi·an gra·mi direct-dial
κατάθεση ① ka·ta·the·si deposit (bank)
κατάλογος ⑪ ka·ta·lo·ghos itinerary
κατάλυμα ⑪ ka·ta·li·ma accommodation
κατάστημα ⑪ ka·ta·sti·ma department store
— για σουβενίρ ⑪ yia su·ve·nir souvenir shop
— ηλεκτρικών ειδών ⑪ i·lek·tri·kon i·thon electrical store
— μουσικών ειδών ⑪ mu·si·kon i·thon music shop
— ρούχων ⑪ ruk·hon clothing store
— των σπορ ⑪ ton spor sports shop
κατεβαίνω ka·te·ve·no get off (train, etc)
κατεύθυνση ① ka·tef·thin·si direction

καύσωνας ⓜ *kaf*·so·nas heatwave
καφέ ka·*fe* brown a
καφενείο ⓝ ka·fe·*ni*·o coffee shop
— **διαδικτύου** ⓝ thi·a·thik·*ti*·u Internet café
καφές ⓜ ka·*fes* coffee
καφεστιατόριο ⓣ ka·fe·sti·a·*to*·ri·o café
κενή θέση ⓣ ke·*ni the*·si vacancy
κέντημα ⓝ *ke*·di·ma embroidery
κέντρο ⓝ *ke*·dro centre
κέντρο της πόλης ⓝ *ke*·dro tis *po*·lis city centre
κέρματα ⓟ pl *ker*·ma·ta coins
κεφάλι ⓝ ke·*fa*·li head
κήπος ⓜ *ki*·pos garden
κινητό ⓝ ki·ni·*to* mobile phone
κίτρινος ⓝ *ki*·tri·nos yellow a
κλειδί ⓝ kli·*thi* key
κλειδωμένος kli·tho·*me*·nos locked
κλειδώνω kli·*tho*·no lock ⓥ
κλείνω *kli*·no close ⓥ
— **θέση** *the*·si book ⓥ
κλεισμένος kliz·*me*·nos closed
κλειστός kli·*stos* shut
κλεμμένο kle·*me*·no stolen
κλήση με αντιστροφή της επιβάρυνσης ⓣ *kli*·si me a·dis·tro·*fi* tis e·pi·*va*·rin·sis collect call
κλονισμός ⓜ klo·niz·*mos* concussion
κόβω *ko*·vo cut ⓥ
κοιμάμαι ki·*ma*·me sleep ⓥ
κοιμητήριο ⓝ ki·mi·*ti*·ri·o cemetery
κόκκινο ko·*ki*·no red
κολιέ ⓝ ko·li·*e* necklace
κολυμπώ ko·li·*bo* swim ⓥ
κολώνα ⓣ ko·*lo*·na column
κολώνια ξυρίσματος ⓣ ko·*lo*·ni·a ksi·*riz*·ma·tos aftershave
κομμωτής ⓜ ko·mo·*tis* hairdresser
κομμώτρια ⓣ ko·mo·tri·a hairdresser
κοντά ko·*da* near • nearby
κοντινός ko·di·*nos* close a
κοντός ko·*dos* short (height)
κόρη ⓣ *ko*·ri daughter
κορίτσι ⓝ ko·*rit*·si girl
Κος ⓜ *khi*·ri·os Mr
κοσμήματα ⓟ pl koz·*mi*·ma·ta jewellery
κοστίζω ko·*sti*·zo cost ⓥ
κοτόπουλο ⓝ ko·*to*·pu·lo chicken
κουβέρτα ⓣ ku·*ver*·ta blanket
κουζίνα ⓣ ku·*zi*·na kitchen
κουμπί ⓝ ku·*bi* button
κουρασμένος ku·raz·*me*·nos tired

κούρεμα ⓝ *ku*·re·ma haircut
κουτάλι ⓝ ku·*ta*·li spoon
— **τσαγιού** ⓝ tsa·*yiu* teaspoon
κουτί ⓝ ku·*ti* box • can • tin
κραγιόν ⓝ pl kra·*yion* lipstick
κρασί ⓝ kra·*si* wine
κράτηση ⓣ *kra*·ti·si booking • reservation
κρέας ⓝ *kre*·as meat
κρεβάτι ⓝ kre·*va*·ti bed
κρέμα ⓣ *kre*·ma cream
— **ξυρίσματος** ⓣ ksi·*riz*·ma·tos shaving cream
κρεοπωλείο ⓝ kre·o·po·*li*·o butcher's shop
κρυωμένος kri·o·*me*·nos cold a
κτηματομεσιτικό γραφείο ⓝ kti·ma·to·me·si·ti·*ko* ghra·*fi*·o estate agency
κτήριο ⓝ *kti*·ri·o building
κυλιόμενες σκάλες ⓟ pl ki·li·*o*·me·nes *ska*·les escalator
κυτίο πρώτων βοηθειών ⓝ ki·*ti*·o *pro*·ton vo·i·thi·*on* first-aid kit

Λ λ

λάδι ⓝ *la*·thi oil
— **αυτοκινήτου** ⓝ af·to·ki·*ni*·tu oil (car)
λαϊκή ⓣ la·i·*ki* street market
λαιμός ⓜ le·*mos* throat
λάστιχο ⓝ *la*·sti·kho tire • tyre
λαχανικά ⓝ pl la·kha·ni·*ka* vegetable
λαιμός ⓜ le·*mos* neck
λεξικό ⓝ lek·si·*ko* dictionary
λεπτό ⓝ lep·*to* minute
λεσβία ⓣ lez·*vi*·a lesbian
λιγότερο li·gho·te·ro less
λίμνη ⓣ *lim*·ni lake
λινό ⓝ li·*no* linen (material)
λιπαντικό ⓝ li·pa·di·*ko* lubricant
λίρα ⓣ *li*·ra pound (money)
λίτρα ⓣ *lit*·ra pound (weight)
λογαριασμός ⓜ lo·gha·riaz·*mos* account • bill • check
λοσιόν ⓣ lo·*sion* lotion
— **για μαύρισμα** ⓝ yia *mav*·riz·ma tanning lotion

Μ μ

μαβής ma·*vis* purple
μαγαζί ⓝ ma·gha·*zi* shop
μάγειρας ⓜ *ma*·yi·ras cook

μαγείρισσα ① ma·*yi*·ri·sa cook
μαγειρεύω ma·yi·*re*·vo cook ⓥ
μαγιό ⓝ ma·*yio* swimsuit
μαζί ma·*zi* together
μαθαίνω ma·*the*·no learn
μακριά ma·kri·*a* far
μακρύς ma·*kris* long a
μαντήλι ① ma·*di*·li handkerchief
μαξιλάρι ⓝ mak·si·*la*·ri pillow
μαξιλαροθήκη ① mak·si·la·ro·*thi*·ki
  pillowcase
μας mas our
μάτι ⓝ *ma*·ti eye
μάτια ⓝ pl *ma*·tia eyes
ματς ⓝ mats game • match
μαυρόασπρο (φιλμ) ⓝ mav·ro·a·spro
  (film) B&W (film)
μαύρος *mav*·ros black
μαχαίρι ⓝ ma·*he*·ri knife
μαχαιροπήρουνα ⓝ pl ma·he·ro·*pi*·ru·na
  cutlery
με ερκοντίσιον me er kon·*di*·si·on
  air-conditioned
μεγάλα φώτα αυτοκινήτου
  ⓝ pl me·*gha*·la *fo*·ta af·to·ki·*ni*·tu
  headlights
μεγάλος me·*gha*·los big • large
μεγαλύτερος me·gha·*li*·te·ros bigger
μέγεθος ⓝ *me*·ye·thos size (general)
μεθαύριο me·*thav*·ri·o day after tomorrow
μεθυσμένος me·thiz·*me*·nos drunk
μενού ⓝ me·*nu* menu
μέσα *me*·sa in • inside
μεσάνυχτα ⓝ pl me·*sa*·nikh·ta midnight
μεσημέρι ⓝ me·si·*me*·ri midday • noon
μεσημεριανό φαγητό ⓝ
  me·si·me·ria·*no* fa·yi·*to* lunch
μετά me·*ta* after
μεταλλικό νερό ⓝ me·ta·li·*ko* ne·*ro*
  mineral water
μετάξι ⓝ me·*tak*·si silk
μετασχηματιστής ⓜ
  me·ta·shi·ma·ti·*stis* adaptor
μεταφράζω me·ta·*fra*·zo translate
μετρητά ⓝ pl me·tri·*ta* cash
μέχρι *me*·khri until
μη καπνίζοντες mi kap·*ni*·zo·des
  nonsmoking
μήνας ⓜ *mi*·nas month
μήνυμα ① *mi*·ni·ma message
μητέρα ① mi·*te*·ra mother
μητρόπολη ① mi·*tro*·po·li cathedral

μηχανή ① mi·kha·*ni* engine • machine
  — εισιτηρίων ① i·si·ti·*ri*·on
  ticket machine
  — φαξ faks fax machine
μηχανική ① mi·kha·ni·*ki* engineering
μηχανικός ⓜ&① mi·kha·ni·*kos*
  engineer • mechanic
μικρό όνομα ⓝ mi·*kro* o·no·ma first name
μικρότερος mi·*kro*·te·ros smaller
μιλάω mi·*la*·o speak • talk ⓥ
μισό mi·*so* half
μόδα ① *mo*·tha fashion
μοιράζομαι mi·*ra*·zo·me share with
μολύβι ⓝ mo·*li*·vi pencil
μόλυνση ① *mo*·lin·si infection
μονό δωμάτιο ⓝ mo·*no* tho·*ma*·tio
  single room
μονοπάτι ⓝ mo·no·*pa*·ti path • track • trail
μόνος *mo*·nos alone
μου mu my • to me
μου αρέσει mu a·*re*·si like ⓥ
μπαγιάτικος ba·*yia*·ti·kos off (spoiled) • stale
μπαίνω *be*·no enter
μπαλάκια από βαμπάκι ⓝ pl
  ba·*la*·kia a·po va·*ba*·ki cotton balls
μπάνιο ⓝ *ba*·nio bath • bathroom
μπάντα ① ba·*da* band (music)
μπαρ ⓝ bar bar
μπαταρία ① ba·ta·*ri*·a battery
μπέιμπι σίτερ ⓝ *be*·i·bi *si*·ter babysitter
μπίζνες κλας *biz*·nes klas business class
μπλε ble blue a
μπλοκαρισμένος blo·ka·riz·*me*·nos
  blocked
μπλουζάκι ⓝ blu·*za*·ki T-shirt
μπότα ① *bo*·ta boot (footwear)
μπουκάλι ⓝ bu·*ka*·li bottle
μπουφές ⓝ bu·*fes* buffet
μπροσούρα ① bro·*su*·ra brochure
μπύρα ① *bi*·ra beer
μπυραρία ① bi·ra·*ri*·a bar • pub
μπωλ ⓝ bol bowl
μυρουδιά ① mi·ru·*thia* smell
μύτη ① *mi*·ti nose
μωρό ⓝ mo·*ro* baby

Ν ν

ναι ne yes
ναρκωτικά ⓝ pl nar·ko·ti·*ka* illegal drugs
ναυτία ① naf·*ti*·a
  nausea • seasickness • travel sickness

νέα ⓝ pl *ne·a* news
Νέα Ζηλανδία ① *ne·a* zi·lan·*thi·a* New Zealand
νέος *ne·os* new • young
νερό ⓝ *ne·ro* water
νοικοκυρά ① *ni·ko·ki·ra* housewife
νοικοκύρης ⓜ *ni·ko·ki·ris* head of the house
νησί ⓝ *ni·si* island
νομικά ⓝ *no·mi·ka* law (study, profession)
νοσοκόμος ⓜ *no·so·ko·mos* nurse
νοσοκόμα ① *no·so·ko·ma* nurse
νοσοκομειακό ⓝ *no·so·ko·mi·a·ko* ambulance
νοσοκομείο ⓝ *no·so·ko·mi·o* hospital
νόστιμος *no·sti·mos* tasty
νότος ⓜ *no·tos* south
ντελικατέσεν ① de·li·ka·*te·sen* delicatessen
ντουζ ⓝ *duz* shower
νύχτα ① *nikh·*ta* night
νωρίς no·*ris* early

Ξ ξ

ξενοδοχείο ⓝ kse·no·tho·*hi·o* hotel
ξένη ① *kse·ni* foreign a • stranger ①
ξένος ⓜ *kse·nos* foreign a • stranger ⓜ
ξενώνας ⓜ kse·*no·nas* guesthouse
ξυπνάω ksip·*na·o* wake • wake (someone) up
ξυπνητήρι ⓝ ksip·ni·*ti·ri* alarm clock
ξυράφι ⓝ ksi·*ra·fi* razor blade
ξυρίζω ksi·*ri·zo* shave ⓥ
ξυριστική μηχανή ① ksi·ri·sti·*ki* mi·kha·*ni* razor

Ο ο

ο καλύτερος ο ka·*li·te·ros* best a
ο μεγαλύτερος ο me·gha·*li·te·ros* biggest
ο μικρότερος ο mi·*kro·te·ros* smallest
οδηγός ⓜ&ⓕ o·*thi·ghos* driver • guide (person)
— **διασκέδασης** ⓜ thia·*ske·*tha·sis* entertainment guide
οδηγώ o·thi·*gho* drive ⓥ
οδοντιατρική κλωστή ①
o·tho·di·a·tri·*ki* klo·*sti* dental floss
οδοντίατρος ⓜ&ⓕ o·tho·*di·a·tros* dentist
οδοντόβουρτσα ① o·tho·*do·vur·tsa* toothbrush
οδοντόπαστα ① o·tho·*do·pa·sta* toothpaste
οδός ① o·*thos* street

οδυνηρός o·thi·ni·*ros* painful
Οθωμανικός o·tho·ma·ni·*kos* Ottoman a
οικογένεια ① i·ko·*ye·ni·a* family
Ολλανδία ① o·lan·*thi·a* Netherlands
όλοι o·li all
ολονυκτίς o·lo·nikh·*tis* overnight
ομάδα αίματος ① o·*ma·*tha e·ma·tos* blood group
όμορφος o·*mor·fos* beautiful • handsome
ομοφυλόφιλος ⓜ o·mo·fi·*lo·fi·los* homosexual
όνομα ⓝ o·*no·ma* name
οπίσθιο ⓝ o·*pi·sthi·os* rear (seat etc)
οπωροπωλείο ⓝ o·po·ro·po·*li·o* grocery
όριο ταχύτητας ⓝ o·ri·o ta·*hi·ti·tas* speed limit
όροφος ⓜ o·ro·fos* floor (storey)
όταν o·tan when
όχι o·hi no • not

Π π

πάγος ⓜ *pa·ghos* ice
παγωμένος pa·gho·*me·*nos* frozen
παγωτό ⓝ pa·gho·*to* ice cream
παζάρι ⓝ pa·*za·ri* fleamarket
παιδί ⓝ pe·*thi* child
παιδιά ⓝ pl pe·*thia* children
παιδικό κάθισμα ⓝ pe·thi·*ko* ka·thiz·ma* child seat
παιδικός σταθμός ⓜ pe·thi·*kos* stath·*mos* crèche
παλάτι ⓝ pa·*la·ti* palace
πάλι pa·li again
παλιός pa·*lios* old a
παλτό ⓝ pal·*to* coat
πάνα ① *pa·na* diaper • nappy
πανεπιστήμιο ⓝ pa·ne·pi·*sti·mi·o* universit
παντελόνι ⓝ pa·de·*lo·ni* pants • trousers
παντρεμένη ① pa·dre·*me·*ni* married
παντρεμένος ⓜ pa·dre·*me·*nos* married
πάνω pa·no on • up
παπούς ⓜ pa·*pus* grandfather
παπούτσι ⓝ pa·*put·si* shoe
πάρα πολύ pa·ra po·*li* too (expensive etc)
παραδίνω pa·ra·*thi·no* deliver
παράθυρο ⓝ pa·*ra·thi·ro* window
παραλαβή αποσκευών ①
pa·ra·la·*vi* a·po·ske·*von* baggage claim
παραλία ① pa·ra·*li·a* beach • seaside
Παραμονή Πρωτοχρονιάς ① pa·ra·mo·*ni*
pro·to·khro·*nias* New Year's Eve

παράπονο ⑩ pa·ra·po·no complaint
παράσταση ① pa·ra·sta·si gig
παρκάρω par·ka·ro park a car
Πάσχα ⑩ pas·kha Easter
πατέρας ⑩ pa·te·ras father
παυσίπονο ⑩ paf·si·po·no painkiller
παχύς pa·his fat
πάω για ψώνια pa·o yia pso·nia
 go shopping
πεζοδρόμιο ⑩ pe·zo·thro·mi·o footpath
πεζοπορία ① pe·zo·po·ri·a hiking
πεζοπορώ pe·zo·po·ro hike ⓥ
πεθερά ① pe·the·ra mother-in-law
πεθερός ⑩ pe·the·ros father-in-law
πεινάω pi·no (be) hungry ⓥ
πελάτης ⑩ pe·la·tis client
πελάτισσα ① pe·la·ti·sa client
πέος ⑩ pe·os penis
περιήγηση ① pe·ri·i·yi·si tour
 — **με οδηγό** me o·thi·gho guided tour
περιμένω pe·ri·me·no wait ⓥ
περίπτερο ⑩ pe·rip·te·ro kiosk
περισσότερος pe·ri·so·te·ros more
περπατάω per·pa·ta·o walk ⓥ
πετάω pe·ta·o fly ⓥ
πετρέλαιο ⑩ pe·tre·le·o petrol
πετρογκάζ ⑩ pe·tro·gaz gas (for cooking)
πετσέτα ① pet·se·ta towel
πετσετάκι ① pet·se·ta·ki napkin
 — **υγείας** i·yi·as
 panty liners • sanitary napkins
πηγαίνω pi·ye·no go
πιάτο ⑩ pia·to dish • plate
πικρός pi·kros bitter ⓐ
πίνακας ⑩ pi·na·kas painting (a work)
πινακοθήκη ① pi·na·ko·thi·ki art gallery
πίνω pi·no drink ⓥ
πιπίλα ① pi·pi·la dummy • pacifier
πιρούνι ⑩ pi·ru·ni fork
πισίνα ① pi·si·na swimming pool
πίστωση ① pi·sto·si credit
πιστωτική κάρτα ① pi·sto·ti·ki kar·ta
 credit card
πλατεία ① pla·ti·a square (town)
πλάτη ① pla·ti back (body)
πλατφόρμα ① plat·for·ma platform
πλένω ple·no wash ⓥ
πληγή ① pli·yi injury
πληγωμένος pli·gho·me·nos injured ⓐ
πληροφορία ① pli·ro·fo·ri·a information
πληροφορική ① pli·ro·fo·ri·ki IT
πληρωμή ① pli·ro·mi payment
πλυντήριο ⑩ pli·di·ri·o launderette •
 laundry • washing machine

ποδήλατο ⑩ po·thi·la·to bicycle • bike
πόδι ⑩ po·thi foot • leg
ποδόσφαιρο ⑩ po·thos·fe·ro football
ποιος pios which • who
πόλη ① po·li city
πολυτέλεια ① po·li·te·li·a luxury
πολύτιμος po·li·ti·mos valuable
πονόδοντος po·no·tho·dos toothache
πονοκέφαλος po·no·ke·fa·los headache
πόνος ⑩ po·nos pain
πόρνη ① por·ni prostitute
πορτοκαλής por·to·ka·lis orange (colour)
πορτοφόλι ⑩ por·to·fo·li purse
ποτάμι ⑩ po·ta·mi river
ποτήρι ⑩ po·ti·ri drinking glass
ποτό ⑩ po·to drink
πού pu where
πουκάμισο ⑩ pu·ka·mi·so shirt
πουλόβερ ⑩ pu·lo·ver jumper • sweater
πούρο ⑩ pu·ro cigar
πρακτορείο εφημερίδων ⑩
 prak·to·ri·o e·fi·me·ri·thon newsagency
πράσινος pra·si·nos green
πρατήριο βενζίνας pra·ti·ri·o ven·zi·nas
 petrol station
πρεσβεία ① prez·vi·a embassy
πριν prin before
πρόγευμα ⑩ pro·yev·ma breakfast
πρόγραμμα ⑩ pro·ghra·ma timetable
προετοιμασία εγγράφων ①
 pro·e·ti·ma·si·a e·gra·fon paperwork
προηγούμενος pro·i·ghu·me·nos
 last • previous
προκαταβολή ① pro·ka·ta·vo·li
 deposit (on house etc)
προμήθεια ① pro·mi·thi·a commission
προμήθειες φαγητού ① pl
 pro·mi·thi·es fa·yi·tu food supplies
προξενείο ⑩ prok·se·ni·o consulate
προορισμός ⑩ pro·o·riz·mos destination
προσαύξηση τιμής ① pro·saf·ksi·si
 ti·mis cover charge
πρόστιμο ⑩ pros·ti·mo fine (penalty)
προσωπική επιταγή ① pro·so·pi·ki
 e·pi·ta·yi check (banking) • cheque
πρόσωπο ⑩ pro·so·po face • person
προϋπολογισμός ⑩ pro·i·po·lo·yiz·mos
 budget
προφυλακτικό ⑩ pro·fi·lak·ti·ko condom
προχθές prokh·tes day before yesterday
πρωί ⑩ pro·i morning
πρώτη τάξη ① pro·ti tak·si first class
Πρωτοχρονιά ①
 pro·to·khro·nia
 New Year's Day

πτήση ① *pti·si flight*
πυρετός ① *pi·re·tos fever*

Ρ ρ

ράδιο ⓝ *ra·thi·o radio*
ραντεβού ⓝ *ra·de·vu appointment • date*
ράφτης ⓜ *raf·tis tailor*
ράφτρα ① *raf·tra tailor*
ρεσεψιόν ① *re·sep·sion check-in (desk)*
ρέστα ⓝ pl *re·sta change (money)*
ρεύμα ⓝ *rev·ma current (electricity)*
ρινική αλλεργία ① *ri·ni·ki a·ler·yi·a hay fever*
ροζ *roz pink*
ρούχα ⓝ pl *ru·kha clothing*

Σ σ

Σαββατοκύριακο ⓝ *sa·va·to·ki·ria·ko weekend*
σακίδιο ⓝ *sa·ki·thi·o backpack*
σάκος ⓜ *sa·kos bag*
σαμπάνια ① *sam·pa·nia champagne*
σαπούνι ⓝ *sa·pu·ni soap*
σε *se at • to*
σεισμός ⓜ *siz·mos earthquake*
σελφ σέρβις ⓝ *self ser·vis self-service*
σεμινάριο ⓝ *se·mi·na·ri·o conference (small) • seminar*
σεντόνι ⓝ *se·do·ni sheet (bed)*
σεντόνια ① pl *se·do·nia bed linen*
σερβιτόρα ① *ser·vi·to·ra waitress*
σεξ ⓝ *seks sex*
σεφ ⓜ *sef chef • cook*
σημειωματάριο ⓝ *si·mi·o·ma·ta·ri·o notebook*
σήμερα *si·me·ra today*
σι ντι ⓝ *si di CD*
σι ντι ρομ ⓝ *si di rom disk (CD-ROM)*
σίδερο ⓝ *si·the·ro iron (for clothes)*
σιδηροδρομικός σταθμός ⓜ *si·thi·ro·thro·mi·kos stath·mos railway station*
σκάλα ① *ska·la stairway*
σκιά ① *ski·a shade*
σκληρός *skli·ros hard (not soft)*
σκοτεινός *sko·ti·nos dark a*
σκουλαρίκια ⓝ pl *sku·la·ri·kia earrings*
σκουπιδοτενεκές ⓜ *sku·pi·tho·te·ne·kes garbage can*
σκούρος *sku·ros dark (colour) a*

σκυλί ⓝ *ski·li dog*
Σκωτία ① *sko·ti·a Scotland*
σλάιντ ⓝ *sla·id slide (film)*
σοκολάτα ① *so·ko·la·ta chocolate*
σορτς ⓝ *sorts shorts*
σουβενίρ ⓝ *su·ve·nir souvenir*
σουγιάς ⓜ *su·yias penknife*
σουτιέν ⓝ *su·ti·en bra*
σπασμένος *spaz·me·nos broken*
σπίρτα ⓝ pl *spir·ta matches (for lighting)*
σπίτι ⓝ *spi·ti home*
σπουδαίος *spu·the·os important*
σπουδαστής ⓜ *spu·tha·stis student*
σπουδάστρια ① *spu·tha·stri·a student*
σπρέι ⓝ *spre·i spray*
σταθμός ⓜ *stath·mos station*
σταθμός λεωφορείου ⓜ *stath·mos le·o·fo·ri·u bus station*
σταθμός μετρό ⓝ *stath·mos me·tro metro station*
σταθμός τρένου ⓜ *stath·mos tre·nu train station*
στάση ① *sta·si stop (bus, tram, etc)*
— λεωφορείου ① *le·o·fo·ri·u bus stop*
— ταξί ① *tak·si taxi stand*
σταχτοθήκη ① *stakh·to·thi·ki ashtray*
στεγνός *stegh·nos dry a*
στήθος ⓝ *sti·thos chest (body)*
στην ώρα *stin o·ra on time*
στόμα ⓝ *sto·ma mouth*
στομάχι ⓝ *sto·ma·hi stomach*
στομαχόπονος ⓜ *sto·ma·kho·po·nos stomachache*
στραμπούλισμα ⓝ *stra·bu·liz·ma sprain*
στρώμα ⓝ *stro·ma mattress*
στυλό ⓝ *sti·lo pen (ballpoint)*
σύζυγος ⓜ&① *si·zi·ghos husband • wife*
συμπεριλαμβανόμενος *si·be·ri·lam·va·no·me·nu included*
συνάδελφος ⓜ *si·na·thel·fos colleague*
συναδέλφισσα ① *si·na·thel·fi·sa colleague*
συνάλλαγμα ⓝ *si·na·lagh·ma exchange*
σύνδεσμος ⓜ *sin·thez·mos connection*
συνέδριο ⓝ *si·ne·thri·o conference (big)*
συνεισφέρω *si·nis·fe·ro contribute*
συνιστώ *si·ni·sto recommend*
σύνορο ⓝ *si·no·ro border*
συνταγή ① *si·da·yi prescription*
σύνταξη ① *si·dak·si pension*
συνταξιούχα ① *si·dak·si·u·kha pensioner*
συνταξιούχος ⓜ *si·dak·si·u·khos pensione.*
σύντομα *si·do·ma soon*
συντροφιά ① *si·dro·fia company (friends*

σύντροφος ⑩ *si·dro·fos companion*
συντρόφισσα ① *si·dro·fi·sa companion*
συστημένο *sis·ti·me·no by registered mail*
σωσίβιο ⑩ *so·si·vi·o life jacket*

Τ τ

ταμείο ⑩ *ta·mi·o cash register*
ταμίας ⑩&① *ta·mi·as cashier*
ταμπόν ⑩ *ta·bon tampon*
ταξίδι ⑥ *tak·si·thi journey • trip*
   — εργασίας ⑥ *er·gha·si·as business trip*
   — του μέλιτος ⑥ *tu me·li·tos honeymoon*
ταξίδι με ωτοστόπ *tak·si·thi me o·to·stop hitchhike* ⑨
ταξιδιωτική επιταγή ① *tak·si·thi·o·ti·ki e·pi·ta·yi travellers cheque*
ταξιδιωτικό γραφείο ⑩ *tak·si·thi·o·ti·ko ghra·fi·o travel agency*
αυτότητα ① *taf·to·ti·ta identification card*
αχυδρομείο ⑩ *ta·hi·thro·mi·o mail • post office*
αχυδρομικό κουτί ⑩ *ta·hi·thro·mi·ko ku·ti mailbox*
αχυδρομικός τομέας ⑩ *ta·hi·thro·mi·kos to·me·as postcode*
αχυδρομώ *ta·hi·thro·mo post* ⑨
αχύτητα φιλμ ① *ta·hi·ti·ta film film speed*
ελεφερίκ ⑩ *te·le·fe·rik chairlift (skiing)*
έλος ⑩ *te·los end*
ελωνείο ⑩ *te·lo·ni·o customs*
ένις ⑩ *te·nis tennis*
έχνη ① *tekh·ni craft • art*
ηγάνι ⑩ *ti·gha·ni frying pan*
ηγανίζω *ti·gha·ni·zo fry* ⑨
ηλεγράφημα ⑩ *ti·le·ghra·fi·ma telegram*
ηλεκατεύθυνση ① *ti·le·ka·tef·thin·si remote control*
ηλεόραση ① *ti·le·o·ra·si television • TV*
ηλεφωνικός κατάλογος ⑩ *ti·le·fo·ni·kos ka·ta·lo·ghos phone book*
ηλέφωνο ⑩ *ti·le·fo·no telephone*
ηλεφωνώ *ti·le·fo·no telephone* ⑨
ης *tis her (ownership/direct object)*
ιμή ① *ti·mi price*
   — εισόδου ⑩ *i·so·thu admission (price)*
   — εξυπηρέτησης ① *ek·si·pi·re·ti·sis service charge*
   — συναλλάγματος ⑩ *si·na·lagh·ma·tos currency exchange • exchange rate*

τίποτε *ti·po·te nothing*
τίτλος κατόχου αυτοκινήτου ⑩ *tit·los ka·to·khu af·to·ki·ni·tu car owner's title*
το πιο κοντινό *to pio ko·di·no nearest*
τοπικός *to·pi·kos local* a
τοστ ⑩ *tost toast*
τοστιέρα ① *to·stie·ra toaster*
του *tu his (ownership/direct object)*
τουαλέτα ① *tu·a·le·ta toilet*
τουριστική θέση ① *tu·ri·sti·ki the·si economy class*
τουριστικό γραφείο ⑩ *tu·ri·sti·ko ghra·fi·o tourist office*
τουριστικός οδηγός ⑩ *tu·ri·sti·kos o·thi·ghos guidebook*
τράπεζα ① *tra·pe·za bank*
τραπεζικός λογαριασμός ⑩ *tra·pe·zi·kos lo·gha·riaz·mos bank account*
τρένο ⑩ *tre·no train*
τρόλεϋ ⑩ *tro·le·i trolley bus*
τρώγω *tro·gho eat* ⑨
τσάντα ① *tsa·da handbag*
τσιγάρο ⑩ *tsi·gha·ro cigarette*
τσιμπιδάκι ⑩ *tsi·bi·tha·ki tweezers*
τσίρκο ⑩ *tsir·ko circus*
τσιρότο ⑩ *tsi·ro·to Band-Aid*
τυρί ⑩ *ti·ri cheese*
τώρα *to·ra now*

Υ υ

υπεραστικό λεωφορείο ⑩ *i·pe·ra·sti·ko le·o·fo·ri·o intercity bus*
υπέρβαρο φορτίο ⑩ *i·per·va·ro for·ti·o excess baggage*
υπηρεσία ① *i·pi·re·si·a service*
υπνοδωμάτιο ⑩ *ip·no·tho·ma·ti·o bedroom*
υπόγειος *i·po·yi·os subway* a
   — σιδηρόδρομος ⑩ *si·thi·ro·thro·mos subway train*
υποδηματοποιείο ⑩ *i·po·thi·ma·to·pi·i·o shoe shop*
υπότιτλοι ① pl *i·po·ti·tli subtitles*
υποχρέωση ① *i·po·khre·o·si engagement • obligation*

Φ φ

φαγητό ⑩ *fa·yi·to food*
   — για μωρά ⑩ *yia mo·ra baby food*
φαγούρα ① *fa·ghu·ra itch*

φάκελος ⓜ *fa·ke·los* envelope
φακοί επαφής ⓜ pl *fa·ki e·pa·fis* contact lenses
φακός ⓜ *fa·kos* lens • flashlight • torch
φαρμακείο ⓝ *far·ma·ki·o* pharmacy
φάρμακο ⓝ *far·ma·ko* medicine
— **για το βήχα** ⓝ *yia to ví·kha* cough medicine
φαρμακοποιός ⓜ&ⓕ *far·ma·ko·pi·os* pharmacist
φερμουάρ ⓝ *fer·mu·ar* zip • zipper
φέρυ ⓝ *fe·ri* ferry
φέτα ⓕ *fe·ta* slice
φθινόπωρο ⓝ *fthi·no·po·ro* autumn • fall
φιλενάδα ⓕ *fi·le·na·tha* girlfriend
φίλη ⓕ *fi·li* friend
φιλμ ⓝ *film* film • movie
φιλοδώρημα ⓝ *fi·lo·tho·ri·ma* gratuity • tip
φίλος ⓜ *fi·los* boyfriend • friend
φλας ⓝ *flas* flashlight
φλυτζάνι ⓝ *fli·dza·ni* cup
φόρεμα ⓝ *fo·re·ma* dress
φούρνος ⓜ *fur·nos* bakery • oven
— **μικροκυμάτων** ⓜ *mi·kro·ki·ma·ton* microwave oven
φουσκάλα ⓕ *fu·ska·la* blister
φούστα ⓕ *fu·sta* skirt
φρένα ⓝ pl *fre·na* brakes
φρέσκος *fre·skos* fresh
φρούτα ⓝ pl *fru·ta* fruit
φτηνός *fti·nos* cheap a
φύλαξη αποσκευών ⓕ *fi·lak·si a·po·ske·von* luggage lockers
φως ⓝ *fos* light
φωτογραφία ⓕ *fo·to·gra·fi·a* photo
φωτογραφική ⓕ *fo·to·ghra·fi·ki* photography
φωτογραφική μηχανή ⓕ *fo·to·ghra·fi·ki mi·kha·ni* camera
φωτογράφος ⓜ&ⓕ *fo·to·ghra·fos* photographer

Χ χ

χαλασμένος *kha·laz·me·nos* broken down • out of order • spoiled (food)
χαλκός ⓜ *khal·kos* copper
χαμένος *kha·me·nos* lost a
χάπι ⓝ *kha·pi* pill
χάρτης ⓜ *khar·tis* map (of country/town)
χαρτί ⓝ *khar·ti* paper
— **υγείας** ⓝ *i·yi·as* toilet paper

χαρτομάντηλα ⓝ pl *khar·to·ma·di·la* tissues
χαρτονόμισμα ⓝ *khar·to·no·miz·ma* banknote
χαρτοπωλείο ⓝ *khar·to·po·li·o* stationer's shop
χαρτοφύλακας ⓜ *khar·to·fi·la·kas* briefcase
χειμώνας ⓜ *hi·mo·nas* winter
χειροποίητο *hi·ro·pi·i·to* handmade a
χέρι ⓝ *he·ri* arm • hand
χιλιόγραμμο ⓝ *hi·lio·gra·mo* kilogram
χιλιόμετρο ⓝ *hi·lio·me·tro* kilometre
χιόνι ⓝ *hio·ni* snow
χορεύω *kho·re·vo* dance ⓥ
χορός ⓜ *kho·ros* dancing
χορτοφάγος ⓜ&ⓕ *khor·to·fa·ghos* vegetarian a
χρήματα ⓝ pl *khri·ma·ta* money
Χριστούγεννα ⓝ pl *khri·stu·ye·na* Christmas
χρόνος ⓜ *khro·nos* year
χρυσάφι ⓝ *khri·sa·fi* gold
χρώμα ⓝ *khro·ma* colour
χτένα ⓕ *khte·na* comb
χτες *khtes* yesterday
χωρίς *kho·ris* without
χώρος ⓜ *kho·ros* venue • place
— **για κάμπινγκ** ⓝ *yia kam·ping* camping ground • campsite
χωροφύλακας ⓜ *kho·ro·fi·la·kas* police officer
χωροφυλακίνα ⓕ *kho·ro·fi·la·ki·na* police officer

Ψ ψ

ψαλίδι ⓝ *psa·li·thi* scissors
ψάρεμα ⓝ *psa·re·ma* fishing
ψηφιακός *psi·fi·a·kos* digital a
ψηλός *psi·los* high • tall
ψιλά ⓝ pl *psi·la* change (money)
ψιχάλα ⓕ *psi·kha·la* drizzle
ψυγείο ⓝ *psi·yi·o* fridge • refrigerator
ψωμί ⓝ *pso·mi* bread
ψωνίζω *pso·ni·zo* shop ⓥ

Ω ω

ώμος ⓜ *o·mos* shoulder
ώρα ⓕ *o·ra* hour • time
ώρες λειτουργίας ⓕ pl *o·res li·tur·yi·as* opening hours

A

B

C

S

When's (the next bus)?	Πότε είναι (το επόμενο λεωφορείο);	*po·*te *i·*ne (to e·*po·*me·no le·o·fo·*ri·*o)
Where's (the station)?	Πού είναι (ο σταθμός);	pu *i·*ne (o stath·*mos*)
How much is it (per night)?	Πόσο είναι (για κάθε νύχτα);	*po·*so *i·*ne (yia *ka·*the *nikh·*ta)
I'm looking for (Ampfilohos).	Ψάχνω για (το Αμφίλοχος).	*psakh·*no yia (to am·*fi·*lo·khos)
Do you have (a local map)?	Έχετε οδικό (τοπικό χάρτη);	e·*he·*te o·thi·*ko* (to·pi·*ko* khar·ti)
Is there a (lift)?	Υπάρχει (ασανσέρ);	i·*par·*hi (a·san·*ser*)
Can I (try it on)?	Μπορώ να (το προβάρω);	bo·*ro* na (to pro·*va·*ro)
Do I need (to book)?	Χρειάζεται (να κλείσω θέση);	khri·*a·*ze·te (na *kli·*so *the·*si)
I have (a reservation).	Έχω (κλείσει δωμάτιο).	e·kho (*kli·*si tho·*ma·*ti·o)
I need (assistance).	Χρειάζομαι (βοήθεια).	khri·*a·*zo·me (vo·*i·*thi·a)
I'd like (to hire a car).	Θα ήθελα (να ενοικιάσω ένα αυτοκίνητο).	tha *i·*the·la (na e·ni·ki·a·so e·na af·to·*ki·*ni·to)
Could you (please help)?	Μπορείς να (βοηθήσεις, παρακαλώ);	bo·*ris* na (vo·i·*thi·*sis pa·ra·ka·*lo*)